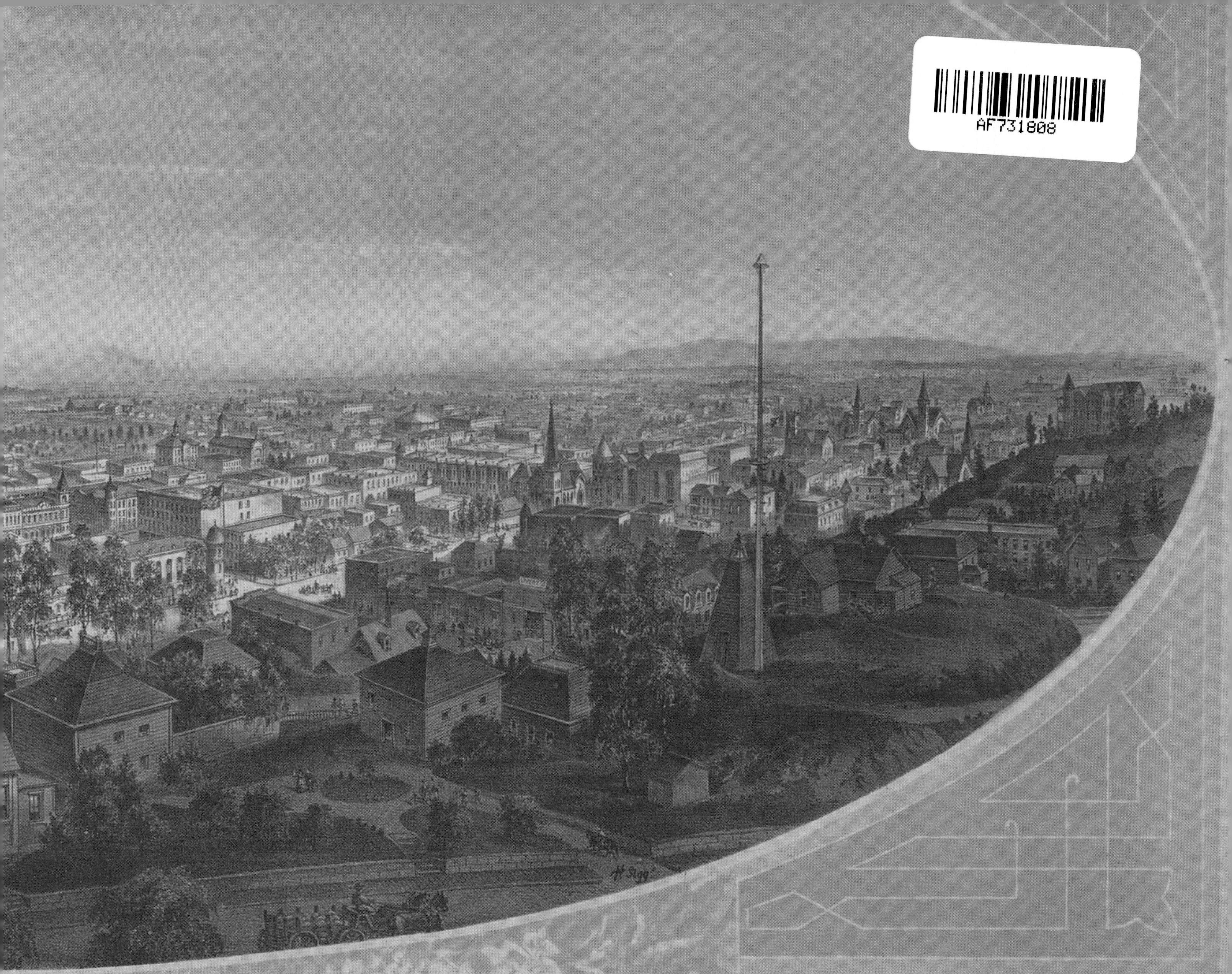

LES CAL.

H & CO. SAN FRANCISCO.

LOST LOS ANGELES

Dedication

Dennis and Eric would like to dedicate this book to Carrie Beavers. Thank you Carrie, for all you do.

Acknowledgments

As authors and historians we want to thank our fellow researchers into Los Angeles' past. We especially want to thank Nathan Masters for his voluminous work about the city's history. We also want to acknowledge the work of Jack J. Feldman at the nonprofit Water and Power Associates who maintain the most comprehensive website with wonderful photos and insightful descriptions on a range of historical themes. This book would not have been possible without two essential photo archives to draw from: Los Angeles Public Library and the California Historical Society Collection hosted by the University of Southern California Digital Archives.

Bibliography

Los Angeles from the Mountains to the Sea by John Steven McGroarty
Before L.A.: Race, Space, and Municipal Power in Los Angeles 1781-1894, by David S. T. Rouff
The History of Forgetting: Los Angeles and the Erasure of Memory by Norman M. Klein
A History of California and an Extended History of Los Angeles by James Miller Guinn

Picture credits

Baseball Hall of Fame Library, pages 100 and 101.
Bruce Torrence Hollywood Historical Collection, pages 22, 29, 40 (bottom left), 41, 82 and 132 (bottom).
California State Library, pages 19 (bottom left) and 28.
Don Ayres, page 85.
Getty Images, pages 74, 102, 103, 116, 117 (bottom right), 128, 129, 130, 138 and 139.
Karl Mondon, pages 10, 11 (top right) 11 (center right), 126 (bottom right), 135 (bottom right).
Helms Bakery Archive, pages 96 and 97.
Huntington Library Photo Archives, pages 64 and 65.
Library of Congress, pages 9 (top), 16 (main), 18, 25, 30, 32, 33 (right), 34 (bottom left), 35, 36, 36-37, 38, 39, 46, 47, 48, 50 (top right), 52, 53 (center right) 53 (bottom right), 56, 58 (bottom left), 59, 60, 61 (bottom), 84, 87, 99, 104, 106, 107, 109, 110, 111, 112, 113, 114, 115, 124, 137 (top) 140, 141, 142 and 143.
Los Angeles Times, pages 12 (bottom center), 69 (bottom center) and 81.
Los Angeles Public Library, pages 9 (bottom), 11 (bottom center), 11 (bottom left), 12 (right), 15 (bottom left), 19 (center), 22, 23 (left), 24, 26 (right), 31 (bottom left), 31 (right), 33 (top center), 42, 45 (bottom left), 50 (center), 51, 55, 62, 63, 70 (top center), 70 (top right), 79, 80, 86 (top right), 90, 91, 92, 93, 94, 95, 98 (top center), 117 (bottom left) and 136.
Los Angeles Unified Schools District, pages 16 (top) and 17 (top right).
Metro Transportation Library and Archive, pages 86 (bottom left), 86 (bottom center), 88 and 89.
Pacific Electric Archive, page 49.
Port of Los Angeles, page 57 (bottom left).
Simon Clay/Chrysalis Image Library, page 133.
University of California, Berkeley, Bancroft Library, page 72 (top).
University of California, Los Angeles, UES Collection, page 20.
University of Southern California/"Dick Whittington" Collection, page 75.
University of Southern California Digital Archive/California Historical Society Collection, pages 14, 21, 26 (left), 27, 31 (bottom center), 34 (right), 37 (bottom), 43, 44, 45 (top right), 54 (center), 58 (bottom right), 66, 67, 68, 69 (top center), 73, 76, 77, 78, 83 (center), 98 (bottom left), 108, 119, 122, 123, 125, 131 (bottom center), 131 (bottom right), and 137 (bottom right).
University of Southern California/California Historical Society, Title Insurance and Trust Collection, pages 8, 120, 126 (bottom left) and 132 (top).
U.S. National Archives, page 57 (center) and 57 (right).

Endpapers

Front: Bird's-Eye View of Los Angeles, circa 1888 (Britton & Rey/Library of Congress).
Back: "See Catalina Island" poster by Otis Shepard, 1935 (Library of Congress).

First published in the United Kingdom in 2014 by
PAVILION BOOKS
an imprint of Pavilion Books Company Ltd.
43 Great Ormond Street, London, WC1N 3HZ, UK

ISBN: 978-1-90981-5599

A CIP catalogue record for this book is available from the British Library.

Reprinted 2016 (twice), 2018, 2020

Repro by Rival Colour
Printed in Singapore

www.pavilionbooks.com

LOST LOS ANGELES

Dennis Evanosky and Eric J. Kos

PAVILION

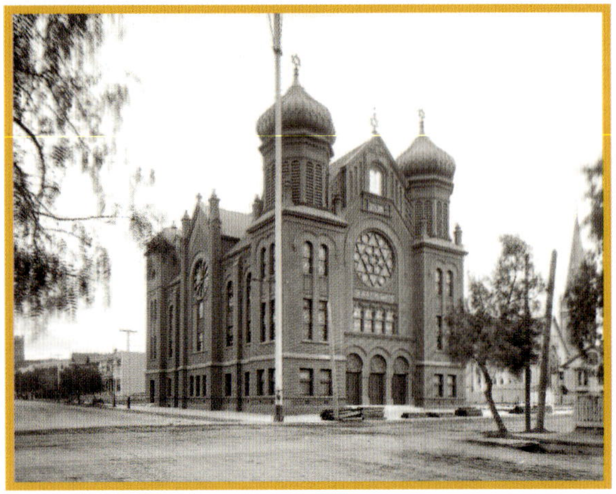

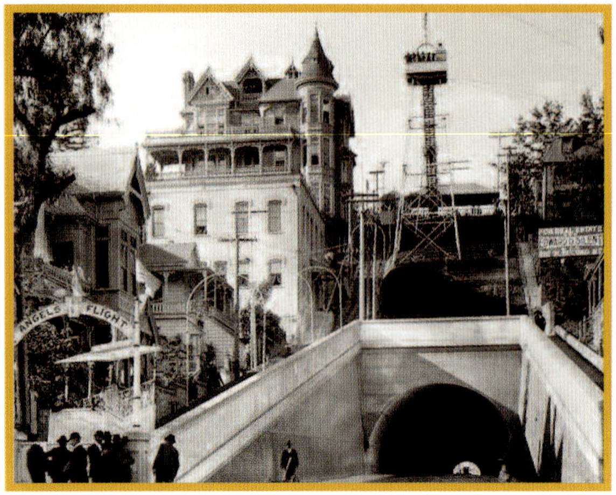
ANGELS FLIGHT

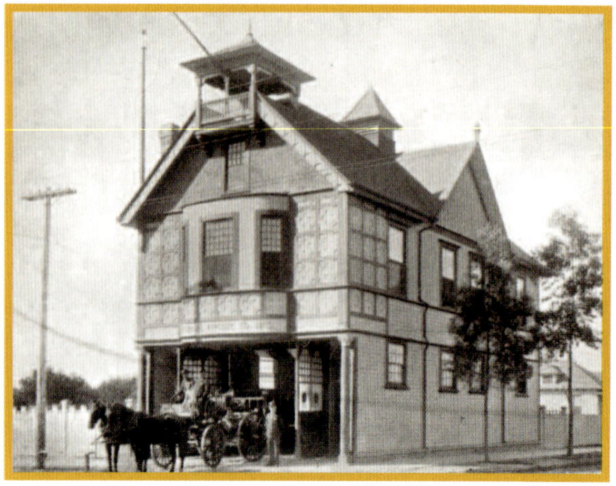

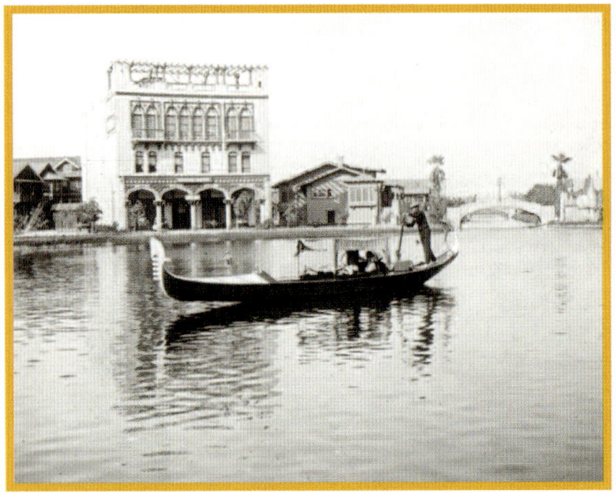

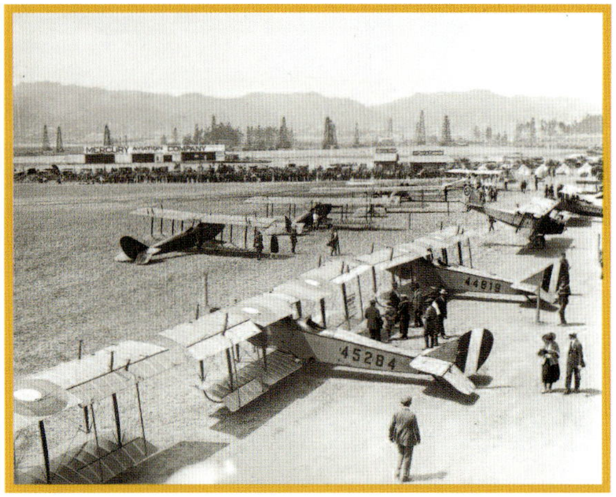
45284

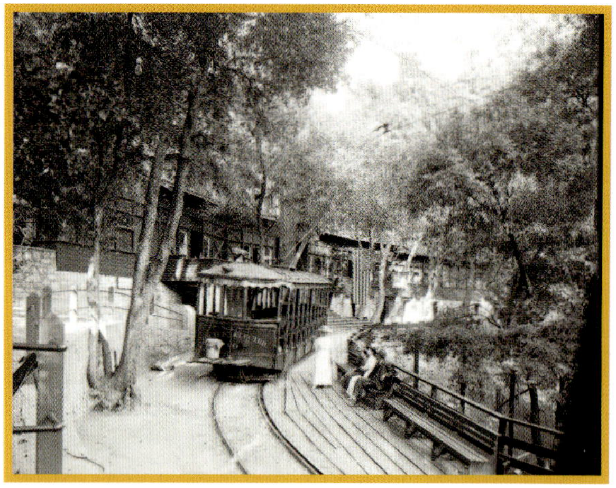

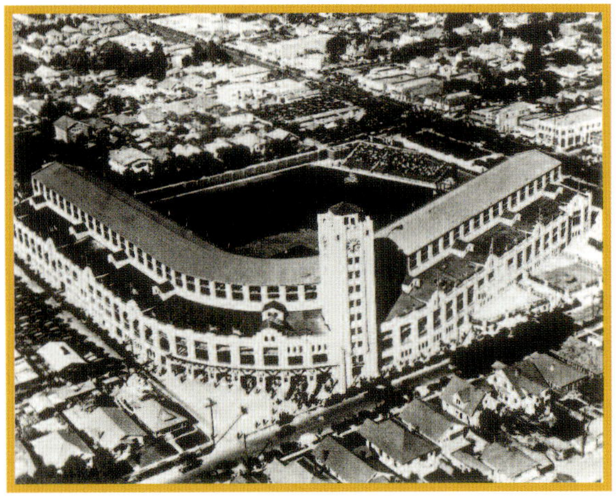

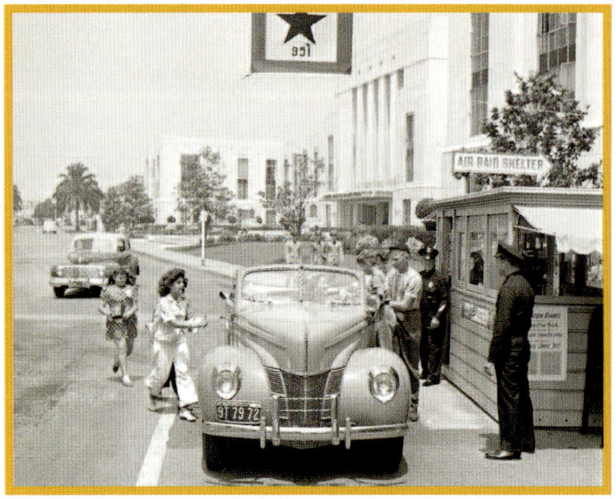
AIR RAID SHELTER

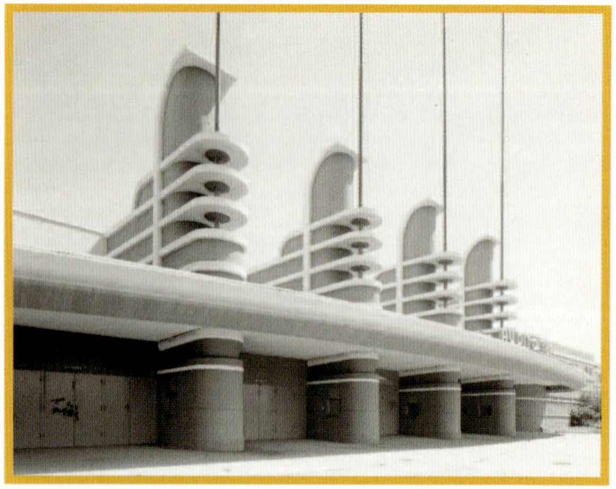

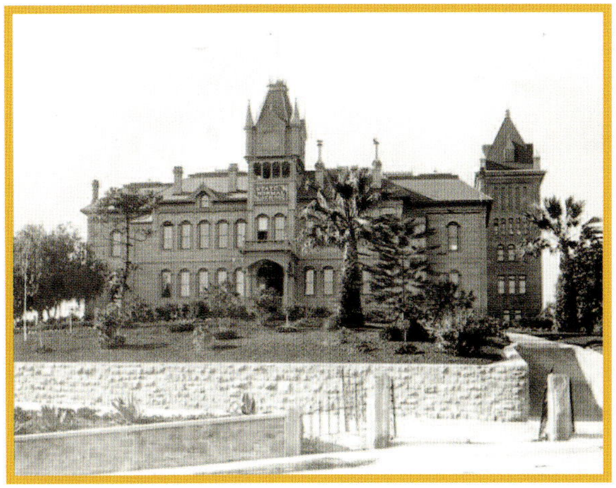

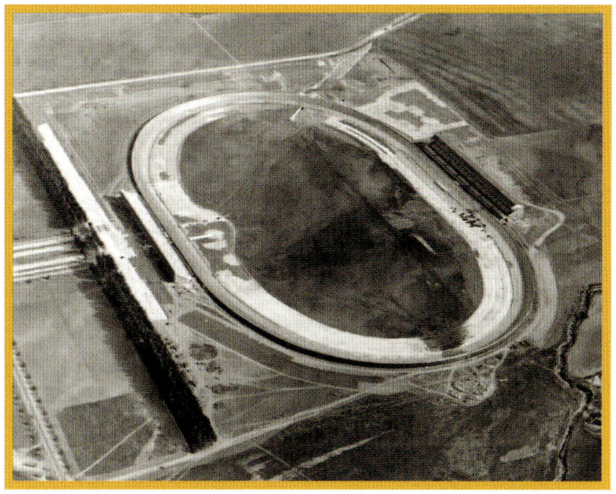

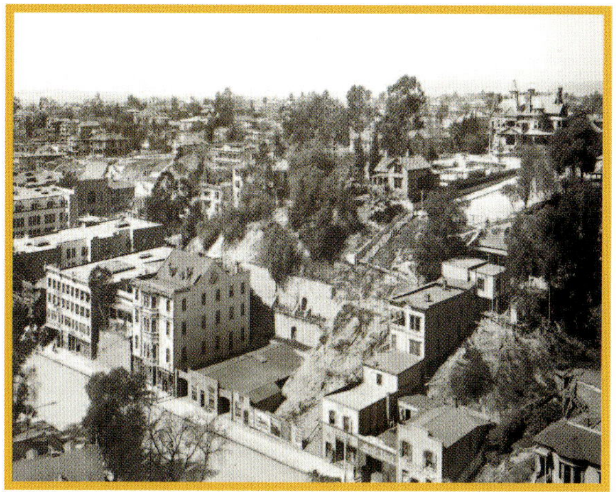

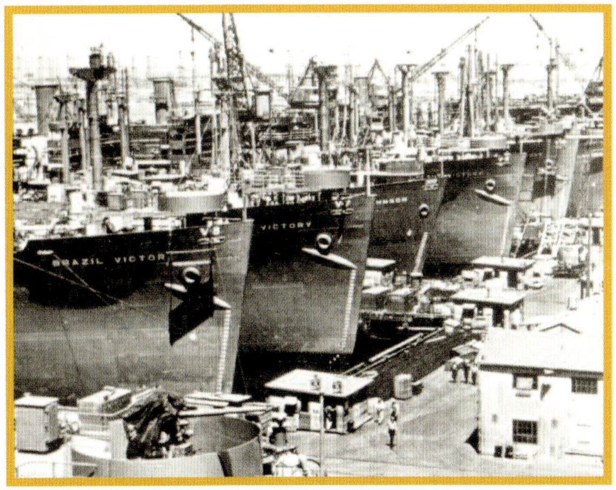

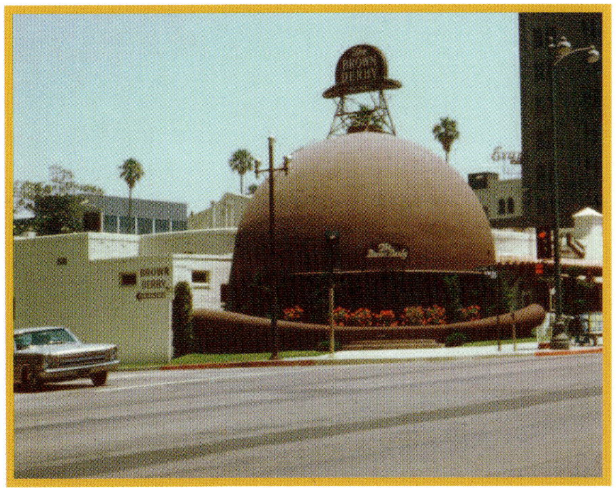

LOST IN THE...

INTRODUCTION

In 1781 under the direction of Governor Felipe de Neve, the Spanish established El Pueblo de Nuestra Señora Reina de los Ángeles where the Gaspar de Portolà expedition had first discovered the Los Angeles river. On September 4, soldiers led a party of priests and 44 settlers to the pueblo, which the governor had ordered laid out. By 1784 the town square included a church.

The settlers built mud-plastered huts and a dam on the river. They channeled water to the pueblo in the *Zanja Madre*, the mother ditch. In 1815, storms flooded the pueblo and forced the settlers to move their village to a new location just to the southwest. This mother ditch still lies beneath the city, and workers occasionally stumble on its remains when excavating foundations. In 1821, Mexico won its independence from Spain and the following year residents worshipped in a new church whose doors opened onto the plaza.

Other Europeans had already arrived, the first by ship in 1805. More would come, first in a trickle then in a flood greater than any from the Los Angeles River. The Americans came to stay from the mid-1840s. As victors in the Mexican-American War they felt entitled to Mexico's land. At first they defended themselves from Fort Hill, which became Fort Moore Hill, then, in turn, home to a Protestant cemetery, the city's first high school. Finally the hill itself was leveled to make room for the 101 freeway.

The story of the demise of Fort Moore Hill is symptomatic of the tale of growth across Los Angeles. The historic Wolfskill adobe was torn down to make way for Southern Pacific's Arcade Station, which fell to the wrecking ball so that the Central Depot could serve rail passengers in its place. Then even Central Depot was demolished with a meat packing plant in the wings to take its place.

When water could be supplied, a desolate Bunker Hill was developed and some of the finest homes in Los Angeles appeared on its crest. Over time the wealthy moved away, smaller homes stood in the place of the mansions and, over time, even these home disappeared.

Technical progress also brought its own brand of change. Cable cars replaced horse-drawn streetcars, which in turn were replaced by electric streetcars and then bus trolleys. Finally the tracks were converted back to roadways. The city bored holes through the hills for the ease of motorists and, over time, even the hills began to disappear.

Development in Los Angeles has done away with entire neighborhoods. Sonora Town, Los Angeles' first barrio, gave way to the city's first Chinatown, which bowed to the needs of the city and its plan for a grand Union Station in the 1930s.

Entire city blocks have also given way to the automobile or grand civic plans. The site that once was home to the Baker Block stood in the path of an extension to the Civic Center. The grand Victorian block was demolished, but the extension never built. Meanwhile the elegant Hall of Records building was too old, too vulnerable to earthquakes and crucially, too out of line with the other institutional buildings around it.

Developments over time have played a role in seeing the city's center move: first from the old plaza to the Temple Block, then from Temple Block to Spring Street and, finally, from Spring Street to today's civic plaza where city hall, the halls of justice and federal office buildings stand. Often this meant the destruction of what came before: Temple Block is nowhere to be found; John and Pliny Temple's legacy laid low by the wrecking ball.

Some buildings and businesses have evolved and survived. The *Los Angeles Times* endured a fatal bombing in 1910 that killed 20 of its staff and destroyed its building. But it has survived the greater challenges of time and fierce competition, while the *Los Angeles Star*, the *Southern Californian* and the *Los Angeles Herald Examiner* are now footnotes in California media history.

The city once boasted a pair of funicular railroads that carried passengers to the top of Bunker Hill, one is gone forever, the other moved to a new place as the buildings that surrounded it have all been torn down and replaced.

Further afield a shipyard that once turned out an impressive array of Victory and Liberty ships has fallen silent and cars now drive over a network of canals intended to be the "Venice of America."

All these things and more, once made up the fabric of Los Angeles and are now part of a past that is lost to us.

The booming California economy of the early 20th century has given Los Angeles the legacy of some of America's most significant art deco buildings. When the city roared out of the Great Depression the style of architecture had evolved to its most refined form in Streamline Moderne and while many of the great buildings remain, such as Helms Bakery and the former ABC Building, others, such as the NBC building and the Pan Pacific Stadium, have been bulldozed or burned. Bullocks department store on Wilshire boulevard has survived with a different occupation, but the Coulter's department store was lost and the magnificent Richfield Oil building was sitting on too valuable a piece of real estate to survive.

Despite the many grievous losses covered in this book, there are restorations, too. Downtown Los Angeles may have lost the site of the original Angels Flight, but the short funicular railway has gone back into service after many years in storage. Some thought it would be gone forever. The Palladium Theatre's distinctive deco frontage (pictured right) was the victim of a makeover which changed its look in the latter half of the 20th century. But stroll past 6215 Sunset Boulevard today and it's hard to tell the difference between the modern restoration and when Sonny Dunham brought his orchestra to the venue in April 1942.

Whether lost forever or restored to their former glory, these places still live on in the pages of this book. To create a comprehensive encyclopedia of Los Angeles' losses would take a lifetime, but hopefully in these pages we have given you an insight into the way the city has changed, and is changing still.

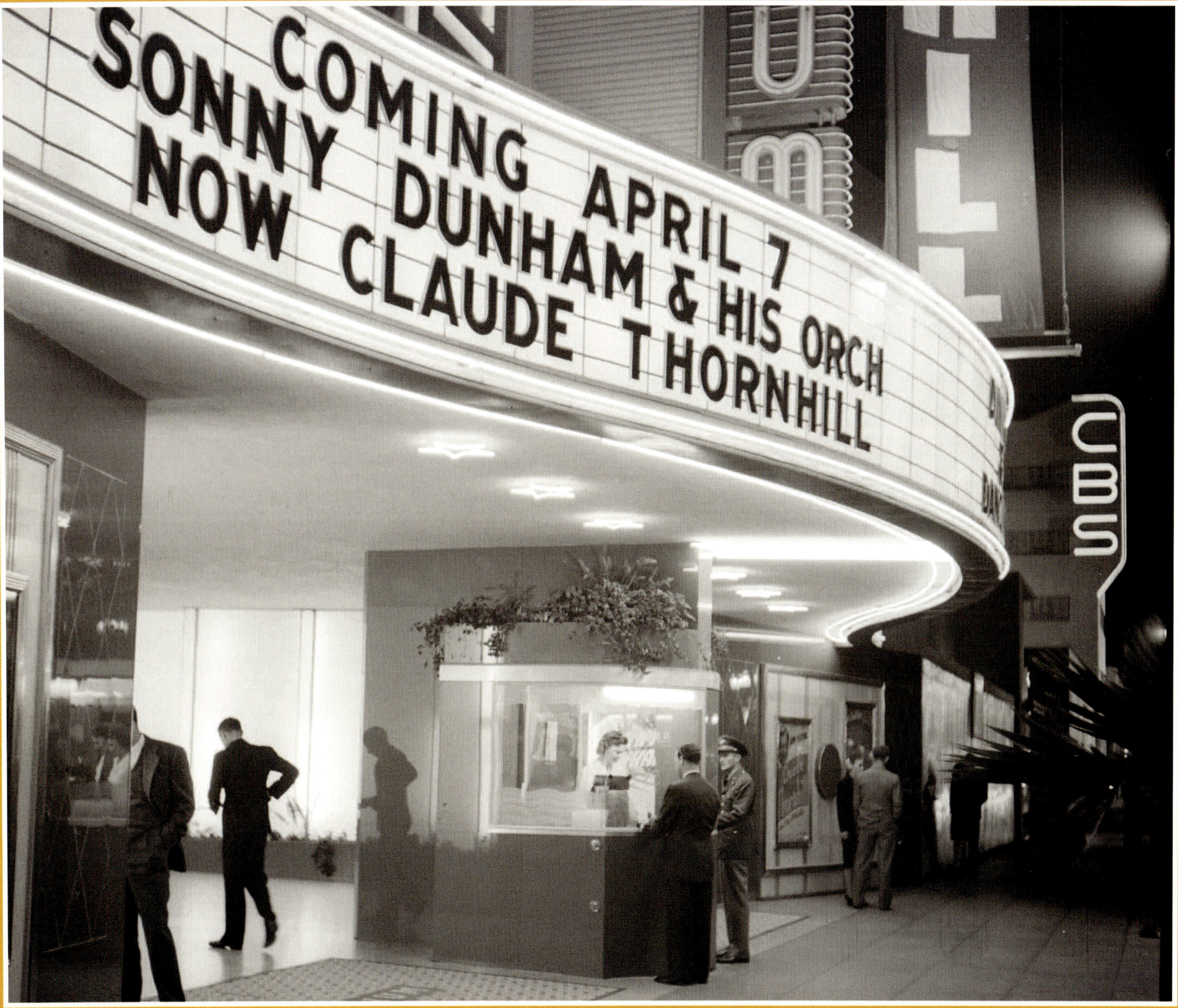
COMING APRIL 7
SONNY DUNHAM & HIS ORCH
NOW CLAUDE THORNHILL
CBS

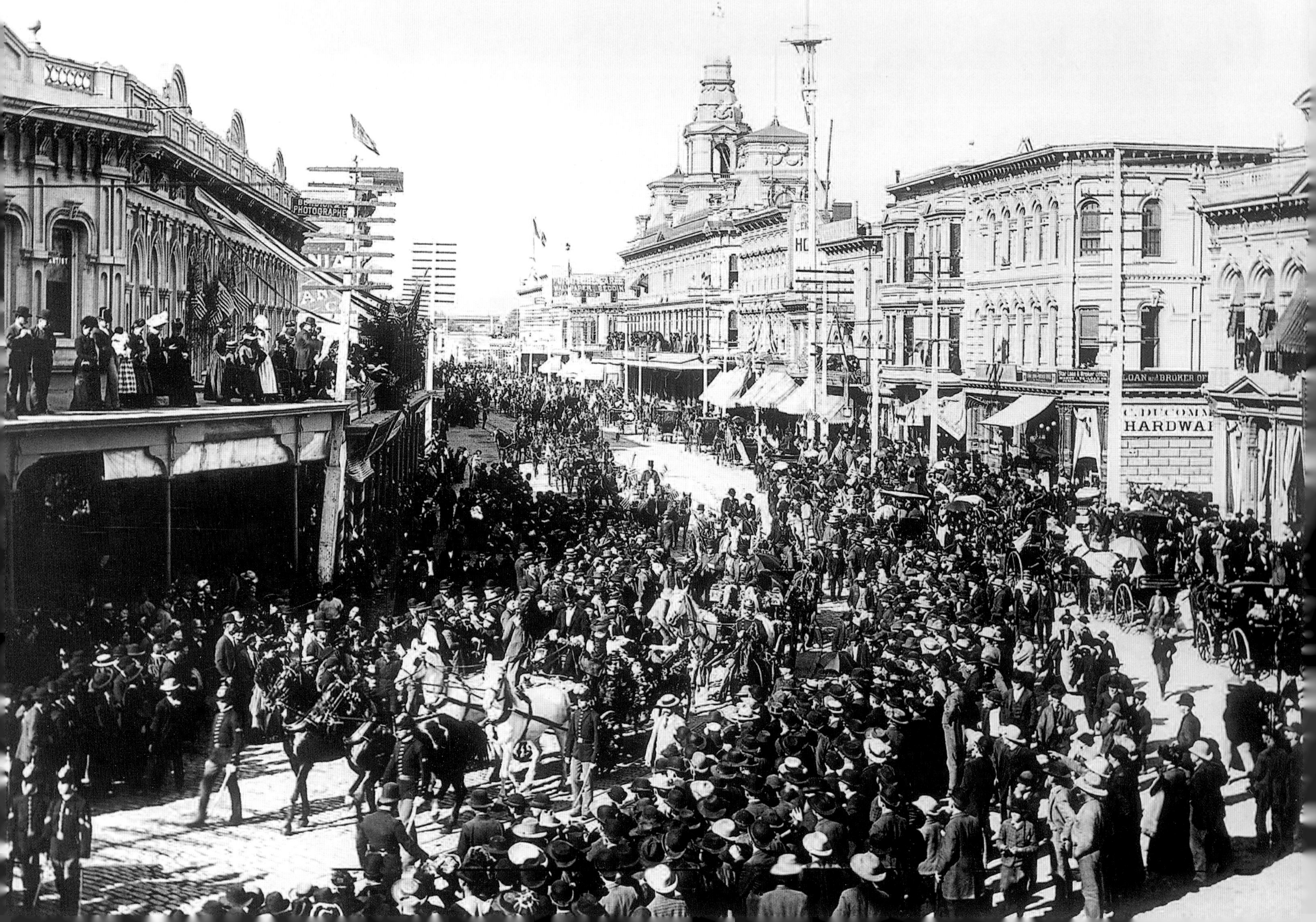
PHOTOGRAPHE
LOAN and BROKER OF
C. DUCOMM
HARDWAI

Electric Light Towers OBSOLETE BY 1900

Public street lighting in Los Angeles dates back to 1867 when the first gas lamps were installed. Prior to that, residents were required, by law, to hang gas lights from their porches to help night travelers find their way. The first gas lights were installed in 1867, 43 of them along Main Street. A lamplighter on horseback rode down Main Street each evening at dusk to light them. By 1873, 136 gas lamps had been installed downtown. They had all disappeared by 1883.

In the 1880s, after Thomas Edison revealed his great invention of incandescent lighting, many West Coast cities electrified their street lighting. Leading the way, the Los Angeles City Council unanimously approved a plan from Charles L. Howland to "illuminate the streets of the city with electric light." Howland fulfilled his promise in dramatic fashion using three 3,000-candle-power lamps on 150-foot towers that bathed the surrounding areas in light as bright as if a full moon were shining.

In 1882, the first two of these standards went up at the intersections of Main and Commercial streets (pictured left), and First and Hill streets. In a ceremony held on December 30th that year, Mayor James Toberman threw a switch and lit the standards for the first time. The next evening, five more masts enjoyed their inaugural lighting: at First Street and Boyle Avenue; Avenue 22 and North Broadway; First Street and Central Avenue; Fourth Street and Grand Avenue; and Sixth and Main Streets. Howland's plant at the corner of Alameda and Banning streets powered them all with a 30-kilowatt steam turbine.

In 1883 Howland and other investors formed the Los Angeles Electric Company and over the next two years, the company created a total of 30 or so standards, scattered around downtown. The sheer height of the masts proved a challenge for engineers though, and they soon needed to be replaced by street lighting that was easier to maintain.

They were replaced by five-globe streetlights closer to the ground (called "Llewellyns"). These were first installed downtown around 1900. These themselves were then replaced around 1910 by two-globe "electroliers."

The ultimate celebration of Los Angeles historic street lighting came in 2008 when Chris Burden revealed *Urban Light* a sculpture at 5905 Wilshire Boulevard featuring 202 antique street lights collected from streets and neighborhoods in and around the city.

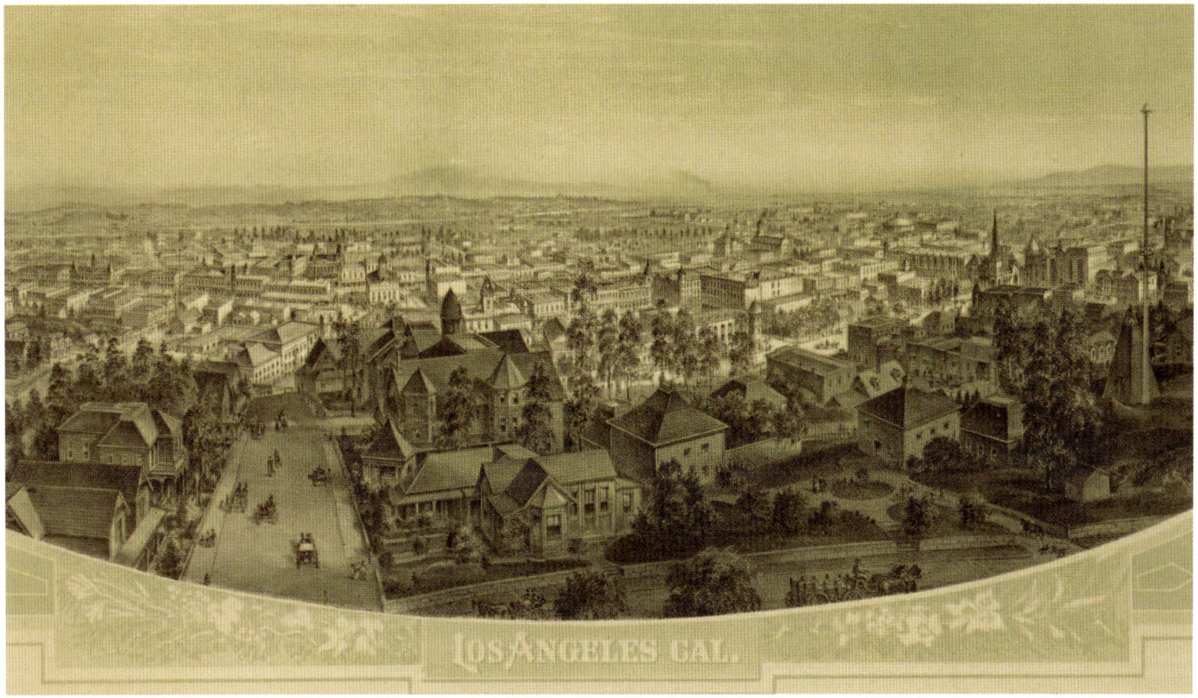

ABOVE *This bird's eye view of Los Angeles printed in 1888 by Britton & Rey of San Francisco depicts one of the city's early electric lighting standards at right.*

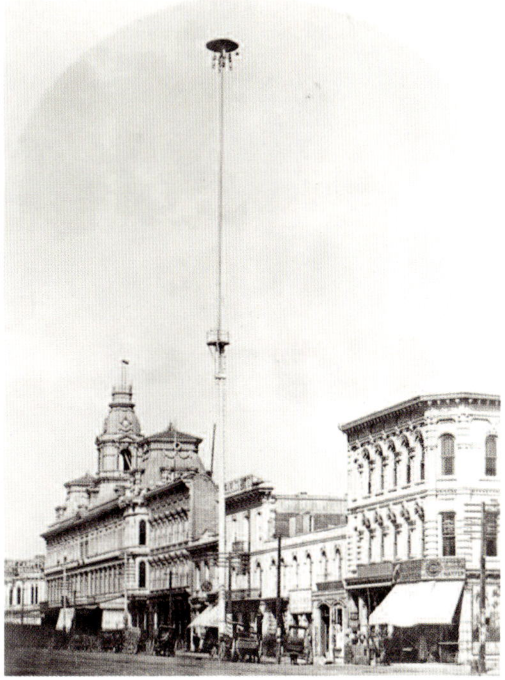

RIGHT AND OPPOSITE *Here the city's first electric streetlight appears out in front of the Baker Block at Main and Commercial streets. The towers are visible in many historic pictures, such as the B'nai B'rith on page 27.*

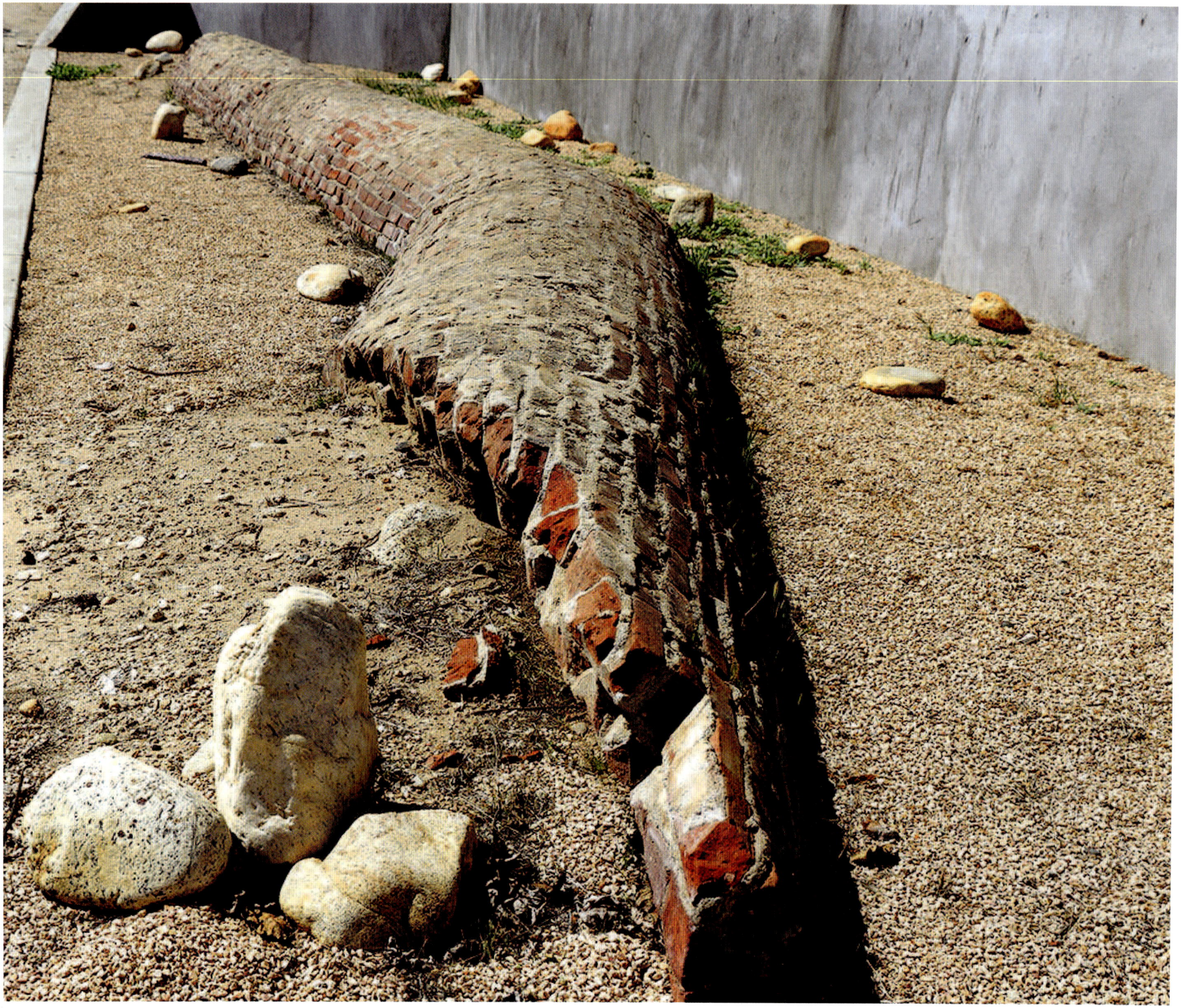

Zanja Madre ABANDONED IN 1904

Once the founding-day ceremonies at El Pueblo de la Reina de los Ángeles had finished, 11 settlers, known as *pobladores*, and their families—44 people in all—got to work building primitive houses of willow branches and mud. The settlers next turned to supplying themselves with their most important commodity, fresh water.

They traveled to a spot on El Río de Nuestra Señora La Reina de Los Ángeles de Porciúncula, modern-day Los Angeles River, about two miles northeast of their settlement. They chose a spot where the river rounded a steep bluff as it flowed around today's Elysian Hills. There they built a *toma*, a dam made of sand and willow poles. In *The Los Angeles River: Its Life, Death, and Possible Rebirth*, Blake Gumprecht writes that the Spanish government held the settlers responsible for not only building the dam, but for digging and maintaining ditches, called *zanjas*, to bring the water from the river to the pueblo.

The settlers got to work and completed the main ditch, the *Zanja Madre* (Mother Ditch) by the end of October 1781. Gumprecht pinpoints the intake from the river to the *Zanja Madre* at where the North Broadway Bridge crosses the river today, near the spot where the Portola Expedition had forded the river in 1769. The open-air ditch carried water to a location just north of the plaza. There it split into two branches: one ran behind the settlers' homes and carried water for domestic needs. The other branch ran further south and brought the water to the fields so the *pobladores* could maintain their crops.

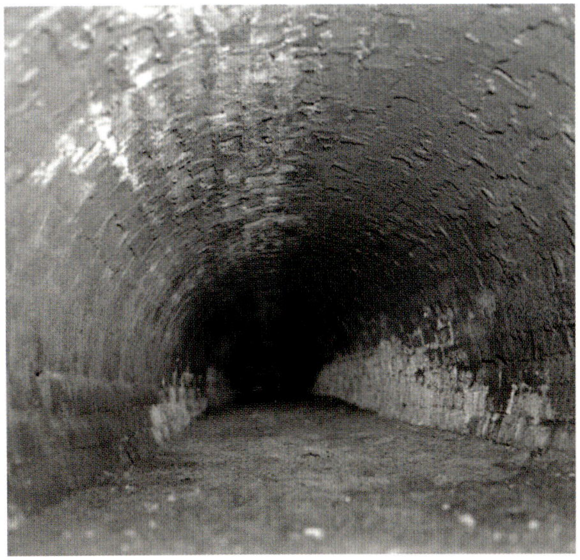

The settlers found the water carried from the river by the Indians more appealing for domestic use than water from the often stagnant *zanjas*. Local Indians capitalized on this. They arrived with fresher, more-palatable water in terra cotta urns calling out "Agua! Agua!"

The *zanja* that carried the water for domestic use became so little used that it does not appear on the earliest map of the pueblo. The mapmaker simply ignored this ditch. Orchards, vineyards and gardens flourished, though, while grain and maize were the first two cash crops. Settlers introduced the grape in 1803 and began planting orange trees in 1815.

In 1857 a large water wheel began taking water up to the *Zanja Madre* and onto the main brick reservoir at the plaza at the end of Olvera Street. In 1877, the city decided for health reasons to cover the ditch with brick to create a tunnel.

The aqueduct was abandoned in 1884 after a flood tore out the wooden dam. Four years later the city planned to put pipes in most of the existing *zanjas*, but couldn't come up with the money. By 1893 some 50 miles of *zanjas* were carrying water throughout the city. The city finally abandoned the *Zanja Madre* in 1904. Now and again workers stumble upon portions of the Mother Ditch; they made a recent find while working on the Blossom Plaza project on North Broadway.

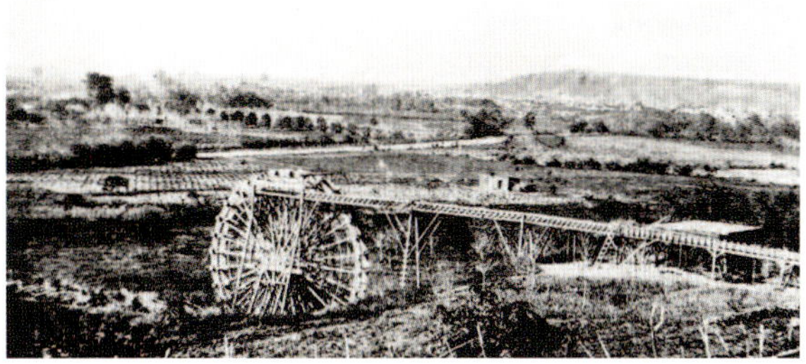

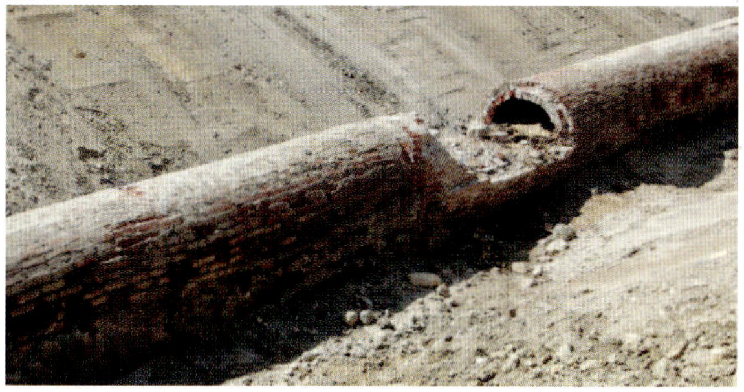

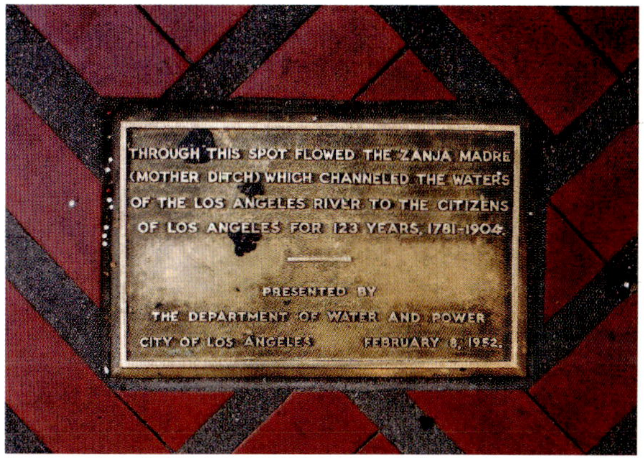

TOP *The antique brick structure of the* Zanja Madre *uncovered in 2014.*

ABOVE *In 1952 the city placed a plaque at the plaza to highlight the* Zanja Madre *once flowed beneath.*

FAR LEFT *The Department of Water and Power photographed the interior of the* Zanja Madre *that workers uncovered along Olvera Street in 1930. They also found traces of the redwood bridge that crossed the ditch.*

LEFT *In 1857, William Dryden rebuilt the* Zanja Madre *adding a water wheel that measured 40 feet in diameter to draw that water from the Los Angeles River. The water flowed though a brick-lined channel to a brick reservoir at the center of the plaza.*

OPPOSITE PAGE *A section of the* Zanja Madre *uncovered and left on permanent display. By 1893 there were around 50 miles of* zanjas *in the city and almost 40 beyond the city limit.*

Crocker Mansion RAZED JUNE 1908

Margaret Eleanor Rhodes married Edwin Bryant Crocker on July 8, 1852. She was Edwin's second wife. Edwin was a California Supreme Court justice who shared the wealth that his brother Charles amassed with the building of the Central Pacific Railroad. The couple had four girls and two boys.

Edwin died in 1875 and Margaret had the three-story Bunker Hill mansion built nine years later. Architect John Hall designed the house, which cost Margaret $45,000. This was not the only place the wealthy widow called home. She also owned houses in Sacramento, Lake Tahoe, San Francisco and New York.

Just a year after Margaret moved into the house on Bunker Hill it became a place of notoriety when Robert Porter Ashe kidnapped his own daughter from the mansion. The child, Gladys (also known as "Alma") was Margaret's granddaughter. Ashe had eloped with Margaret's daughter Aimee and (so the story goes) spent his time frittering away Aimee's inheritance of $10 million buying race horses and investing in prize fighters. Ashe held Alma captive for two days until a judge ordered her return to her mother. Margaret took her granddaughter to Europe to keep the young girl away from her father.

Margaret moved out of the Bunker Hill mansion in 1891. She maintained ownership of the property while renting it out to commercial ventures and boarders. She advertised that space in the "Crocker Mansion" was available to rent.

When workers began digging through Bunker Hill in 1900 to create the Third Street Tunnel, Margaret complained that the work was making the mansion "a veritable death trap." More digging commenced the following year when James Ward Eddy's company, the Los Angeles Incline Railway, began constructing Angel's Flight, which opened on New Year's Eve 1901. The funicular railway carried passengers from Third and Hill streets up to its terminus on Olive Street practically at the mansion's doorstep.

Margaret did not live to see the completion of Angel's Flight, she died on December 2, 1901, at her home in New York. The children took over the mansion when Margaret died, except for Aimee, that is; Margaret had disinherited her.

On July 17, 1906, the Elks Club purchased the mansion. "Negotiations for the purchase with Crocker heirs were concluded yesterday through K. D. Silent & Co., the reported consideration being $65,000," the *Los Angeles Herald* reported. J. W. Eddy was living in the mansion at the time. The Elks wanted to refurbish the mansion but the builders talked them out of it, saying that the frame was too weak. The Elks had the house razed in June 1908.

"The local lodge of the Elks has decided to demolish the old Crocker Mansion at Third and Olive streets and erect an up-to-date club building instead of remodeling the three-story, wood-frame structure," the *Los Angeles Herald* subsequently reported on June 21, 1908. Construction on the building that replaced Margaret's home began three months later.

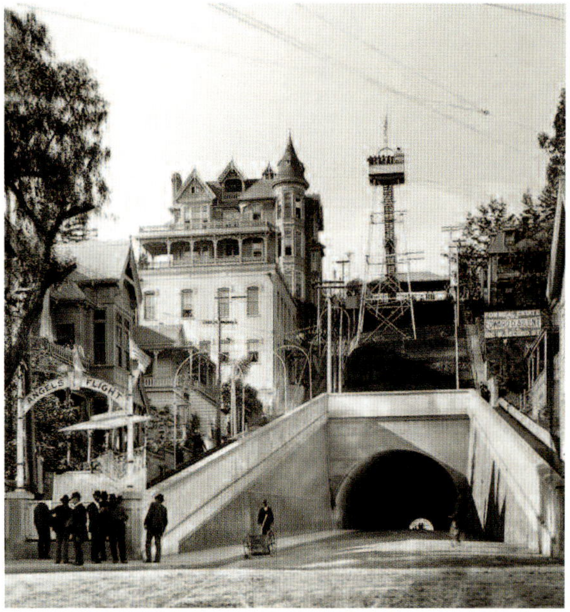

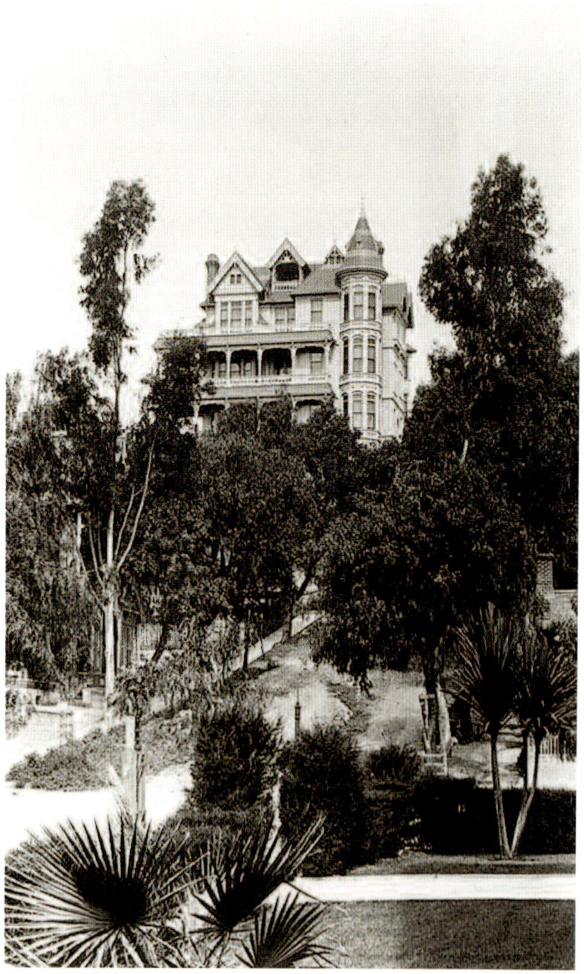

RIGHT *People crowd the observation tower in the center of this photograph taken on the opening day of Angels Flight, New Year's Eve, 1901. More than two thousand people took the ride that ended almost at the doorstep of the Crocker mansion; seven years later the mansion would be gone.*

FAR RIGHT *Crocker Mansion, Bunker Hill: The photographer stood on Hill Street and looked up Third Street to Olive Street to get this early shot of Margaret Crocker's home atop Bunker Hill. The house was the predominant Queen Anne-style home on Bunker Hill, if not in the entire city.*

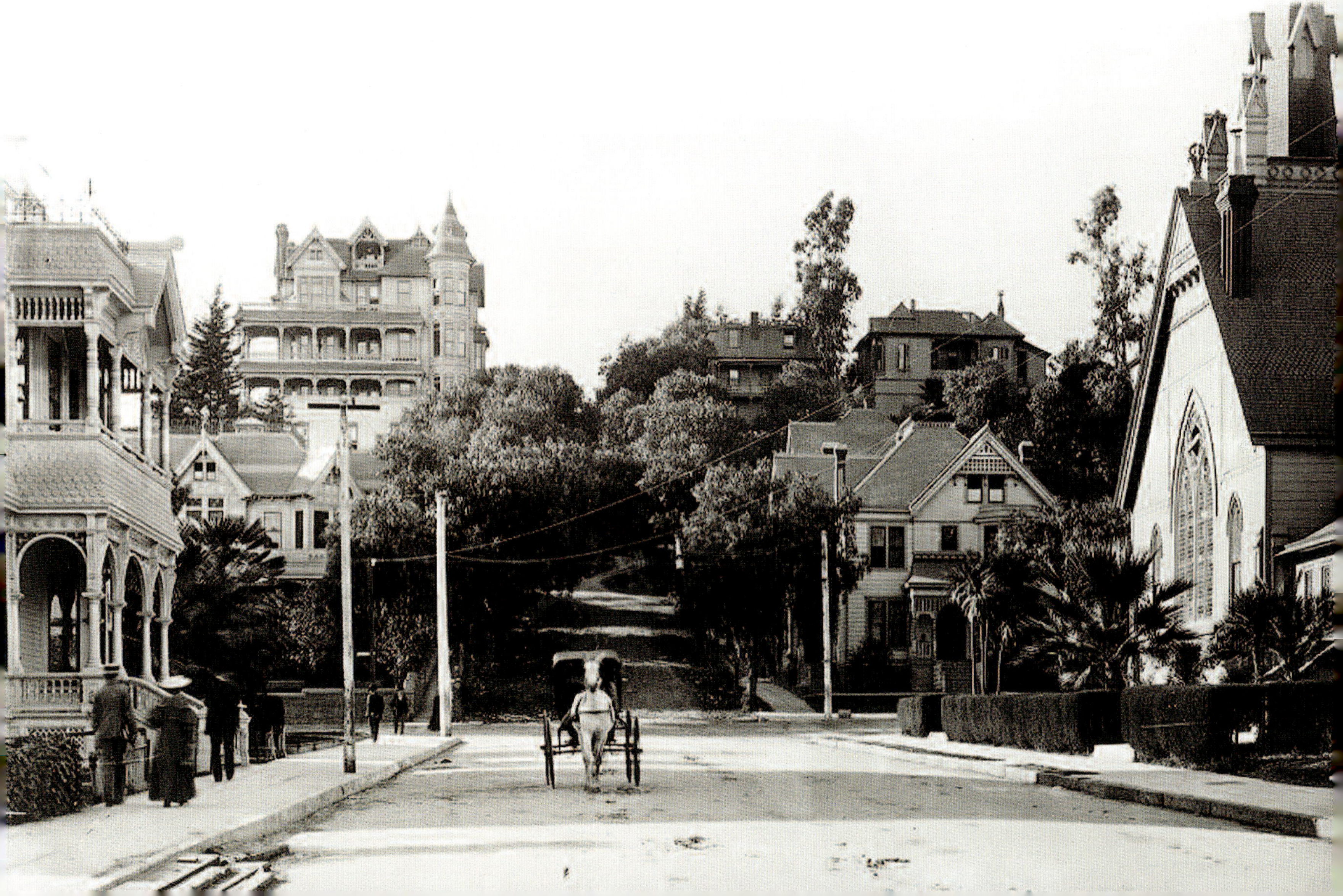

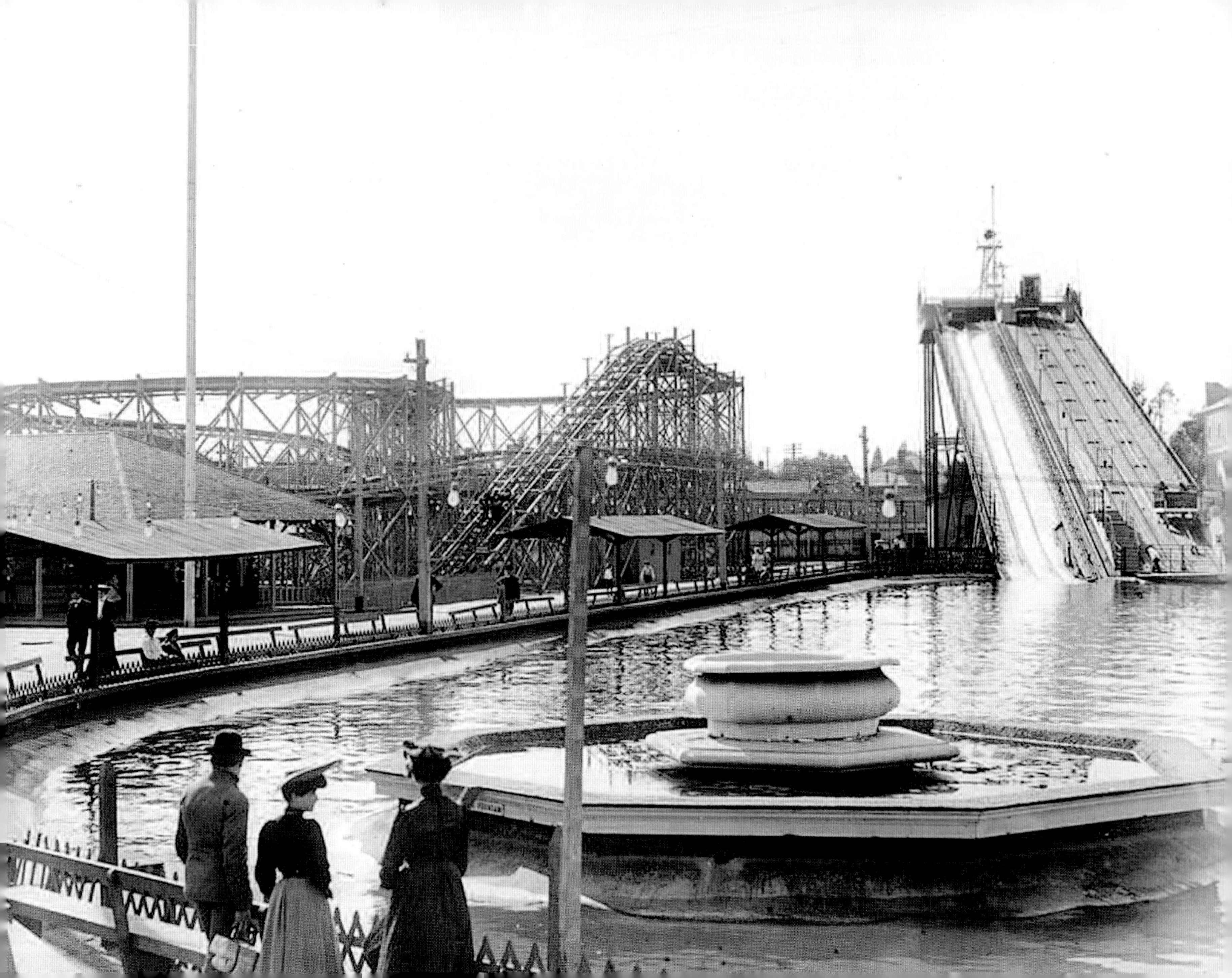

Chutes Park CHUTES DEMOLISHED 1910

Amusement park rides featuring a boat launched down a steep waterslide have captivated Americans since well back in the 19th century. The first recorded ride of this sort is attributed to J. P. Newberg whose ride entertained park-goers in Rock Island, Illinois. The modern version of the ride is a "log flume," and in the Victorian era the 500-foot greased wooden track proved so popular, Newberg set up more rides in Chicago.

Amusement parks featuring chutes began appearing across the nation, named after Paul Boyton's 1894 Water Chute version of the ride in Chicago. Boyton's name for the ride: "Shoot the Chute" became "The Chutes" for short. In some places, like Los Angeles, an entire 35-acre amusement park would take the name, "Chutes Park" to capitalize on the popularity of the ride.

Los Angeles' chutes were constructed on property owned by David V. Waldron bounded by Grand Avenue, Washington Boulevard and Main and 21st streets, at Waldron's trolley park. It was also the site of John Lang's 1873 Sulphur Springs Hotel. Trolley parks, often controlled by a railroad company, offered recreational attractions like picnicking, dancing or fireworks at the end of trolley lines. These entertainments tended to blossom into full-blown amusement parks with Ferris wheels, swimming pools and sports fields, guaranteeing riders on the line.

Waldron had to construct his own horsecar line to connect to the city's streetcar lines since his property sat so far outside the city limits. He planted an orange grove, set up animal exhibits and a small pavilion for shows and dancing. In 1899 Waldron sold the struggling park to the Los Angeles County Improvement Co. which, as its name would imply, began improving the property. The company put up a theater, created a fishing pond, ran a circus and offered daily hot-air balloon rides.

By 1910, Chutes Park had grown into a considerable resort with a 1903 roller coaster and a 10,000-seat baseball park that opened in 1900 as the original home of the Los Angeles Angels and Vernon Tigers of the Pacific Coast League. The mechanism running the chutes now boasted electric power. That year, the park became part of roller coaster designer and amusement park mogul Frederick Ingersoll's empire, and was renamed "Luna Park" just like all his other parks worldwide. The new Luna Park featured improvements including a miniature railway and more rides than ever, but the chutes ride was removed.

Soon after opening, the site was sold to a group who formed a short-lived plan to make the site into an exclusive location for the amusement of African Americans. By 1914 the site had been named Horsley Park and housed a zoo owned by British film pioneer David Horsley. The rides had all been demolished.

The Angels remained the largest baseball franchise in town and played out of Washington Park until 1925 when they moved to Wrigley Field. The ballpark was demolished in the 1950s as more intense commercial development encroached. Today, the location of decades of amusement, Chutes Park, is a parking lot.

FAR LEFT *Today's version of this ride, the log flume, is just as popular as its forerunner The Chutes. The ride pictured measured 75 feet tall and 300 feet long.*

BELOW LEFT *One of the first improvements made to the park after selling to the Los Angeles Improvement Company was the construction of the 4,000-seat Chutes Theater, offering vaudeville and later, moving picture productions.*

BELOW *Sixteenth Street School appears in the distance of this 1905 photo looking north over Chutes Park.*

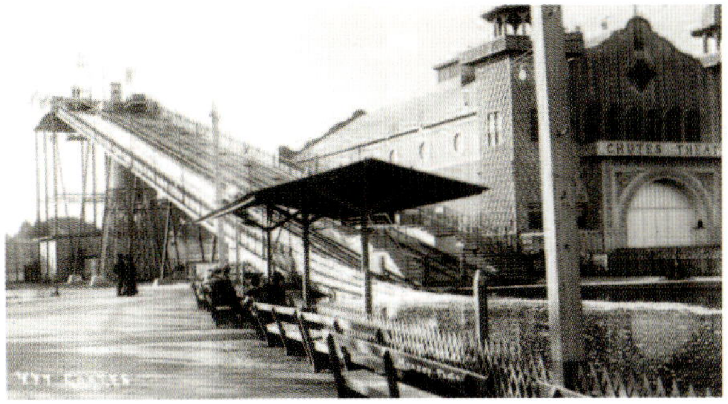

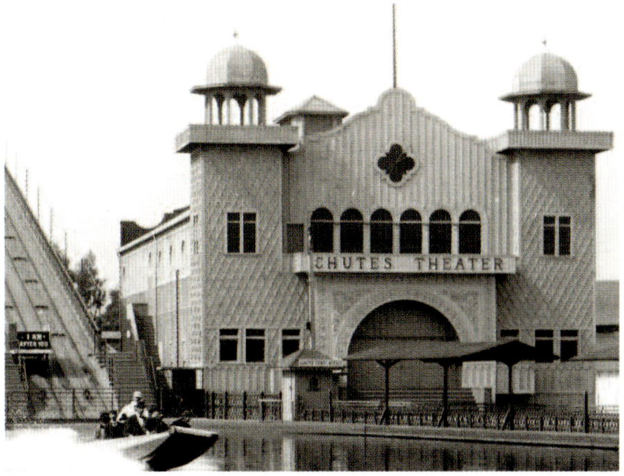

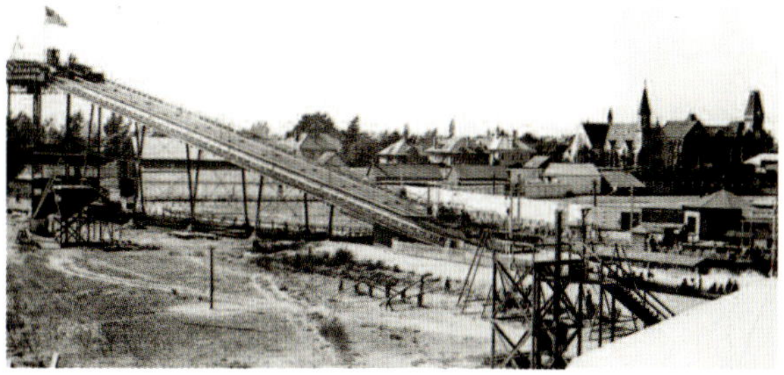

St. Vincent's RENAMED 1918

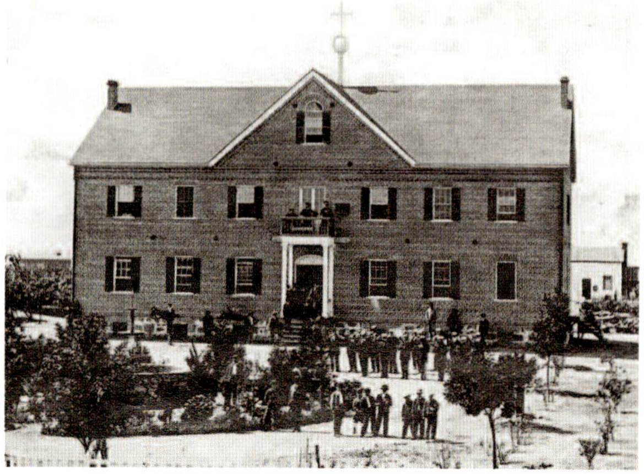

The Fathers of the Congregation of the Mission, better known as the Vincentians, had a long tradition of serving immigrant children. In August 1865 they opened a school in rented rooms at the Lugo Adobe on the plaza. They named the school St. Vincent's for St. Vincent de Paul, the founder of their order.

In August 1867 they learned that Ozio W. Childs had donated six acres of land for a campus. The following March, the priests moved into their new school, which was located at present-day Hill Street and Broadway between Sixth and Seventh streets.

On the Feast of the Assumption, August 15, 1869, St. Vincent's received a charter from the state of California. This empowered the school to grant college degrees to its students.

Austrian Archduke Ludwig Salvator visited the school in September 1876. The school "is situated in the west end of town in a pleasant garden," the archduke wrote. When he visited the school, the Vincentians welcomed him into a two-story brick building. The architect had set the main entrance with its portico below a large single gable that faced Broadway. The balanced setting of the windows echoed Federal-style buildings on the East Coast.

In June 1883 the Vincentians added an extra wing to this building to accommodate growing enrollment; it wasn't enough. Less than two years later the priests purchased some real estate at the intersection of today's Washington Boulevard and South Grand Avenue. In 1887, St. Vincent's moved into a brand new building that J. V. McNeil Construction had put up on the site. The building included a modern furnished college library. Three years after the students and faculty moved in, St. Vincent's celebrated its silver anniversary.

About this time the Very Reverend J. W. Hickey was serving as the rector at St. Vincent's. In an advertisement he wrote for the school he bragged

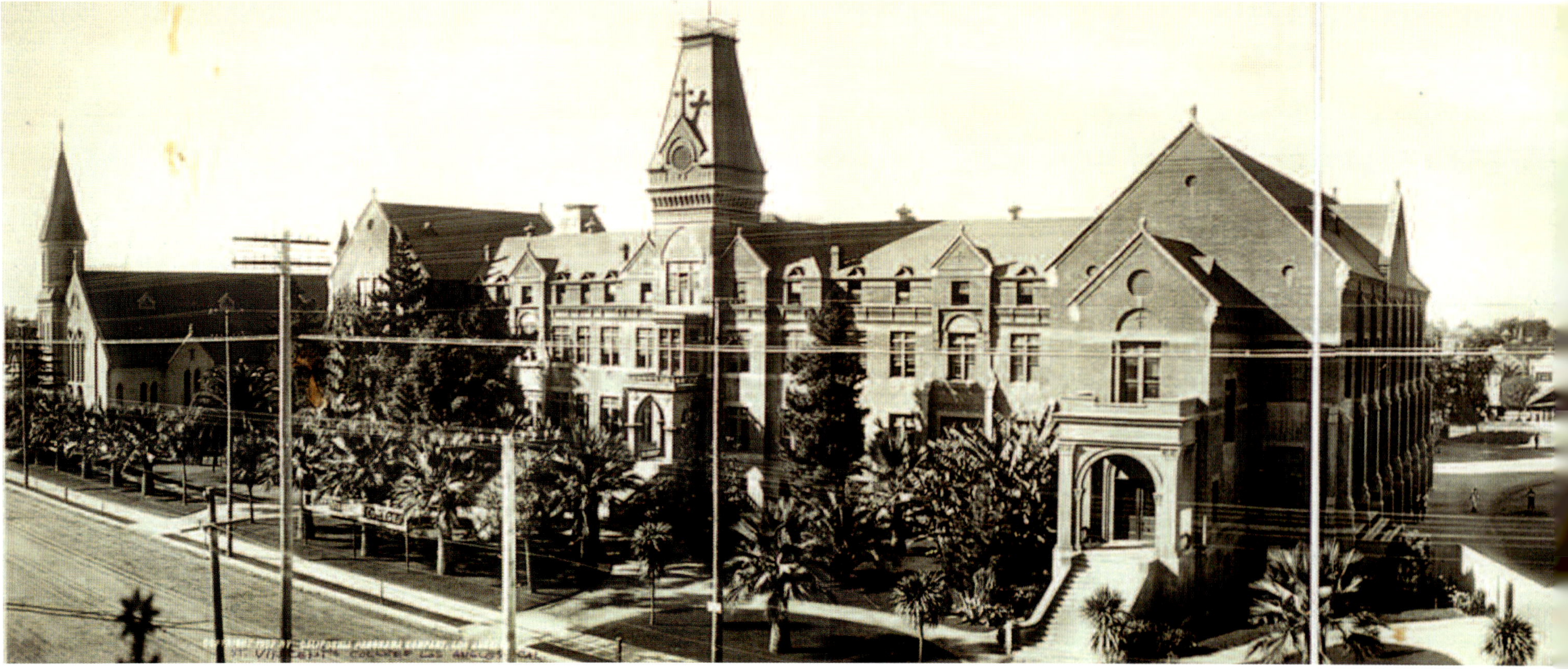

about Los Angeles, which he said was "proverbial for the salubrity of its climate and the beauty of is scenery." He pointed out that St. Vincent's receives students at any time of the year. "The College is open to all over ten years old, no matter of what denomination they may be," he wrote. He made it clear that he only wanted students "disposed to comply with the rules of the College, which, though strict, are mild and parental."

In September 1911 the Vincentians decided to give up running St. Vincent's and the Jesuits took over. They stepped in and renamed St. Vincent's "Los Angeles College." This college's first president, Reverend Richard Gleeson, turned to J. V. McNeil, who had put up the school's Grand Avenue buildings in 1890. Gleeson built the Jesuits a new campus in Highland Park.

In March 1914 the Jesuits changed the Highland Park school's name back to St. Vincent's, but four years later had a change of heart and renamed the school for their founder, Ignatius of Loyola. The name "St. Vincent's" would be no more.

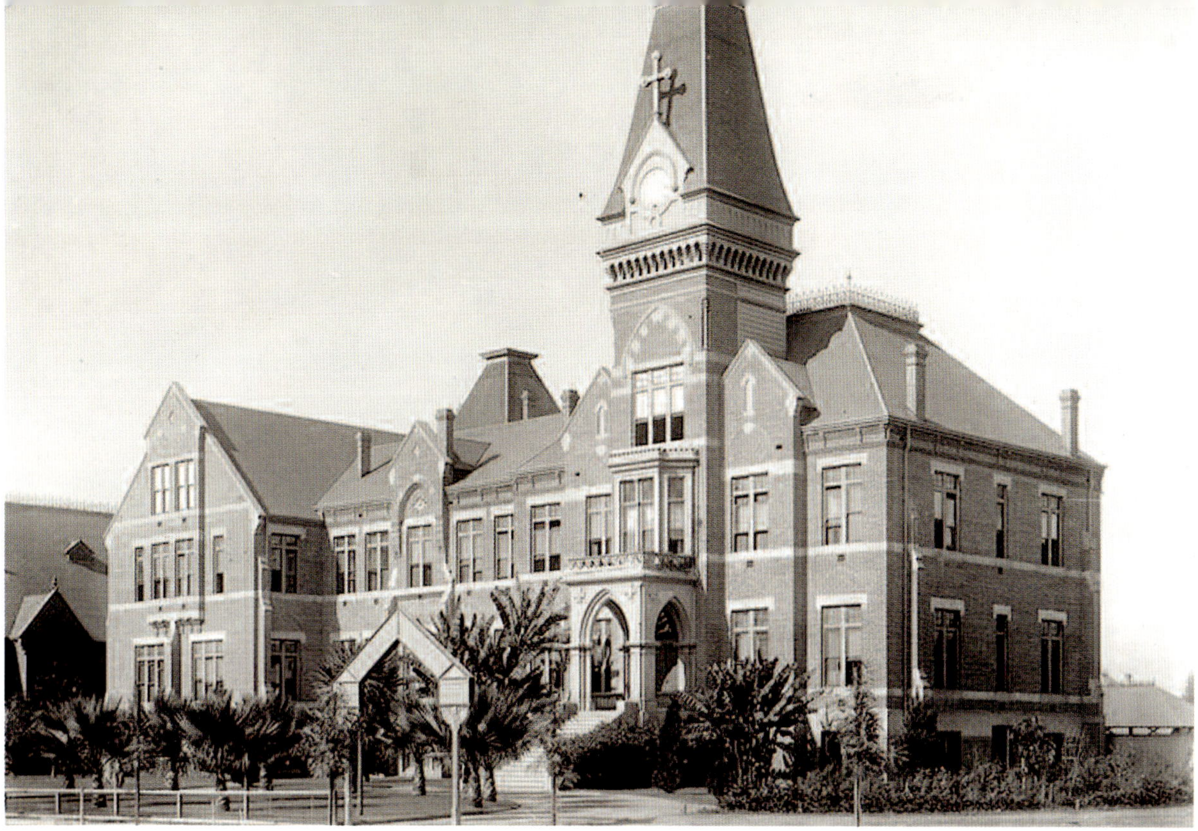

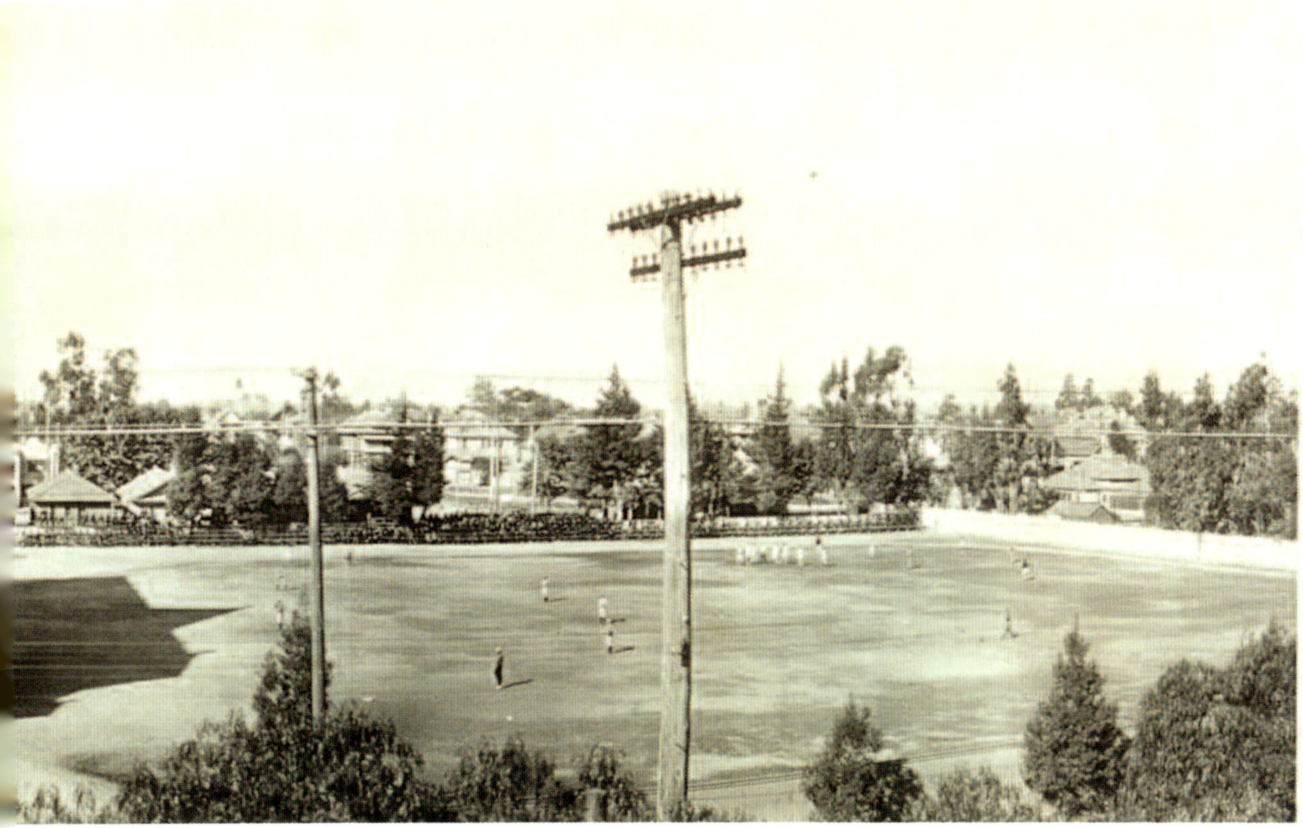

ABOVE *The school photographed in 1905.*

ABOVE LEFT *Students, including some with musical instruments pose for the camera about the year 1875 in front of St. Vincent's College. The school's campus faced Broadway and was bounded by Broadway, Hill Street and Sixth and Seventh streets, the site of today's St. Vincent's Court.*

LEFT *The school moved from Broadway in 1887 to South Grand Avenue between West Eighteen Street and West Washington Boulevard. The Vincentian fathers built a school of brick and stone and a wooden church just up the street. This panoramic photo from circa 1908.*

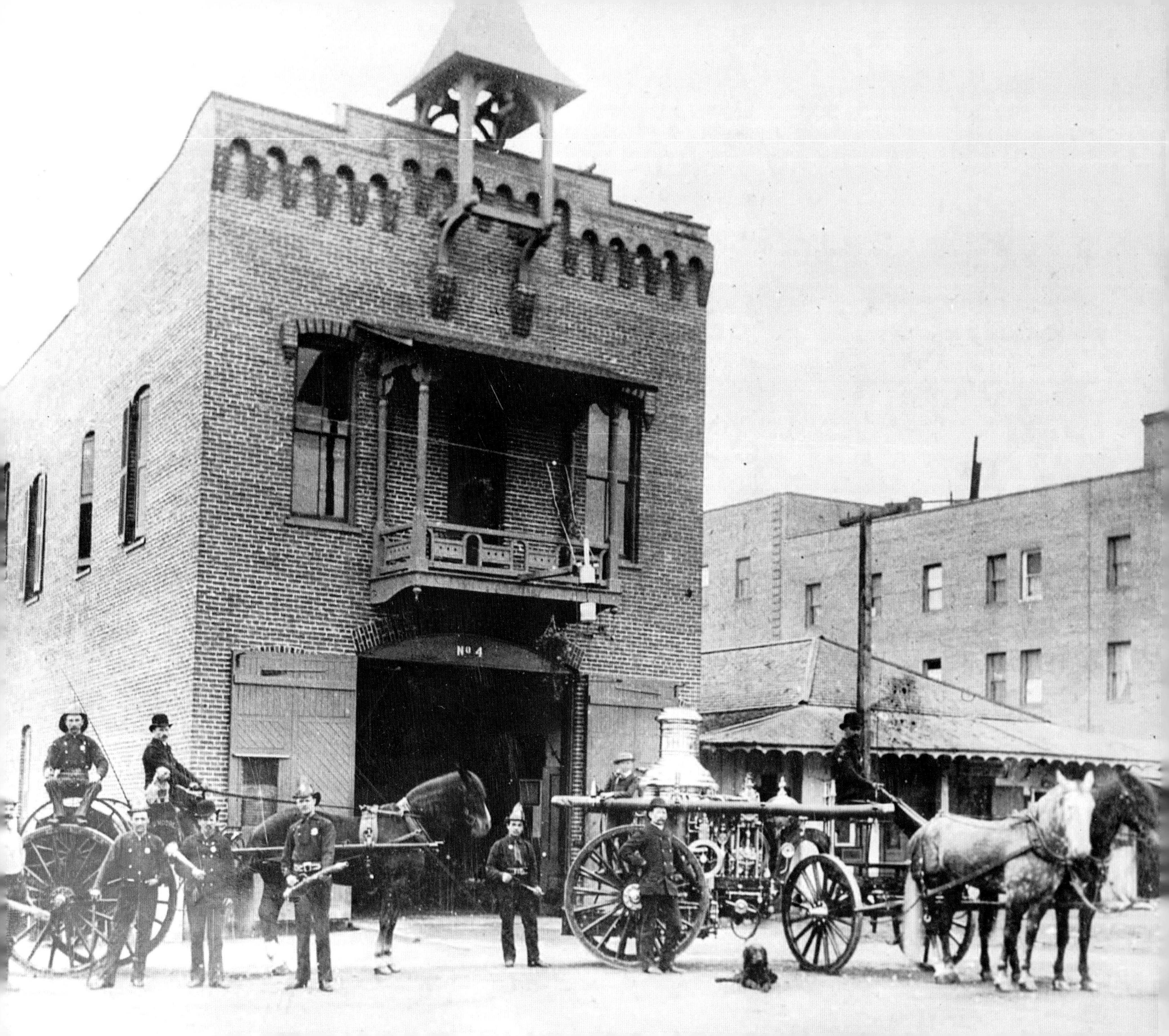
No 4

Los Angeles Fire Horses RETIRED 1921

When fire broke out in Los Angeles before September 30, 1871, the city had no organized firefighters who could respond. County Clerk George M. Fall put an end to that dilemma when he organized Engine Company No. 1. Because they had no horses, members of Fall's new company arrived at a fire pulling the fire engine themselves along with a two-wheel cart containing the rolled hose, known as a "hose jumper."

In 1874 members of Engine Company No. 1 petitioned the city for horses. The City Council refused their request and the company disbanded. On April 14, 1875, 38 members of the former company organized as the "Thirty-Eights No. 1." The following month, more firefighters stepped up and formed Engine Company No. 2, calling themselves the "Confidence Engine Company."

In 1877 the city finally gave in and purchased two horses for its firefighters; the "Era of the Horse" had begun. In 1878 the "Park Hose Company No. 1" appeared on the scene. The city's fourth volunteer company, the "East Los Angeles Hose Company," formed in 1883. That same year the fifth and final volunteer fire company took the stage as the "Morris Vineyard Hose Company No. 3."

All five engine companies were in service until February 1, 1886, when the city commissioned a paid fire brigade, bringing the Los Angeles Fire Department into existence. The new department started life with 31 paid firefighters and 24 reserves. These firefighters manned four stations and worked with two steam-pump fire engines, a pair of hose reels, a hose wagon, a 65-foot aerial ladder truck and 11 horses.

In 1893 the fire department held an inspection in front of Fire House No. 1, the Plaza Fire House, at the time, the home of Chemical Company No. 1. All seven engine companies, both chemical companies and the hose company, all paraded in wagons pulled by horses. Assistant Chief Dan Moriarity and Chief Engineer Walter S. Moore also appeared at the inspection in their horse-drawn wagons. The inspection included the department's 24 horses—a far cry from a time just 19 years earlier when the City Council had refused to buy even a single horse for the volunteers.

By 1900 the department had 120 full-time firefighters working from 18 stations. The new century brought change and the department began to phase out the horses and motorize. The department purchased its last horse in 1915; by 1921 the job was done and the department retired the rest of its horses to Griffith Park.

The era of the horse ended in Los Angeles on July 19, 1921, when the Los Angeles Fire Department took its last horse-drawn apparatus—the Gorter Water Tower assigned to Engine Company 24—out of service and sent it to the workshops. The mechanics fitted a motorized tractor onto the tower to replace the horses. The department used this tower—an apparatus that allowed firefighters to aim a hose from 75 feet up in the air—from the time Henry Gorter designed it in 1898 until its retirement in 1971.

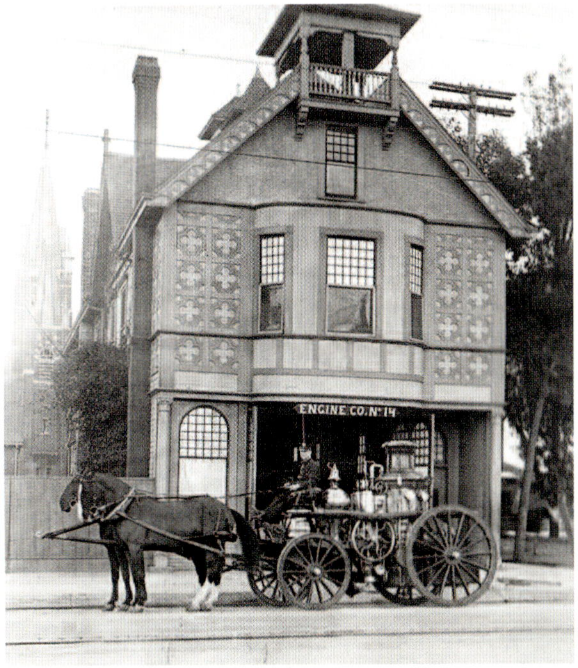

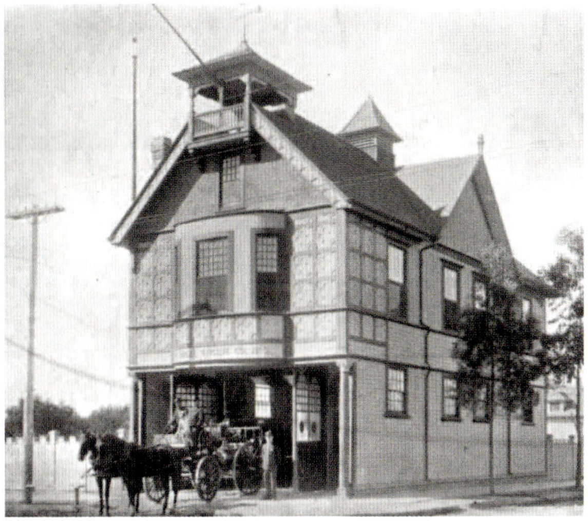

LEFT *Engine Company No. 14 at East Thirty-Fourth Street and Central Avenue, was 14 years old when this photograph was taken in 1914. In 1906 an accident happened on the very spot the photographer stood. "Los Angeles firemen were roused almost to the lynching point when Frank B. Willits, driver of the combination hose and chemical wagon of Engine Company No. 14, sustained injuries in a collision in front of the company house," the* Los Angeles Examiner *reported. "Vernon avenue streetcar No. 342, collided with Willits and his apparatus."*

ABOVE *Two firemen and a "fire dog" sit atop a horse-drawn engine, and another fireman stands to their left. Chemical Engine Company No. 2 was organized in 1891 and had their station at 137 South Belmont Street. The following year the company was assigned to share quarters with Engine Company No. 14 at Central Avenue and 34th Street. This station was rebuilt in 1950. The new building stands at the same location.*

OPPOSITE *The first occupants of the Plaza Fire Station were the Volunteer Thirty-Eights, so called because all 38 men had served as volunteers before the paid department was formed. Engine Company No. 1 occupied this building from 1884 to 1889. Shown here in 1887 it was later abandoned and used variously as a cigar store and a flophouse until it was bought in 1950 by the State of California and restored as a fire house museum.*

State Normal School DEMOLISHED IN 1923

A "normal" school trained high school graduates how to teach; it took its name from the "norms," or teaching standards, the school established. George Washington Minns established such a school in 1857 in San Francisco as the Minns Evening Normal School. Minns was a Harvard-educated attorney who began teaching grammar school in San Francisco. The State of California took over Minns' school in 1862 and renamed it the California State Normal School. The school moved to San Jose in 1870. In March 1881, after heavy lobbying by Los Angeles residents, the California State Legislature authorized the creation of a southern branch of the school in downtown Los Angeles.

The State Normal School at Los Angeles opened on August 29, 1882, on today's West Fifth Street, the site of the city's Central Library. The building stood on a knob of Bunker Hill that students quickly dubbed "Normal Hill." The beautiful brick building had numerous tall windows, several chimneys, gabled dormers, a tower with a balcony and ornate grill. A set of stairs on either side led to the main entrance. The facility included an elementary school where teachers-in-training could practice their teaching techniques on children. That elementary school is similar to the present-day Lab School at the University of California at Los Angeles. In 1887, the school became known as the Los Angeles State Normal School.

In 1914, the school moved to a new campus on the 800 block of Vermont Avenue, now the site of Los Angeles City College in East Hollywood. Three years later, University of California Regent, Edward Augustus Dickson, the only regent representing Southern California, joined forces with Ernest Carroll Moore, Director of the Normal School, to lobby the State Legislature to enable the school to become the second University of California campus, after Berkeley.

They met resistance from Berkeley alumni, Northern California members of the state legislature, and Benjamin Ide Wheeler, who served as president of the University of California until 1919. They all vigorously opposed the idea of a southern campus for the university.

However, David Prescott Barrows took over the presidency of the university from Wheeler and did not share his predecessor's objections. On May 23, 1919, the Southern Californians' efforts were rewarded when California Governor William D. Stephens signed Assembly Bill 626 into law. This new law merged the Los Angeles Normal School with the University of California as the southern branch of the University of California. This bill added the College of Letters and Science into the mix, and the new campus opened on September 15, 1919. The school offered a two-year undergraduate program to 250 Letters and Science students and admitted an additional 1,250 students to the Teachers College.

The old Normal School building met the wrecking ball in 1923. Once the building was out of the way, workers straightened out Fifth Street and prepared the site for the construction of the city's new public library, which rose up on the site three years later.

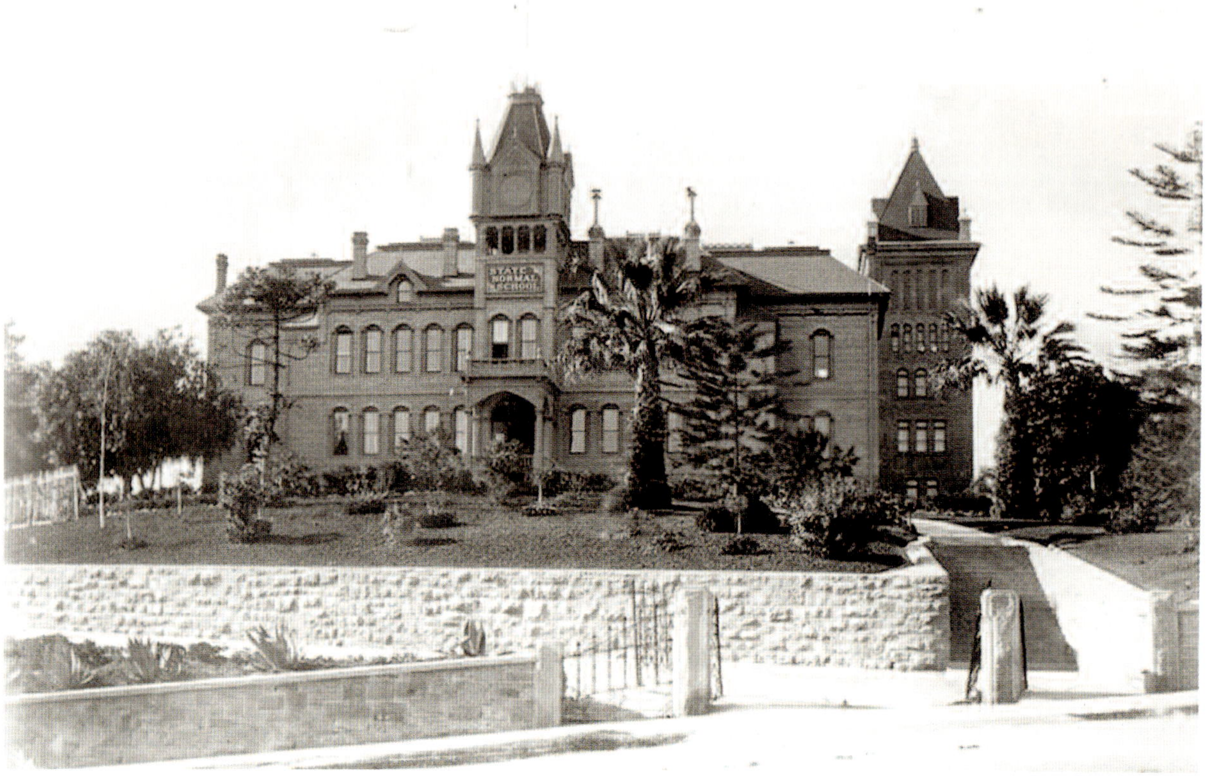

ABOVE *A slightly earlier image of the Los Angeles State Normal School. This photograph was taken after the 1894 addition to the school opened. The tower on the building's right-hand side belies the size of the new structure, which the school built to accommodate new classrooms and an assembly hall.*

OPPOSITE PAGE *The State Normal School sits impressively on a knoll of Bunker Hill in this circa 1925 photograph.*

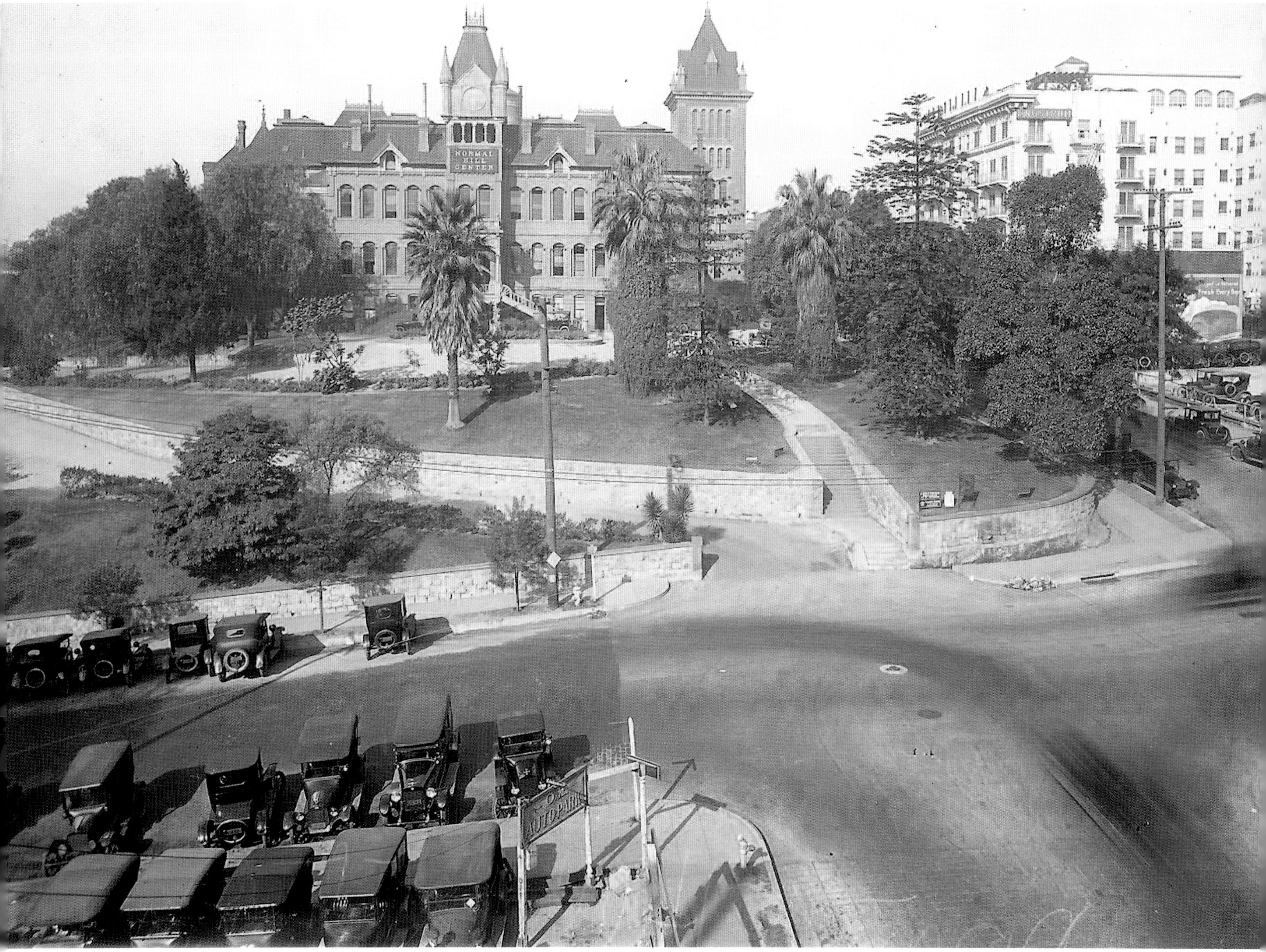
NORMAL
HILL
CENTER

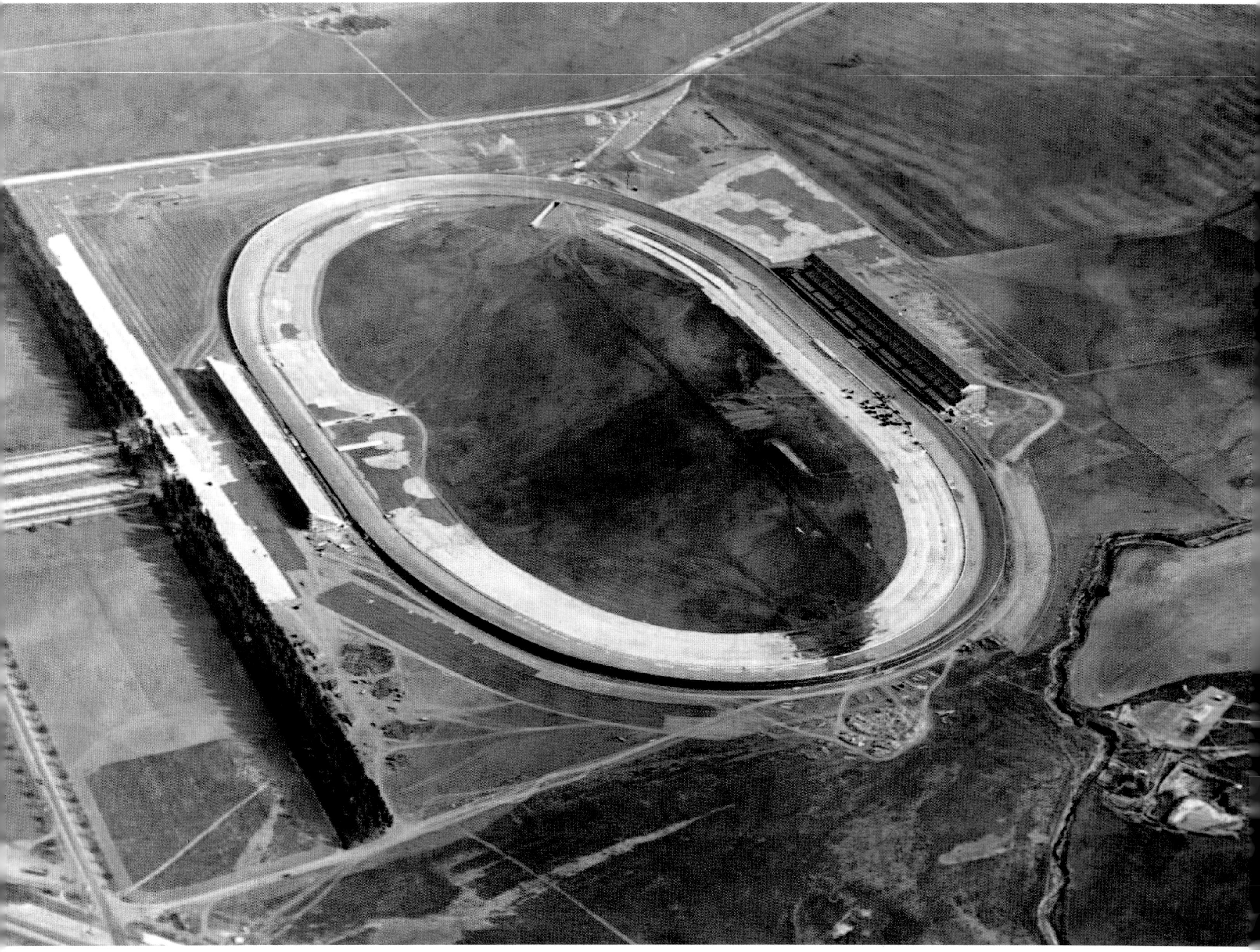

Beverly Hills Speedway REDEVELOPED 1924

Towards the close of World War I, a group of Los Angeles businessmen formed an association to further their passion for automobiles. Combined with this passion came the love for speed, and the newly formed Beverly Hills Speedway Syndicate gave themselves one main goal: to build the fastest racetrack in the nation.

The resultant Beverly Hills Speedway covered a 275-acre site that today includes the Beverly Wilshire Hotel, and the area between Wilshire and Olympic boulevards, and South Beverly and Lasky drives. Previously a bean farm, the site sold at $1,000 an acre to the 11-member association that included General Motors' founder William C. Durant's son, Cliff, and future three-time winner of the Indianapolis 500, Louis Meyer. Quite considerately, the association waited for the farmer to harvest his bean crop before beginning construction in 1919.

The one-and-a quarter-mile wooden board track was not the first in Los Angeles. When the Los Angeles Motordrome opened in 1910 in nearby Playa Del Rey, it created a sensation as the first wooden track built specifically for the purpose of racing motorized vehicles. The Motordrome shuttered after burning two short years later.

The track that became the Beverly Hills Speedway was the first in the nation to have banked turns with mathematically calculated curves. Designers Jack Prince and Art Pillsbury used techniques developed when laying railroad tracks.

The first race, held on February 28, 1920, saw Jimmy Murphy race 250 miles to victory in his Duesenberg at an average speed of 103.2 miles per hour. Some 50,000 people turned out for the event. Tragedy struck on Thanksgiving Day that same year when a collision involving Gaston Chevrolet (brother of Chevrolet Motor Company founder Louis Chevrolet) and Eddie O'Donnell, during a 250-mile race, took the lives of both drivers along with Chevrolet's riding mechanic the next day.

The speedway operated for four more years hosting a wide variety of events including motorcycle races, horse shows and movie shoots. A promotional film, *Beverly Hills Board Track Racing* (1921) showcased the excitement of racing an Indian Motorcycle Company bike. Early timber racetracks like the Beverly Hills Speedway (sometimes referred to as "murderdromes") offered plenty of danger to both cyclist and spectator alike. Accidents, made worse by the track's banking, could spark fires or worse.

The city rapidly encroached on the property, eventually making it far too valuable a site. At its final race in 1924, Harlan Fengler broke the world record for a 250-mile race averaging 116.6 miles per hour in front of a crowd of 80,000. The association tore down its 70,000-seat stadium and moved to Culver City in 1924. They sold the property at ten times the price they paid and within four years the Beverly Wilshire Hotel rose on the track's former northwest turn.

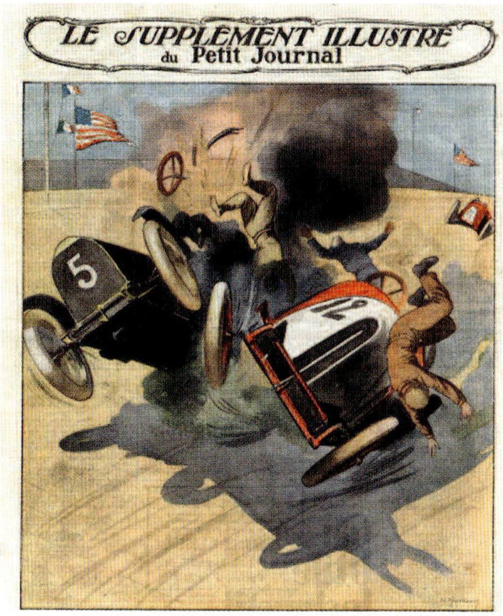

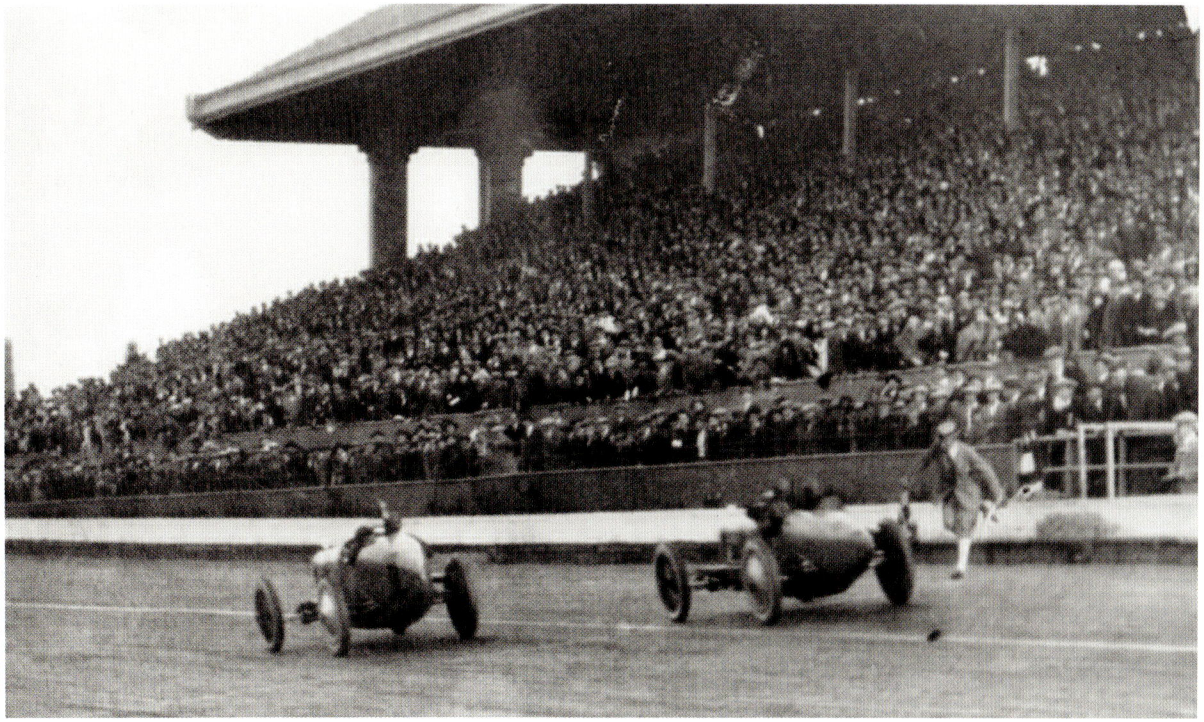

LEFT *The Speedway consistently drew big crowds for races and speed events.*

ABOVE *A French publication covered the accident at Beverly Hills Speedway that killed Louis Chevrolet's brother in 1920.*

OPPOSITE PAGE *This aerial photo of the speedway was taken around 1920.*

Temple Block DESTROYED 1927

Pliny Temple's building rose up on Temple Street in 1874 and lasted till 1927.

In the late 19th century, the three-sided space formed by the intersections of Main, Spring and Temple streets was established as the city's commercial heart. Main Street was Los Angeles' first *Calle Principal*; it connected the pueblo with Mission San Gabriel. Mapmaker Edward Ord put Spring Street or *Calle Primavera* on the map. He named the street for his Spanish girlfriend Trinidad Ortega, whom he affectionately called "Primavera." Temple Street bears Jonathan Temple's name. He got his name onto Ord's map by paying for the project.

California historian Nathan Masters writes that professionals of all stripes—lawyers, bankers, photographers and hatters—jockeyed for the offices that overlooked the yawning, open space that the intersection of these three streets created.

Los Angeles pioneer Jonathan Temple owned so much of the property here that the junction became informally known as Temple Square. Temple had arrived here in 1827 from Massachusetts. He quickly learned to assimilate, converting to Catholicism and changing his first name to "Juan." Temple opened a general store at the junction's northwest corner soon after he arrived. He served as the city's first *alcalde* (magistrate) after United States forces captured the pueblo during the Mexican-American War.

Temple made his eponymous square more attractive by installing rudimentary sidewalks and planting Peruvian pepper trees. He moved on to San Francisco, where he died in 1866. In 1871, his brother, Pliny Fisk Temple, built a three-story Italianate-style structure in place of Jonathan's adobe building. Pliny called it the New Temple Block and leased out space to the city's professionals, especially lawyers. In fact, so many attorneys had offices there that people called the building the "Lawyer's Block."

Pliny Temple got some competition from John G. Downey, who built his own eponymous block across the street. In 1874, the city's first streetcar line chose Temple Square as its northern terminus. In 1884, grocer and dry goods merchant Harris Newmark installed a seven-foot-tall fountain in the square. The city stepped up and provided the water for free. Newmark topped his fountain with a nude female figure. As a prank, the firemen of the Confidence Engine Company provided her with a blue dress.

As the 20th century dawned, commercial activity moved away from Temple Square. Retail shops opened along Broadway and the city's financial center moved to Broadway and Spring Street. The end came in 1926 with the creation of the city's new Civic Center. The project straightened out Spring Street, doing away with Temple Square's three-sided intersection. The steam shovels arrived in 1927 and made short work of what remained of the Temple Block.

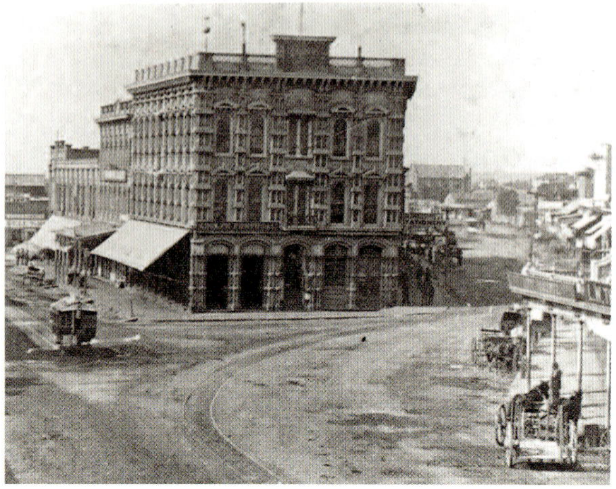

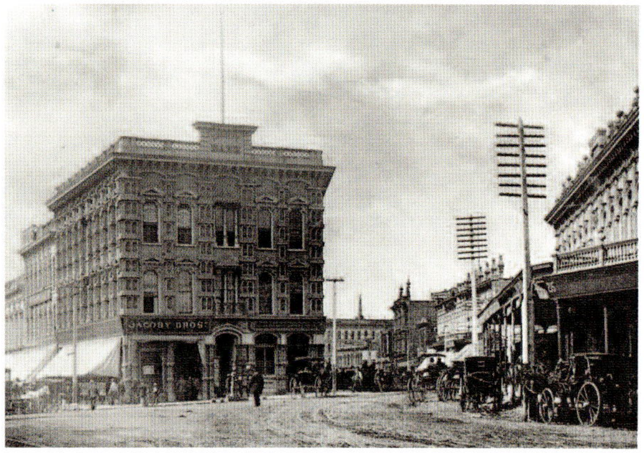

TOP AND ABOVE RIGHT *Two views of the New Temple Block in the 19th century, showing the early streetcar tracks that looped round the block. At this time, banks and lawyers were in residence at this important Los Angeles intersection.*

RIGHT *The Temple building shows its wear in this photo taken just a few years before the wrecking ball arrived. Comparing this photograph with earlier ones shows how the building and the quality of the tenants deteriorated after businesses began to concentrate on Broadway.*

OPPOSITE PAGE *A stereo card image of "Temple's Block" from around 1879. The four-story flagpole across the street, outside the United States Hotel, was said to be the tallest man-made object in Los Angeles from the time of the Civil War.*

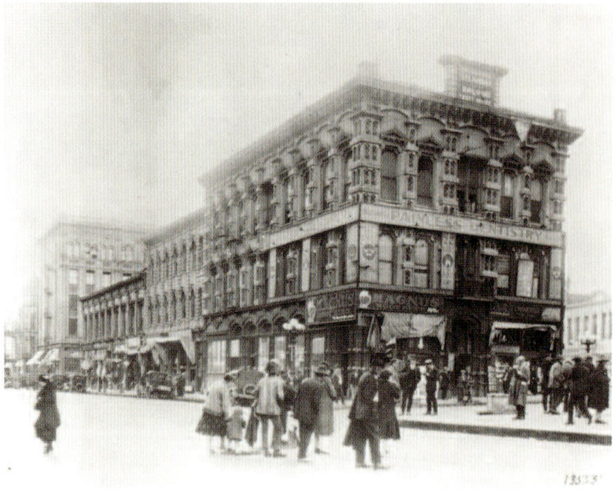

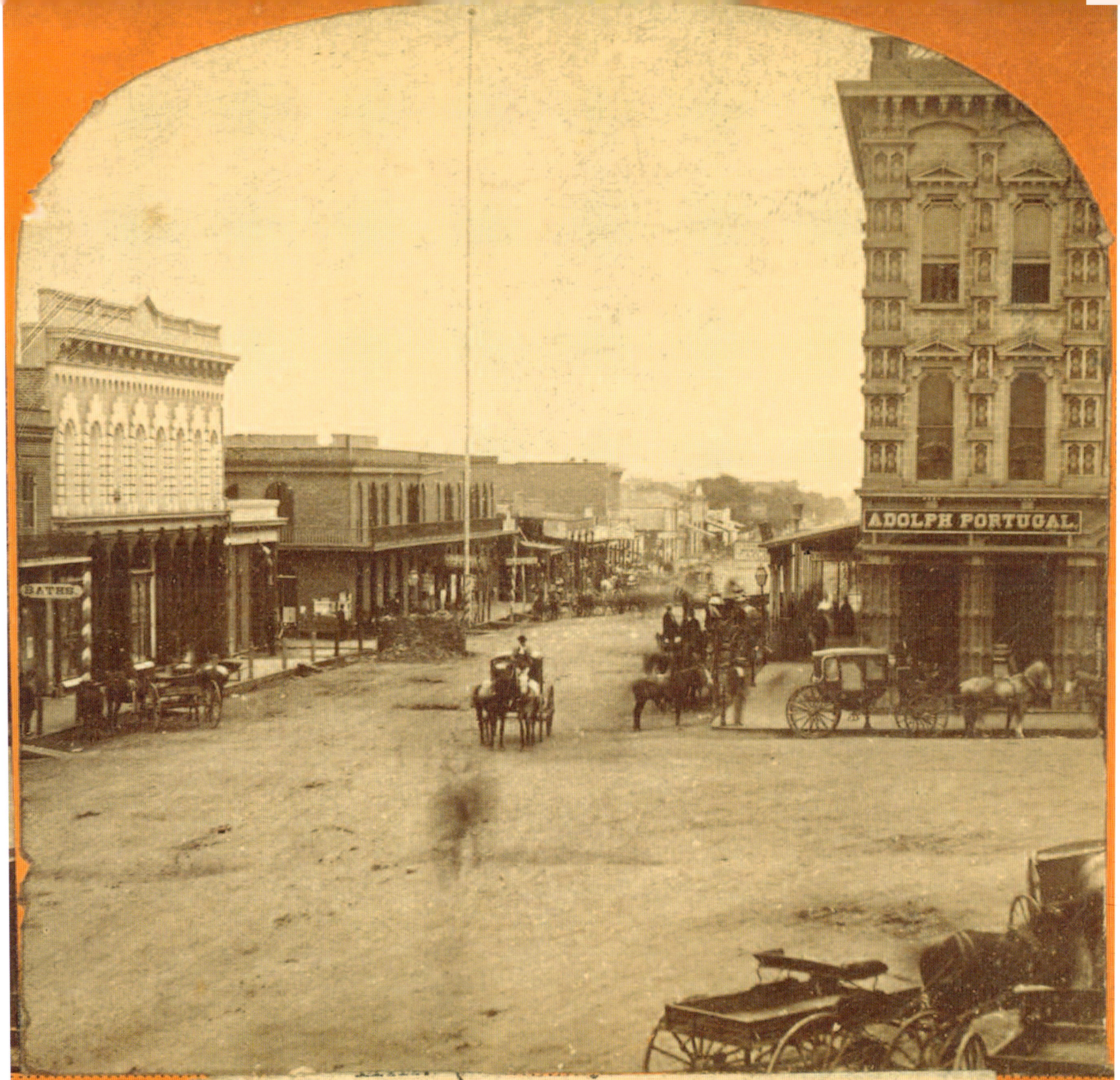

23. Temple's Block, Main street, Los Angeles.

B'nai B'rith Synagogue VACATED IN 1927

Just after California became a state in 1850, a census was taken through Los Angeles, tallying numbers, occupations and ethnicities of each household that was visited. The census tallied 1,610 people in Los Angeles at that time, about ten of whom were of Jewish descent.

Just seven years earlier in a New York City café, recently displaced German Jews founded what is known as the world's oldest Jewish service organization. B'nai B'rith, or "Children of the Covenant," was formed to help Jewish people as they settled into their new homes in America. Founders wished to address the "deplorable condition of Jews in this, our newly adopted country." The group provided aid to the sick, orphans, widows and seniors, and also aimed to unite the Jewish community against anti-Semitism.

Formal Jewish services in Los Angeles weren't organized until the arrival of Joseph Newmark in 1854. His rabbinical training brought him to the forefront of the community where he remained until his death in 1881. A group of Polish-born Jews formed Congregation Beth El in 1861, only to be absorbed by the more populous Germanic B'nai B'rith congregation formed soon after.

Newmark oversaw construction of the city's first Gothic brick synagogue in 1873 located on the east side of Fort Street (now Broadway) between Second and Third Streets. He invited Rabbi Abraham Edelman from San Francisco to lead services at the new temple as the city's first officially ordained rabbi. This first structure, once described in the *Los Angeles Star* as "the most superior church edifice in Southern California" was razed in 1896. Congregation B'nai B'rith then moved into a new building located on the corner of Ninth and Hope streets and began to adopt Reform Judaism.

Both this synagogue and its successor, the 1929 temple on Wilshire, were the designs of architect Abram M. Edelman, the son of Rabbi Abraham Edelman.

The main entrance to the red brick temple on Hope Street led visitors to a wide hall with a tiled floor inlaid with Arabesque designs. Two staircases led to the second-floor vestibule. "The main hall is a dream in color," the *Los Angeles Times* reported the day after the temple opened. The newspaper described the room's dark red carpet that complemented the white pews and wainscoting.

The space featured a great Moorish arch and an organ. Just below the organ stood a pair of "slender carved pillars," between them a seven-branched candelabra fashioned out of silver and onyx. At the back of the room, nestled in a recess, a light burned in an exquisite lamp of ruby glass and polished silver.

The early 1900s saw an influx of Jewish immigrants to Southern California, mostly seeking a better climate. New congregations formed including the first Orthodox congregation, Beth Israel, and the first Conservative congregation, Congregation Sinai, in 1906.

B'nai B'rith combined with a Wilshire group and built a magnificent new temple in 1929, at Wilshire and Hobart, with a Byzantine-revival dome. The temple still stands and at one time served the largest Jewish congregation in California. Featuring black marble, gold inlay, fine mosaics, rare woods and murals by Hugo Ballin, the temple is an architectural masterpiece.

In the much-repeated story of *Lost Los Angeles*, the site of the city's first synagogue is today a parking garage on Broadway. The second site of the congregation at Ninth and Hope, with its unique red brick domes on its two front towers, was soon demolished after being sold in 1927 to a private developer. This location has also become a parking lot.

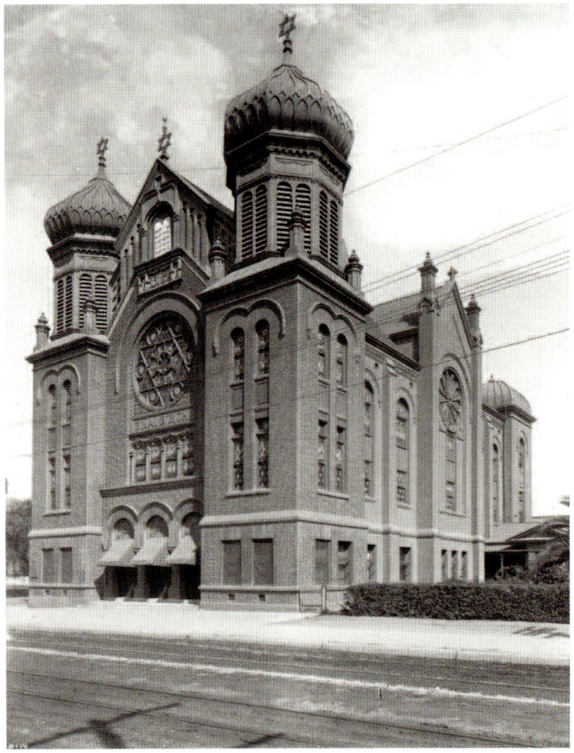

LEFT *The second B'nai B'rith Temple at Ninth and Hope Streets.*

RIGHT *The 1896 synagogue appears in this 1926 photograph shortly before its demolition. Descriptions of the building reference its deep red carpeting, plush-cushioned pews and chandelier containing sixty bulbs, said to be the largest in the city.*

OPPOSITE PAGE *The 1896 temple shortly after it was completed.*

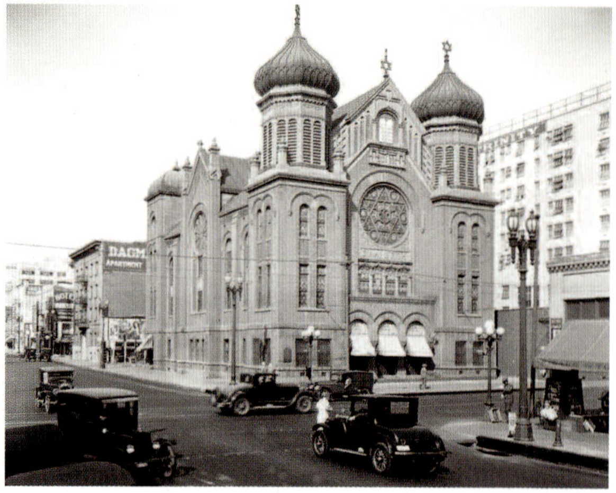

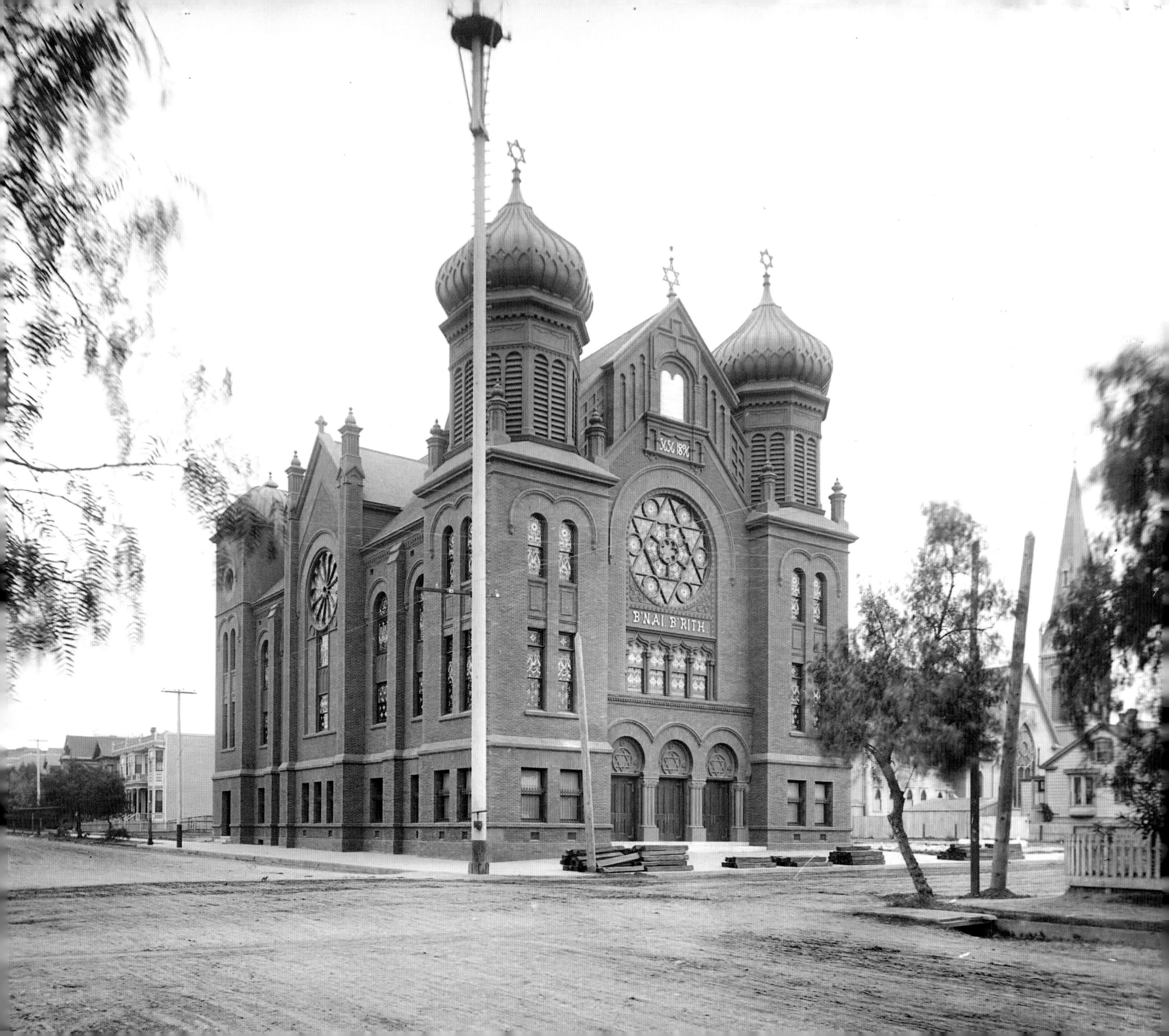

5656 1896
B'NAI B'RITH

Hollywood Bowl Band Shell ORIGINAL REPLACED 1927

The world-famous amphitheater set against a backdrop of the Hollywood hills and the Hollywood sign, the Hollywood Bowl, has hosted an incredible series of performers since opening at Daisy Dell in Bolton Canyon.

Christine Stevenson, heiress to the Pittsburgh Paint fortune, arrived in Hollywood in 1918 and wanted to present religious plays and outdoor theatrical performances. She chose the natural amphitheatre of Daisy Dell. Stevenson established the Theater Alliance, and along with developer C. E. Toberman's help, she bought the land for $49,000 in 1919. In 1920 it was sold to the Community Park and Art Association.

At first just a simple awning covered the rudimentary stage, but from 1926 Allied Architects constructed permanent seating and a shell for the stage. Deemed acoustically unpleasant and stylistically out of date with its murals of wooden tall-masted ships during an era of oil and steel, the shell was turned over to Frank Lloyd Wright's architect son, Lloyd, for the 1927 season at the Bowl. Wright's construction used recycled materials from a production of *Robin Hood* and took a pyramidal shape, which improved sound quality, but didn't please the aesthetic sensibilities of the organizing committee. Wright was asked to rebuild the shell for 1928 using curves. The new fiberglass version featured concentric 120-degree arches with movable panels used to tune the acoustics. The structure wouldn't survive the winter.

Allied Architects returned to construct yet another shell, this time using transite, a cement-asbestos mixture, over a metal frame. This structure, while acoustically inferior to the Wright shells, remained in use until 2003. In later years, the shell's performance declined. Efforts were taken in the 1970s and 1980s to mitigate the shell's deterioration. Large cardboard tubes that helped increase the resonance of the shell were later replaced by Frank Gehry-designed fiberglass tubes. These efforts created a more pleasing sound quality, but as ambient noise in the city had increased so dramatically since the 1920s, extensive use of electronics was required to amplify the sound so it could be heard everywhere in the amphitheater.

Visual changes included the addition of a proscenium and a reflecting pool which echoed the happenings on stage from 1953 to 1972.

During the summer of 2003, the shell underwent a complete renovation, removing all memory of the 1929 construction. The new shell, by architects Hodgetts and Fung, was acoustically approved, but appalled local preservationists. Proponents of the new shell argued the historic shell wasn't functioning up to expected standards even at its construction, but had since become an "acoustic liability" as the transite shell hardened. (Not to mention its potentially carcinogenic properties.)

The 2004 shell incorporated elements of the previous shells, including the prominent front arch of the 1926 shell, the broad profile of the 1928 shell, the unadorned white finish and most of the general lines of the 1929 shell, and by the end of the 2004 season, sound engineers had perfected the best quality sound the Bowl had yet heard. During the renovation, the theater itself received an upgrade of four new video screens and towers, giving the audience close-up views of the performers through remote cameras hidden in the shell.

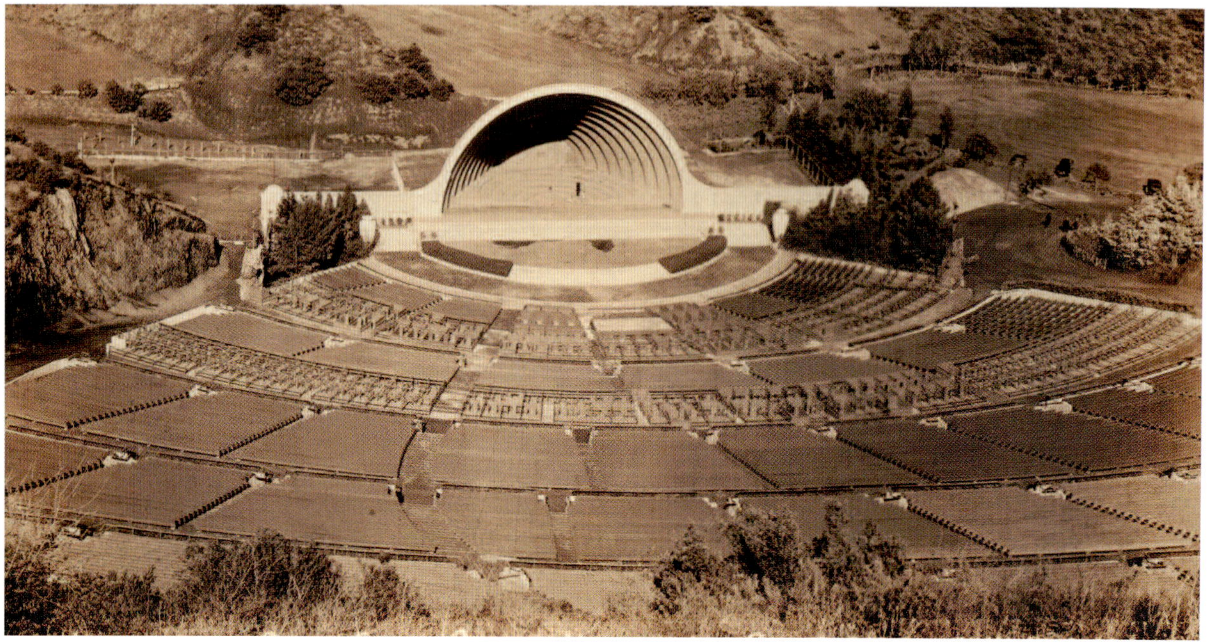

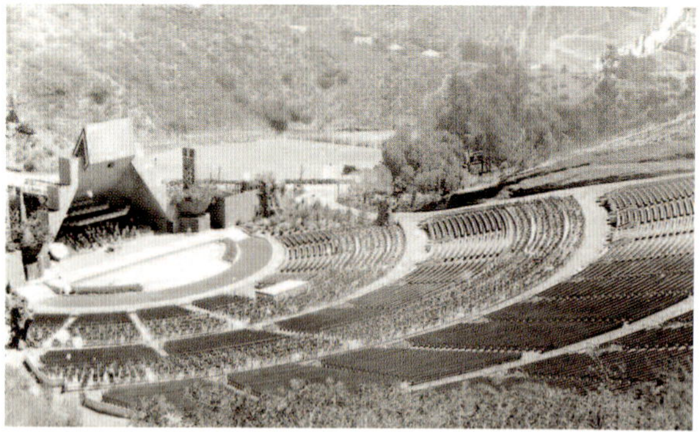

TOP *The 1929 band shell, with concentric rings, lasted 70 times longer than its predecessors.*

ABOVE *Lloyd Lloyd-Wright's pyramid stage lasted a single season. Its design has been echoed by the world-famous Glastonbury Festival in England, whose main stage is The Pyramid Stage.*

OPPOSITE PAGE *The original band shell was deemed to be old-fashioned in style and construction and also lasted a single season.*

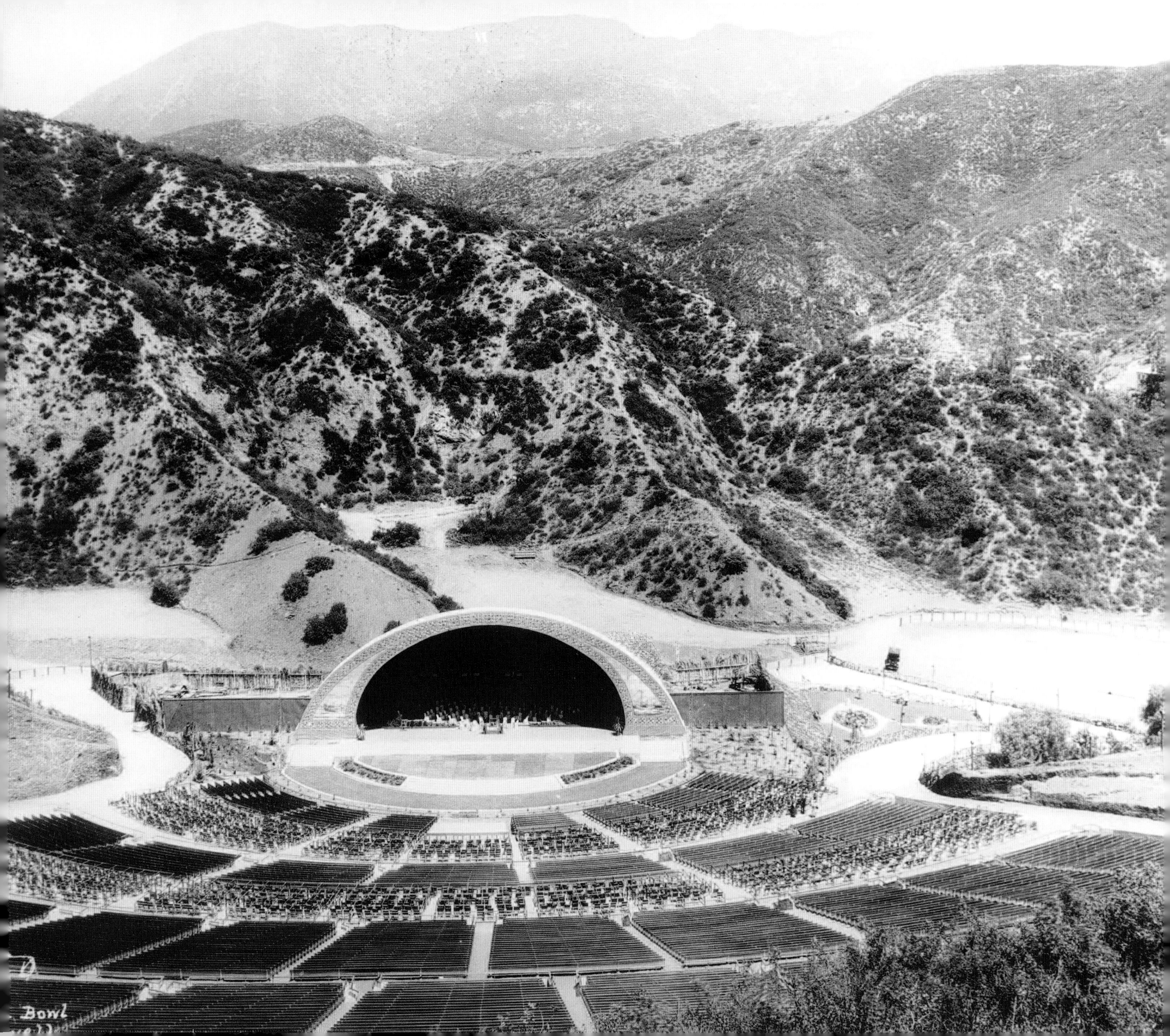
Bowl

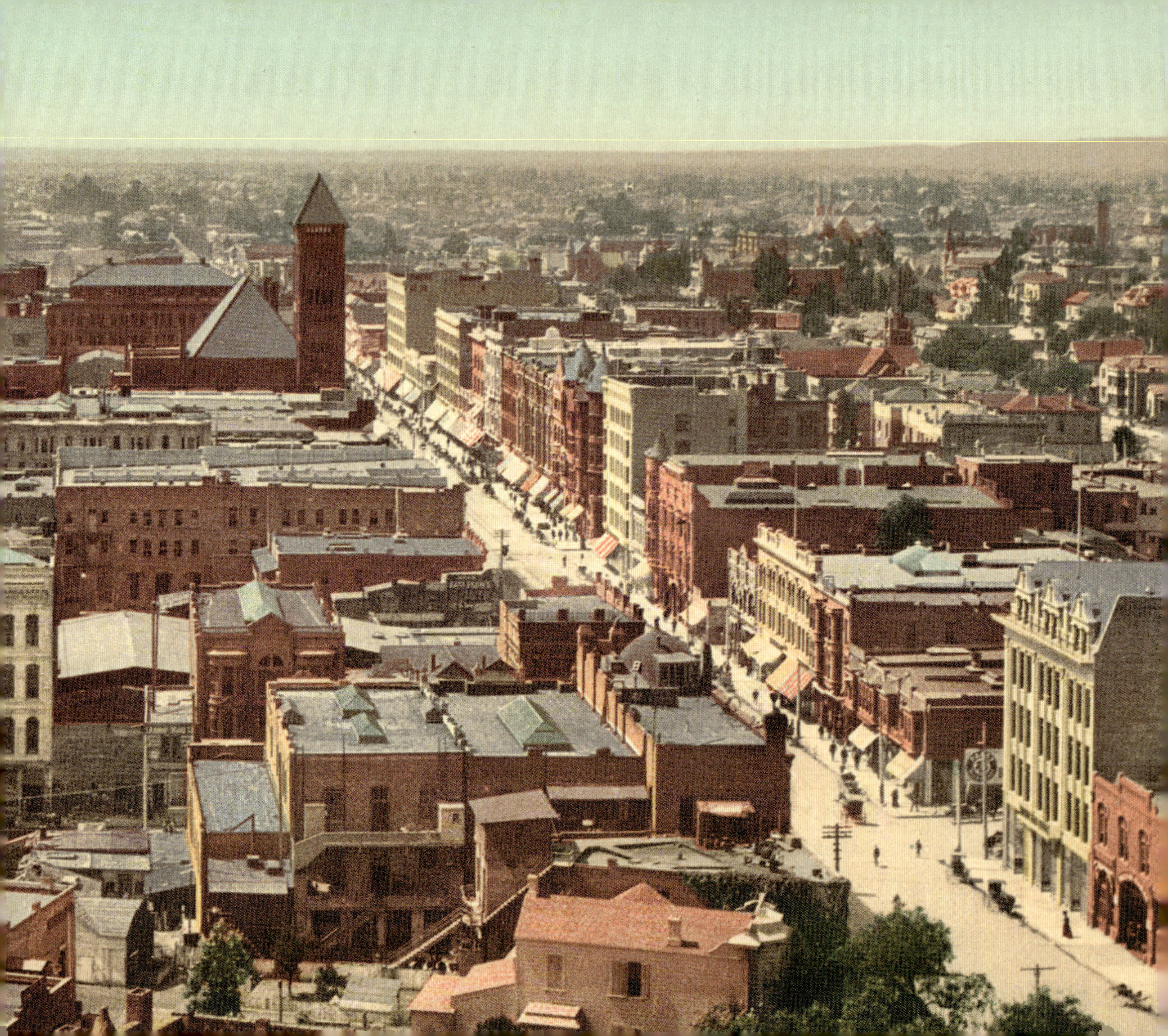

Third City Hall DEMOLISHED 1928

Two years after the third city hall opened its doors the city changed its address from Fort Street to Broadway. One story goes that the Germans in town had trouble distinguishing between the pronunciation of "Fourth" and "Fort" streets. Fred Lind Alles petitioned the city to change Fort Street's name. Alles was the vice-president of the Los Angeles Printing Company, which was located at the intersection of Fourth and Fort streets.

Beginning in 1850, when the city of Los Angeles incorporated, city fathers had conducted much of their business in rooms they rented in hotels and other establishments. In the 1860s the city hall found its first real home at a rented adobe house on Spring Street. Visitors to the Clara Shortridge Foltz Criminal Justice Center now park their cars on this site. For the second city hall the city used rooms in the Los Angeles County Courthouse.

Architects Eugene Caulkin and Solomon Haas designed Los Angeles' third City Hall, which stood on Fort Street/Broadway between Second and Third streets, from 1888 to 1928.

The city accepted Caulkin and Haas's plans on July 7, 1887, and work began immediately. The building, which came in under the city's $150,000 budget, rested on a square colonnade base. Caulkin and Haas designed a broad flight of stone steps that led to a three-arched porch. They capped their creation with a gabled roof and a buttressed tower.

Brick, sandstone and terra cotta accented the graceful Romanesque Revival style that the architects employed. The building's design echoed a style popular for late-19th-century public buildings. The size of this new building allowed the city to house most of its municipal departments under one roof for the first time. The city council met here, and the mayor, the city attorney, city surveyor and the city clerk all had offices here. The city housed many of its services in this building as well, including the public library and the boards of education, public works and health.

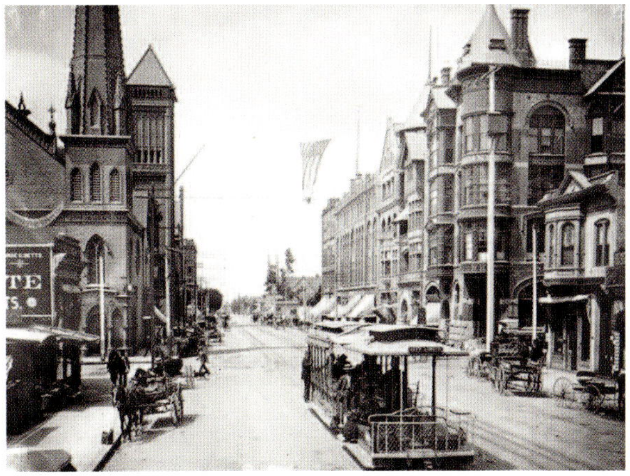

The rapidly growing city generated a larger and larger bureaucracy and planners began considering an even larger city hall in the early part of the 20th century. In 1910 land for the new building was purchased. But it wasn't until June 5, 1923, that voters authorized the expenditure of $7.5 million to build a new city hall on that property. Ground was broken in 1927 and on January 2, 1928, the first city offices moved into the city's present-day city hall.

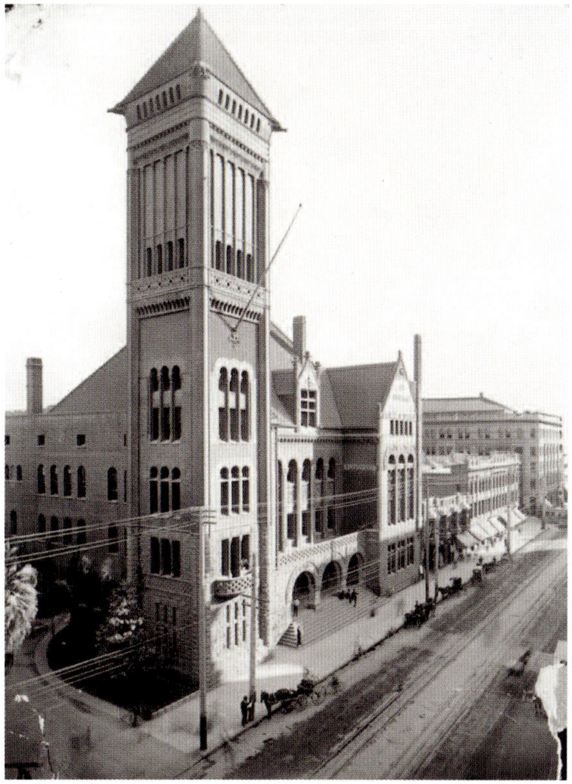

Eight days later the city held an auction on the front steps of its third city hall. A crowd of anxious buyers crowded Broadway to bid on the furnishings from the former seat of local government. "The city dismantled the building and auctioned it off piece by piece," *Los Angeles Times* writer Cecilia Rasmussen wrote. Later that same year the city demolished the building.

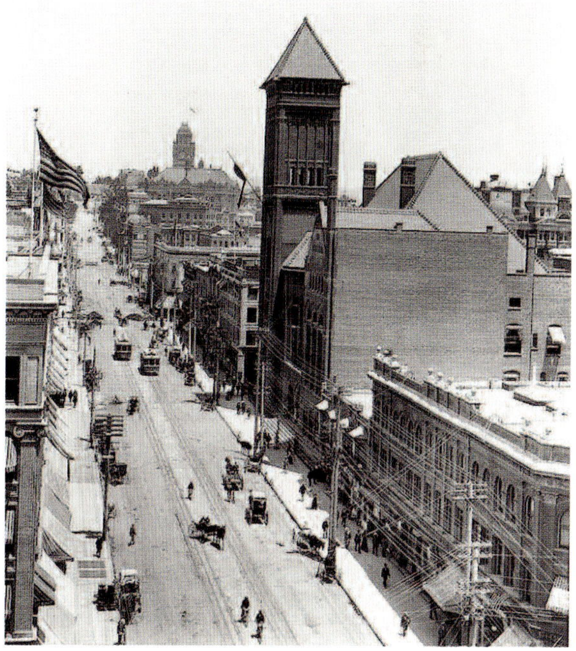

ABOVE *City Hall around 1900.*

FAR LEFT *Passengers enjoy a ride on a Los Angeles Cable Railway Car in this photograph taken by C. C. Pierce in 1889. They've just ridden past the First Presbyterian Church and City Hall. The building across from City Hall, the Potomac Building, holds shops like the Ville de Paris and The City of London that sold lace, curtains and draperies.*

LEFT *The late afternoon sun bathes City Hall in this photograph looking south toward Third Street.*

OPPOSITE PAGE *An early colorized photograph of Los Angeles looking down Broadway with the Romanesque Revival tower dominating the street.*

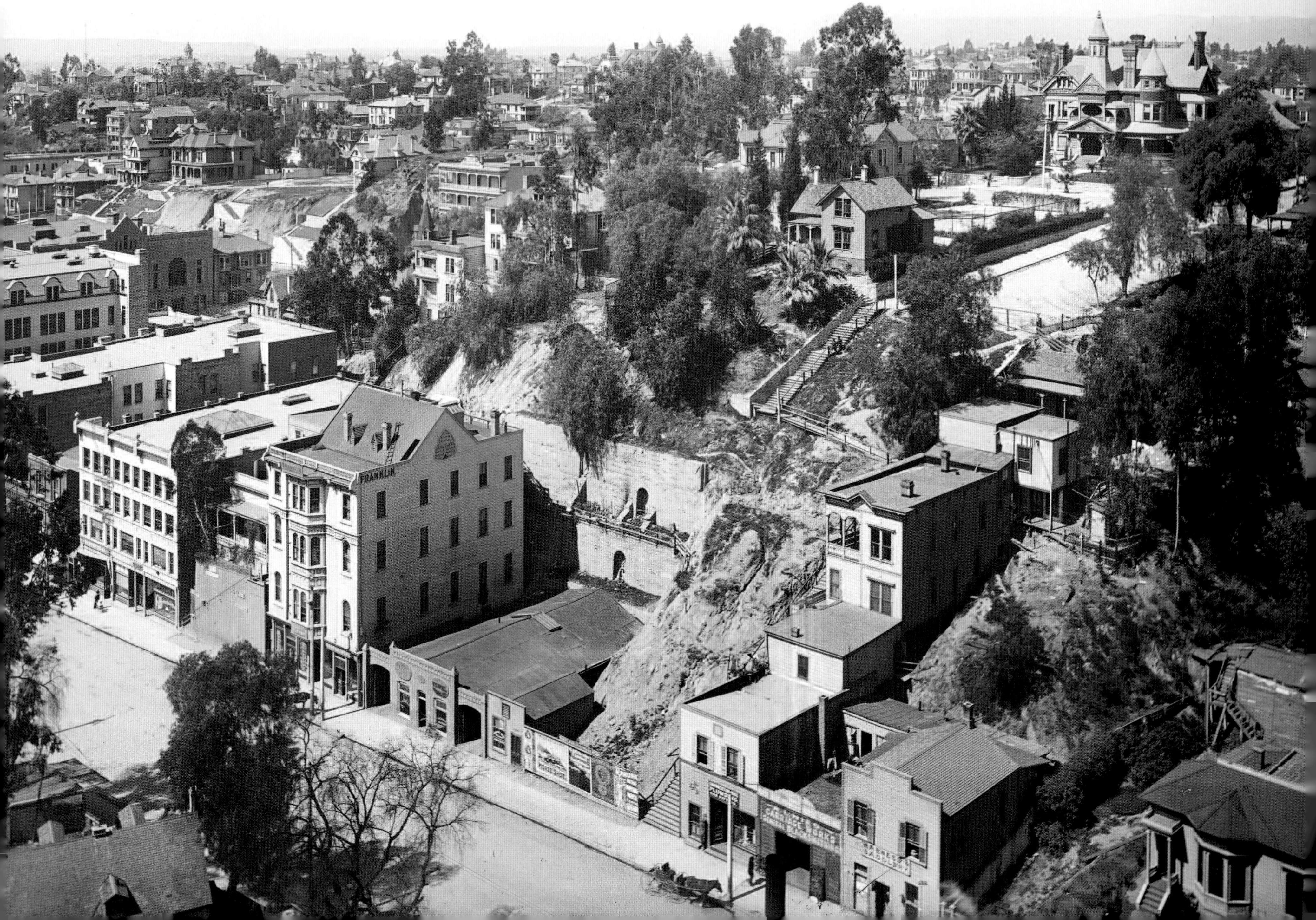
FRANKLIN

Bradbury Mansion DEMOLISHED 1929

In 1887, Los Angeles County Clerk J. W. Potts purchased a lot on Court Hill at the intersection of Hill and Court streets. He commissioned architects Samuel and Joseph Cather Newsom to build a 35-room Queen Anne-style mansion complete with five chimneys and five turrets. The Newsom brothers, who had already made a name for themselves as designers of homes for the well-heeled, charged Potts $80,000 for the house. That same year Potts sold the property to wealthy mining tycoon Leonard Lewis Bradbury for $125,000. Bradbury had moved to Los Angeles from Oakland with his wife Simona hoping to find a climate that was friendlier to his asthma.

In 1890 *Picturesque and Artistic Homes and Buildings* described the home as the finest residence on Bunker Hill with a "handsomely polished" interior and an exterior of "granite, marble, wood and shingles."

Bradbury, the scion of a wealthy family from Bangor, Maine, made his own fortune mining gold and silver in the Sierra Madre Mountains in Mexico. He began buying up shares in the "Tajo vein" in Sinaloa, and by 1873 he owned the controlling interest. In 1880, Bradbury moved to California, first settling in Oakland and then buying the house in Los Angeles.

Bradbury invested the wealth he extracted from Mexico in California real estate. That included a portion of the Rancho Azusa de Duarte about 22 miles west of Los Angeles in the foothills of the San Gabriel Mountains. The present-day city of Bradbury recalls the family's presence there.

Bradbury used his money to put up a pair of buildings on Broadway: the Bradbury Building at Third Street and the Tajo Building, two blocks away at First Street and Broadway. He named the building for the mine where he struck it rich. The Bradbury Building boasted 288 radiators, 50 fireplaces, 215 wash basins and the largest plate-glass windows in Los Angeles. Italian marble, Mexican floor tiles, delicate water-powered bird-cage elevators built in Chicago transported people to the upper floors and down again. Ira Yellin lovingly restored the Bradbury Building in 1991.

Bradbury lived in his grand Victorian home until his death in 1892. He didn't live long enough to see either the Bradbury Building completed in 1896 or the Tajo Building open its doors in 1897. Simona moved back to the family home in Oakland shortly before her death in 1902.

By 1912 the home had fallen into other hands. Bradbury's daughter, Minerva, married Isaac Polk and the couple built "Chateau Bradbury," a spacious home on the family's property in Bradbury. The following year J.A.C. Film Manufacturing moved into the house. Charlie Chaplin used the house as a filming location in 1915.

Filmmaker Harold Lloyd transformed the home into a studio, but he found it so drafty that he dubbed the place "Pneumonia Hall." The film industry moved elsewhere, and the Bradbury mansion served as a restaurant where judges working at the nearby courthouse ate lunch, and finally as a boarding house. It met the wrecking ball in 1929.

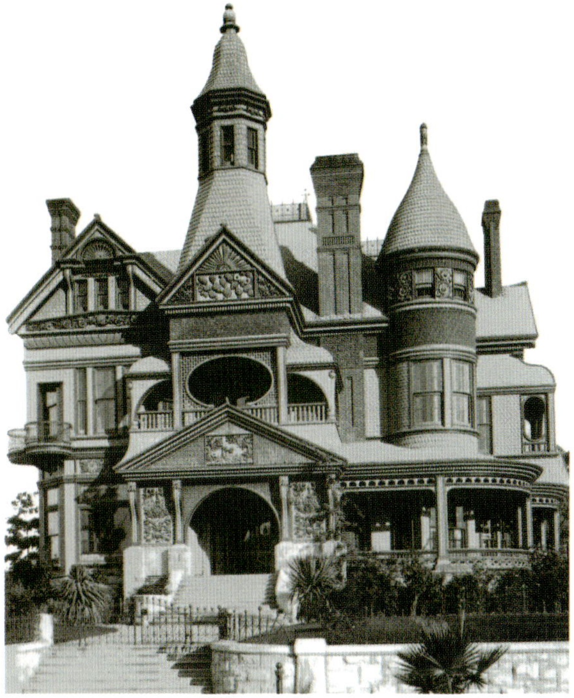

LEFT *The Bradbury family may not have been at home when this photo was taken in 1890. They spent four months of that year in Europe. Lewis was taking care of business while his wife, Simona, traveled in style with the couple's children. The 1890s were not a happy time for the family. Lewis died in 1892, and Simona moved to the family home in Oakland for a while. She purchased a lot at Mountain View Cemetery in Oakland and laid her husband to rest there.*

OPPOSITE PAGE *The Bradbury mansion crowns Bunker Hill in this 1899 panorama.*

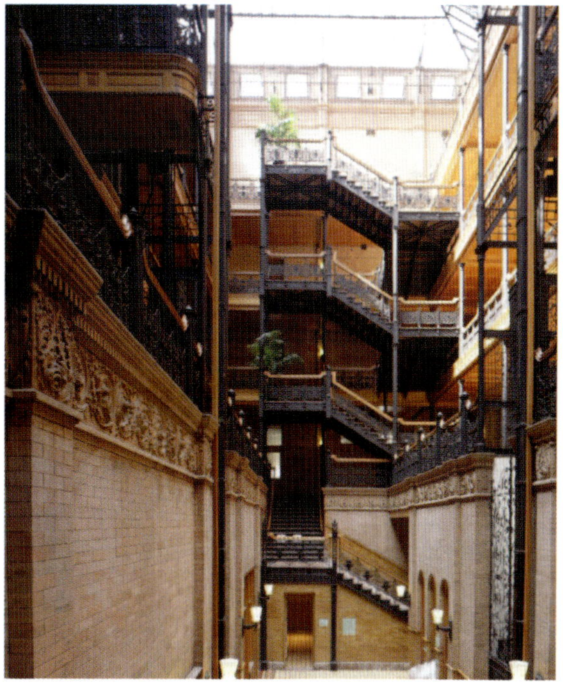

ABOVE *The unique interior of the Bradbury Building at Third Street. Its financier never saw it finished. Over the years movie producers have transformed the space into a London military hospital, a garment factory, an architectural firm and an exotic hotel.*

Abbott Kinney's Canals MOSTLY PAVED IN 1929

In 1904 Abbott Kinney purchased 160 acres of land just south of Santa Monica, property that was once part of the Ballona Wetlands. He told his friends that he wanted to develop "The Venice of America." He hired architects Norman Marsh and C. H. Russell to design a project that consisted of a Grand Canal, a network of smaller canals and a central lagoon—all this right next door to a pier and an amusement park. Kinney was convinced his creation would bring a cultural renaissance to Southern California.

Marsh and Russell laid out seven canals in an irregular grid pattern. Their design included four islands with one, United States Island, shaped like a triangle. The widest of these manmade waterways, the Grand Canal, led to a saltwater lake.

To create these canals, crews dredged some two miles of waterways out of the marshlands. Marsh and Russell spanned the canals with arched bridges that echoed those in Venice, Italy. Kinney even imported gondolas from Venice and hired Venetian gondoliers to guide these boats through the canals.

At first Kinney used mule teams to dredge the marshland. When he saw how slowly the animals worked though, he brought in the Marion Steam Shovel Company to complete the task. The machines did the job and the canals opened to traffic on July 4, 1905, to coincide with opening day at the adjacent amusement park along the Pacific Ocean. Soon after Kinney's canals opened a second set of canals were built just to the south. Named the "Short Line" canals after the interurban transport system, these canals would be the only ones to survive.

Kinney died in 1920 and five years later Venice became part of the city of Los Angeles. By then the automobile was king and the canals that had invoked the charm of Venice, Italy, were viewed as impediments to progress. Due to the haste in which they had been constructed many of the banks started to crumble and drainage was poor. When

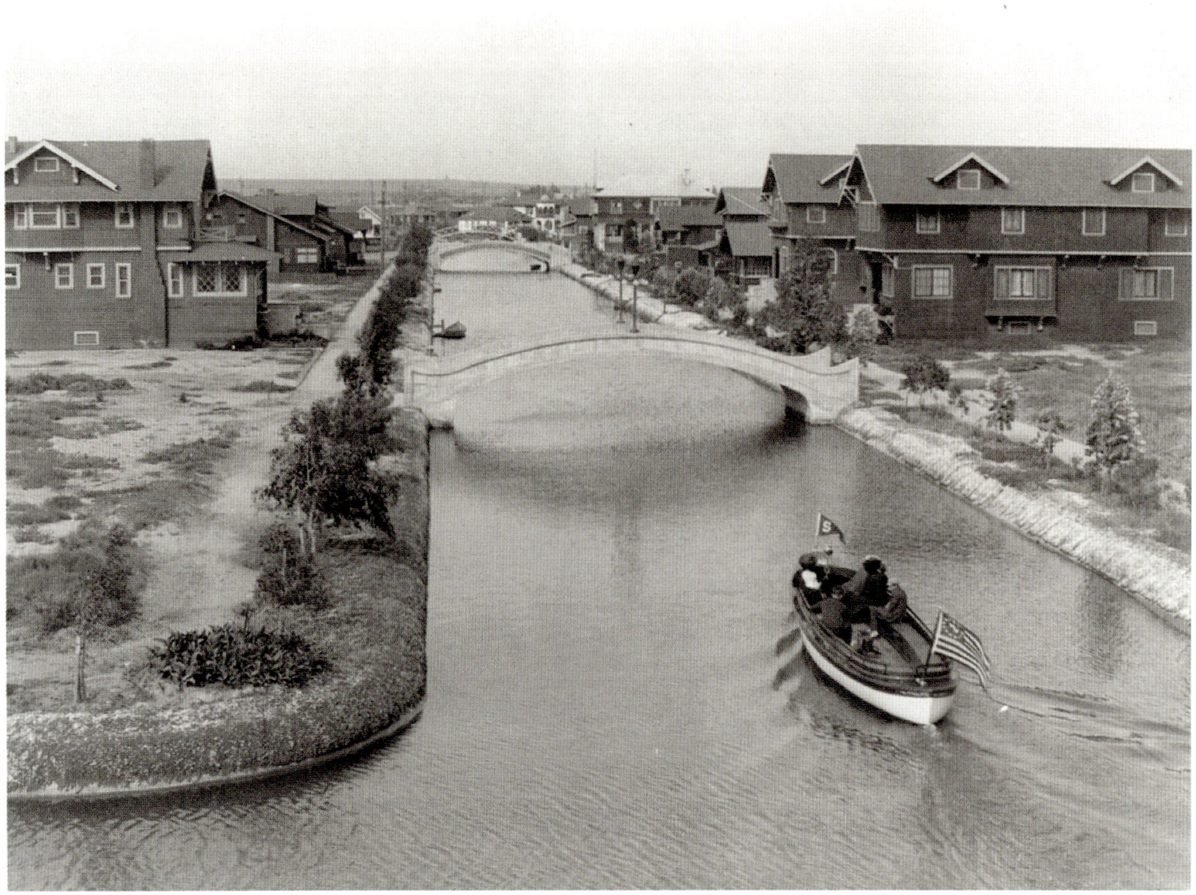

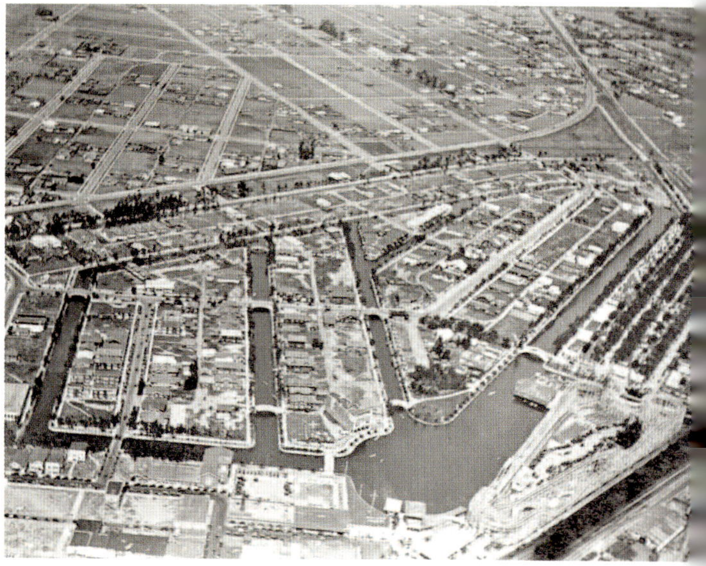

LEFT *A boat carries passengers down the Aldebaran Canal toward the Rovigo and Rialto bridges in this photograph taken in February 1911. Abbot Kinney named three of his canals for heavenly bodies, the stars Altair and Aldebaran, and the planet Venus.*

ABOVE *An aerial view of the canals in 1918 shows the Grand, Lion and Coral canals feeding directly into the bathing lake, which was later named Venice Lagoon.*

OPPOSITE PAGE *A gondolier posed with his passengers in front of the Antler Hotel on Venice Lagoon in November 1912. A roller coaster called "Race through the Clouds" opened across from the hotel the year before this picture was taken.*

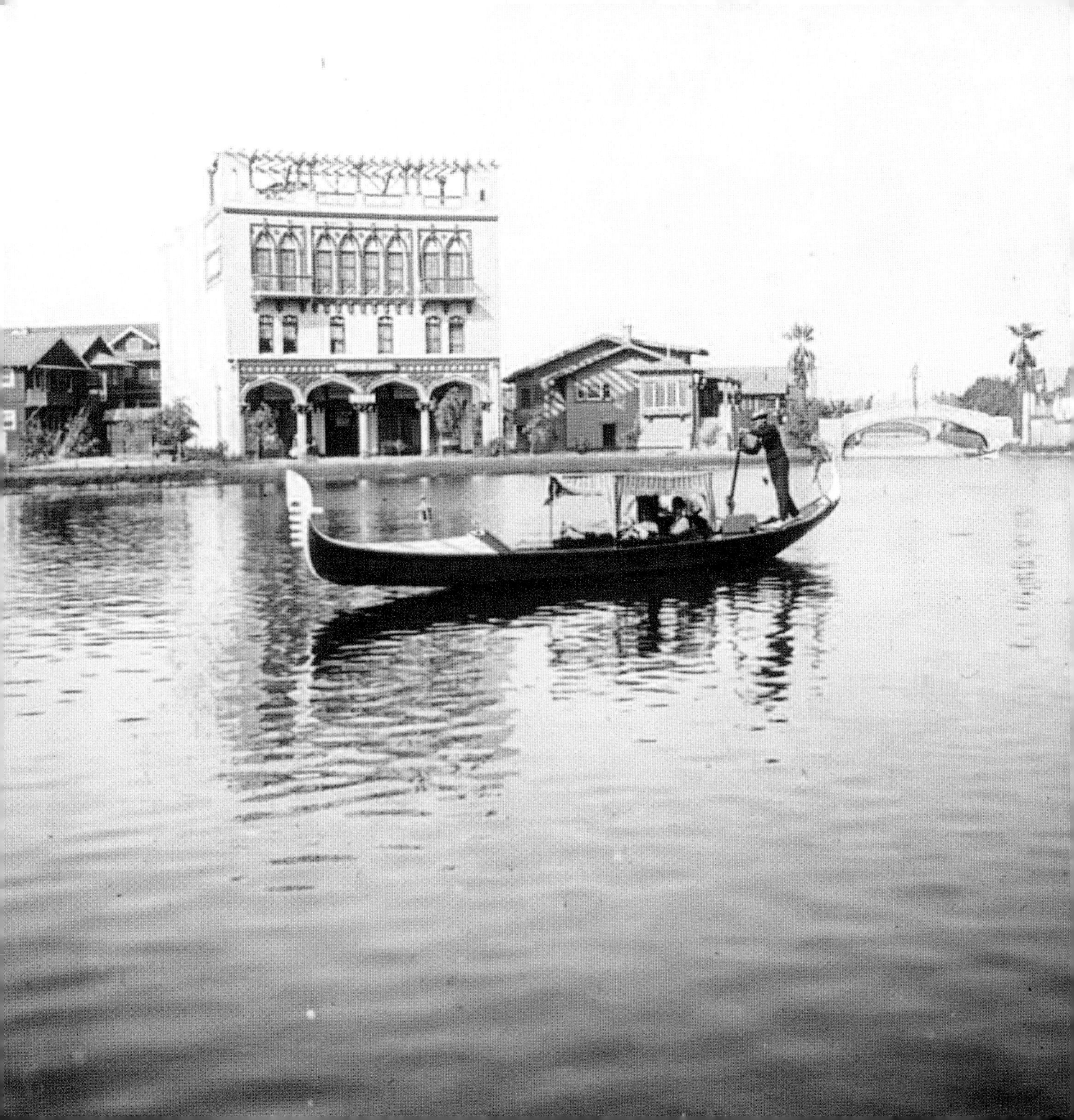

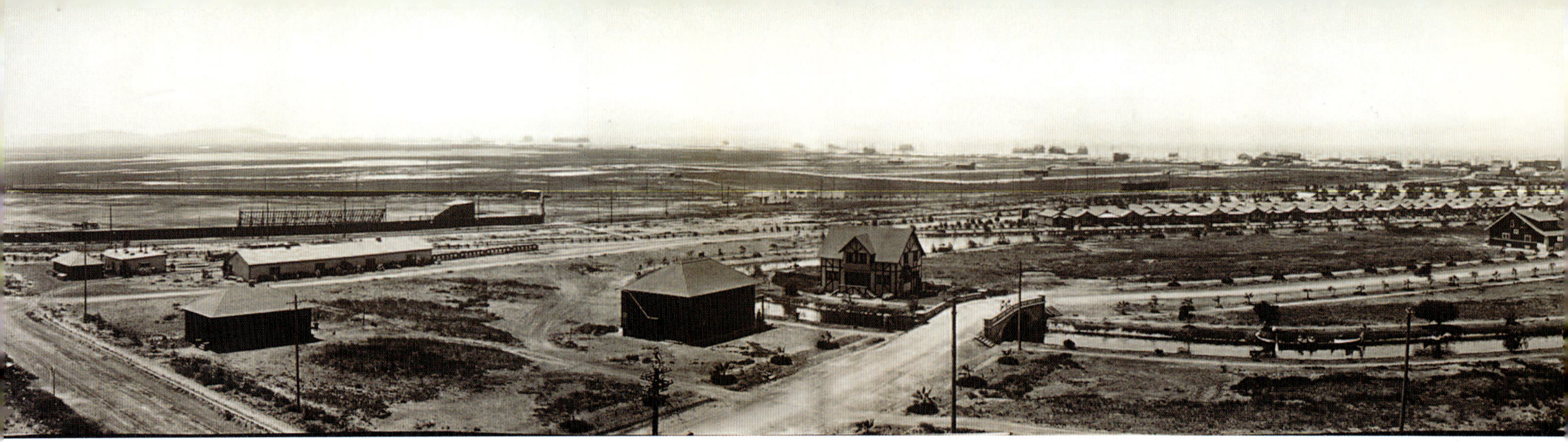

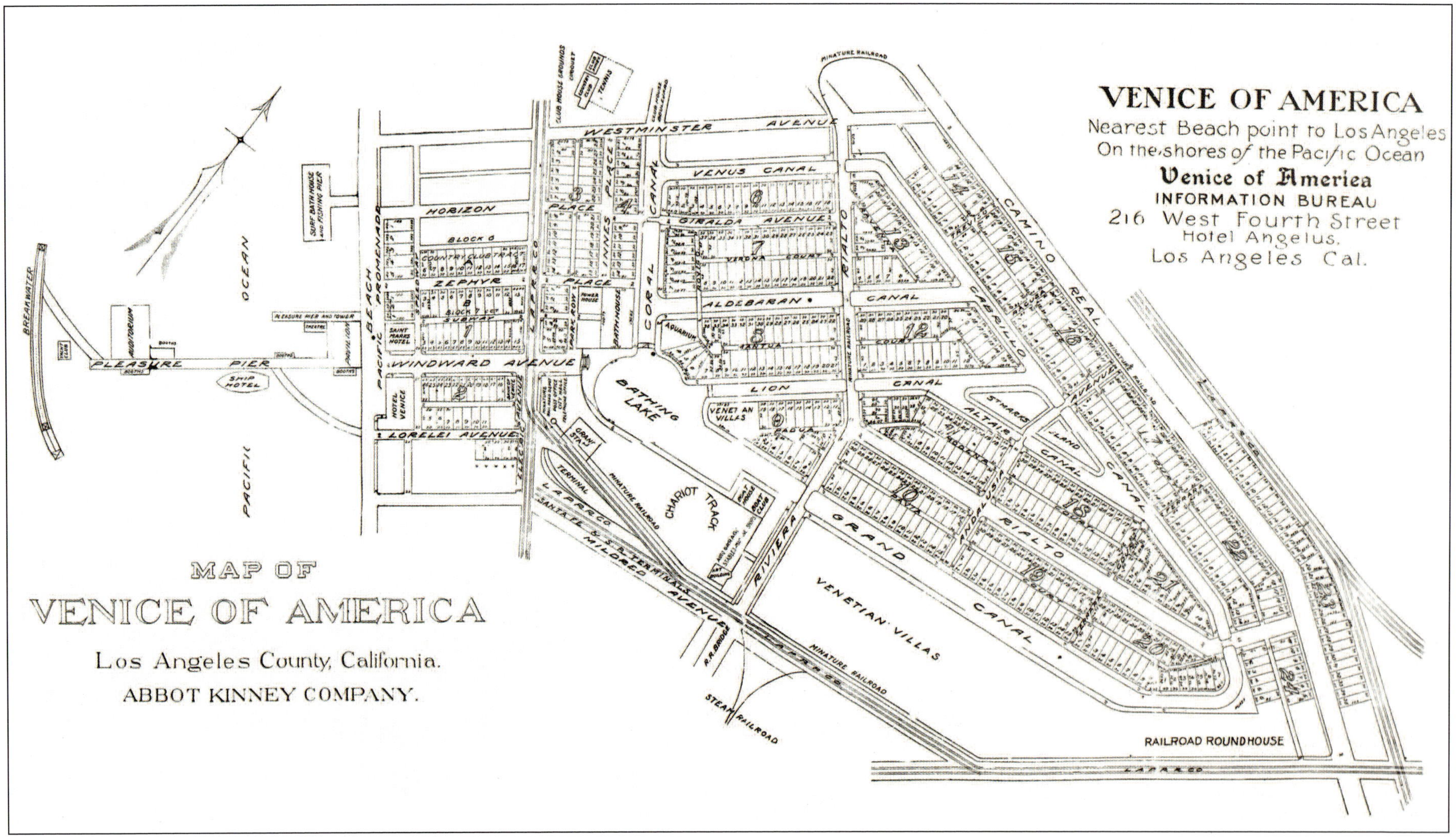

VENICE OF AMERICA
Nearest Beach point to Los Angeles
On the shores of the Pacific Ocean
Venice of America
INFORMATION BUREAU
216 West Fourth Street
Hotel Angelus.
Los Angeles Cal.
MAP OF
VENICE OF AMERICA
Los Angeles County, California.
ABBOT KINNEY COMPANY.
PACIFIC
OCEAN
BREAKWATER
PLEASURE PIER
SHIP HOTEL
AUDITORIUM
SURF BATH HOUSE AND FISHING PIER
PLEASURE PIER AND TOWER
BEACH PROMENADE
HORIZON
ZEPHYR
WINDWARD AVENUE
LORELEI AVENUE
HOTEL VENICE
SAINT MARKS HOTEL
WESTMINSTER AVENUE
VENUS CANAL
GIRALDA AVENUE
ALDEBARAN
CANAL
LION
CORAL CANAL
BATHING LAKE
AQUARIUM
CHARIOT TRACK
VENETIAN VILLAS
GRAND CANAL
RIVIERA
RIALTO
CABRILLO
CAMINO REAL
MINATURE RAILROAD
STEAM RAILROAD
MILDRED AVENUE
RAILROAD ROUNDHOUSE
L.A.P.R.R.CO.

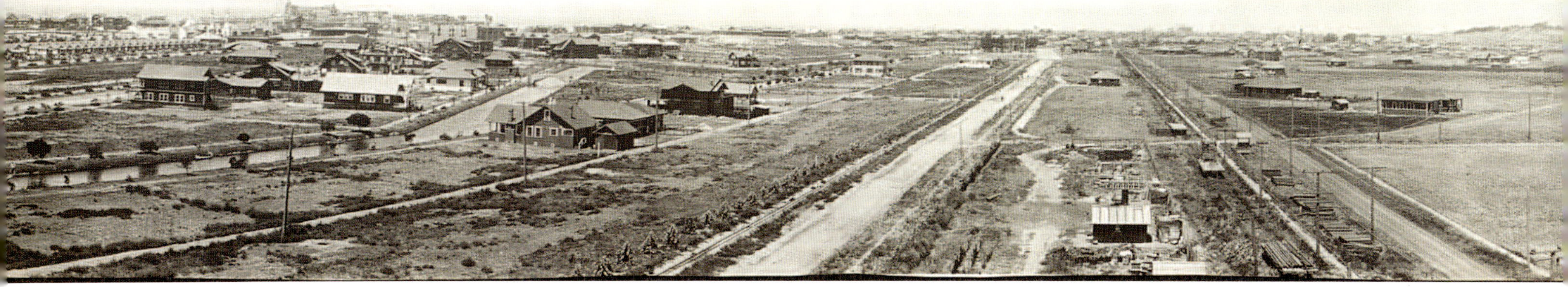

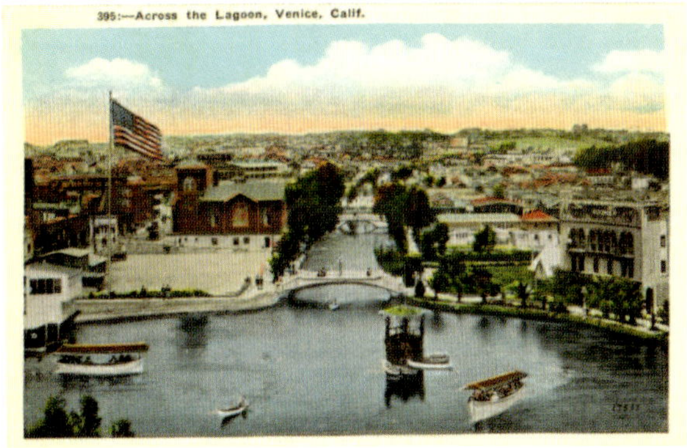

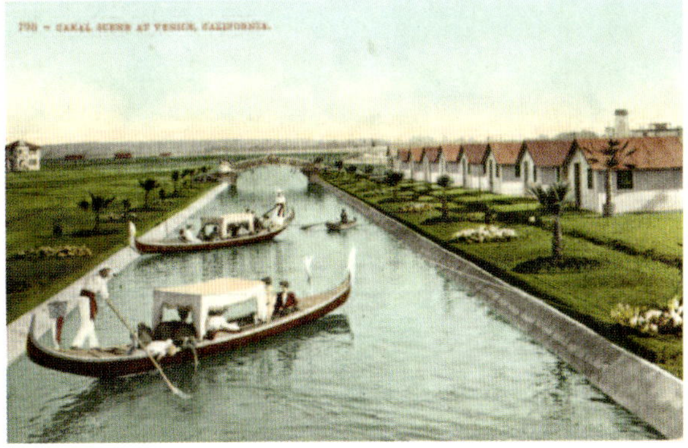

TOP *Pleasure boats ply their trade on this postcard view depicting the Lagoon.*

ABOVE *Expert Venetian gondoliers were brought in to add authenticity to the scheme. With no current running through the canals they have angled their gondolas purely to give a better effect for the camera.*

Abbot Kinney designed his canals in 1904 scarcely anyone owned an automobile. That had all changed by the 1920s. In 1924, Venice Beach's Civic Betterment League proposed paving over the city's canals and the streetcar tracks to make room for the automobile. The Kinney family went along with the scheme by deeding over all the canals north of Venice Boulevard to the city. Disgruntled property owners took the city to court, and on August 6, 1924, a judge put a stop to the project. The case went all the way to the California Supreme Court. In 1927 the court ruled in favor of the city of Los Angeles, which had taken over Venice Beach in 1925.

Dump trucks arrived the morning of July 1, 1929, and began dumping dirt into the Coral Canal. They followed suit with Kinney's other canals. By the time they were finished these trucks had entombed Abbot Kinney's grandest canals and his Venice Lagoon under 90,000 cubic yards of dirt.

Three of these canals kept their own names after they became streets: Cabrillo Canal became Cabrillo Avenue, Altair Canal became Altair Street and Grand Canal was transformed into Grand Boulevard. Three others lost their identities: Coral Canal became Main Street. Venus Canal morphed into San Juan Avenue, and Aldebaran Canal became Market Street. They filled Venice Lagoon to create a traffic circle.

The Great Depression stepped in and put a stop to the work and only the "Short Line" canals were spared. The city of Los Angeles neglected these remaining canals and they fell into disrepair. In 1992, they were drained and renovated.

ABOVE *This photo from the California Panorama Company is dated to 1908.*

OPPOSITE PAGE *The Kinney Company opened an office in the Hotel Angelus to sell lots along the newly created canals in the "Venice of America." Amenities included an aquarium, a bathing lake and a miniature railroad.*

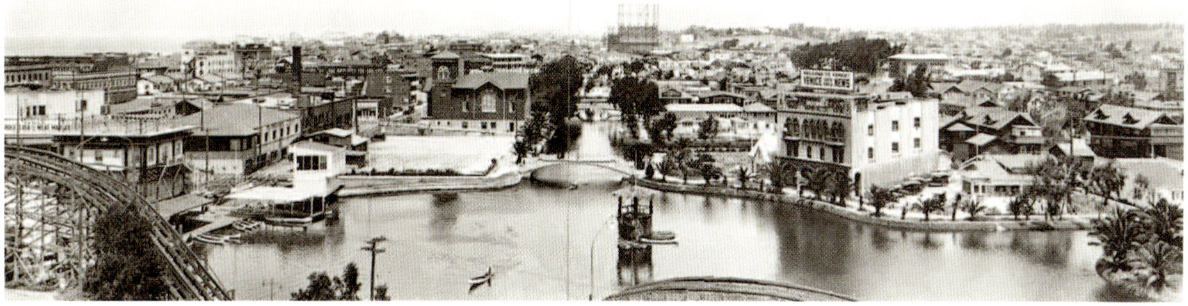

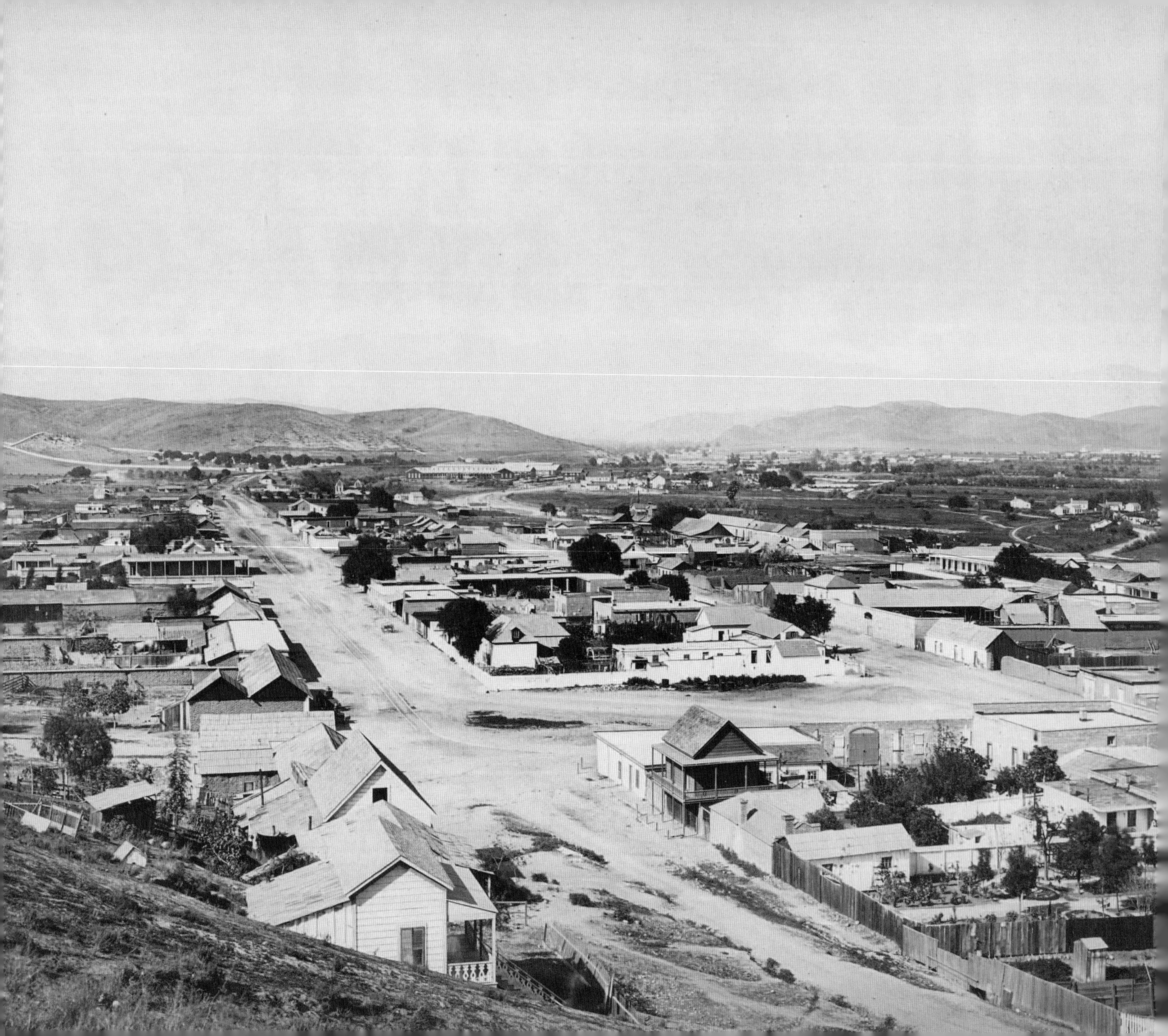

Sonora Town ABSORBED INTO CHINATOWN BY 1930

Some of the first miners to arrive in California's gold country hailed from Sonora, Mexico. Indeed one of first towns founded along the mother lode was called Sonora because so many people from that region of Mexico settled there.

Some of these gold seekers passed through Los Angeles on the way to the mines. They discovered that they were among friends: the Mexican settlers who had founded the city and their descendants welcomed them. Some decided to stay in Los Angeles. They settled just north of the town's plaza and the neighborhood took on the name of the place they had left behind. Sonora Town, which historian Nathan Masters has dubbed Los Angeles' first barrio.

The residents lived in adobe houses or in housing courts, ramshackle structures built around a central area. Most of these courtyard dwellings had two rooms, each with one window; a kitchen with a small wood-burning stove and a table and second room with only a bed and a chair. Sonora Town residents whitewashed their homes on the inside. They painted them either brown or red on the outside. The homes had neither electricity nor plumbing. Residents lit their homes with candles and shared a common outhouse.

These Mexicans were, of course, not the only people to settle in Los Angeles after the gold rush. The Yankees arrived and essentially took over the city. The United States had won a war with Mexico and established the Treaty of Guadalupe Hidalgo. As part of the treaty the United States took over some 525,000 square miles of land that included California.

ABOVE RIGHT *Jose Mascarel's adobe house located at 721 Castelar Street, between Ord and Alpine streets in Sonora Town. Mascarel was a French sea captain who served as mayor of Los Angeles.*

OPPOSITE PAGE *This photograph taken from Fort Hill shows the Calle de la Eternidad, Eternity Street, leading to the Calvary Cemetery, which is visible in the distance. The first intersection in the photo is Ord Street, and Alpine Street lies just beyond. Calle de la Eternidad passed through Sonora Town, became part of Broadway and is today's North Broadway.*

This meant that the Mexicans living in Los Angeles no longer governed the city that their forebears were instrumental in founding. Newcomers segregated the descendants of the city's founders and their fellow countrymen into a small section of town north of where the city was born. Despite this, Sonora Town remained a vibrant Hispanic community. Those who chose to live here kept the city's Latin culture alive.

The white population looked toward Sonora Town with prejudice and disdain. They considered the city's original neighborhood as that part of town better avoided by respectable people not interested in overindulging in alcohol, gambling their earnings away or spending time with cutthroats and prostitutes. According to some who lived outside the city's first barrio, cockfights were common. Outsiders also pointed to Sonora Town's dilapidated housing and said that such surroundings bred crime, sickness and poverty.

By the time the 20th century dawned many Sonora Town residents had decided to move out. In one final flurry of activity, the town and the nearby plaza served as the center of revolution. Anarchist Flores Magon led his Partido Liberal Mexicano party in strikes and uprisings in Mexico. He used Sonora Town as his base of operations, and many consider Los Angeles as the birthplace of 20th century Mexican-American political and social activism. By this time Chinese immigrants had begun to outnumber the Latinos and by 1930 Sonora Town had become the city's first Chinatown.

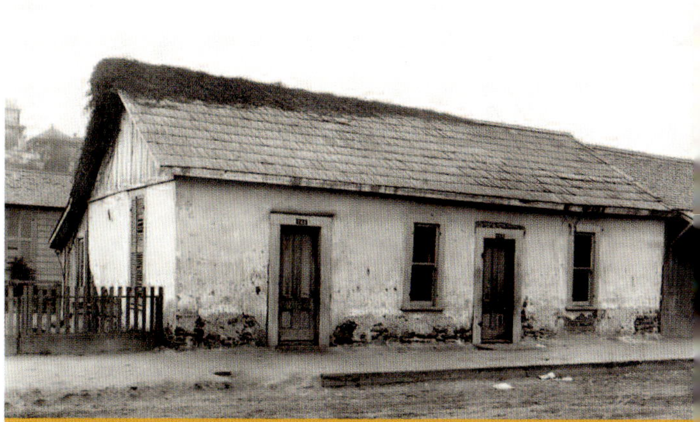

ETERNITY STREET

Los Angeles once had a street known as *Calle de la Eternidad,* Eternity Street. The name was fitting because it led to Calvary Cemetery. From 1826, when the pueblo got its first resident priest, Angelenos had buried their dead at the *Campo Santo* (consecrated ground) near the town's plaza. A marker stands on Olvera Street reminding passersby that the dead once rested there. That cemetery filled up in 1844. The cemetery's register lists more than 650 burials. That year the Catholic Church established Calvary Cemetery on an abandoned, windswept hill north of the plaza. They moved the bodies interred at *Campo Santo* to the new burial ground. Calvary Cemetery opened on November 3, 1844, and mourners now carried their dead through Sonora Town. To reach the cemetery, they processed along Eternity Street. In 1890 *Calle de la Eternidad* died its own death when the city incorporated the street into Broadway. Six years later the Catholic Church closed the cemetery and moved the bodies some seven miles away to East Los Angeles. Since 1925, students at Cathedral High School have been studying on the land that once held the dead at Calvary Cemetery. Fittingly the school's athletic teams are known as the "Phantoms."

Chaplin Airfield REDEVELOPED 1931

Film pioneer Charlie Chaplin often shared credit for his success with his older half-brother Sydney, or "Syd," who looked after Charlie though their difficult childhood in London. Essentially parentless by age 18 and 14 respectively, Syd and Charlie ventured into performing on the vaudeville circuit, with Syd supporting them using money he'd saved working as a sailor. In 1910 the vaudeville outfit sent Charlie to America and within five years, he had landed the largest salary paid to anyone in Hollywood up to that time: $670,000.

As Charlie's film career blossomed, Syd managed his brother's business affairs and decided to take a venture into the brand new field of aviation with Charlie tagging along. In 1910 the nation's first major air show took place at Los Angeles' Dominguez Field—now the site of Cal State's Dominguez Hills campus—and became a regular event. Among the Hollywood luminaries impressed by the new possibilities of flight were Syd Chaplin and Cecile B. DeMille, the most commercially successful man in Hollywood at the time.

DeMille went on to found the Mercury Aviation Company in 1918. DeMille's Field No. 1, across from today's Fairfax High School, was among the first places that offered commercial flights, offering sightseeing and charter rides in surplus World War I Jennys. A bit later he'd moved to DeMille Field No. 2 at the corner of Wilshire Boulevard and Fairfax Avenue, right around the time Chaplin Airfield opened on the other side of Wilshire in 1919.

The Chaplins' operation occupied the area bounded by Wilshire, Fairfax and San Vicente Boulevard. Syd teamed up with pilot Emery Rogers, forming the first privately owned domestic airline: Syd Chaplin Airline Company. This venture, while lasting just a year, built the first-ever showroom to display their collection of Curtis planes; conducted the first roundtrip flight from Los Angeles to San Francisco in just one day, and operated what was called "the largest airfield in the west." Many of the Chaplins' Hollywood buddies would later claim to have flown for the first time in one of Syd's planes, including Charlie himself.

Just a few years later, in 1922, DeMille shuttered Mercury Aviation after having transported some 25,000 people without injury. Flying was just too expensive for the general public. Chaplin's company experienced similar problems, its regular flights to San Diego cost $150 in the days when the average annual salary ran to about $1,500. Right around that time the government took a hand in regulating aviation, and Syd bowed out of the industry as well, selling to his partner Rogers who renamed their location Rogers Field.

For about a decade Rogers continued operation, including incorporating DeMille's former airfield, but real estate in his neighborhood continued to increase in value. By 1931, the site of both airfields lay under developments along Wilshire Boulevard's Miracle Mile.

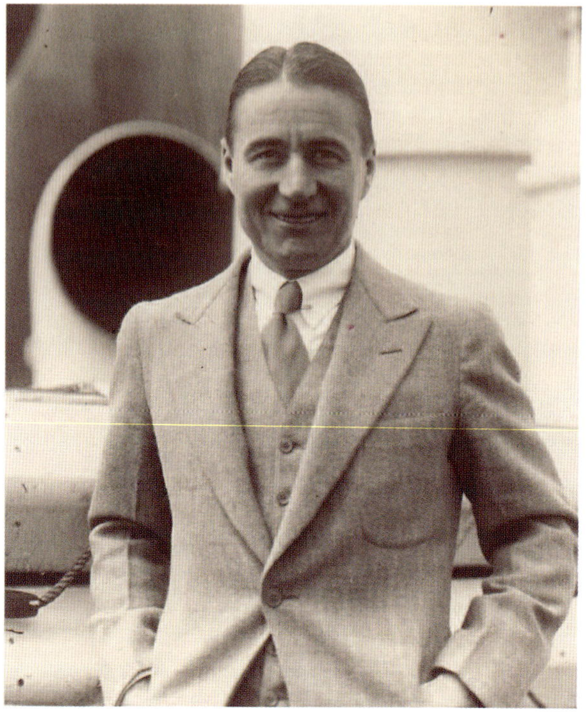

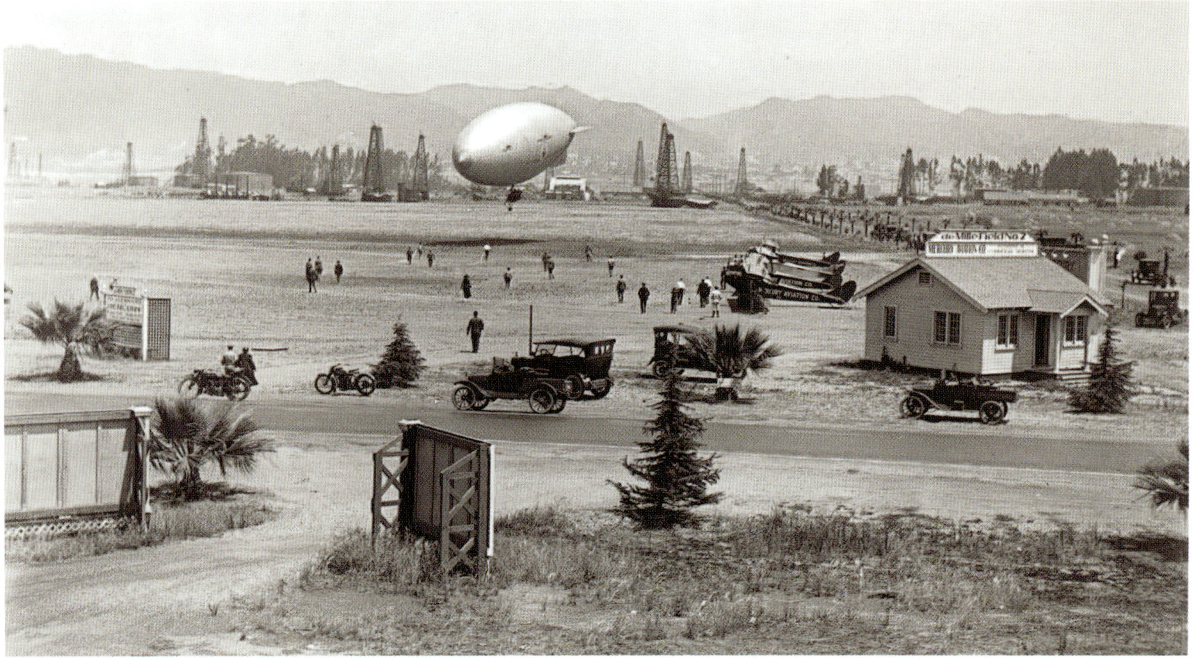

ABOVE *Former sailor, Syd Chaplin was Charlie's elder half-brother and managed his business affairs, including the short-lived aviation business.*

LEFT *DeMille Field No.2 around 1920.*

RIGHT *The Chaplin Airfield around 1920 hosting an aero display.*

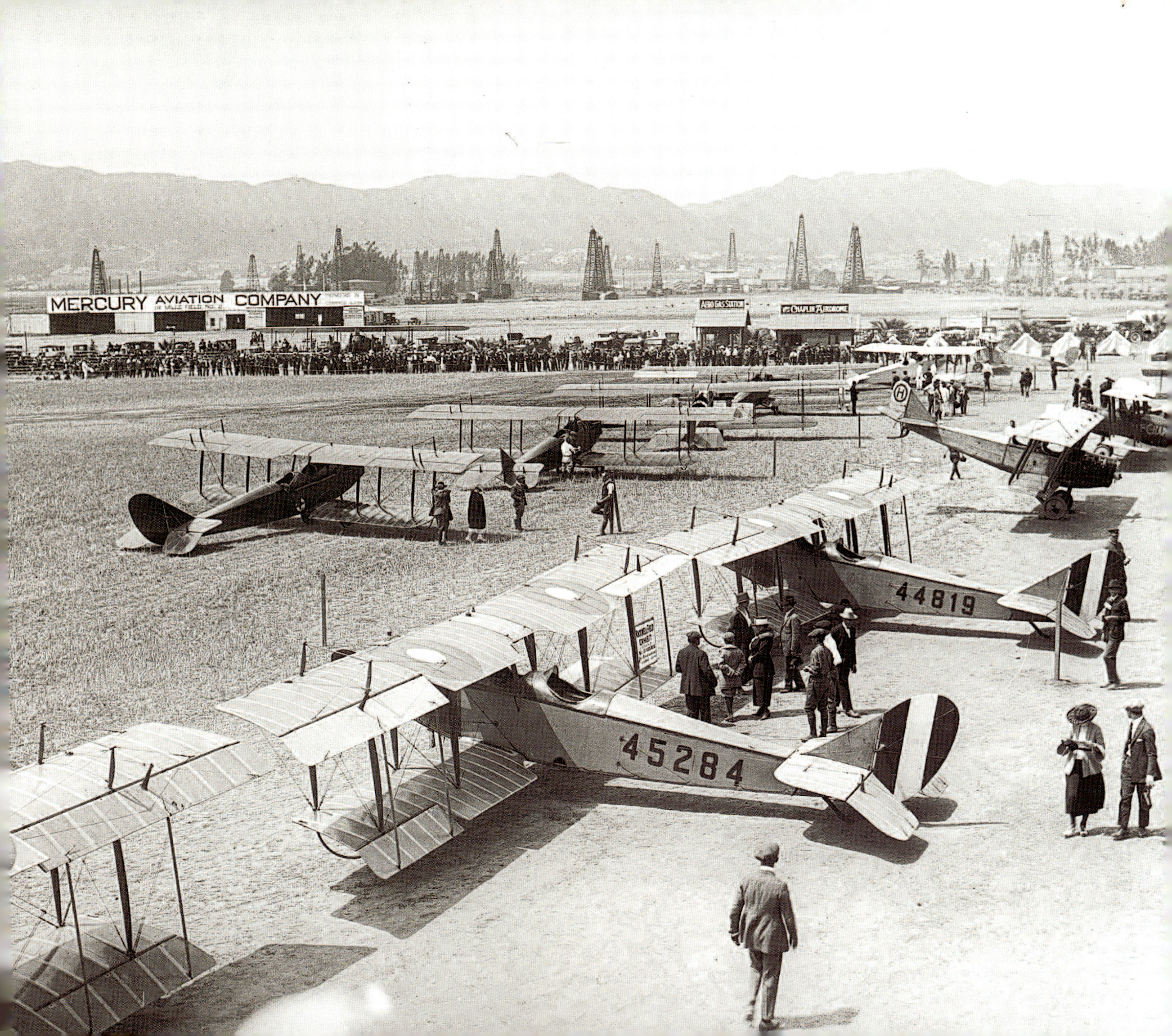
MERCURY AVIATION COMPANY
DE MILLE FIELD NO. 2
AERO GAS STATION
CHAPLIN AERODROME
44819
45284

Los Angeles County Courthouse **RAZED 1935-1936**

Los Angeles County built its showcase red sandstone courthouse on Poundcake Hill, at Temple and Spring streets, on the former site of Los Angeles High School.

It had been located in John Temple's Clock Tower Courthouse since 1861, but the burgeoning business of city and county meant that a far bigger building was required. The county hired the San Francisco architectural firm of Curlett, Eisen and Cuthbertson to design the building. One of the partners, Walter Cuthbertson, worked as the city architect for the City and County of San Francisco. Another partner, William Curlett, had designed the Mechanical and Electrical Engineering Building, at the University of California, Berkeley, in 1893.

Construction began in 1887, and when the courthouse opened four years later, admirers called the structure one of the finest examples of Richardsonian Romanesque Revival architecture on the West Coast. The building's design split the structure into three parts: two side pavilions on either side of a grand central entry.

The architects calculated the approach to the courthouse to impress. A round driveway took visitors to the building as its massive tower loomed overhead. The courthouse's entrance shrouded the main door in dark shadows, which gave the building the air of a medieval monastery.

The impressively detailed building could not withstand the March 10, 1933, Long Beach Earthquake, which registered a strong 6.3 on the Richter Scale. When a severe aftershock struck, the county voted to demolish the already abandoned building. The Great Depression left little available money to complete the task. The county decided to demolish the top two floors and remove the tower, with a view to reusing what remained. When Angelenos ridiculed the result as an "objectionable eyesore," the county turned to the federal government for help, which came in 1935. Work finally got underway in January 1936.

"Los Angeles County's eyesore, the old red stone Courthouse at Temple Street and Broadway, which has stood for a number of months in a partly wrecked condition, is to be removed," the *Los Angeles Times* reported on January 10, 1936, under the headline "W.P.A. Will Take Over Razing Old Courthouse."

The process of obtaining funding and getting approval for a replacement for the demolished courthouse dragged on. The Great Depression and then World War II stood in the way. It was not until the mid-1950s that construction would begin on Los Angeles County's fourth courthouse. The county had set aside a portion of the tower from the 1891 building and incorporated it into the east facade of the new courthouse, which has been located close to the site of its Romanesque Revival predecessor.

OPPOSITE *The Los Angeles County Courthouse along New High Street in this photograph taken about 1900. The small building snug against the courthouse is the first hall of records. Temple Street runs up Poundcake Hill on the right.*

BELOW FAR LEFT *The Los Angeles County Courthouse with the Hall of Records circa 1906.*

BELOW LEFT *The Hall of Records has dwarfed the Los Angeles County Courthouse in this photograph from 1928.*

BELOW *A reverse view showing the main entrance to the Courthouse in the early 1930s as the new City Hall looms over it.*

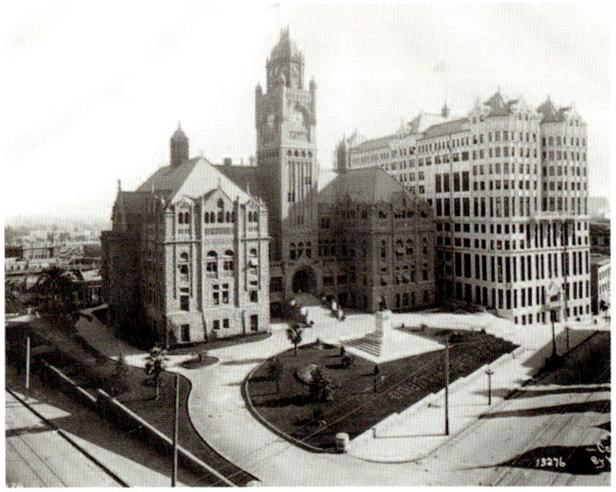

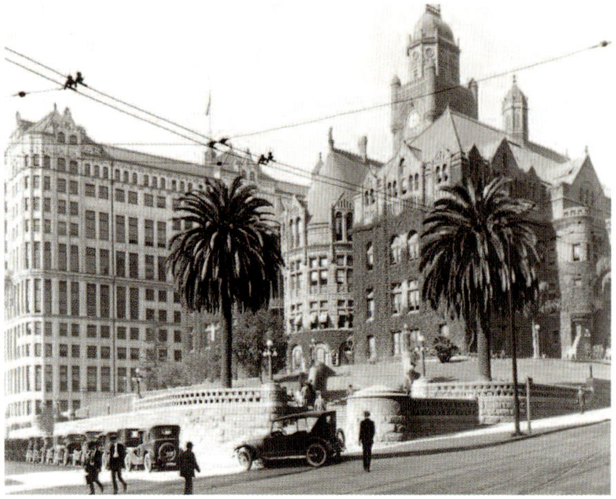

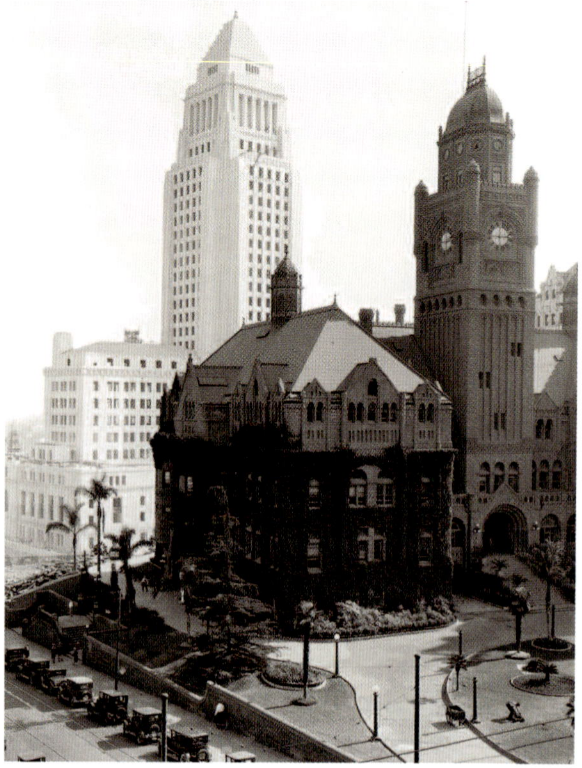

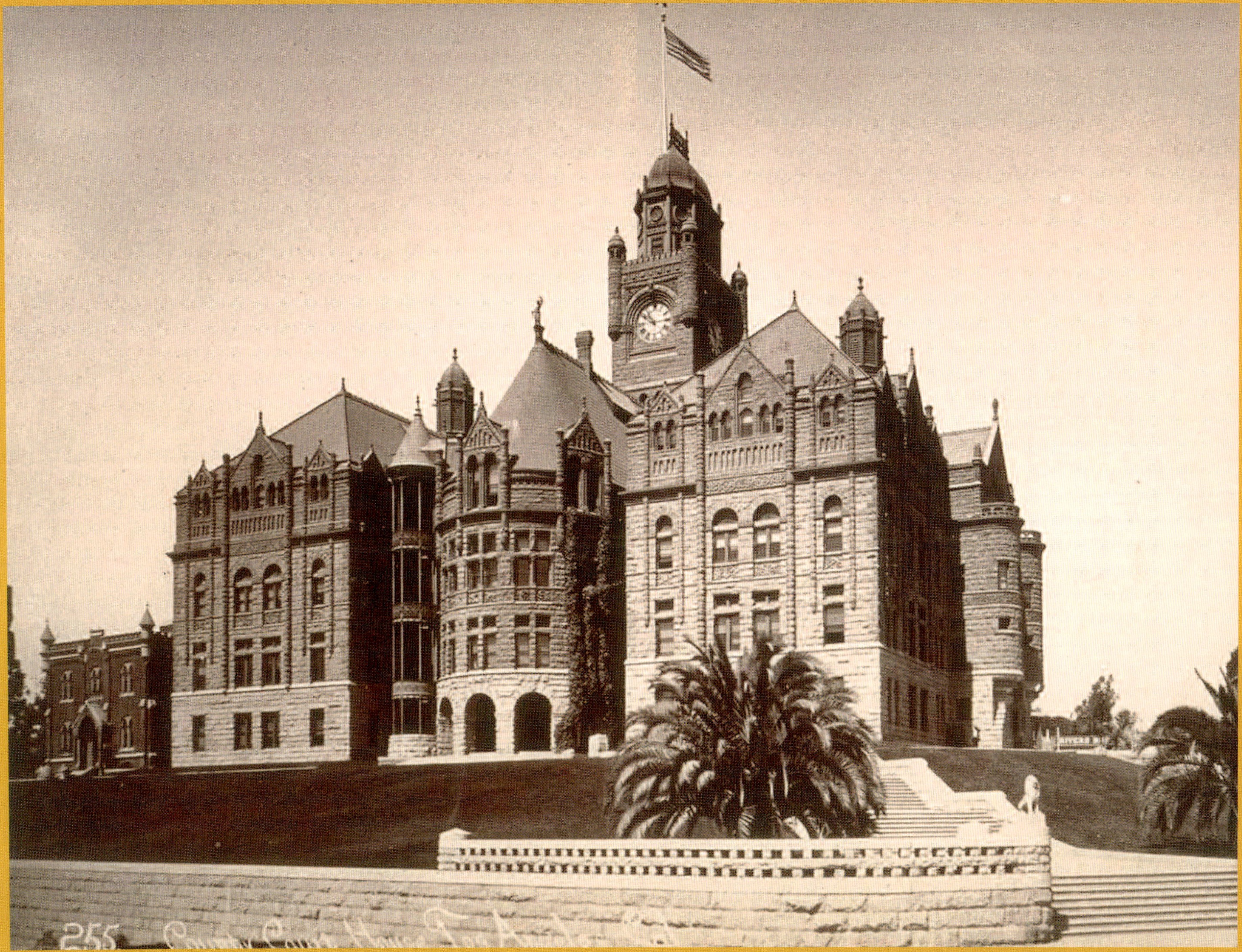
255

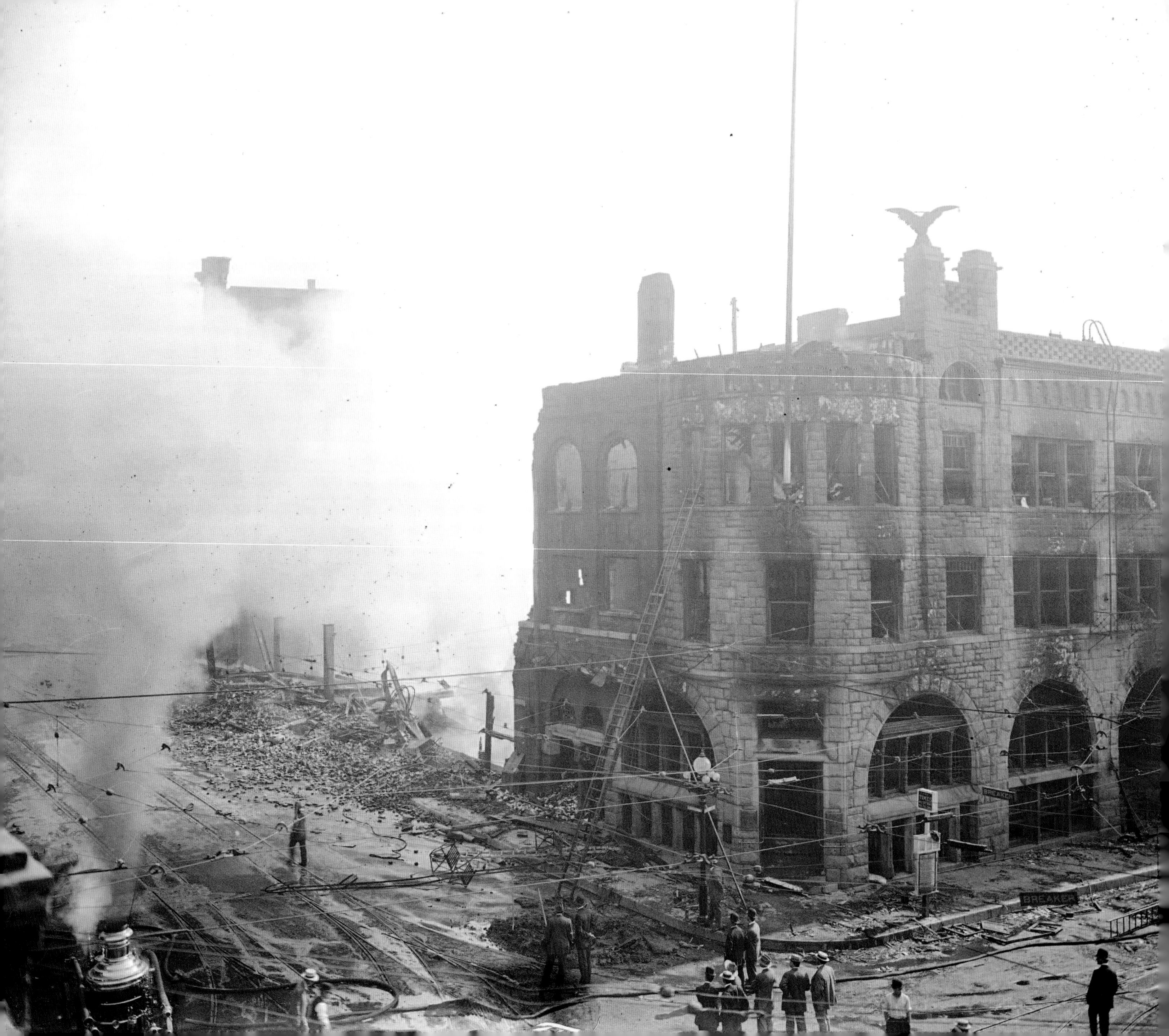
BREAKER

Los Angeles Times Building RAZED 1937

The *Los Angeles Times* began its life in a simple one-story building at Temple and New High Streets. Family homes, rather than businesses, had occupied the real estate here; the newspaper's first home was built on the site of the Schumacher family home.

In 1887 Harrison Gray Otis took over as the owner and publisher of the *Times*. He moved his newspaper to a handsome Romanesque Revival building at First Street and Broadway. In 1891, Otis commissioned Gutzon Borglum to fashion the *Times* eagle, which was emblematic of the owner's motto: "Stand fast, stand firm, stand sure, stand true."

Borglum's creation weighed more than 200 pounds and had a wingspan of seven and one-half feet. It has perched atop three *Times* buildings beginning December 5,1891, on the First and Broadway building.

Otis's attitude toward his workers and his militant anti-union stance brought trouble to his doorstep. In 1910 workers in the metal trades were threatening to organize. Otis's anti-union editorials fueled the fires of discontent.

On the evening of September 30, 1910, the discontented acted. The brothers James and John McNamara spearheaded a conspiracy to destroy Otis and all that he stood for. They packed 16 sticks of dynamite into a suitcase which was due to go off at 4:00 a.m. when the Times building would be empty. Instead, the bomb detonated just after 1:00 a.m, with a late-night team still producing an extra edition for the Vanderbilt Cup. The explosion set off a natural gas main and the ensuing fire collapsed the building. The explosion rocked the city awake in the early morning hours of October 1.

Twenty men working inside the building lost their lives; some 20 more men were injured, some so severely that they were no longer able to work. James McNamara, who set the dynamite, was sentenced to life in prison. Otis showed his defiance by quickly repairing the damaged building. He opened it with a dedication timed for the second anniversary of the bombing.

When Otis died in 1917, his son-in-law, Harry Chandler, took over the newspaper. In 1935 Chandler built the newspaper's present headquarters at First and Spring streets. The art deco building made a statement to the city as to just how powerful the *Los Angeles Times* had become. Chandler was a powerhouse whom many credit with bringing the 1936 Olympic Games to Los Angeles. When he died in 1944 his son Raymond took the reins. Under his leadership a ten-story addition to the newspaper's empire went up at Third and Spring streets.

The Chandler family sold the paper to the *Chicago Tribune* in 2000.

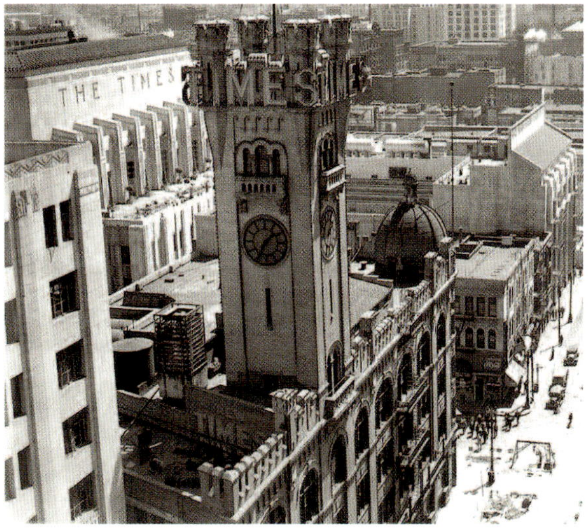

ABOVE *The* Los Angeles Times*' third home can be seen In the distance in this 1934 photograph just beyond the clock tower that Harrison Gray Otis added to the newspaper's second place of business. Otis's son-in-law, Harry Chandler, had the new building put up and tore down his father-in-law's building two years later. Famed clockmaker Nels Johnson designed the tower's clock. He called his products "century clocks" because he designed them to last one hundred years. The Eagle changed roosts from the 1912 building to the 1935 building, but in 1956 was moved inside the lobby to protect it from the elements.*

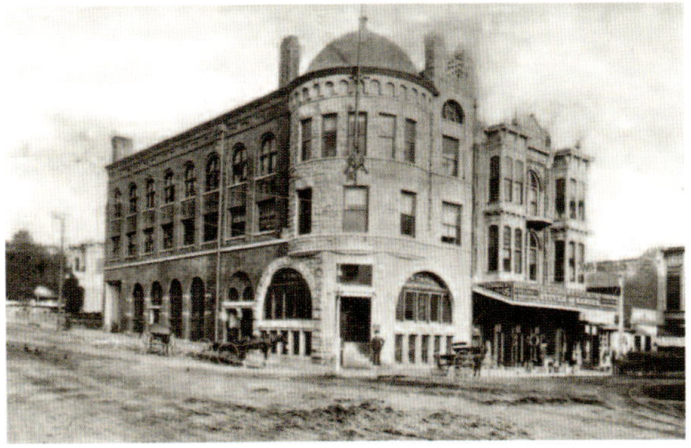

RIGHT *The tower on the renovated Los Angeles Times Building pierces the skyline in the middle of this photograph. Publisher Harrison Gray Otis added the tower to the building as part of renovations after the October 1, 1910, bombing. Otis opened the refurbished building on October 1, 1912, on the second anniversary of the bombing.*

LEFT *Harrison Gray Otis built the* Los Angeles Times *a second home in this building at First and Broadway. The newspaper's first home was a modest affair at Temple and New High streets on the site of the old Schumacher family home.*

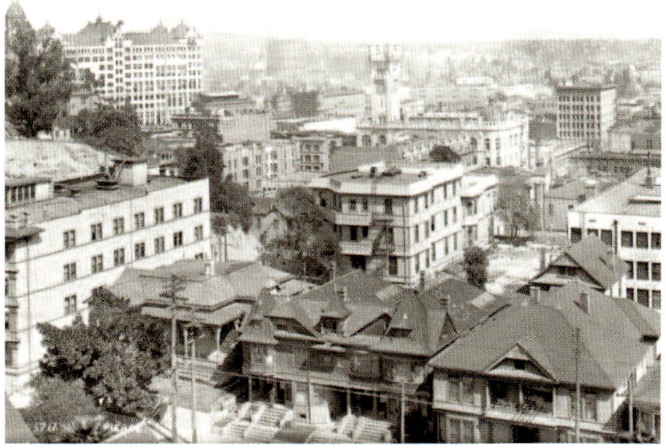

Original Chinatown RELOCATED 1938

The Chinese first appeared in Los Angeles in 1852. They were mostly men who found work in laundries and tending the gardens of the wealthier "Anglo" settlers. These were some of the few jobs they were allowed to do as laws had already been passed that prohibited the Chinese from owning any land.

By 1870, about 200 Chinese were living together on *Calle de los Negros* near the Mexican barrio Sonora Town. The street took its name from Mexicans with darker complexions who lived there in the earlier part of the 19th century.

On October 24, 1871, a mob of white men marched on *Calle de los Negros*. They ransacked every home and hanged some of the Chinese living there. This mass lynching was in retaliation for the accidental shooting of a white man named Robert Thompson.

"A simmering, small-scale turf war involving three Chinese gangs exploded into a riot that engulfed the small, but growing town of Los Angeles," Scott Zesch writes in *Chinatown War*. "A large mob of white Angelenos, spurred by racial resentment, rampaged through the city and lynched some 18 people before order was restored."

Most of the Chinese had joined one of a number of Chinese community associations. These associations provided job placement and other services, but they were involved in extortion and illicit businesses, including prostitution. In 1870 the largest of these associations, the See-Yup Company, began a battle among the Chinese. During this battle some of the crossfire accidently killed Thompson and sparked the riot that caused the death of so many.

The Chinese recovered and Chinatown expanded. By 1890, some 3,000 Chinese called Los Angeles home. By 1910 they had settled in some 200 buildings on 15 streets and alleys. They enjoyed their own theater, worshipped in three temples and had their own telephone exchange and newspaper.

Then they were forced to move. The threat of relocation was nothing new. In 1913, L. F. Hanchett had paid $2 million for most of Chinatown's land. He wanted to convert the property into an industrial and warehouse spread and add a railroad terminal but his plans disintegrated.

In 1931 the threat was back. The California Supreme Court sided with the idea of building Union Station on the property where the Chinese lived. Chinese-American engineer Peter Soohoo stepped up. He formed the Los Angeles Chinatown Project Association, whose 28 members became known as "the founders" and began raising funds to begin construction of a new Chinatown. The grand opening took place on June 25, 1938.

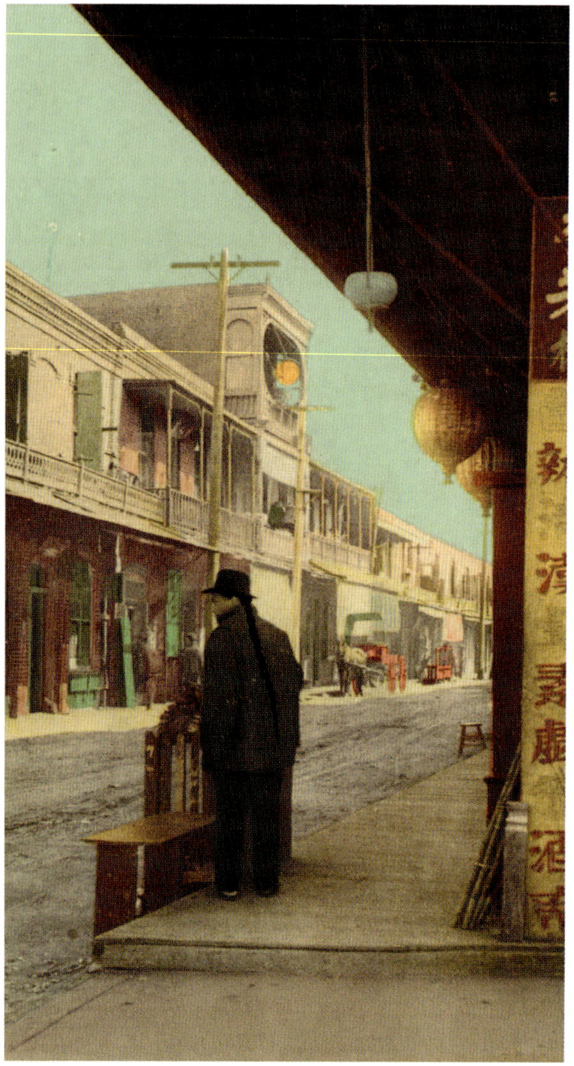

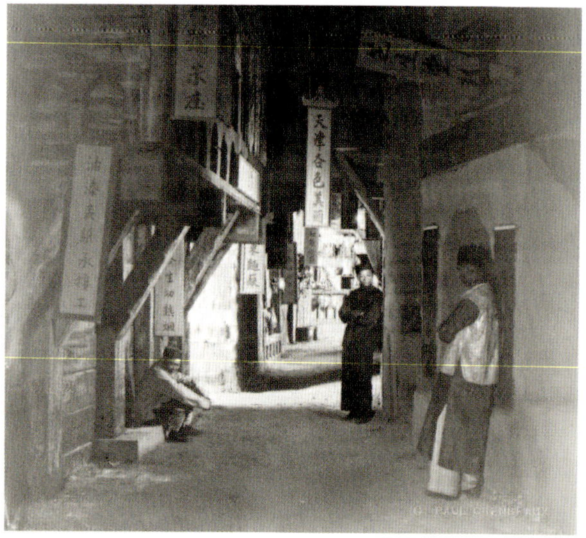

LEFT *By 1900, when this photograph was taken in Chinatown, the Chinese had been in Los Angeles for almost 50 years. Their neighborhood would survive for almost another 30 years.*

ABOVE *Neighbors linger in a Chinatown alley about 1922. People living in Chinatown at this time had their own telephone exchange. The neighborhood also boasted an opera house, three temples and a Chinese language newspaper.*

OPPOSITE PAGE *This 1922 picture shows Chinese men reading some news posted on a wall in Los Angeles' first Chinatown which was centered on Alameda and Macy streets. By the time these men had gathered, Chinatown had about 200 buildings spread over 15 blocks.*

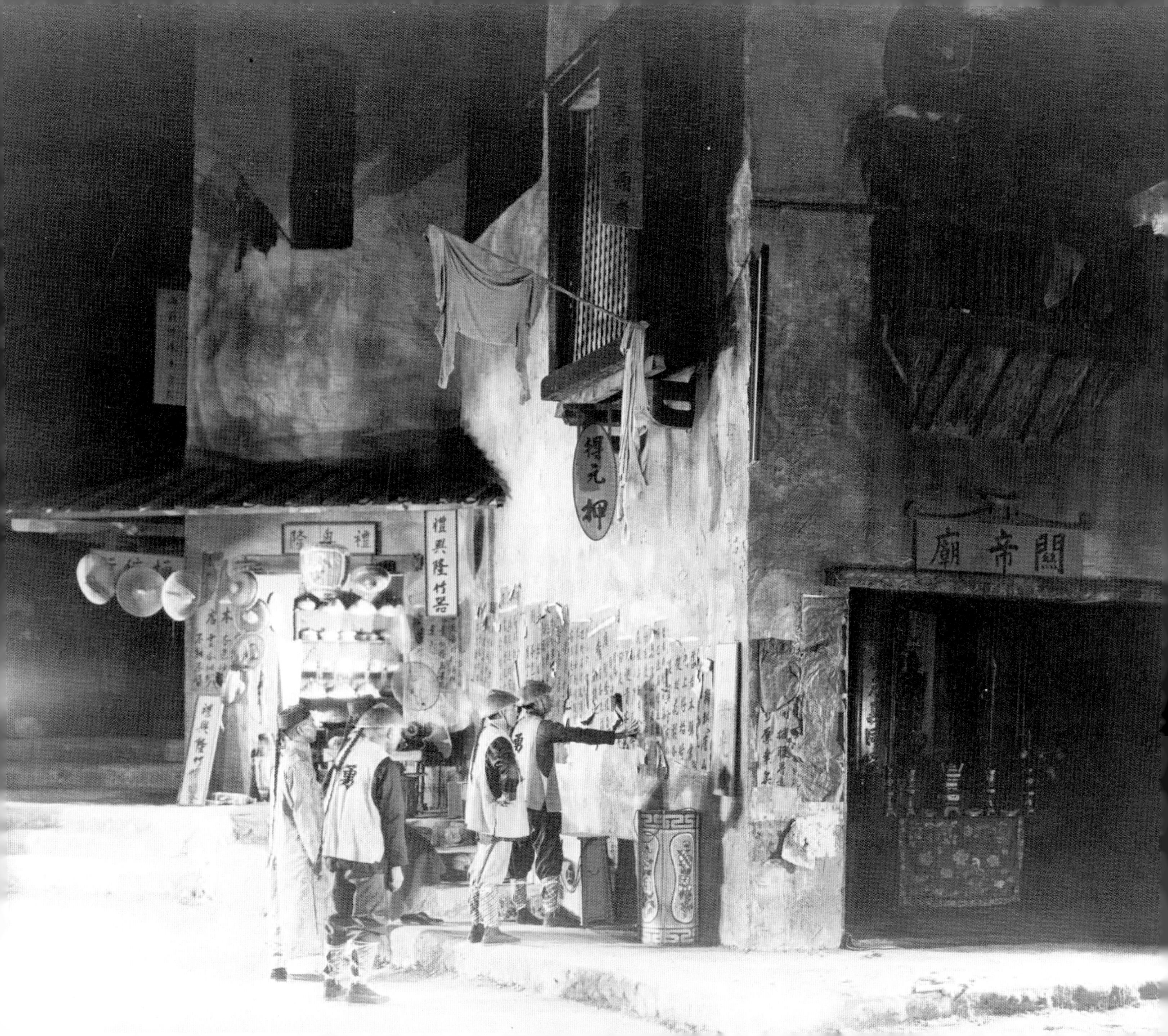

禮興隆
禮興隆竹器
得元押
關帝廟
勇

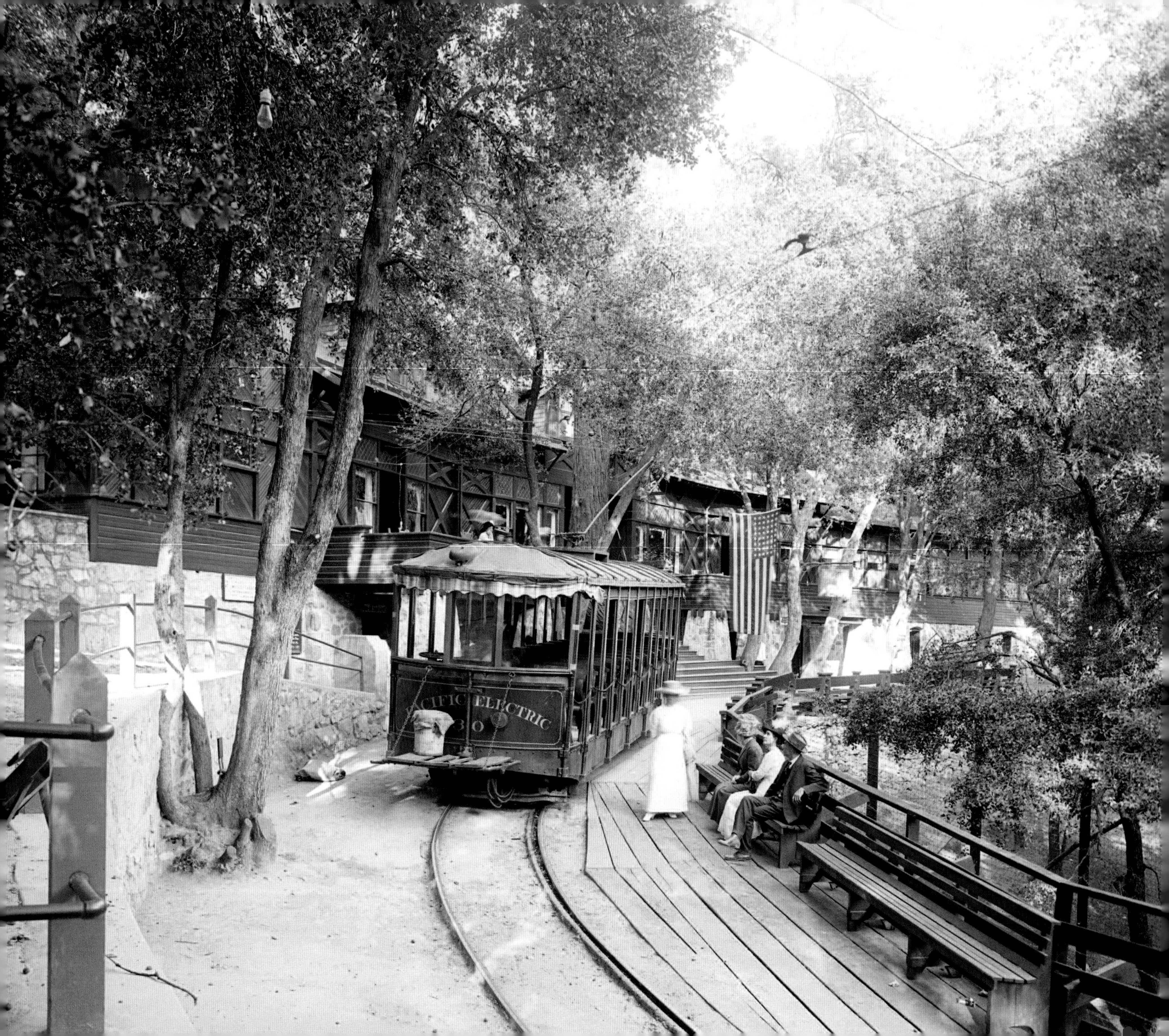

ACIFIC ELECTRIC

Mount Lowe Railway CLOSED 1938

At a celebration fitting for Independence Day in 1893, the Mount Lowe Railway opened. The Pasadena & Mount Wilson Railroad Company's seven miles of track took residents of Pasadena to the crest of the San Gabriel Mountains purely for scenic purposes. Company president Thaddeus S. C. Lowe and engineer David J. Macpherson devised a plan to satisfy Pasadena residents' desire to scale the mountains easily.

Professor Lowe earned his reputation as an inventor, scientist and aeronaut. A pioneer in the military use of balloons, President Abraham Lincoln had dubbed him Chief Aeronaut of the Union Army Balloon Corps during the Civil War. Lowe made observations over Mechanicsville, Virginia, and the Battle of Seven Pines during the Peninsula Campaign of 1862. Disputes over his pay forced his resignation from the army in 1863, but Lowe continued experimenting, attempting to complete a transatlantic flight in a balloon.

In 1887, he moved to Los Angeles and promptly made a fortune in ice making, using a chemical process he patented. A portion of his fortune went to create the railway that scaled the 6,100-foot Echo Mountain. In 1892, the mountain was renamed to celebrate Professor Lowe.

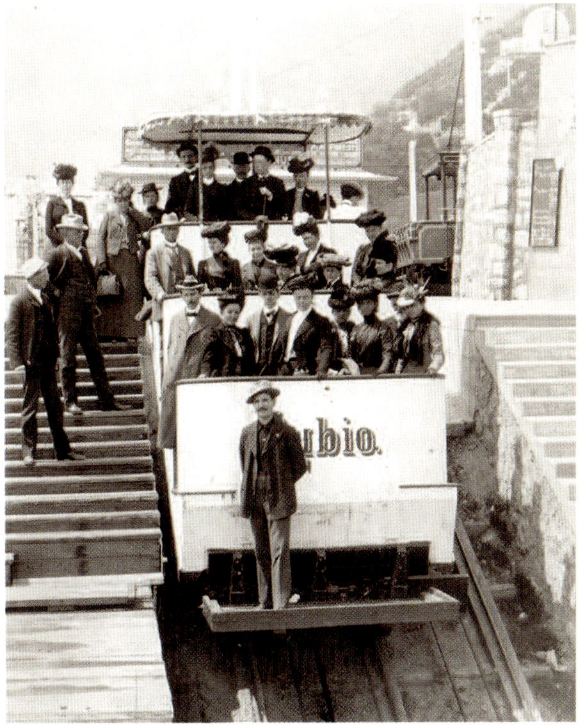

Starting from Altadena, a fairly standard rail car ride took passengers up Lake Avenue into Rubio Canyon. It terminated at a 12-room hotel, the Rubio Pavilion, where those destined for the crest of the mountains boarded a funicular which climbed to the top of Echo Mountain promontory where the 70-room Echo Mountain House stood, along with the 40-room Echo Chalet, an observatory, casino, dance hall and menagerie. Another trolley line continued to Crystal Springs and Ye Alpine Tavern where riders enjoyed tennis, wading pools and mule rides. And the tavern, of course.

While it may have been the only scenic railway of its kind in the nation, the Mount Lowe Railway never prospered under Lowe's leadership. Most travelers couldn't afford the trip to the Altadena hillside, never mind the admission up the mountain. Lowe soon learned fares wouldn't cover the debts he'd incurred from construction and sold out in 1899. Eventually the railway became part of Henry Huntington's Pacific Electric Railway. Huntington's huge streetcar empire helped support the fringe effort at Mount Lowe from 1902 until its eventual closure in 1938.

The attractions atop the hill were woefully distant from the city's fire-fighting capabilities, and fires took their toll. A blaze in 1900 took out Echo Mountain House, and five years later, another destroyed everything but the observatory. A flood in 1909 washed away the Rubio Pavilion, while gale-force winds knocked down the observatory and its 14-inch telescope in 1928. An electrical fire destroyed the Alpine Tavern in 1936. Two years later torrential rains washed everything else off the hillsides.

The railway's ruined remnants became listed on the National Register of Historical Places in 1993. Today, visitors to the area can hike the 5.8-mile Mount Lowe Railway Trail that accesses the ruins of Ye Alpine Tavern. A non-profit organization dedicated to the memory of the Mount Lowe Railroad—The Mount Lowe Preservation Society, Inc.—maintains an incredible collection of artifacts and ephemera related to the now-lost railway.

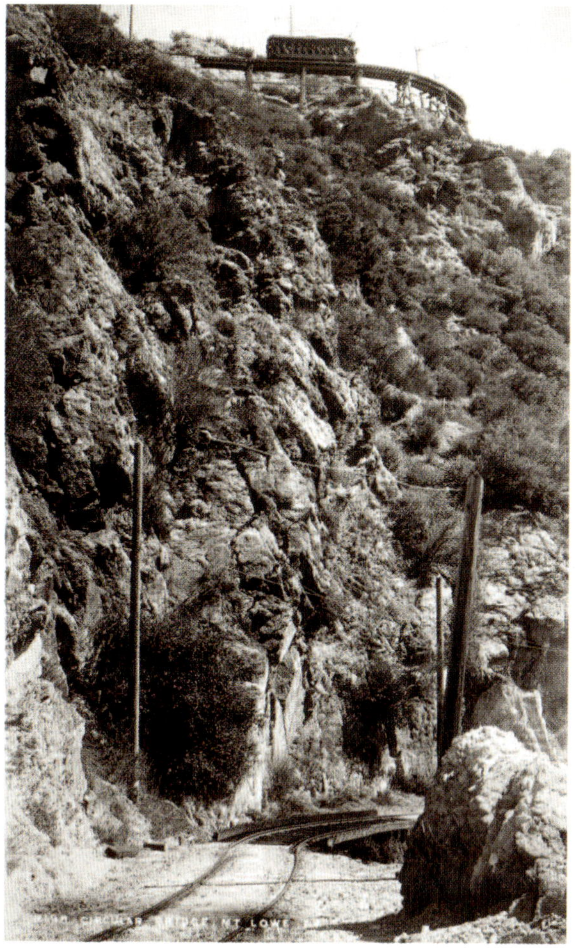

LEFT *This photograph from 1899 shows passengers about to begin their journey down Mount Lowe's cable incline funicular to the Rubio Pavilion.*

ABOVE *Cars would wind their way up Flores Canyon to the trestles of the Circular Bridge. It combined breathtaking views with a precipitous journey. After the bridge, passengers traveled through the Devil's Slide and Devil's Gate before arriving for a restorative drink at Ye Alpine Tavern.*

OPPOSITE PAGE *The electric trolley at Ye Alpine Tavern plies the rails sometime between 1902 and 1910.*

The Baker Block DEMOLISHED 1942

Colonel Robert Symington Baker put the finishing touches to the ornate three-story Baker Block in 1878. The building housed offices, shops and apartments. The structure rose up at the intersection of Main and Arcadia streets on the site of Abel Stearns' adobe, which locals called *El Palacio*, the palace. The adobe was known for the parties that Stearns hosted in his grand ballroom.

Stearns died in 1871 and three years later his widow, Arcadia—for whom Stearns had named Arcadia Street—married Baker. In 1875 Baker had the Stearns adobe torn down and began putting the Baker Block up in its place. Much of Baker's wealth was in land and sheep farming. He owned Rancho San Vicente, which he had purchased from the Sepulveda family for $55,000. The rancho included all of Santa Monica. Baker sold a portion of the rancho to Nevada Senator John Percival Jones for $162,500. Jones described Rancho San Vicente as the most beautiful place he'd ever seen. Jones and Baker would team up to create the city of Santa Monica.

"Baker wanted a grand home and replaced *El Palacio* with a three-story, 64,428-square-foot building," Susan Cook wrote in the *Santa Monica Mirror*. The Bakers rented the first two floors to commercial businesses. They lived on the top floor. Locals pointed to the structure as the largest and the most expensive building in the city, possibly the most expensive one south of San Francisco. It had cost the Bakers the tidy sum of $25,000 and was Los Angeles' first steel-framed building and the first with tiled floors.

"An ornate building, it expressed the aesthetics of the 'Gilded Age' in which they lived," Cook wrote. "The large, land–grant families—the Sepulvedas, Reyes, Lugos, Machados and Wolfskills among them—were frequent guests at famous dances and parties hosted by the Bakers."

The Baker Block's impressive staircase had a pair of bronze Roman soldiers holding up the gas lights on the top landing that led to the Baker's sumptuous home. The building also had an elevator. Baker died in 1894 and Arcadia moved to Santa Monica.

Goodwill Industries of Southern California purchased the building in 1919. By 1936 critics were calling the Baker Block a "relic of the cast-iron age." *Los Angeles Times* columnist Timothy G. Turner called the building a "magnificent pile" in a story he wrote that same year. The city purchased the old Baker Block from Goodwill in 1941 with the intention of using the site for an extension to the Civic Center and demolished the building a year later.

The building had its champions to the end. The Metropolitan Garden Association tried to persuade the city to move the Baker Block and use it as a public recreation center. Arthur E. Briggs led some of his fellow city councilmen to raise funds to keep the building just where it stood and turn it into the city's history museum. It was all in vain.

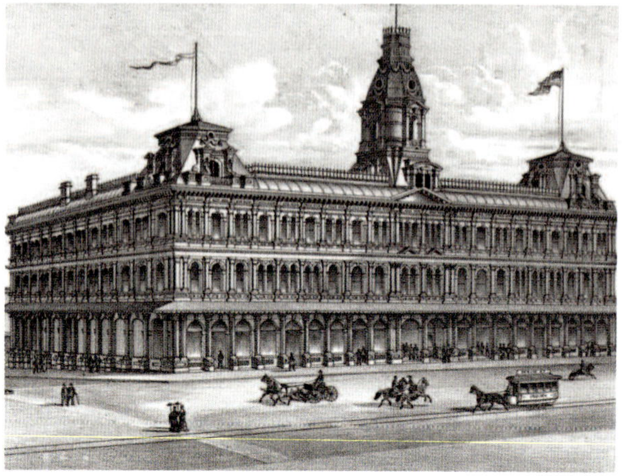

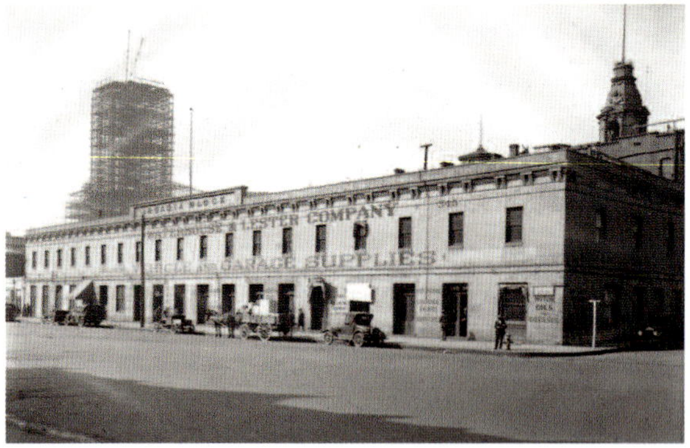

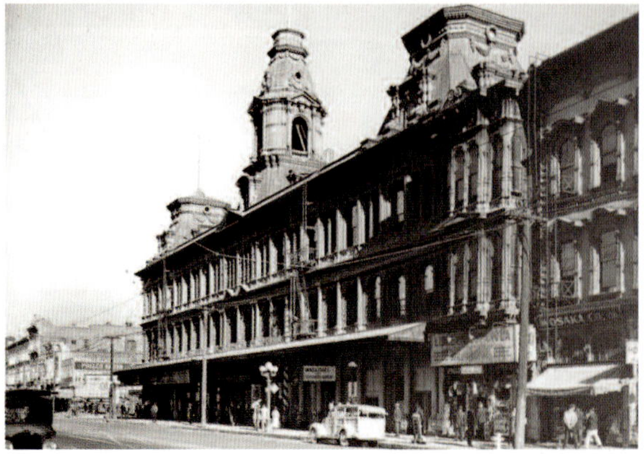

ABOVE *An early illustration, from around 1880, of the Baker Block soon after completion.*

LEFT *In 1858, Abel Stearns built this two-story business block on Los Angeles Street. He called it the "Arcadia Block" after his young bride. It was the first brick building in Los Angeles. The tower from the Baker Block peeks over the Arcadia Block at right. That's Los Angeles' new city hall going up on the left. The block was demolished in 1927, the same year this picture was taken.*

LEFT *By the time this photograph was taken in 1938, the block across the street had been cleared and the Federal Building was going up.*

OPPOSITE PAGE *Photographer Carlton Watkins took this picture of the Baker Block in 1880, five years after the building opened. Watkins, already famous for the Yosemite photographs that influenced Abraham Lincoln to make Yosemite a national park, sold his Los Angeles photographs for use in a stereo cards under the title "California Views."*

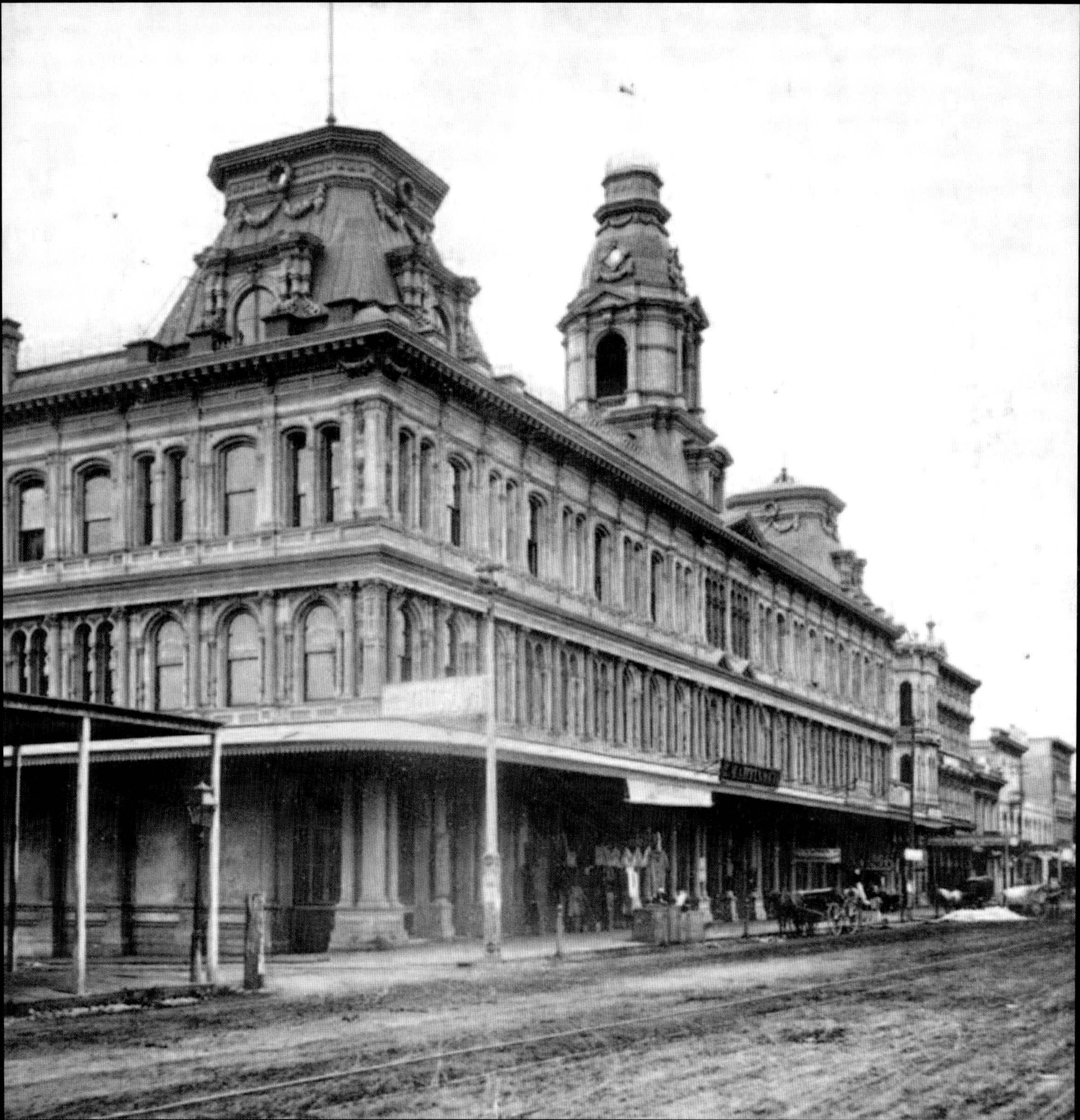

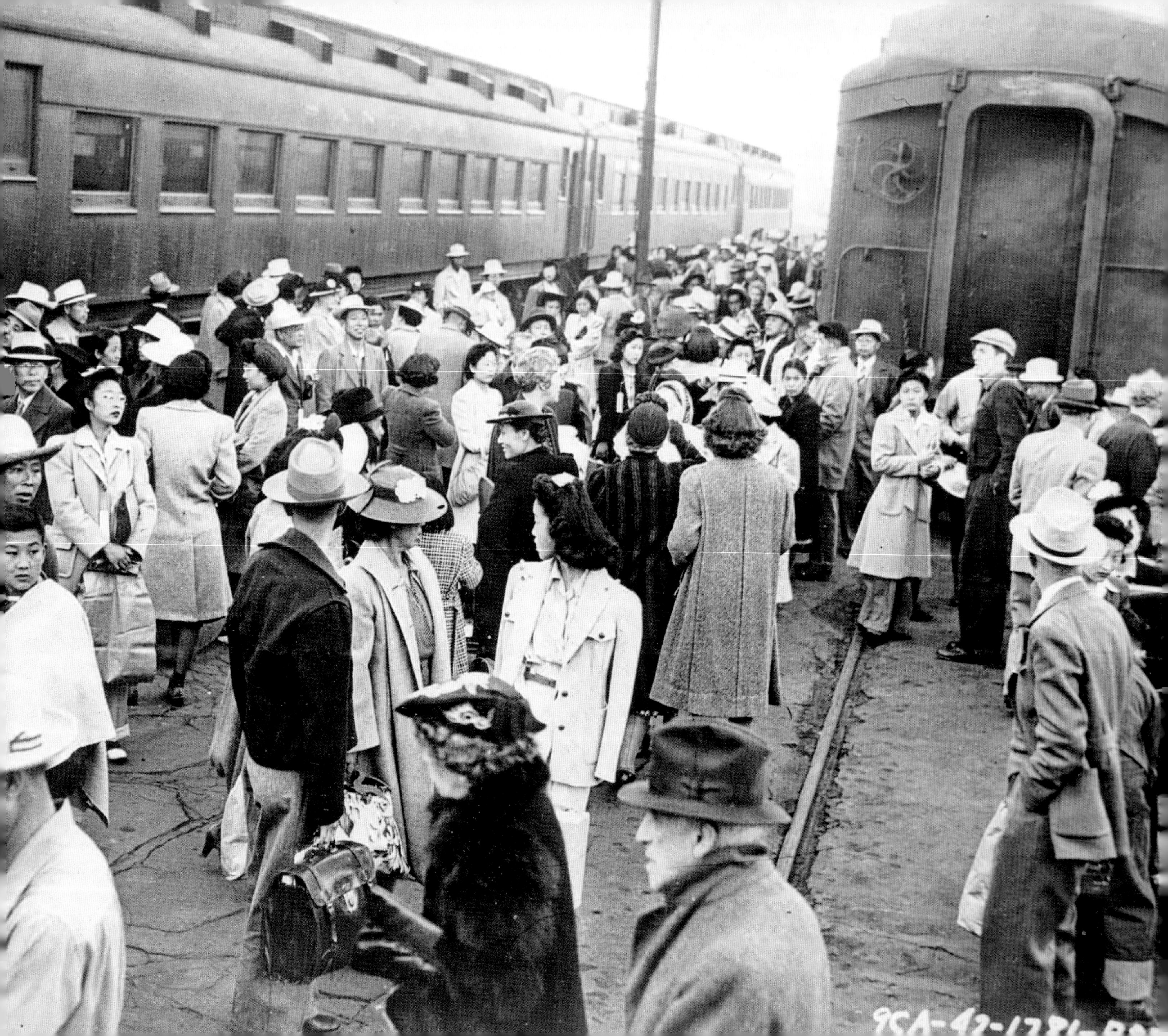

Original Little Tokyo **INTERNED 1942**

Immigrants to America throughout history faced xenophobia and a language barrier on arrival, often causing them to band together and settle in areas where they could create their own economies. Japanese immigrants to Southern California settled in a location that became known as Little Tokyo, a one-square-mile area now largely occupied by the Los Angeles Civic Center.

The settlement is said to have begun with the establishment of Kame Restaurant in 1885, the creation of shipwrecked sailor Hamanosuke "Charles" Hama Shigeta. The restaurant operated at 340 East First Street. The original Little Tokyo offered shopping along First Street and vegetable markets along Central Avenue, a retail outlet for the many Japanese truck farmers in Southern California. Bounded by Temple Street, Judge John Aiso Street, First Street and Los Angeles Street, and with a maximum population of 30,000, Little Tokyo's growth was limited by the 1924 Japanese Exclusion Act which disallowed any future migration to the area.

Fears about Japanese Americans' loyalty during World War II led to Japanese internment via Executive Order 9066, signed by Franklin D. Roosevelt on February 19, 1942, which allowed authorized military commanders to designate "military areas from which any or all persons may be excluded." This applied primarily to Japanese but also to Italian and German Americans and indeed anyone a military commander considered a threat. The result was the systematic emptying of Los Angeles' Little Tokyo and many ethnic communities like it.

In a story paralleled by San Francisco's Fillmore District, once the Japanese left Little Tokyo, African American and some Native Americans moved into the vacated properties and opened notable nightclubs and restaurants. Soon the area took the name Bronzeville. At the close of hostilities in 1945, Japanese Americans returning to the neighborhood found their former homes occupied by others and mostly settled elsewhere. The 1950 construction of the Los Angeles Police Department's Parker Center, one block east of City Hall, displaced a thousand residents and 50 Little Tokyo businesses.

Some 30 years later, a new Little Tokyo began taking shape. As Japanese corporations thrived and expanded into American markets, many chose Los Angeles for their U.S. headquarters. New corporate buildings, shopping plazas and hotels appeared among the historic buildings along First Street in a neighborhood that in recent years has also gained the reputation as an arts district.

While few Japanese Americans still reside in the area, Little Tokyo remains a locus of Japanese investment and community. Activists successfully had the First Street district established as historic in 1986 but not before the loss of many significant buildings during the 1950s including: the 1885 Amelia Street School, the 1925 Olympic Hotel, the 1905 Filipino Christian Church and Fellowship, the 1920 Rafu Dojo and the 1923 Paris Hotel, home to Toyo Miyatake's first photo studio.

Miyatake's photos, taken while he was interned at Manzanar—the main Japanese internment camp near Los Angeles—have become an incredibly important record of the wartime relocation of Japanese Americans. The photo studio, though now located in San Gabriel, remains in the family, run by Miyatake's grandson, Alan.

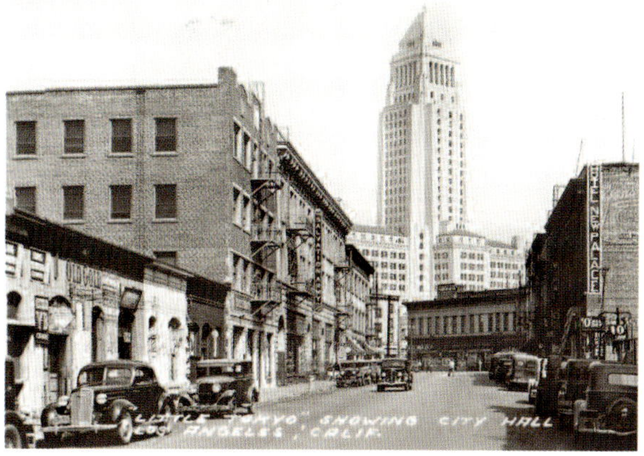

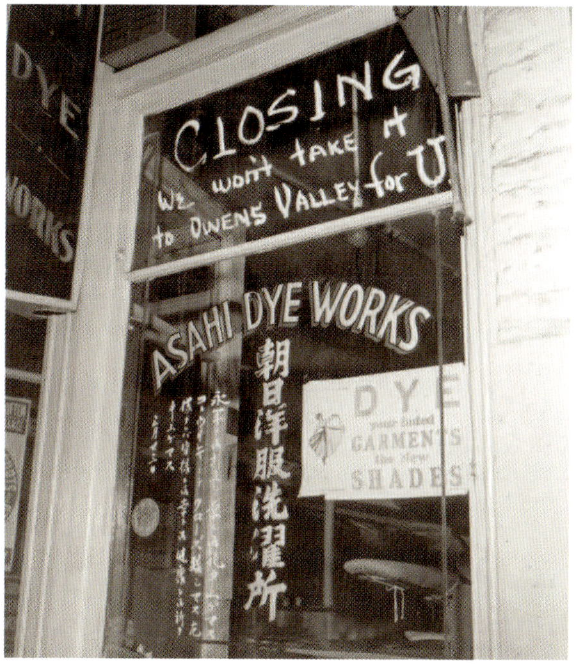

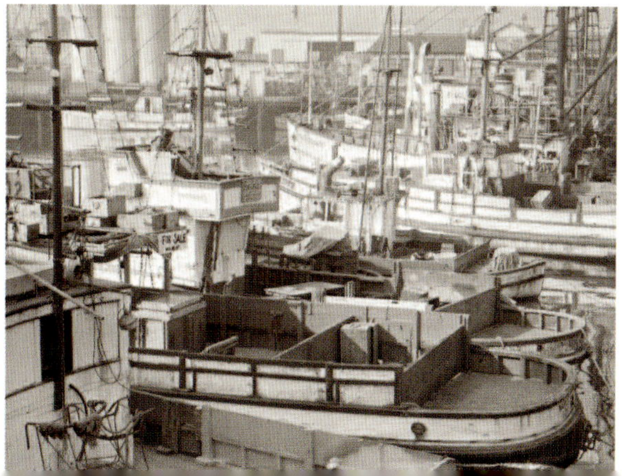

TOP RIGHT *A view of Little Tokyo in the shadow of City Hall.*

RIGHT *One of the many Japanese businesses forced to close its doors after FDR's Executive Order.*

BELOW RIGHT *Fishing boats that once belonged to Japanese residents of Los Angeles tied up for the duration of World War II in San Pedro Harbor in this April 1942 photograph from the U.S. War Relocation Authority.*

OPPOSITE PAGE *Japanese internees await transport in Los Angeles to inland detention camps where they would be held for the duration of World War II, sometime in early 1942. Most likely they'd be taken to Manzanar, a site 230 miles northeast of Los Angeles in the Owens Valley.*

Court Flight ABANDONED 1943

A forerunner to railroads everywhere, the Reisszug, a wooden rail line constructed in 1515 Salzburg, Austria, served the Hohensalzburg Castle as a sort of glorified dumb waiter powered by humans or animals hauling hemp ropes. Long since replaced with steel mechanisms, the Reisszug still operates and is the world's oldest funicular: a railroad designed strictly to get up a particularly steep embankment. Most funiculars consist of two passenger cars counterbalancing each other on opposite sides of a cable passing through a pulley, while being constricted to roll along a track. The counterbalancing reduces the amount of energy needed as gravity performs a lot of the work.

Perhaps the world's next most famous funicular is Angels Flight of Los Angeles, now a fully restored tourist destination in the Bunker Hill district downtown, whose taller, steeper sister, Court Flight, first started service in 1905.

Court Flight opened as part of a business venture by real estate investors R. E. Blackburn and Samuel G. Vandegrift. It gave rides to passengers going from Broadway between Temple and First streets to Court Street. The opening of the flight was delayed because of rains on the last day of 1904 which washed elements of the partially constructed railway down the hill onto Broadway. Blackburn incorporated as the Observation Tower Company, apparently with the idea of having passengers pay admission to use Court Flight to access the "One Big Look" tower. The tower sat atop what is thought to be the highest viewpoint in the city prior to the construction of City Hall in 1928.

Riders from the bottom of Court Flight rose 200 feet in height in just 200 feet of distance. Court had to conform to the city's anti-trust ordinance. Offering competition in the get-up-the-hill market, a stairway was constructed next to Court Flight. Climbers navigated 47 steps to the first landing and 96 more to the top. The railway didn't charge for rides down the hill in a further nod toward serving the public.

An advertisement in the March 29, 1906, *Los Angeles Herald* maintained that Court Flight offered the "finest view of the city, mountains and islands of the ocean… this grand viewpoint is the mecca of all sightseers… fare 5 cents." The tourist destination doubled as a means of developing the wealthy Court Hill neighborhood. Court Flight's designers had no idea it would one day serve busy courthouse workers accessing convenient parking on the hill above.

Operator Sam Vandergrift, his wife Annie, and Sam's popular co-pilot, Tom the cat, eventually gained ownership of Court Flight from his business partner. After Sam died in 1933, the flight struggled. A fire in 1943 damaged Court Flight's wooden ties and with few men available to operate it during wartime, the flight was abandoned that same year.

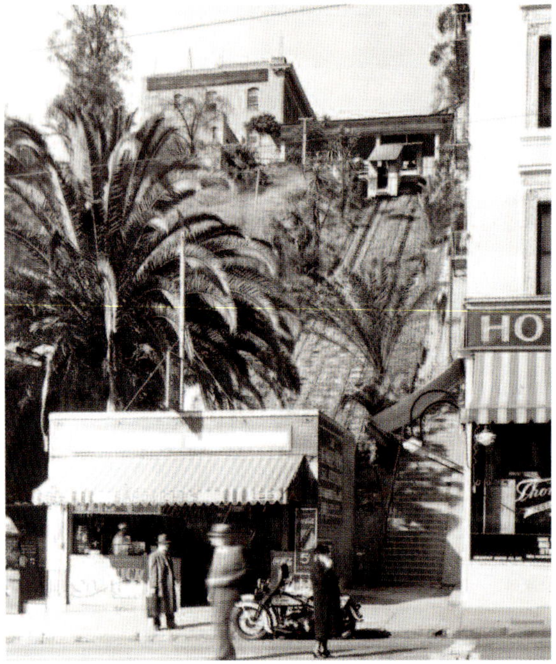

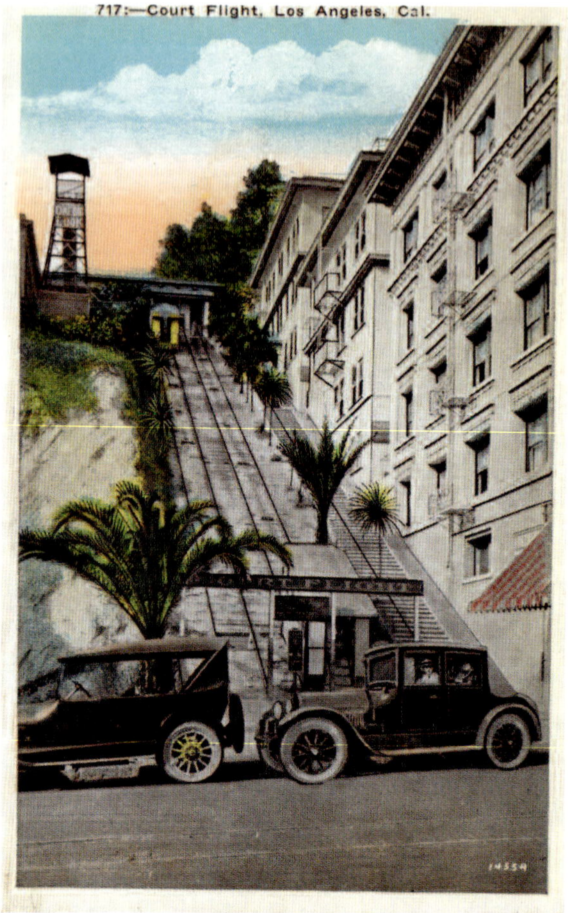

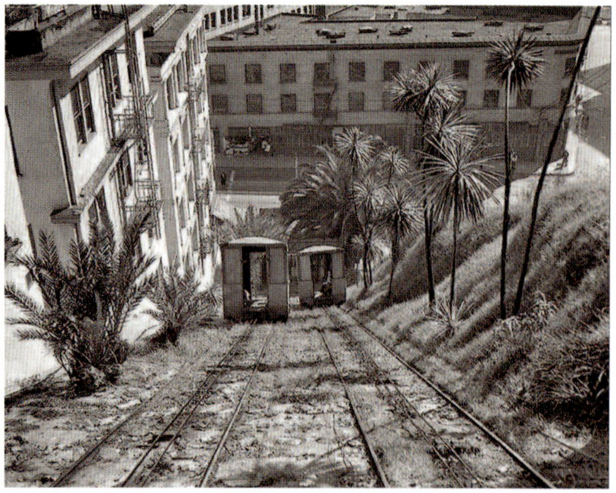

ABOVE *Court Flight as it looked in the mid-1930s.*

ABOVE RIGHT *This postcard view of Court Flight captures the flight sometime in 1930.*

RIGHT *Court Flight went into decline after the death of its founder Sam Vandergrift.*

OPPOSITE PAGE *The recently completed New Hotel Broadway appears to the right of Court Flight in this circa 1925 photograph.*

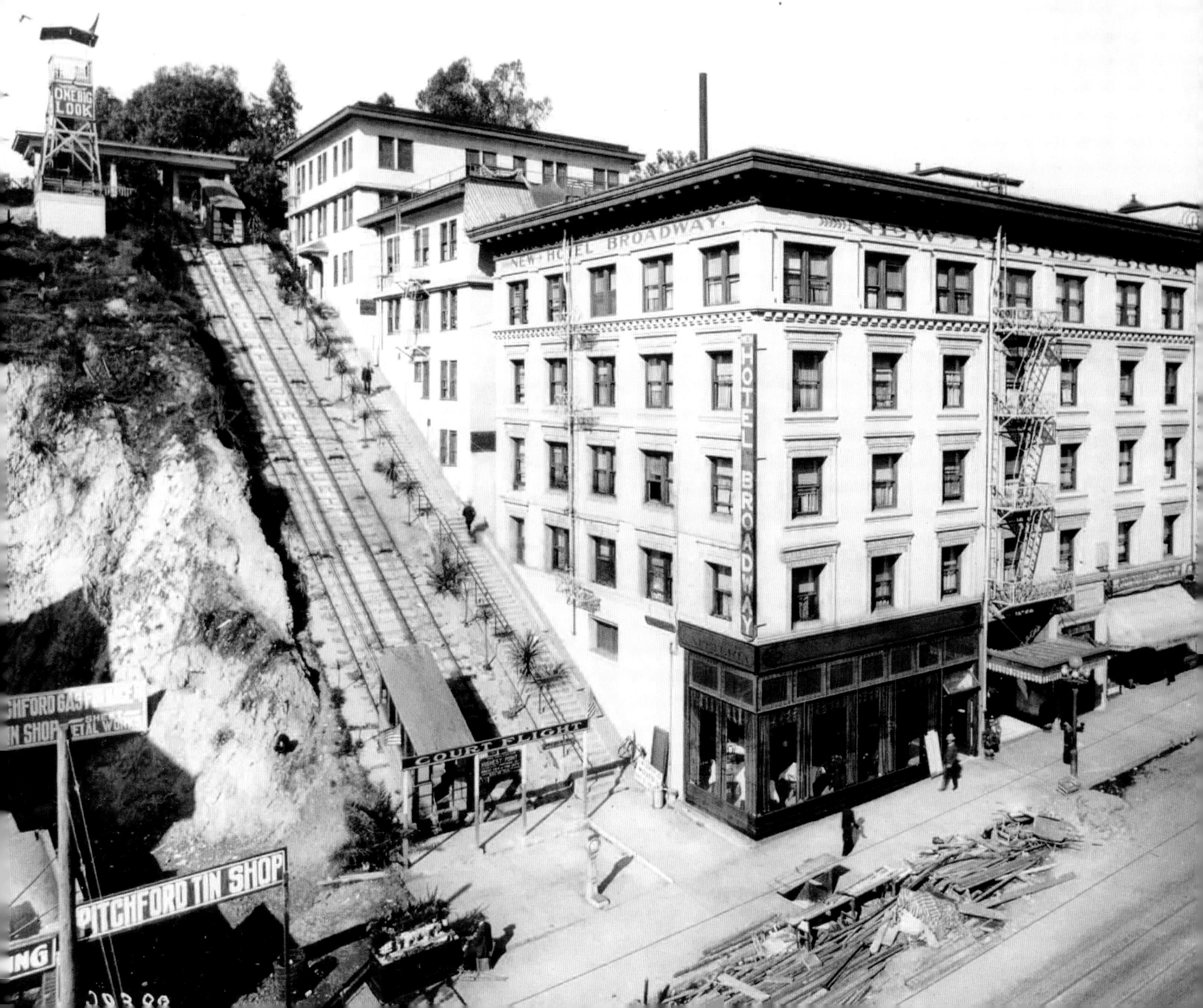
ONE BIG LOOK
NEW HOTEL BROADWAY
HOTEL BROADWAY
COURT FLIGHT
PITCHFORD TIN SHOP

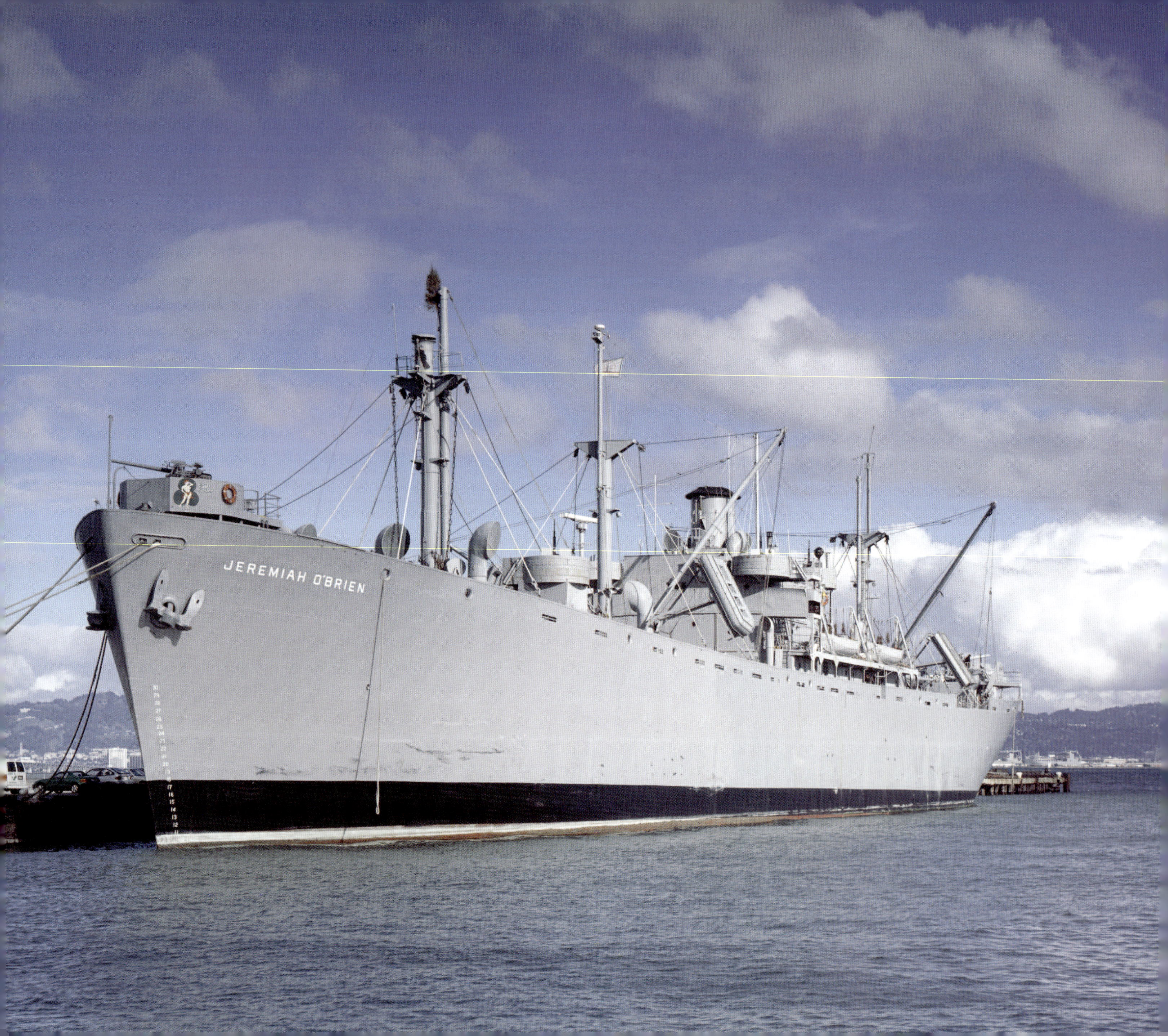
JEREMIAH O'BRIEN

Wilmington Shipyards CLOSED ON OCTOBER 25, 1945

While sailing up the coast of today's Southern California in 1540, Juan Rodriguez Cabrillo discovered a natural harbor. He dropped anchor and claimed the place for Spain. He named his discovery "San Pedro," for Peter of Alexandria (Egypt), the fourth century saint whose day the Spanish were celebrating.

The Spanish largely ignored San Pedro for more than 200 years. Then about 1770 San Pedro Harbor became an important trading post for the Mission San Gabriel Arcángel. The Americans arrived here in 1805 aboard the 74-ton *Lelia Byrd* out of Salem, Massachusetts. She was not the last; by the time the city of Los Angeles incorporated in 1850, San Pedro harbor had turned into a thriving port.

Phineas Banning arrived and founded the city of Wilmington. Banning, who many consider the "father of Los Angeles Harbor" laid the foundation for future business at the port. In 1897, thanks largely to the efforts of United States Senator Stephen White, San Pedro Harbor became Los Angeles' official port. Ten years later, Los Angeles established a Board of Harbor Commissioners. In 1909, Los Angeles annexed the cities of San Pedro and Wilmington.

When World War II arrived, the federal government commissioned the port to conduct only war-related business. Shipbuilding and boat repair shifted into high gear. The government built what it termed "emergency yards" to ramp up shipbuilding. One of these, the California Shipbuilding Corporation, or CalShip, sprung up in February 1941 with eight ship-launching ramps, known in the business as "ways."

CalShip sat on Terminal Island, a marshy, weed-infested island that had previously been home to a Japanese American community just outside Wilmington and San Pedro. To accommodate shipbuilding the company converted the marshland into artificial land supported by 57,000 wooden piles or "stilts." CalShip became known as the "shipyard on stilts."

CalShip launched the S.S. *John C. Fremont*, on September 27, 1941, ten weeks before the Japanese attacked Pearl Harbor. As the war progressed the number of ways were increased from eight to 14. At its peak, CalShip was employing some 40,000 people. Before the war was over these workers built 467 cargo ships for the Liberty and Victory fleets.

CalShip delivered the amazing figure of 111 ships in 1942, more than any other yard in the United States. In June 1943, it broke the record again by delivering 20 ships that month. CalShip employees broke a third record in December 1943, when they built 23 ships.

The company launched its last Victory ship, S.S. *Council Bluffs Victory*, on October 25, 1945 and closed its doors. In 1946, Howard Hughes moved his "Spruce Goose" airplane from Culver City to Terminal Island. The plane's first (and only) test flight took off from the Island on November 2, 1947. That same year the National Metal & Steel Corporation stepped in and opened a scrap yard on the spot. In a touch of irony the National Metal and Steel facility scrapped 55 of the Liberty and Victory ships that CalShip built on the same spot.

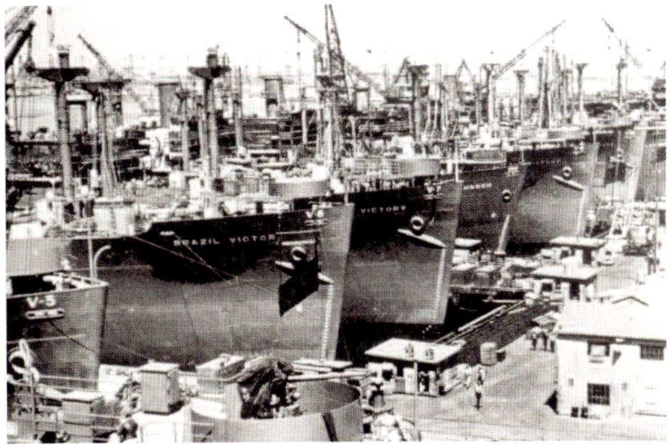

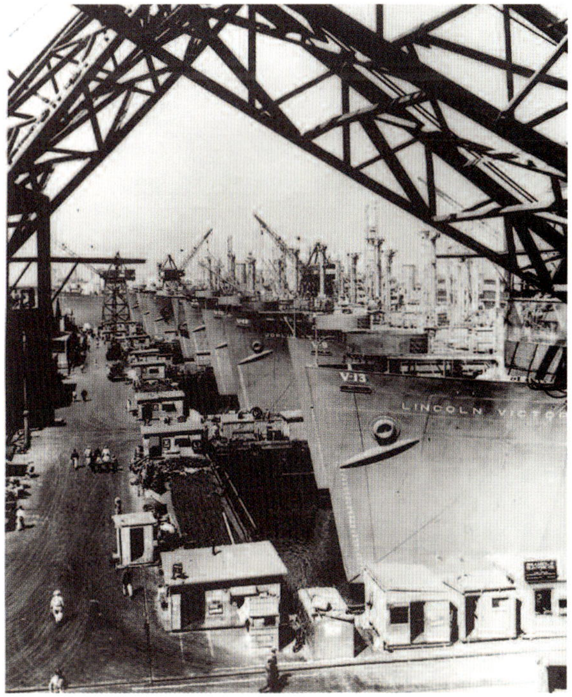

LEFT *Victory ships line up at the Wilmington Shipyards In April 1942. Among the ships pictured are* Philippines Victory *(V-5),* Brazil Victory *(V-8) and* Mexico Victory *(V-7).*

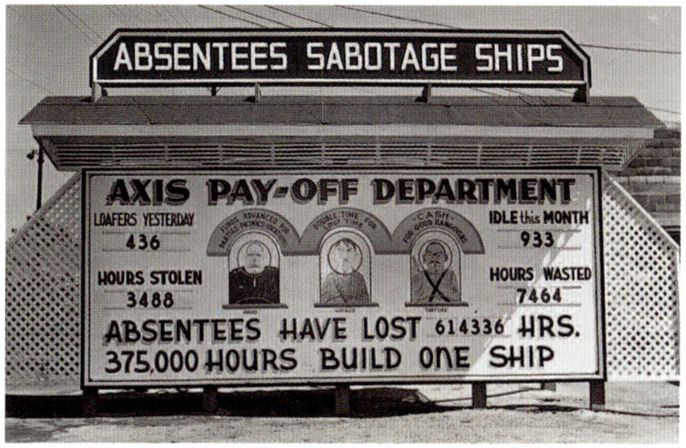

ABOVE *Regularly updated absentee posters were a feature of factories during the World War II years, usually featuring Adolph Hitler, General Tojo and Benito Mussolini. The yards at Wilmington were no different.*

OPPOSITE PAGE *The S.S.* Jeremiah O'Brien *is the only surviving Liberty Ship. Although typical of the kind of ship turned out by CalShip she was actually built in Maine and is currently berthed as a museum in San Francisco. The* Jeremiah O'Brien *made eleven English Channel crossings carrying men and supplies for the D-Day invasion in 1944. In 1994 she returned to Normandy to celebrate D-Day's fiftieth anniversary.*

La Grande Depot DEMOLISHED 1946

The Atchison, Topeka and Santa Fe Railway Company once operated La Grande Depot on Santa Fe Avenue near the west bank of the Los Angeles River between today's Second and Third streets. The late Victorian-era structure was an architectural delight, fashioned from red sandstone and brick. Turquoise domes, turrets and chimneys and squat arches set the building apart from any other train station in Los Angeles.

Fred Thomas Perris, chief civil engineer of the Atchison, Topeka, and Santa Fe Railroad designed the ornate station with Moorish influences.

The depot cost the Atchison, Topeka and Santa Fe $50,000. The design dispensed with gas lighting and included the use of electricity throughout the station. The project called for pressed brick with Flagstaff sandstone trimming. Oregon pine and redwood set off the interior of the 320-foot-long depot.

The first shovelful of earth for the new station was turned on December 21, 1892. The first trains rolled into the station the following July 29. The same year that the station opened the Atchison, Topeka, and Santa Fe Railroad Company changed "Railroad" to "Railway" in its name and became the Atchison, Topeka, and Santa Fe Railway Company.

In 1914, the railroad renovated the station's interior, enlarging the space for both the ticket offices and the newsstand and giving a part of the men's waiting room over to the women.

In 1932, comedian and actor Harold Lloyd immortalized La Grande Depot in his talking motion picture *Movie Crazy*. Lloyd plays a bumpkin who arrives in Los Angeles at La Grande where he is met by filmmakers who offer him work.

On March 10, 1933, the Long Beach Earthquake, which registered a strong 6.2 on the Richter Scale, put the building temporarily out of commission as a passenger terminal. The damage to La Grande's signature Moorish dome was severe enough to force the railroad to remove it.

Plans were already in the works for a new downtown station. As its name implies The Union Passenger Terminal (Union Station for short) was a joint venture built to accommodate all three railroads that served Los Angeles—the Atchison, Topeka and Santa Fe, the Southern Pacific, and the Los Angeles Terminal Railway. Voters approved the new station in 1926, but it took almost a decade to agree on the 48-acre site and raze part of Chinatown to make room for the joint venture.

La Grande Depot closed on May 7, 1939, the day Union Station, opened. Two years later the railroad re-opened the station to allow Warner Brothers to film *King's Row* there. The onslaught of World War II put an end to demolition plans. In 1943 the federal government used the depot as a staging area to transport Japanese Americans to the Santa Anita Racetrack where they were interned.

On a happier note, Metro Goldwyn Mayer featured La Grande in the Judy Garland hit movie *The Harvey Girls*. Garland's rendition of the hit song "On the Atchison, Topeka and Santa Fe" won an Oscar in 1946, the same year the station met the wrecking ball.

BELOW FAR LEFT *The La Grande station had been welcoming passengers on the Atchison, Topeka & Santa Fe Railroad for 17 years when this photograph was taken in 1910.*

BELOW LEFT *A colorized postcard of La Grande shows the rich red tone of its red brick and sandstone construction. The Moorish dome was turquoise.*

BELOW *In 1927, car dealer William M. Murphy used the Santa Fe station as a backdrop to publicize just how fast the Hudson-Essex 6 could get its owners to Death Valley. That team of burros and their wagon would have taken 16 days, but the Hudson-Essex 6 could make the journey in just six hours and 19 minutes. Today, drivers can make that same trip in about an hour and 25 minutes.*

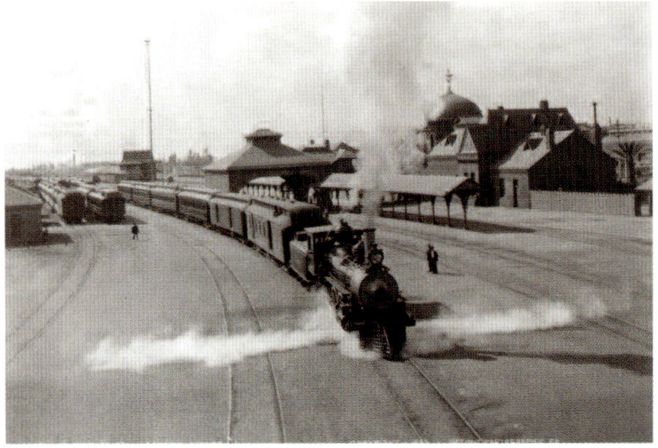

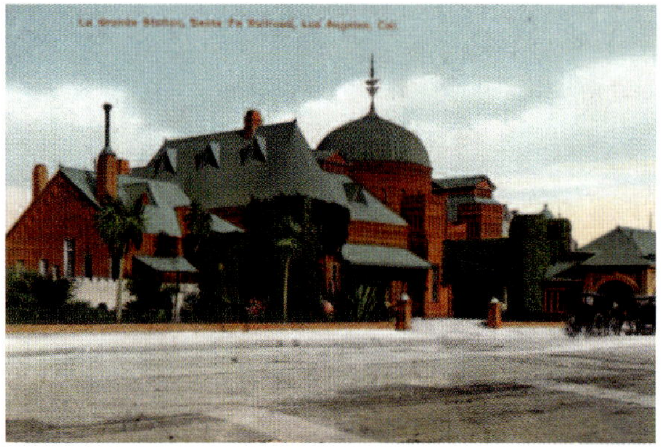

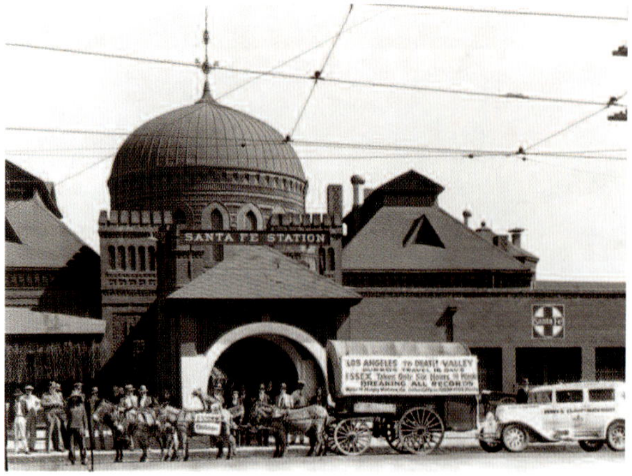

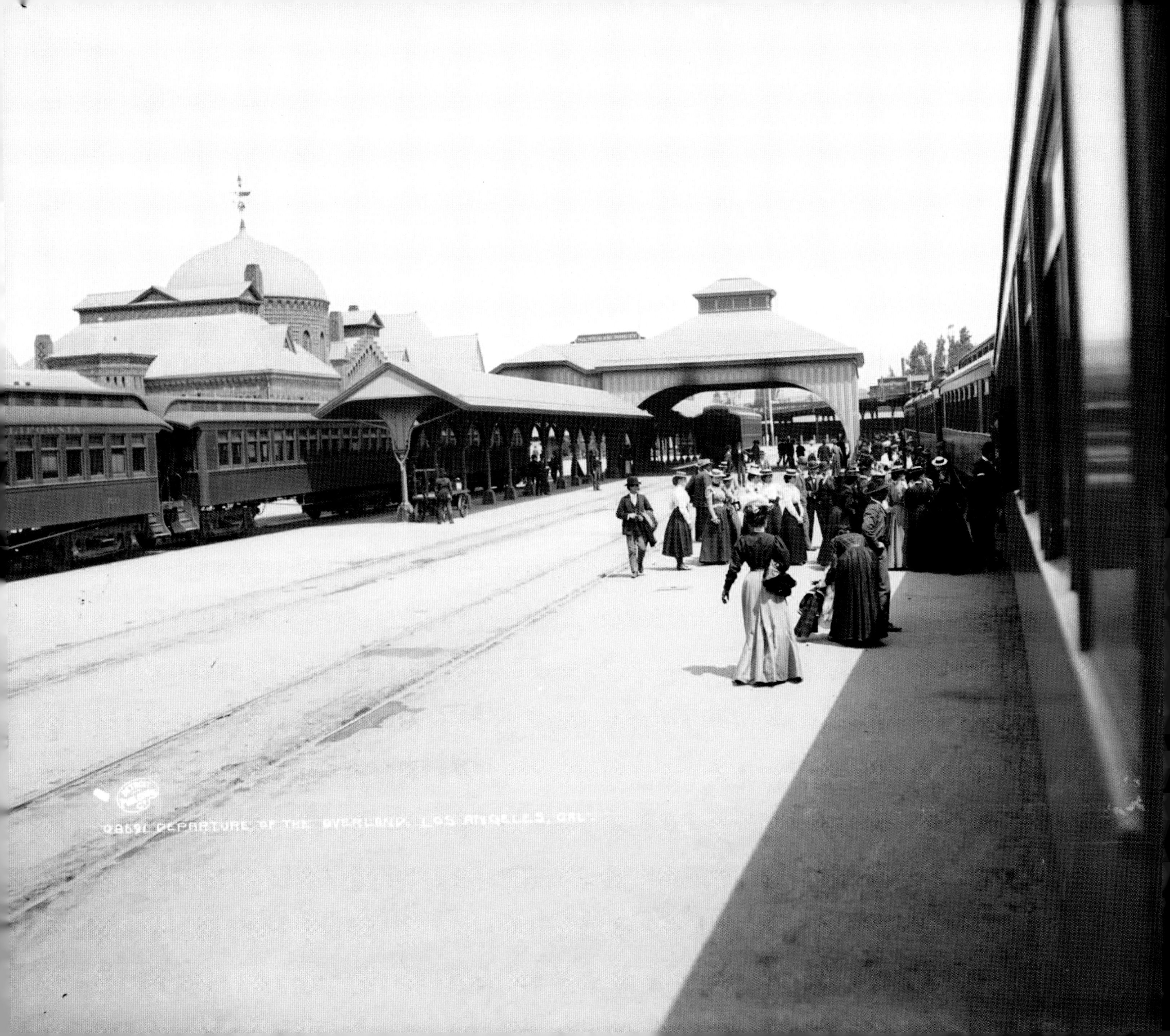
03691 DEPARTURE OF THE OVERLAND, LOS ANGELES, CAL.

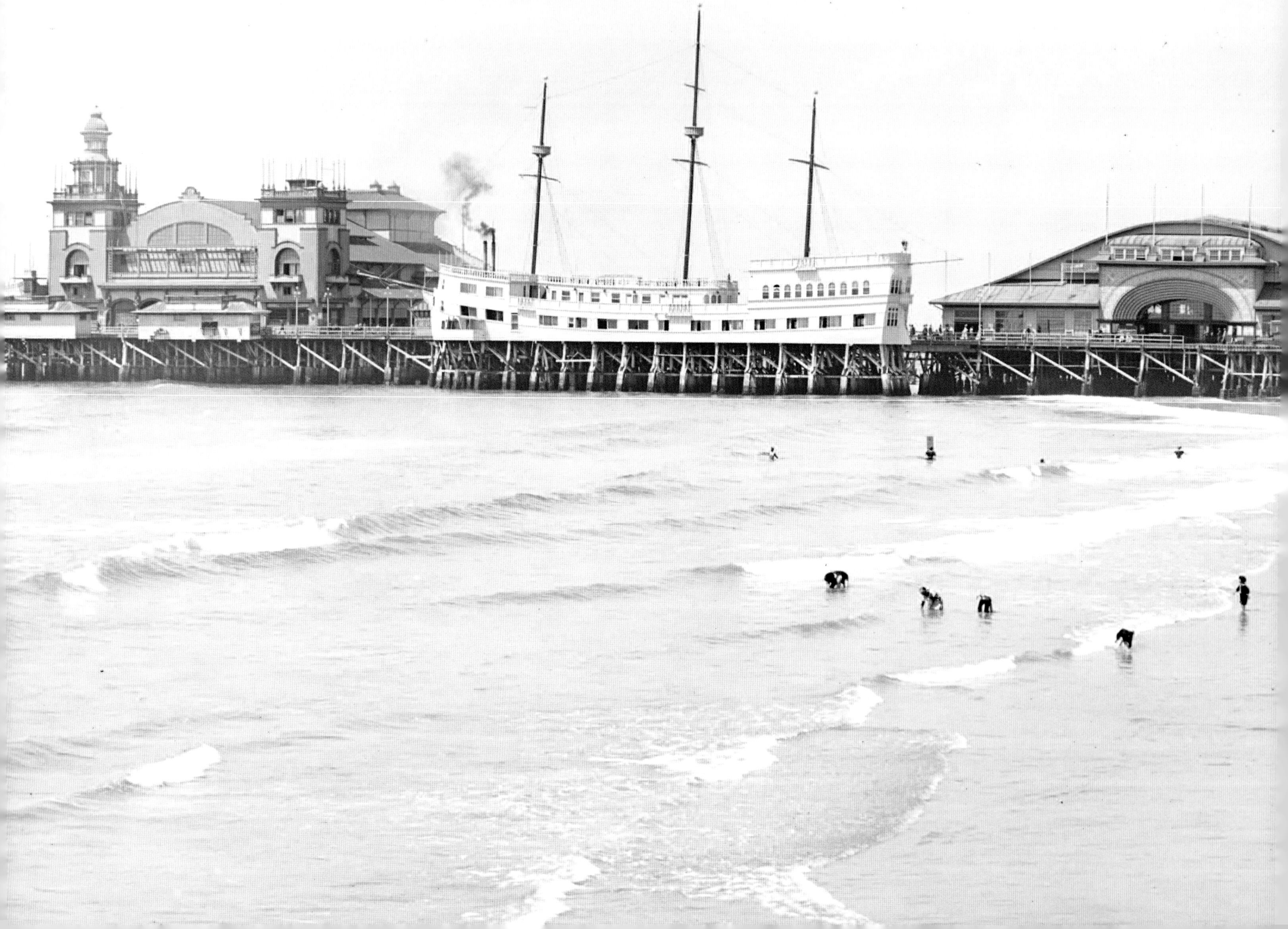

Venice Pier BURNED FOR THE FINAL TIME 1947

Abbot Kinney opened the Venice Pier on July 4, 1905. The pier that beachgoers visited that Fourth of July, however, was not the first to grace the site, but the second.

The first pier was never used because winter storms had wrecked it. Kinney set his crews to work around the clock rebuilding the pier so it could open in time. He added an additional 100 feet to the new design, so instead of the original 1,100-foot-long pier, the rebuilt pier stretched 1,200 feet into the Pacific. Kinney built a breakwater to protect the new pier from any further disaster.

When it opened, the new pier boasted an auditorium, a dance pavilion, bowling alley, a fun house, a roller-skating rink, as well as an aquarium. By the time New Year's Day 1906 arrived, the Kinney Company had added an amusement park on the edge of the nearby Grand Lagoon complete with a miniature steam train that circled the attractions.

Just after midnight on October 26, 1908, fire broke out in the Venice Theater on the pier but firefighters were able to douse the blaze in time to save the dance hall next door. Abbott Kinney died on November 8, 1920. The man who made his fortune in the tobacco industry had succumbed to lung cancer. His son Thornton took over the business.

Just six weeks after Kinney's death a fire destroyed his beloved pier. The blaze started the evening of December 20, 1920, in the dance hall. Flames quickly spread to the theater auditorium. Forced to use extreme measures firefighters used dynamite in a vain attempt to stop the fire spreading beyond the pier's outer boundary. However a change in the wind direction help them get the blaze under control. A lack of insurance meant the attractions were slow to be rebuilt.

Venice and its pier sorely felt the effects of the Great Depression; business was so bad during the summer of 1932 that the Kinney Company defaulted on its bond interest payments. The company went into temporary receivership.

The Kinney Company's tidelands lease expired on January 13, 1946. To the company's great surprise the Los Angeles Parks and Recreation Department would not renew the lease. With annual revenues of $100,000 the company was now making money. In addition, the company had recently built a new pier entrance and repaired the planking on the pier's deck. But the city had its eye on widening the beach and Kinney's pier was simply in the way.

The Venice Amusement Pier closed on midnight Saturday, April 20, 1947. The city gave the Kinney Corporation until May 15 to clear out. All the rides except for the Bamboo Slide and the intricate roller coaster were either sold or scrapped. On May 23, 1947, vandals set fire to the slide. The fire spread to the roller coaster and the "Coney Island of the Pacific" was lost forever.

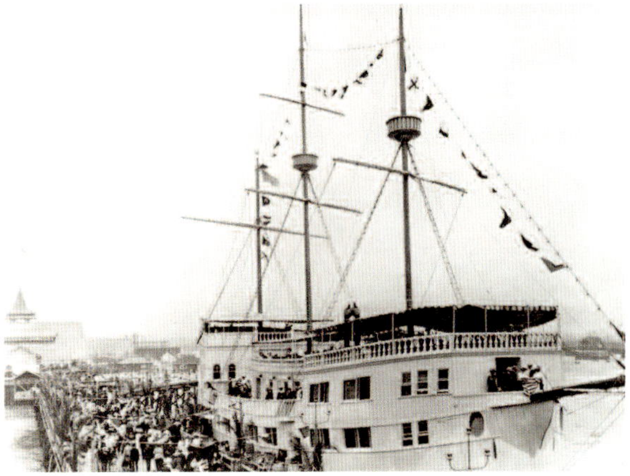

LEFT *Kinney modeled his hotel-restaurant after Spanish explorer Juan Cabrillo's ship and named it fittingly "The Cabrillo." The expensive restaurant's employees were decked out in uniforms that resembled those Kinney imagined 16th-century naval officers would wear.*

BELOW *This panorama of Ocean Park Beach features the city's 1905 Moorish-style baths. The three-story-tall structure featured five domes. Its promoters claimed it had the largest swimming pool in the country. The Venice Pier is at right.*

OPPOSITE PAGE *A view of Abbot Kinney's Pier shows, from left to right, the auditorium, which seated 300 people, the ship café and the dance hall, whose spacious floor could accommodate 800 couples.*

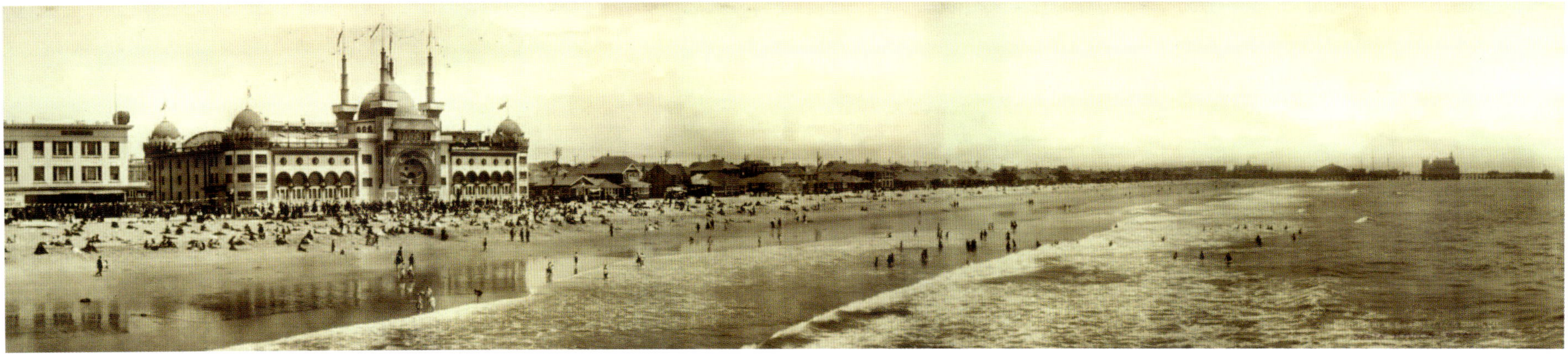

Schaber's Cafeteria ORIGINAL LOCATION SOLD 1947

After the rioting that broke out in 1992 and spread across Los Angeles, the built environment changed in surprising ways. Structures that had stood for decades suddenly faced vandalism and fire. The original Schaber's Cafeteria, a Spanish Colonial-style building on South Broadway between Sixth and Seventh streets, had all but its facade and mezzanine destroyed.

The cafeteria, named for German immigrant Alfred T. Schaber, actually didn't last long in the building on South Broadway. Schaber got his start as a bus boy in the restaurant business from the four Boos brothers (his cousins) who opened one of the first Los Angeles cafeterias on the south side of Second Street, between Spring Street and Broadway, in 1906. Cafeterias offered "food you could see" that patrons carried to their tables on trays.

Schaber spent some $400,000 to open his own cafeteria in 1928 in a building that could serve 10,000 people per day according to the *Los Angeles Times.* Architect Charles F. Plummer designed the two-story cafeteria on the former site of the Platt Music Company Building. The popular eatery featured Spanish décor, helped along by famed Los Angeles muralist Einar Peterson's image depicting three Spanish women and a ten-piece orchestra performing "Spanish selections." Advertising touted the remarkable Sturtevant "air washer" that purified the air inside. During the Depression, advertising promised "a distinct lack of Depression" inside the cafeteria.

Alfred and his cousin Erhard grew their chain with apparent success through the 1950s and 1960s, but had already sold the original location in 1947, for $517,000 to Clarence M. Hayman's Forum Cafeterias of America. The original Schaber's was renamed Forum Cafeteria.

Other locations continued to be called Schaber's, with Erhard in charge until he sold the business in 1976 to Michael Weinreich. Weinreich continued operation at the North Hollywood Schaber's until well into the 1990s when its mostly aging clientele could sense their favorite eatery's days were numbered—it closed in 1998. In 1973, the Broadway location changed hands and names, becoming the Broadway Cafeteria into the 1980s. When shoppers started to prefer suburban shopping malls and fast food was replacing the linen tablecloth, the Broadway Cafeteria began to falter. By the mid-1980s the place had been converted to a Carl's Jr. burger joint.

The building was given a $2.5 million rehabilitation by new owner Walter Thomson in 1994 as part of the city's ten-year plan of "Bringing Back Broadway" a scheme which encouraged restoration of classic and historic downtown buildings.

Since 2013 the tradition of fine dining has returned to the site of the original Schaber's Cafeteria with a French bistro, Les Noces de Figaro, which operates with a 1930s-era restoration of the cafeteria. Restorers brought back as many historic details as possible in the 9,000-square-foot space that now houses the 24-hour restaurant and its retail bakery outfit.

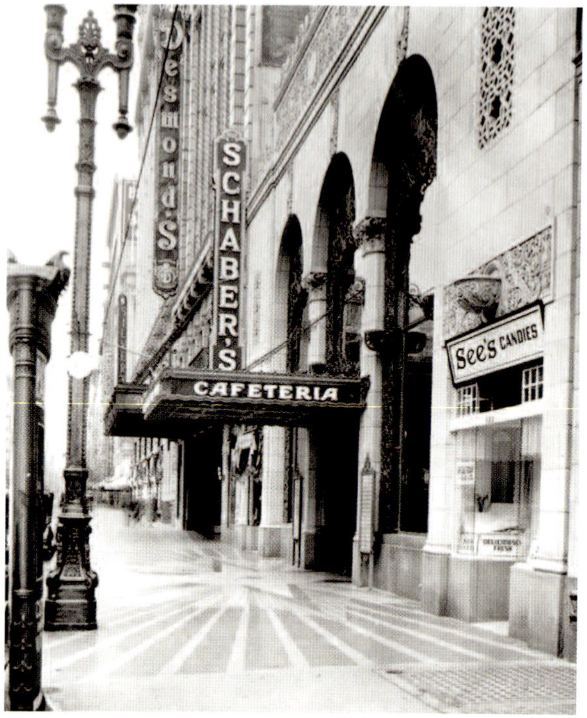

ABOVE *Schaber's next-door neighbor, Desmond's, was a men's clothing store founded by Daniel Desmond who came to Los Angeles in 1869 to start a hat business. On the other side of Schaber's sat one of the earliest shops in See's Candies empire. Founded in 1921 on Western Avenue in Los Angeles, the company expanded to 30 shops in the city during the Depression era.*

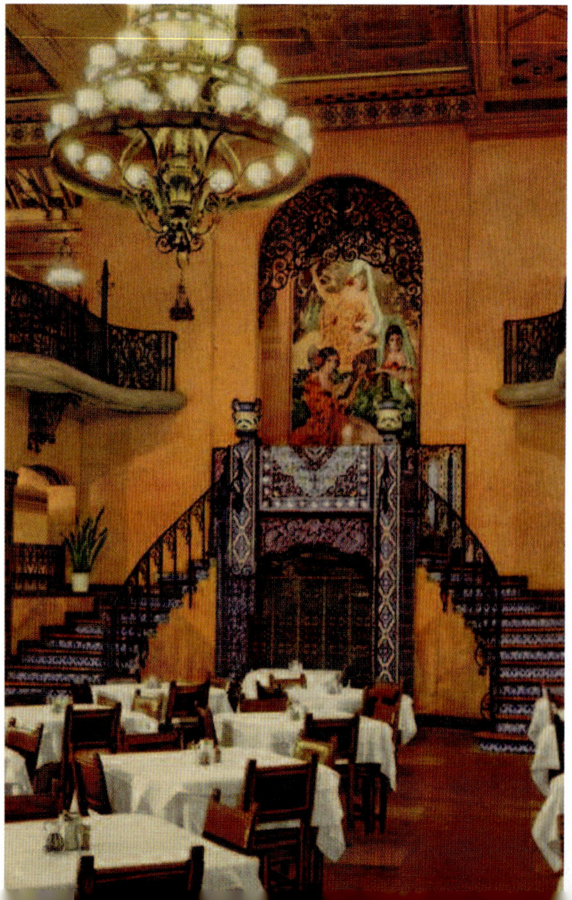

LEFT *Einar Peterson's vivid mural at the head of the tiled staircase.*

OPPOSITE PAGE *Schaber's Cafeteria around 1940.*
BELOW *The grand Spanish-Colonial facade circa 1930.*

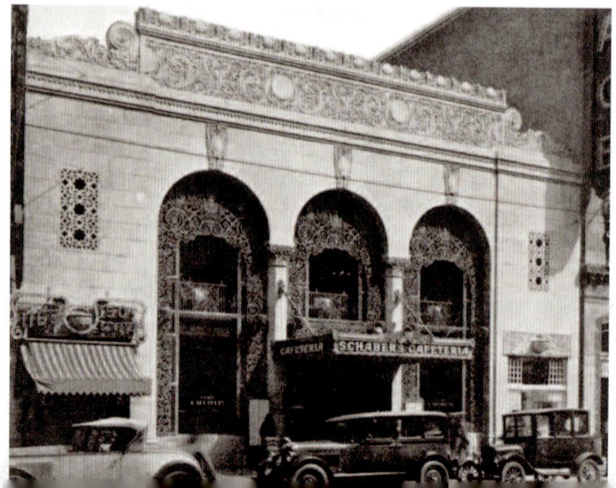

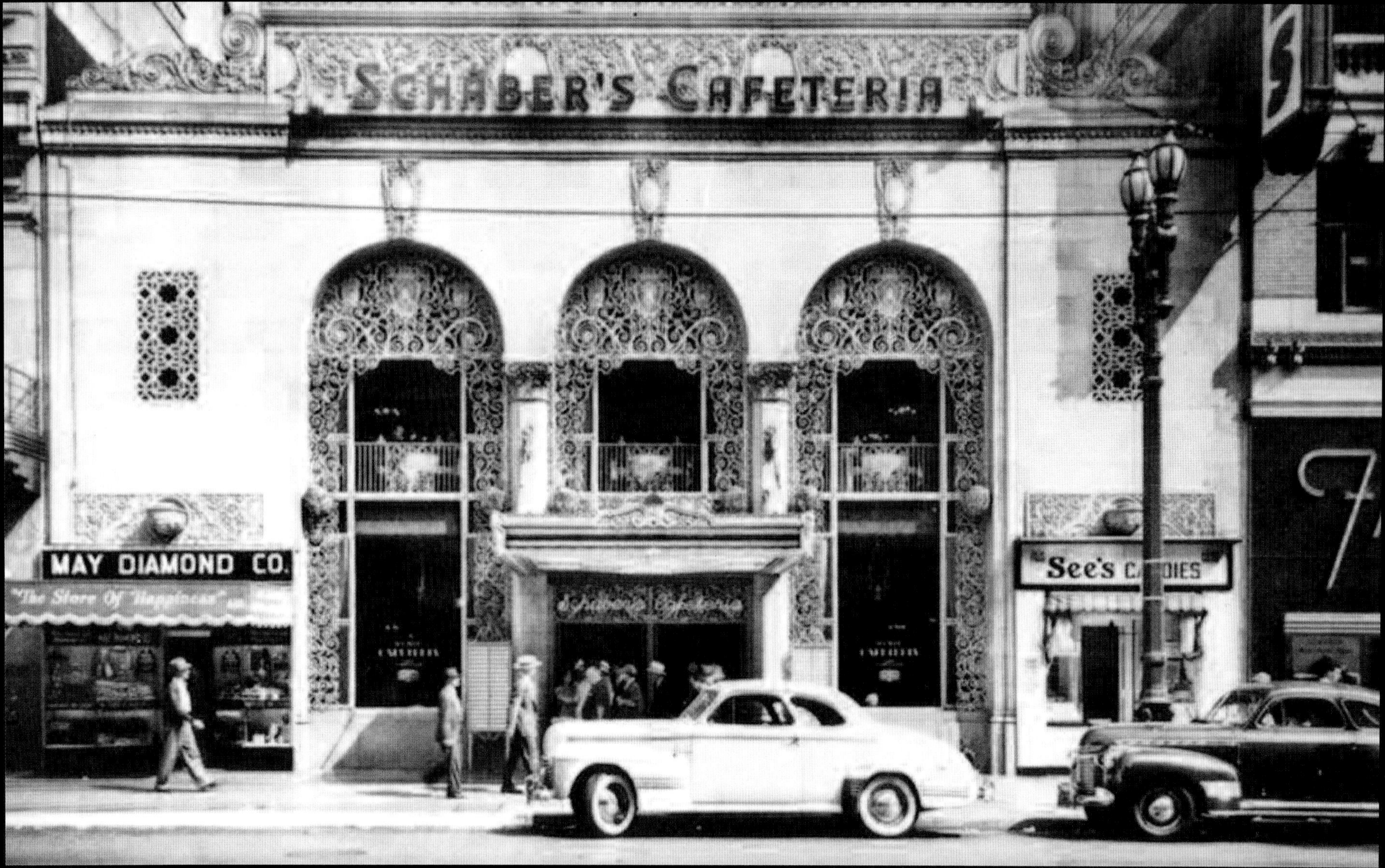
SCHABER'S CAFETERIA
MAY DIAMOND CO.
"The Store Of Happiness"
See's CANDIES

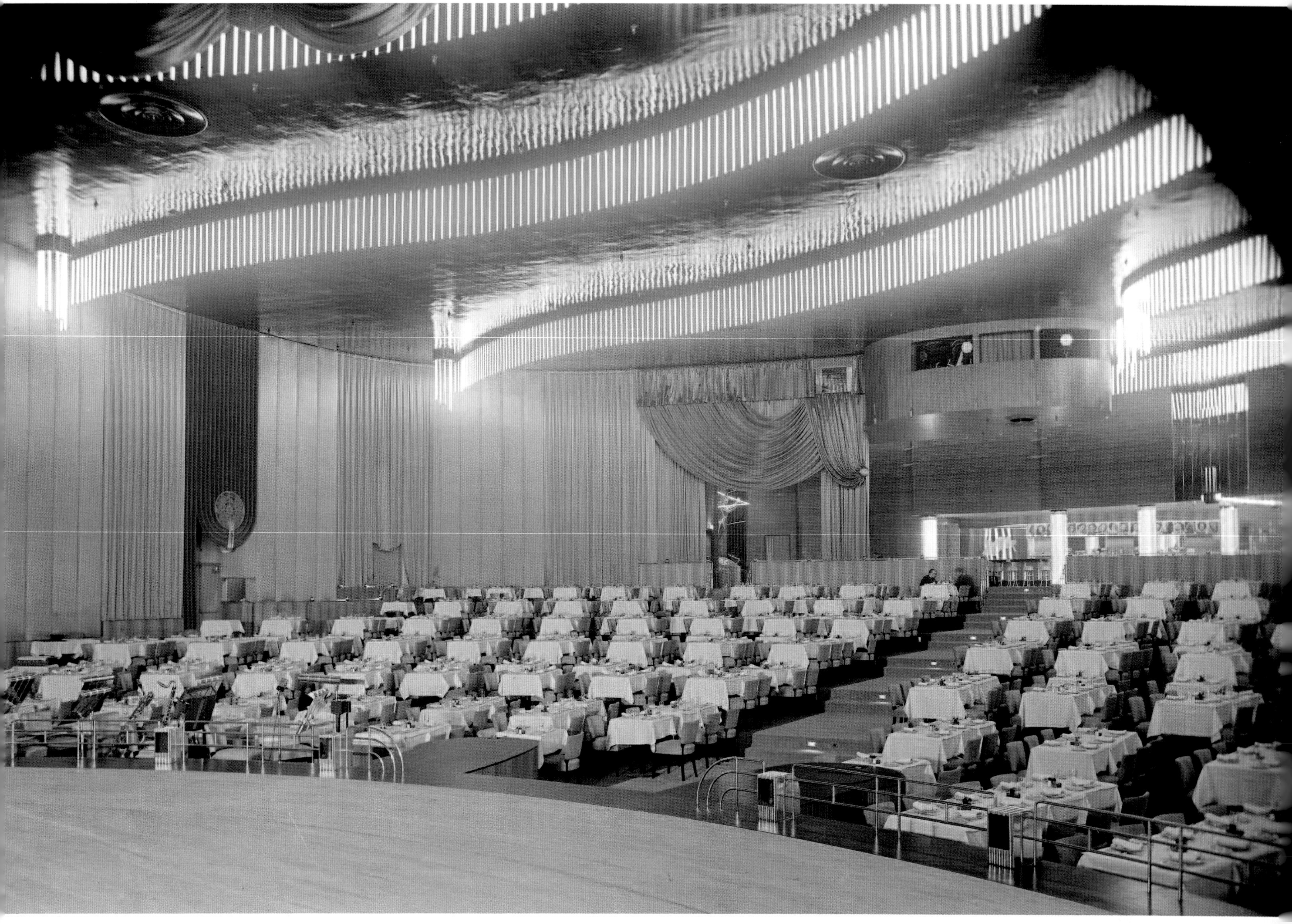

Earl Carroll Theater RENAMED IN 1948

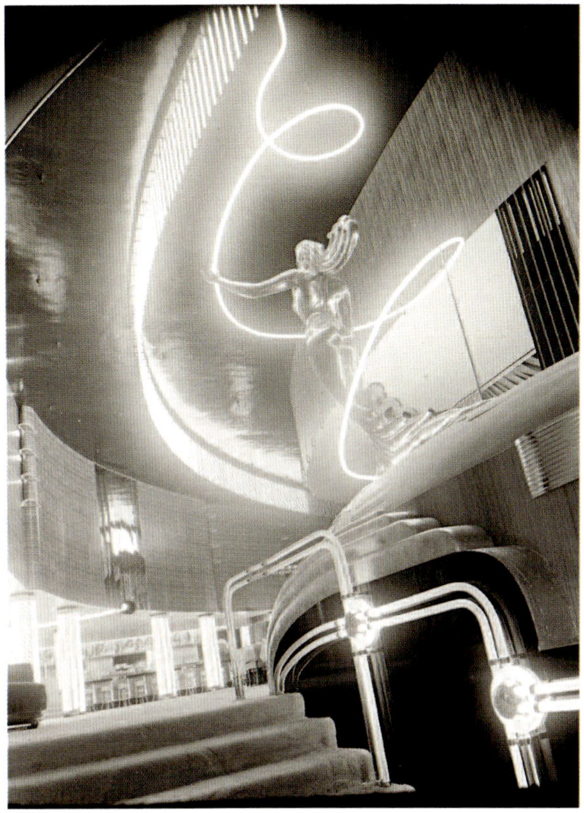

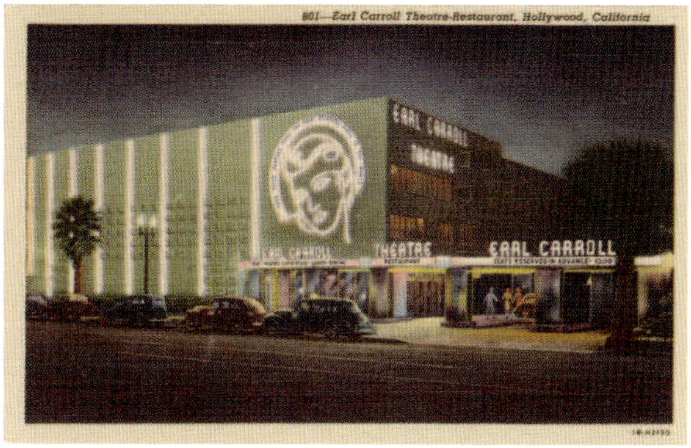

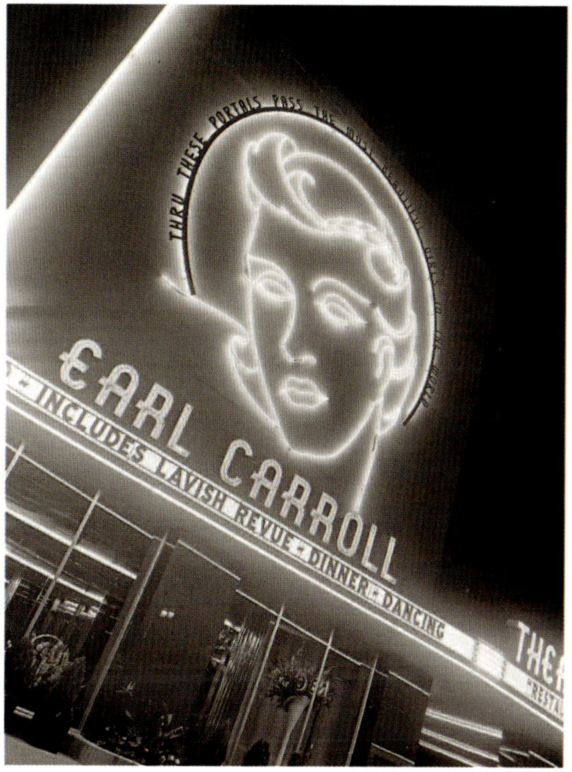

On December 26, 1938, Earl Carroll opened a theater at 6230 Sunset Boulevard that boasted the world's largest double-revolving stage. The opening night gala entertained the likes of Clark Gable, Carole Lombard, Marlene Dietrich, Tyrone Power, Betty Grable, Jack Benny, Claudette Colbert, Robert Taylor and Bob Hope.

Daryl Zanuck, Errol Flynn, Jack Warner, W. C. Fields, David O. Selznick and Louis B. Mayer also enjoyed the show. The theater could seat one thousand guests for dinner. Architect Gordon B. Kaufman designed the playhouse, which bore Carroll's name and featured a 20-foot-high neon likeness of Carrol's girlfriend, Beryl Wallace, on the wall along Sunset Boulevard.

This was not Carroll's first large theater. He had already built one in New York that was so successful that he enlarged it in 1931. Carroll had these words emblazoned by the neon depiction of his wife's profile: "Thru These Portals Pass the Most Beautiful Girls in the World." He billed himself as the "Troubadour of the Nude," and onstage his girls performed as close as legally possible as "the barest in the world."

He produced and directed Broadway musicals, which included 11 editions of *Earl Carroll's Vanities*, *Earl Carroll's Sketch Book*, and *Murder at the Vanities*. The latter was made into a film starring Jack Oakie. Carrol's Vanities all featured scantily clad girls combined with low humor.

Carroll wrote many scores for Broadway shows. His show credits include *So Long Letty, Canary Cottage* and *The Love Mill.* He also wrote popular songs of the day.

But on June 17, 1948, his world came crashing down. Earl Carroll, along with Beryl Wallace and 42 others, died in a plane crash over Mount Carmel in Pennsylvania. They were on their way to New York. They rest together at Forest Lawn Memorial Park Cemetery in Glendale in the Gardens of Memory, a private section with Mary Pickford and Humphrey Bogart as their neighbors.

Ownership of the theater changed; the Earl Carroll name was removed from the marquee along with the neon image of Beryl Wallace. The building operated as the Moulin Rouge in the 1950s. From 1965 until early 1968 it was the Hullabaloo Theatre. In 1968 it became the Kaleidoscope. In late 1968 it was renamed the Aquarius for a run of the hippy musical *Hair.* The Aquarius got a psychedelic makeover which included a massive, gaudy mural painted all round the building. Earl Carroll would not have recognized the place, although he would have recognized the commercial sense in *Hair*'s notorious nude scene.

In 1977 it was known as the Longhorn Theatre. It was also called the Chevy Chase Theatre. Since 1997 Earl Carroll's pride and joy has housed West Coast productions for the Nickelodeon cable channel. Called Nickelodeon on Sunset, the lobby boasts a seven-foot-tall poster of Beryl Wallace. Nickelodeon placed the poster there in December 2013 to help celebrate Earl Carroll Theater's 75th anniversary.

TOP LEFT *When it opened in 1938, the theater was the height of art deco expression with elegant curves and bright neon.*

TOP CENTER *A postcard view from the 1940s.*

TOP *The original facade featuring Beryl Wallace's image.*

OPPOSITE PAGE *Carroll's new theater re-set the standard for many post-war Las Vegas show rooms that combined glamorous stage shows with dining.*

Los Angeles High School SECOND SCHOOL RAZED 1948

"Always a hill, always a tower, always a timepiece," runs a Los Angeles High School motto, echoing a tradition that began with the appearance of the city's first high school on Poundcake Hill. Dignitaries laid the cornerstone for the school on July 19, 1872. The building, a wooden affair that cost the school district $20,000 to build, opened in 1873 with Dr. William T. Lucky serving as principal. The building sat above and faced Fort Street, which later became part of Broadway. Students had to climb a steep wooden staircase to reach their classrooms. Seven students were members of the school's first graduation class in 1875.

The two-story wooden structure was so big and grand it was regarded as the finest school south of San Francisco at the time, with classic lines and a tower with a clock in it. Teachers appreciated the wide corridors, walnut banisters, and well-lit classrooms.

By 1884 the city had abandoned the old Protestant cemetery on Fort Moore Hill. Vandals had been desecrating the place for years. The Board of Education purchased part of the site in 1884 with a view to building a school there at some time in the future. Three years after the school board purchased the Fort Moore Hill property, the school district learned its Poundcake Hill School had to go: the county wanted the space to build a courthouse.

Instead of selling up and moving on, the school district decided to move Los Angeles High School—lock, stock and barrel—to Sand Street just west of North Hill Street and below the south side of Fort Moore Hill.

They hired a certain Mr. Hickam, who said that his workers could do the job with scaffolding, rollers and horses. He got the contract and his men got to work. They rolled the school off the hilltop and on to Temple Street. They got the building halfway up Temple Street when Hickam ran out of money. He dismissed his workers, took the horses back to the stables and left the schoolhouse right in the middle of the street.

The original schoolhouse finally made it to Sand Street. The venerable edifice that once graced Poundcake Hill became a school for the lower grades. It survived the 1933 Long Beach Earthquake, which did a lot of damage to the newer buildings in downtown. By April 1936, nearly 300 children attended school there. The building fell victim to highway construction the following year.

The high school transferred to a new building atop Fort Moore Hill. In 1890, construction began on a new red brick schoolhouse facing North Hill Street on Fort Moore Hill between Sand Street and Bellevue Avenue (today's Cesar Chavez Avenue). The school district hired architect Jasper Newton Preston to design the school. Preston also designed the Los Angeles County Courthouse as well as the addition to the State Normal School. The school's entrance tower accented Preston's Romanesque Revival building, echoing his courthouse and Normal School designs.

The school district moved its students to a new school in 1917 on Olympic Boulevard. The second high school on Fort Moore Hill became a school for truants. That building was razed in 1948. Fort Moore Hill itself was leveled the following year to make way for the Hollywood Freeway. The Fort Moore Pioneer Memorial now stands on all that remains of the site of the cemetery and high school.

BOTTOM LEFT *When Los Angeles County authorities decided to build a courthouse on Poundcake Hill, they told the school district that it had to move the high school. Mr. Hickam signed on for the job. However, he walked away and left the building in the middle of Temple Street when he ran out of money. People were forced to cope with having the old high school in the middle of the road. Eventually the building was moved from Temple Street to Sand Street, where it stayed until 1937.*

BOTTOM CENTRE *This view of Fort Moore Hill shows Los Angeles' first two high schools. The white building on the left housed the city's first high school classes on Poundcake Hill. This building was moved here and finally razed in 1938. The large brick building on the right-hand side of the hill was home to Los Angeles' second high school until 1917. This building met the wrecking ball in 1948. Even Fort Moore Hill is gone, leveled in 1949.*

BELOW *The first Los Angeles High School surveys a relatively undeveloped neighborhood.*

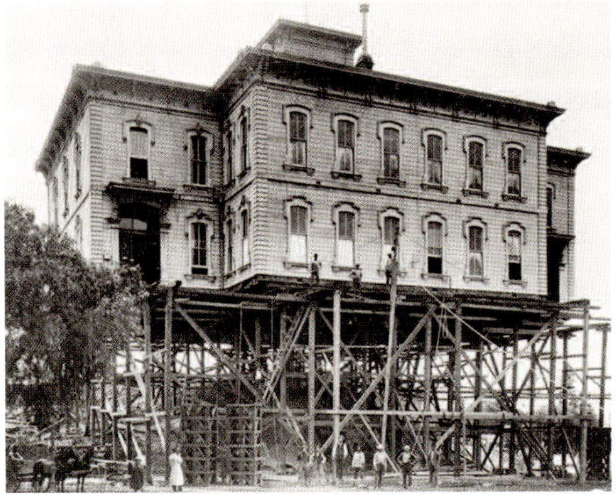

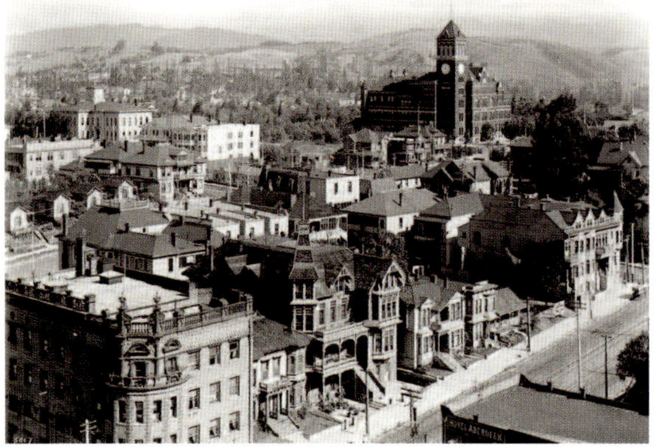

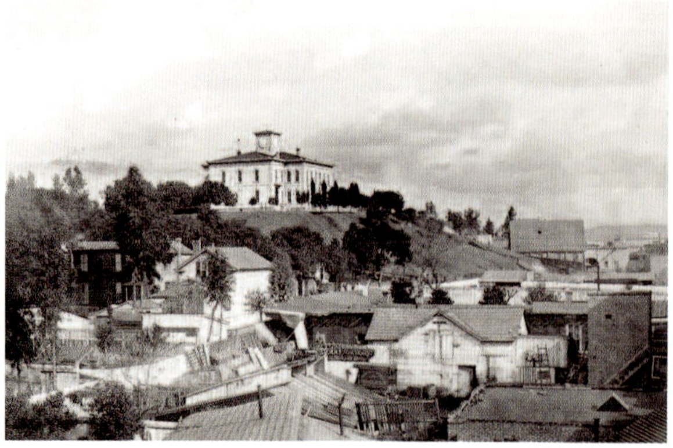

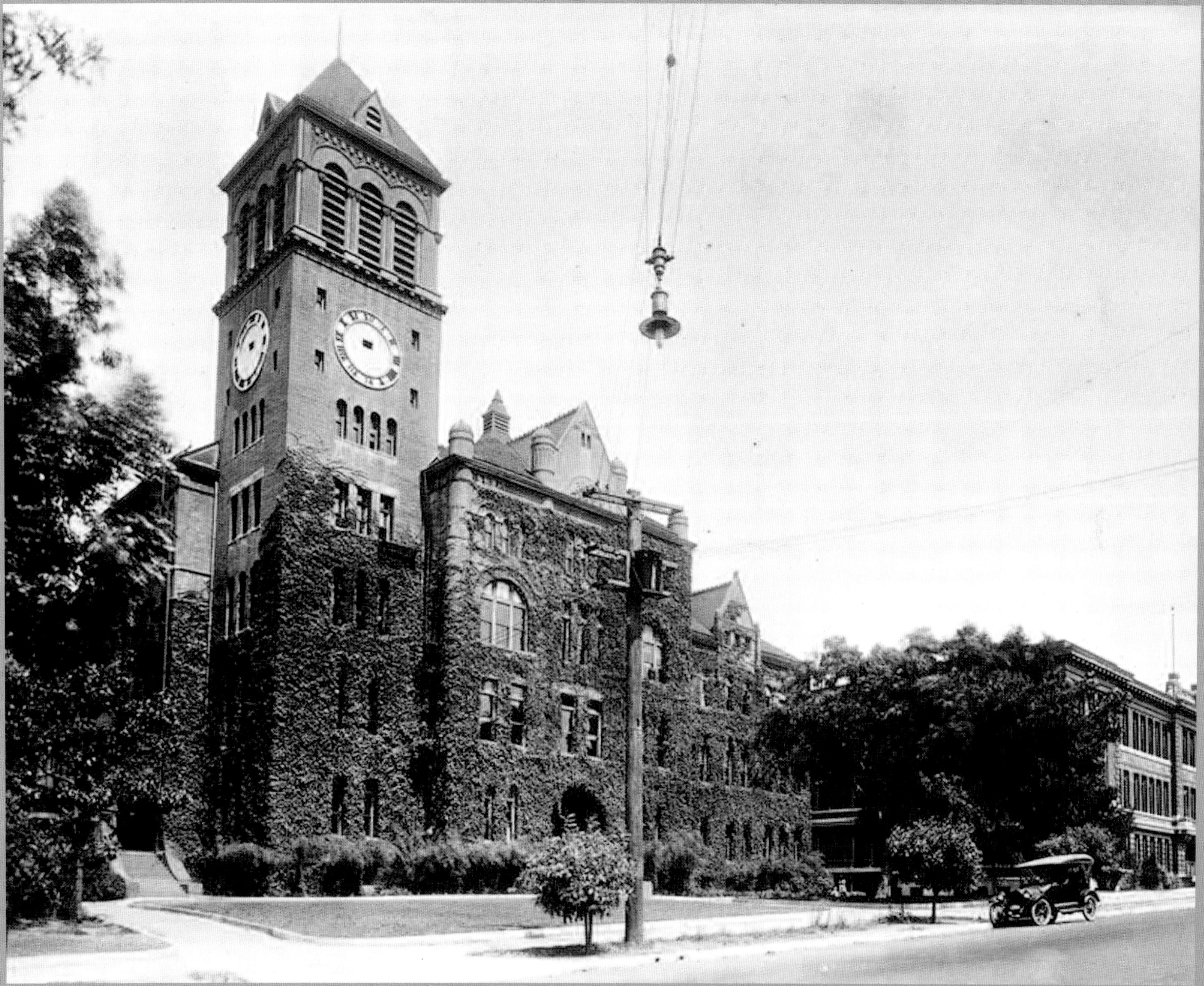

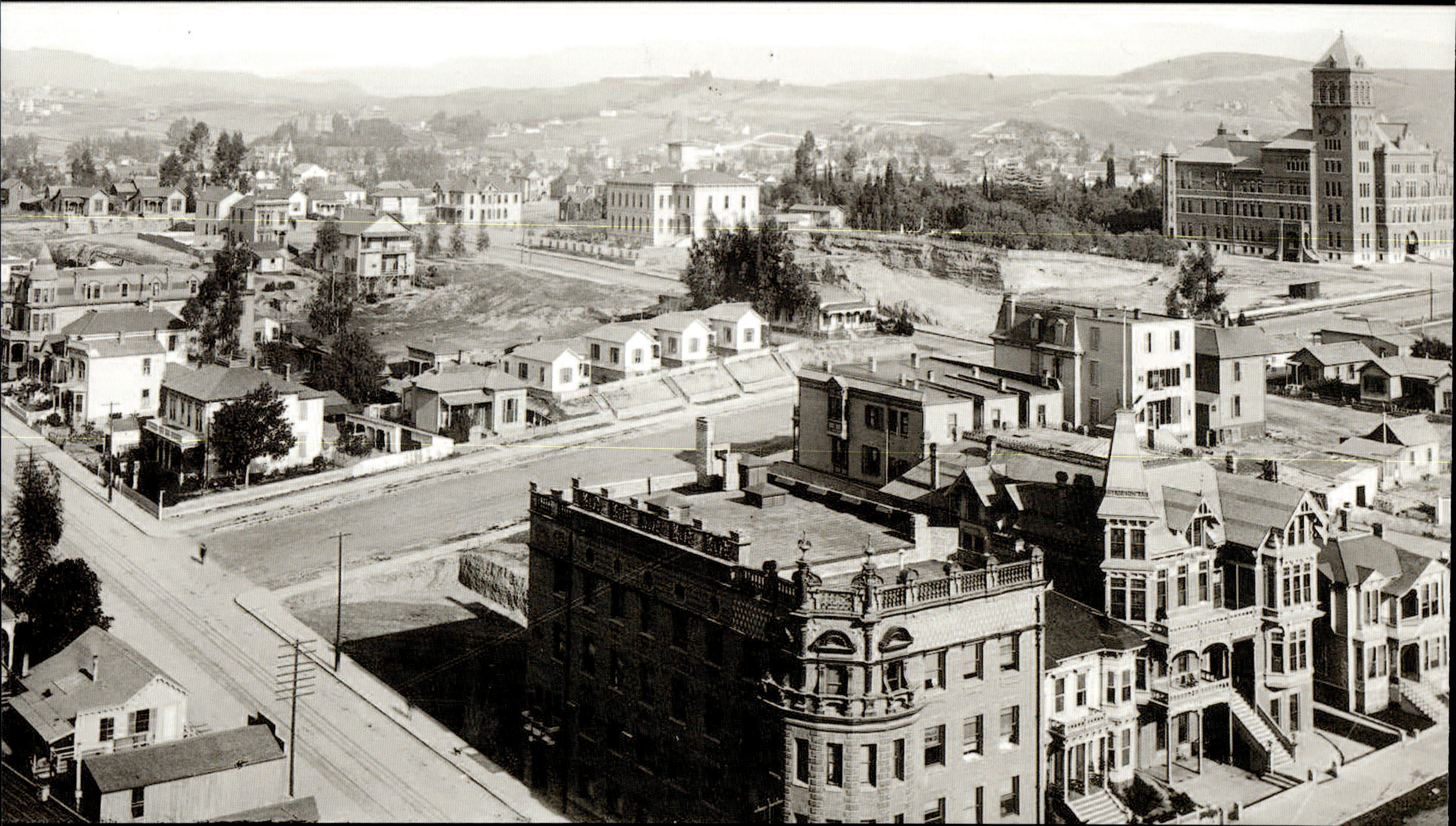

Fort Moore Hill FLATTENED 1949

The Spanish settlers did not have a name for the hill that overlooked the plaza in the heart of the pueblo of Los Angeles, but its commanding view of the city made it a strategic location. The hill remained barren until September 22, 1846, when United States Marine Corps Captain Archibald H. Gillespie and the 50 men under his command erected a temporary barricade of earth-filled sacks and mounted some cannon there.

Soldiers under Navy Commodore Robert F. Stockton's command had taken the pueblo from the Mexican government five weeks earlier. Stockton left Gillespie in command with a small contingent of soldiers to control the Californios. Twenty days after Stockton left they revolted.

"On the 22nd of September, at three o'clock in the morning, a party of 65 Californians and Sonorenos made an attack upon my small command quartered in the government house," Gillespie later told the *Sacramento Statesman* newspaper. "We were not wholly surprised, and with 21 rifles we beat them back without loss to ourselves, killing and wounding three of their number."

Gillespie and his men took refuge on what came to be known as Fort Hill. The temporary barricades he erected were not enough. Mexican General Jose Maria Flores issued an ultimatum: surrender within 24 hours or suffer the consequences. The Americans surrendered and abandoned Fort Hill and Los Angeles.

Stockton returned in force and retook Los Angeles on January 10, 1847. This time the Americans built in earnest atop Fort Hill. The Mormon Battalion arrived in March and the following month they were hard at work. They completed their task just in time for the Fourth of July celebrations. They named the place Fort Moore, for Benjamin Moore, who had been killed fighting the Mexicans on December 6, 1846, in San Diego. The hill took on the fort's name. Instead of "Fort Hill" locals now called it "Fort Moore Hill."

Fort Moore was decommissioned in 1853 and the hill served the pueblo as a cemetery until 1882. Jacob Phillippi arrived that year and transformed the place into a beer garden. The raucous beer drinkers at this establishment did little to endear themselves to the Angelenos living below. Phillippi sold his establishment to a wealthy widow.

Mary Hollister Banning converted the former military bastion and drinking hole into what historian Nathan Masters calls "one of the city's first upscale neighborhoods." Masters writes that "many of Los Angeles' so-called first families followed Banning up the steep slope, building elaborate mansions."

In 1886 the city's board of education moved the high school from Poundcake Hill to Sand Street on Fort Moore Hill at Sand Street.

By the 1940s, the hill was simply something in the way of progress, hemming in the planners' options. The city had already built a tunnel under the hill, but now it stood in the way of the new 101 Freeway. In 1949, construction crews set to work converting the former viewpoint and stronghold into more workable real estate and by the end of the year, the contours on the map of Los Angeles had been changed.

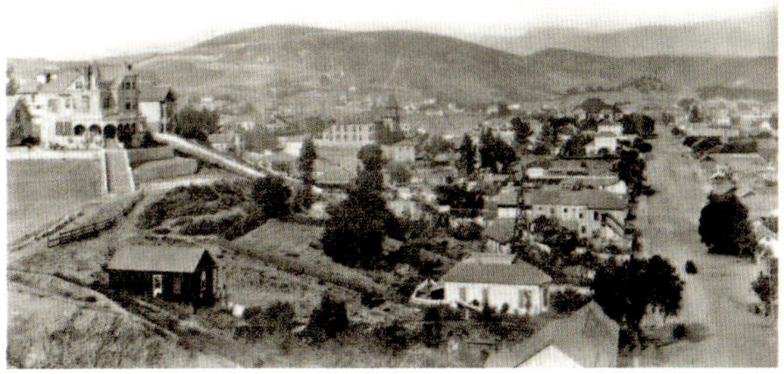

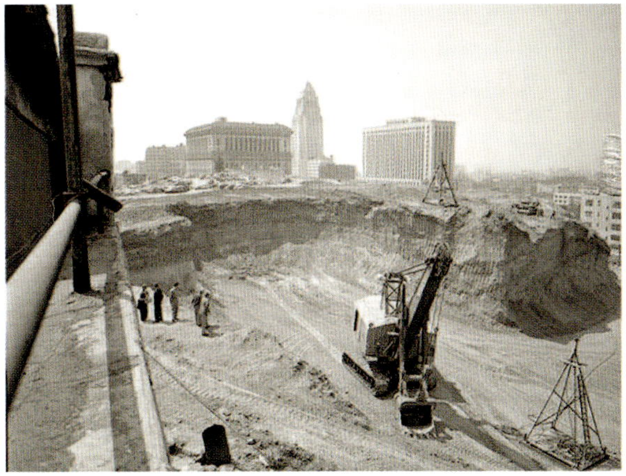

LEFT *The J. W. Robinson mansion on the left dominates this photo taken from Fort Moore Hill about 1895. Robinson, who owned Boston Dry Goods, hired architects Samuel and Joseph Cather Newsom, who also designed the Bradbury mansion. Robinson added a winged gargoyle to watch over the house, which cost him $10,000 to build. A single wagon is the only traffic on Castelar Street, which ran through Sonora Town below Robinson's mansion.*

BELOW LEFT *By the time this photograph was taken in 1949, work was well underway to create space for the 101 Freeway to make its way through what was once Fort Moore Hill.*

OPPOSITE PAGE *In 1893 a photographer aimed his camera from the tower of the Los Angeles County Courthouse at Temple Street and Broadway to get this photograph. Fort Moore Hill has turned into a respectable neighborhood since its days as a fort and a cemetery. The first two Los Angeles high schools are visible: the venerable white building with the flag flying from its clock tower and the larger brick building with its more impressive tower that took its place.*

Lugo Adobe DESTROYED FEBRUARY 1951

Antonio Maria Lugo was a Californio, a descendant of one of the earliest Spanish settlers of Alta California. His father, Francisco, was born in Sinaloa, Mexico, around 1740 and served in the army at Monterey. Francisco was one of the soldiers who escorted Los Angeles' first settlers from Mexico.

Antonio was born in 1775 at *Mission San Antonio de Padua*, about 80 miles south of Monterey. Like his father before him, Antonio served in the army, stationed at the presidio at Santa Barbara. When Antonio retired in 1810 the government rewarded him for his service by giving him Rancho San Antonio, a 29,514-acre spread that encompassed the modern-day Los Angeles County cities of Bell, Bell Gardens, Maywood, Vernon, Huntington Park, Walnut Park, Cudahy, South Gate, Lynwood and Commerce.

Antonio served the pueblo at Los Angeles as *alcalde* (magistrate) from 1816 to 1819. This role put him in charge of the 1818 move from the pueblo's original site to where the plaza stands today.

Sometime around 1838—the exact date is lost to us—he built a two-story adobe across the plaza from the Church of Our Lady of the Queen of the Angels. The home's second story made it unique among the more sprawling one-story homes in early Los Angeles. Antonio lived in the home with his wife, and their eight children.

In 1855, Antonio partitioned the rancho among his five sons. He died five years later, and the children further divided the rancho among themselves. Antonio's son Vicente lived in the adobe with his family until 1865. The home then served that community as a boy's school that later became St. Vincent's College. St. Vincent's was the first college in Southern California and grew to become Loyola Marymount University.

By the 1880s the neighborhood had become part of old Chinatown and the home served the Chinese both as a rooming house and a place of business. In 1890 the adobe was home to Leeching Hung & Co. The building also housed Fook Wo Lung Curio Co. and Ying's Art Shop. It also served the community as a stage coach stop.

Later photographs showed that builders had added a hipped roof and dormers to match the Colonial Revival style. Workers had also encased the rear of the building in brick and added windows to the shops on the ground floor. By 1950 the building was so altered that it scarcely resembled the 1838 Lugo family home.

The Lugo adobe was among 19 buildings demolished in 1951 to make way for the 101 freeway. Bulldozers and cranes arrived on February 7, 1951, and every building within a rectangle bounded by Sunset Boulevard, Alameda Street, Los Angeles Street and Ferguson Alley came down.

Despite last-minute efforts to save the Lugo family's old home, the 113-year-old building came down. A little more than four months later, on June 20, Los Angeles Mayor Fletcher Bowron presented Loyola University president Rev. Charles Casassa with a fragment of the Lugo house, a board that commemorated the school's early ties to the house. That board is all that remains of the Lugo house today.

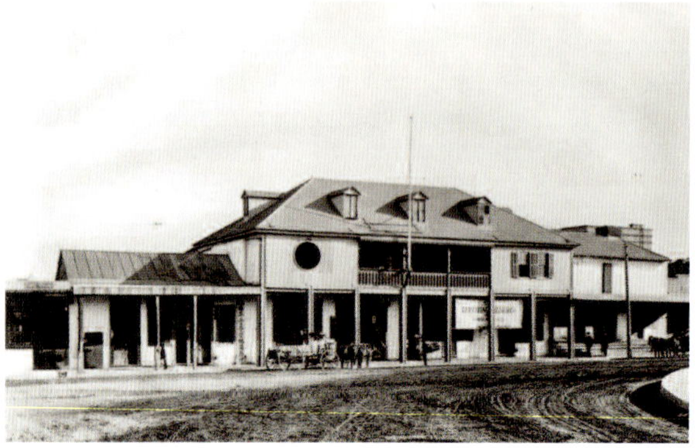

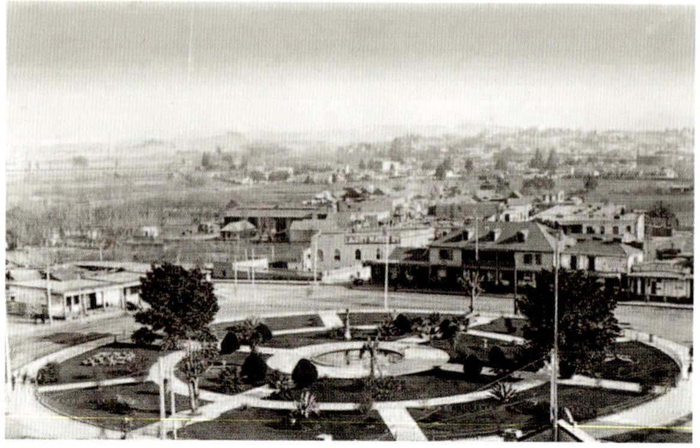

ABOVE LEFT *When this photograph was taken sometime in the 1890s, the Lugo family adobe had become part of Chinatown and Leeching Hung & Co. did business out of the old house.*

ABOVE *The Lugo house had stood on the plaza for more than 50 years when this photograph was taken in 1890. By that time all the Californio families had moved and the city had adopted the place where it was born and turned it into a park. Streets had been renamed and the house stood on the southeast corner of Los Angeles and Alameda streets.*

OPPOSITE PAGE *The Lugo family would not have recognized their two-story adobe by the time this photo was taken in the early 1940s. A Colonial Revival-style roof had been added to the home, which had become part of Chinatown and housed the Canton Bazaar.*

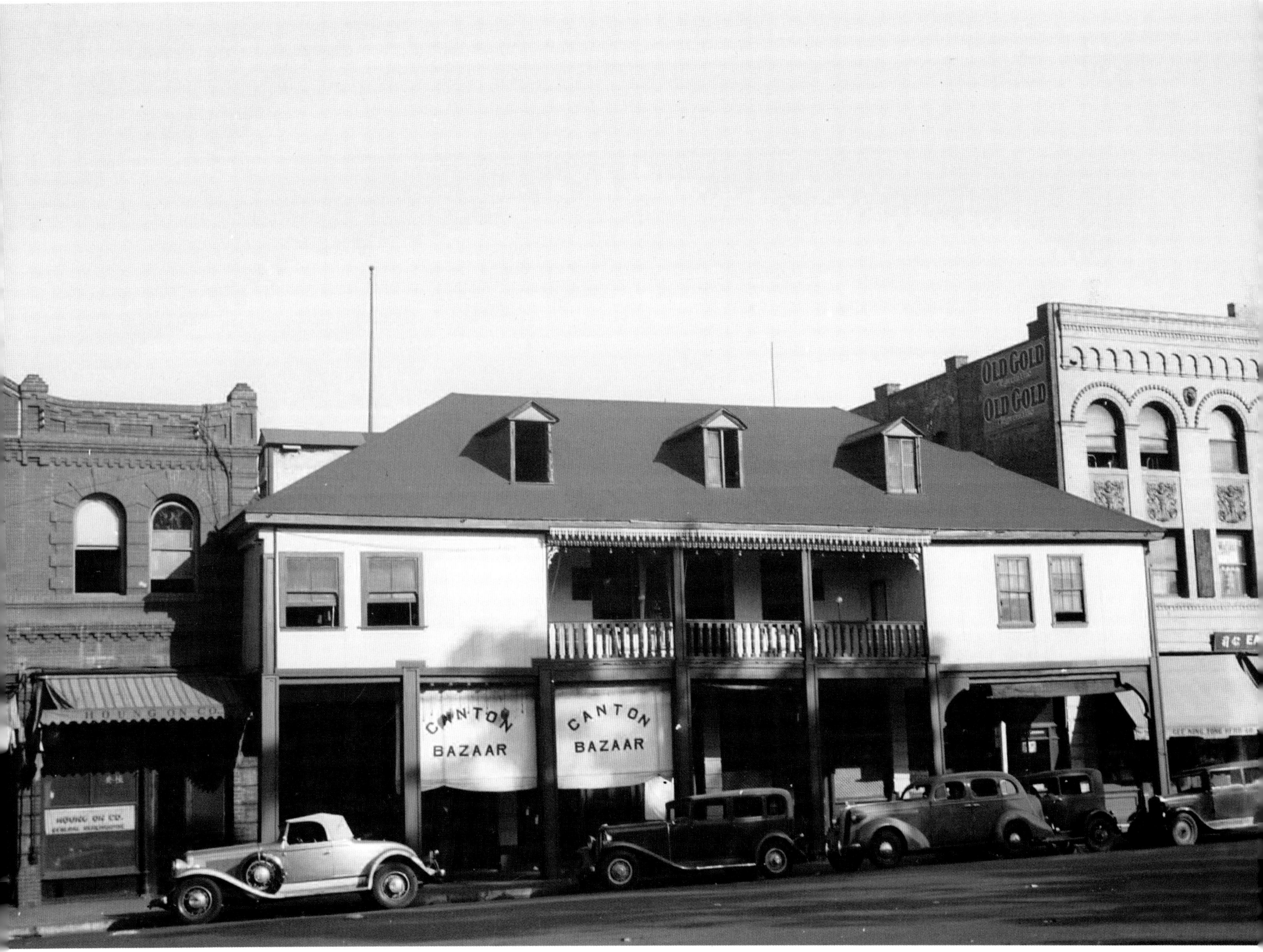

OLD GOLD
OLD GOLD
CANTON
BAZAAR
CANTON
BAZAAR

Los Angeles Orphan Asylum MOVED 1953

In 1856, the Daughters of Charity of St. Vincent de Paul, also commonly known as the Sisters of Charity and "God's Geese" because of their wing-like headgear, opened an orphans' home in former mayor Benjamin D. Wilson's recently vacated mansion.

In 1869, the orphanage, which initially took just girls, was incorporated as the Los Angeles Orphan Asylum in a move to settle any dispute as to who was the owner of the site.

As the population of the city surged during the late 1880s, the Daughters looked for a new site in Boyle Heights to house their growing number of orphans, now both boys and girls. After fund-raising for the new site, a location at Boyle Avenue and Whittier Boulevard was purchased for $12,000, and work began in 1890. The following year, at Thanksgiving 1891, the imposing Romanesque Revival-style building was ready to receive its small souls. The new orphanage cost $150,000 and could provide home for 400 orphans.

Unlike many buildings of the Victorian era, the Orphan's Asylum lasted 60 years, though there were scares along the way. Building work on the nearby extension of Sixth Street in the 1930s involved dynamiting the hillside and this reportedly weakened the building's foundations.

On March 10, 1933, the Long Beach earthquake struck, which rang the school's Angelus bell right at 6 p.m. The earthquake caused extensive damage to the roof and cupolas and resulted in falling brickwork and a temporary evacuation of the third-floor dormitories. Once the after-shocks had passed, the orphanage set about removing the weakened bell tower, with bricks and tiles sent down an elaborate wooden chute from the top of the building, but classes still went on.

The death knell to the old building was rung by the post-war freeway construction through Boyle Heights. The Daughters decided to take up the offer of Carrie Estelle Doheny who donated land in Rosemead in the San Gabriel Valley together with funds for the construction of a new campus. This was matched by fund-raising from the Los Angeles Orphanage Guild. In 1953 they moved to the new campus, named Maryvale, where they continue their mission today.

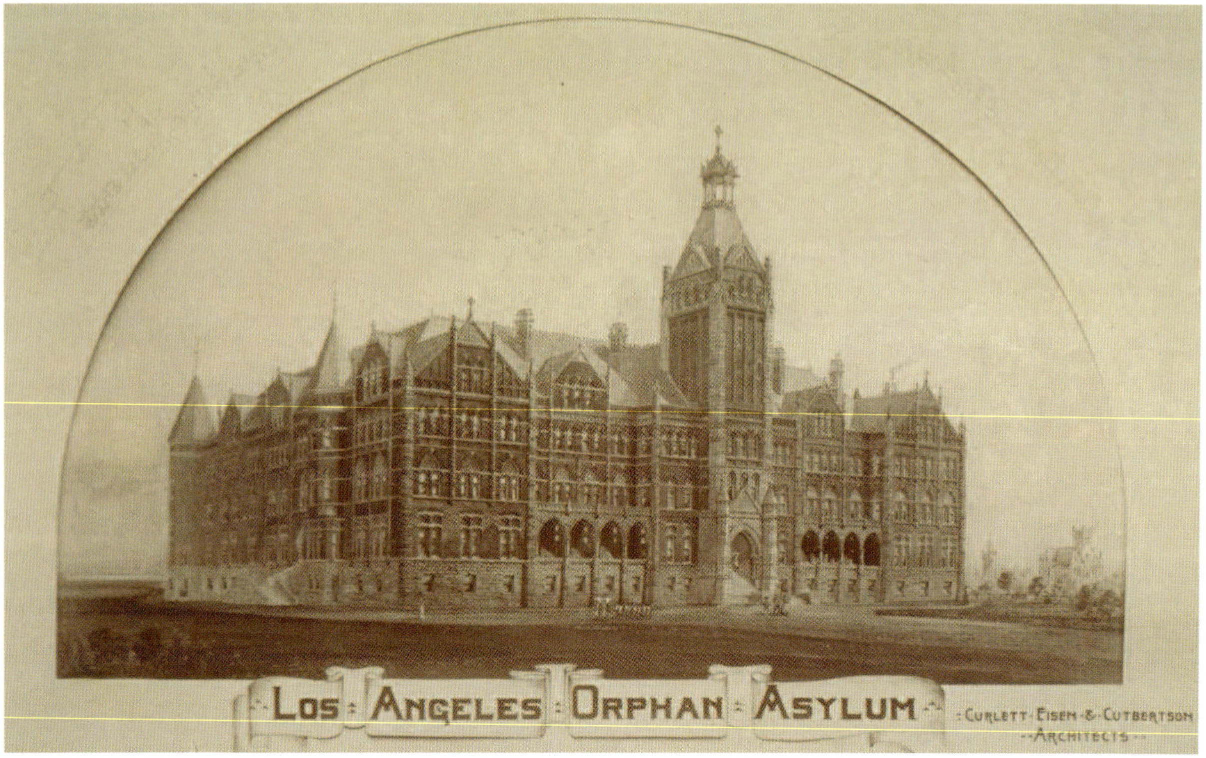

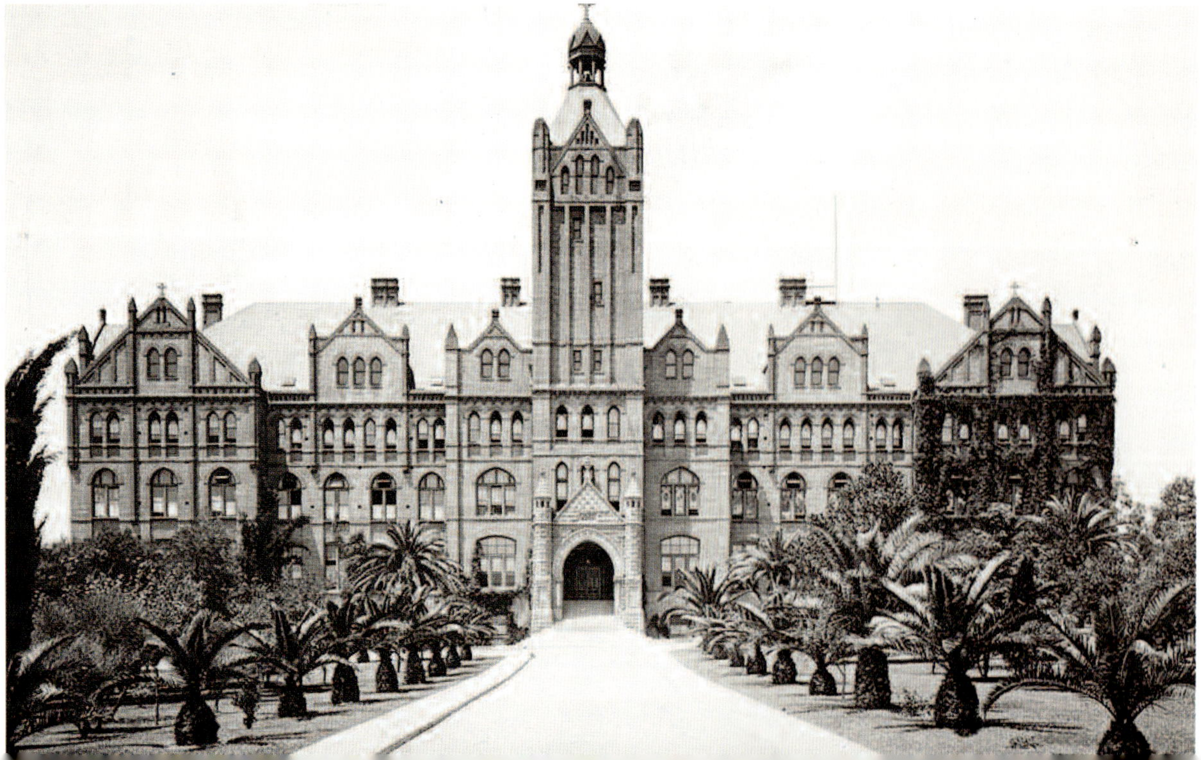

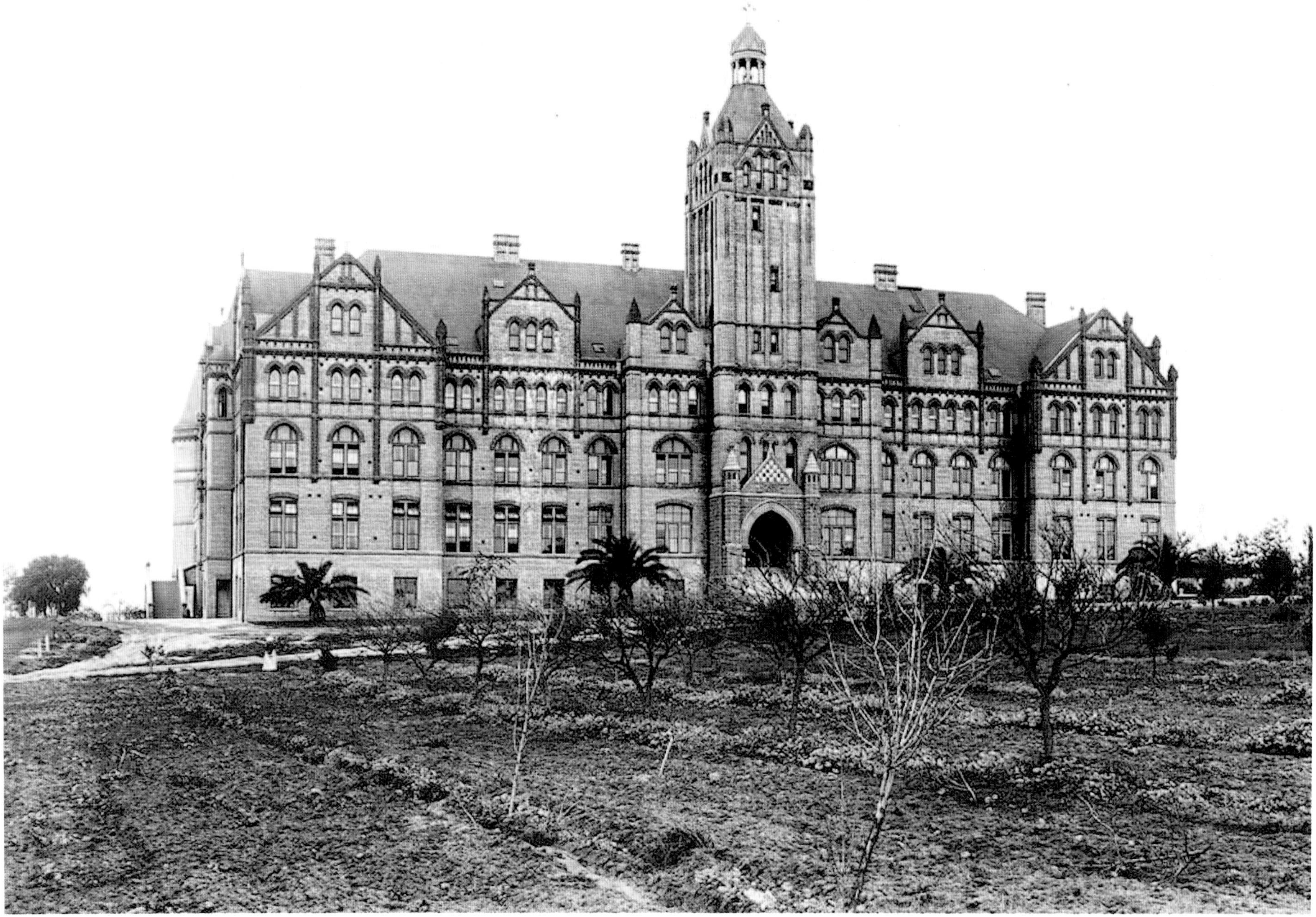

ABOVE *The Daughters were led by the inspirational figure of Sister Scholastica. To celebrate her fiftieth year as a Daughter, in 1889, a fund was set up to raise money for this new building in Boyle Heights.*

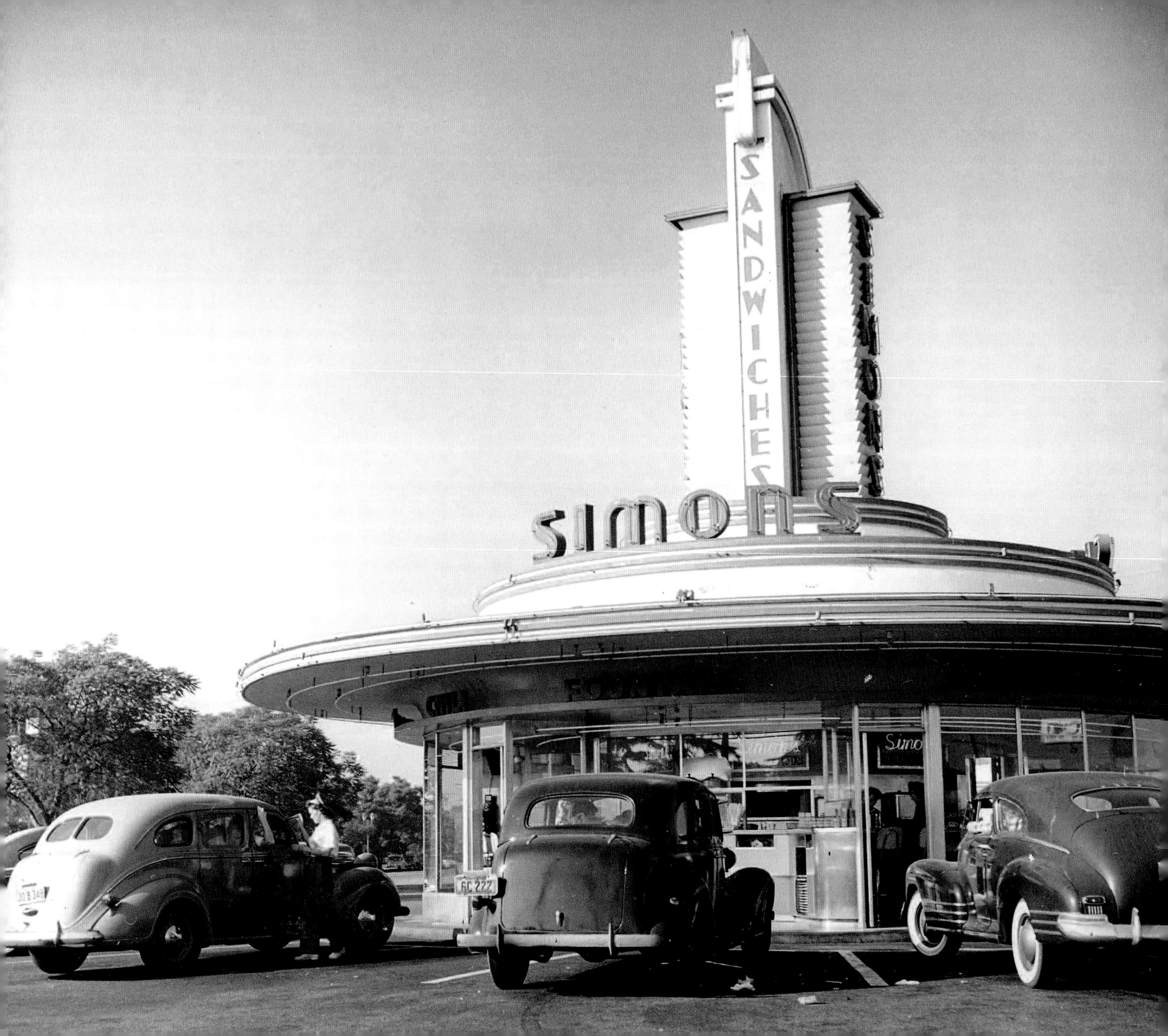
SANDWICHES
SIMONS

Simon's Drive-In DEMOLISHED 1955

Across the sweep of human history, many an architect has toiled away in their field with little or no recognition. Architects specializing in vernacular uses, such as restaurants, faced an even steeper climb to acclaim. Los Angeles Architect Wayne McAllister took that climb to the top.

McAllister's leisure architecture career began in Mexico with a hotel and casino project in 1928 when he was just 20 years old. In the 1930s he designed a series of drive-in restaurants that would define the Streamline Moderne style of restaurant design. McAllister embraced car culture as the wave of the future, and his buildings elegantly solved the problem of serving drivers food in their cars.

In the 1930s, drive-in restaurants appeared everywhere in Los Angeles. Carpenter's, McDonnell's, Herbert's—McAllister worked for them all. They all had door-less buildings surrounded by a sea of parking so uniformed carhops could easily access customers in their cars. Herbert's owner, Sydney Herbert, hired McAllister in the early 1930s to create a unique look for his eatery at the corner of Beverley Boulevard and Fairfax Avenue. The result became an icon. The neon-lined circular roof and advertising pylon formed the basis of several more McAllister designs, but this time for a more prominent chain.

William Simon had an eye on building restaurants in all the booming areas of the city: The Miracle Mile, Sunset Boulevard and Ventura Boulevard. Simon approached McAllister about designing unique buildings for him that would catch a motorist's eye, day or night.

The Simon's at Wilshire Boulevard and Fairfax appeared in 1935 on the site of the Chaplin Airfield. Like a theater's blade sign, letters spelling Simon's blazed out into the night in neon on the building's central pylon, echoing Herbert's. A second McAllister design stood further down Wilshire at Hoover Street. This building's unique three-tiered roof, like a wedding cake, and other elements of McAllister's design were copied all over the nation.

A major contributor to the "Googie" style of architecture, which featured bold sweeps and space-age shapes, McAllister would be remembered for taking restaurant design a step further. The style, he said, was "influenced by the automobile, not the architect."

McAllister moved to Washington, D.C. in 1956 to oversee the construction of some of Marriott's first hotels, but returned to Los Angeles in 1962 and began working to develop a coin-operated vending machine that photocopied documents.

Today, neither Los Angeles Simon's survives. On the site of the original Simon's, demolished in 1955, stands Johnnie's Coffee Shop, a building used in several films and designated a landmark in 2013 as one of the best remaining examples of the Googie style. The Simon's at the corner of Sycamore has become a BMW dealer.

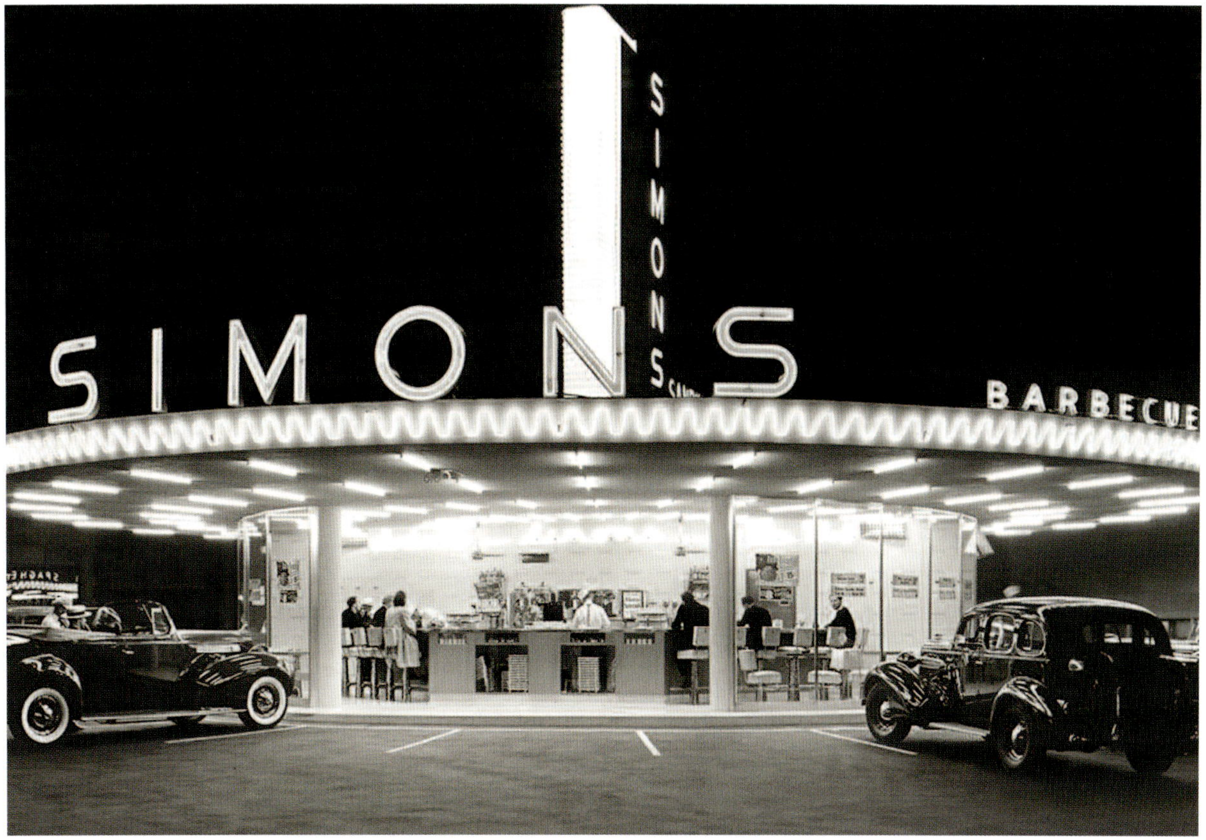

LEFT *Open day and night, the contrast in the use of typeface on Simon's neon signs shows that McAllister evolved his style.*

OPPOSITE PAGE *A waitress serves a customer at Simon's Drive-In at Wilshire and Hoover in the late 1930s.*

Southern Pacific Central Depot **RAZED 1956**

In March 1838 Kentuckian William Wolfskill purchased 100 acres of land he dubbed the Wolfskill Ranch. The property was bounded on the north by today's East Third Street. The ranch stretched south to modern-day East Ninth Street and was bounded on the east and west by Alameda and San Pedro streets respectively.

William married Magdalena Lugo. The couple lived in a large adobe on today's Alameda Street, between Third and Fourth streets. The home stood until 1887 when it was razed to make room for the Southern Pacific Railroad's Arcade Station, which opened the following year at Fourth and Alameda streets.

Arcade Station survived for 25 years. In 1914 the *Los Angeles Times* described the edifice as "ancient" and "unsightly and inadequate." Southern Pacific hired architects John Parkinson and George Bergstrom to design the new Central Station, which would stand right next to the Arcade Station.

The new station opened to passengers on December 1, 1914. Shortly afterwards wreckers arrived to dismantle Arcade Station and put outdoor loading platforms for the new Central Depot in its place. Parkinson and Bergstrom chose a neoclassical design for the imposing new station that they covered with white stucco.

The station's five soaring arched windows impressed travelers, while on the inside, the building offered passengers an elegant waiting room with chandeliers hanging above them and marble wainscoting surrounding them in the station's waiting room. Amenities included carpeted lounges, a restaurant, a lunch counter and even a medical center. The depot itself stretched 500 feet along Alameda Street. Its rail shed featured skylights and an arched roof that soared 90 feet above the platforms below.

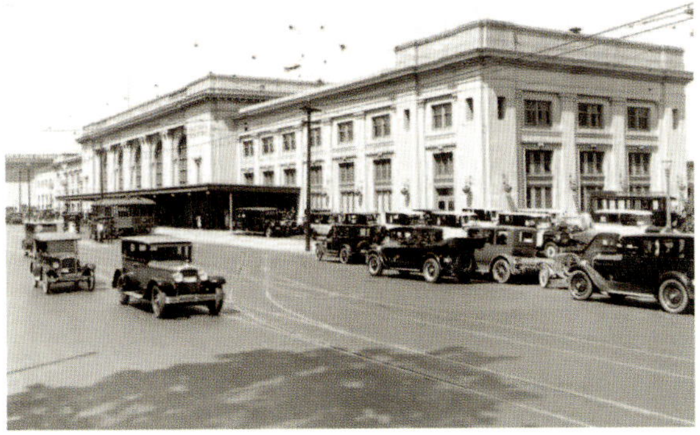

The station's designers used every opportunity to incorporate sub-tropical planting around the building to emphasize California's mild climate. Outside the station's entrance a fully-grown Washington palm greeted arrivals from the chilly Midwest.

The Young Market Co. acquired the site where Central Depot stood. In 1956, the new owners demolished Parkinson and Bergstrom's creation and built a meat-packing plant in its place.

But something does survive. The palm tree that once stood in front of Arcade station was moved in 1914 when the Southern Pacific built Central Depot. The tree stands today in front of the Los Angeles Coliseum in Exposition Park.

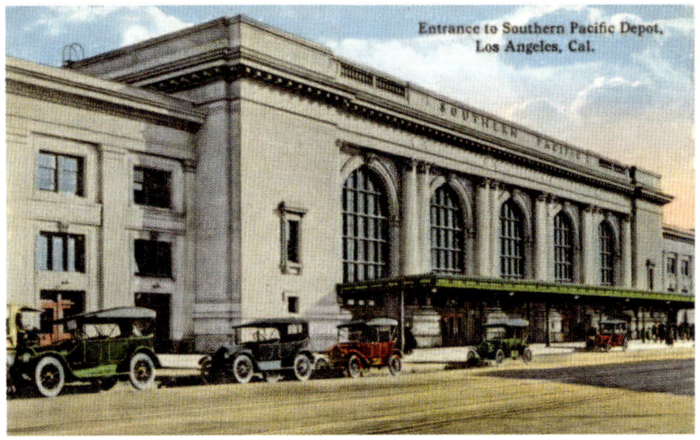

ABOVE *An early color postcard of the Southern Pacific terminal.*

LEFT *Automobiles, a streetcar, taxis and even a bus parked on the side of the station transported people arriving at and departing from Southern Pacific Railroad's Central Station. From 1920 until the station closed, passengers rode the Bonnie Brae line's successor, the narrow-gauge "D" line to reach the station.*

OPPOSITE PAGE *The Depot in the early 1920s.*

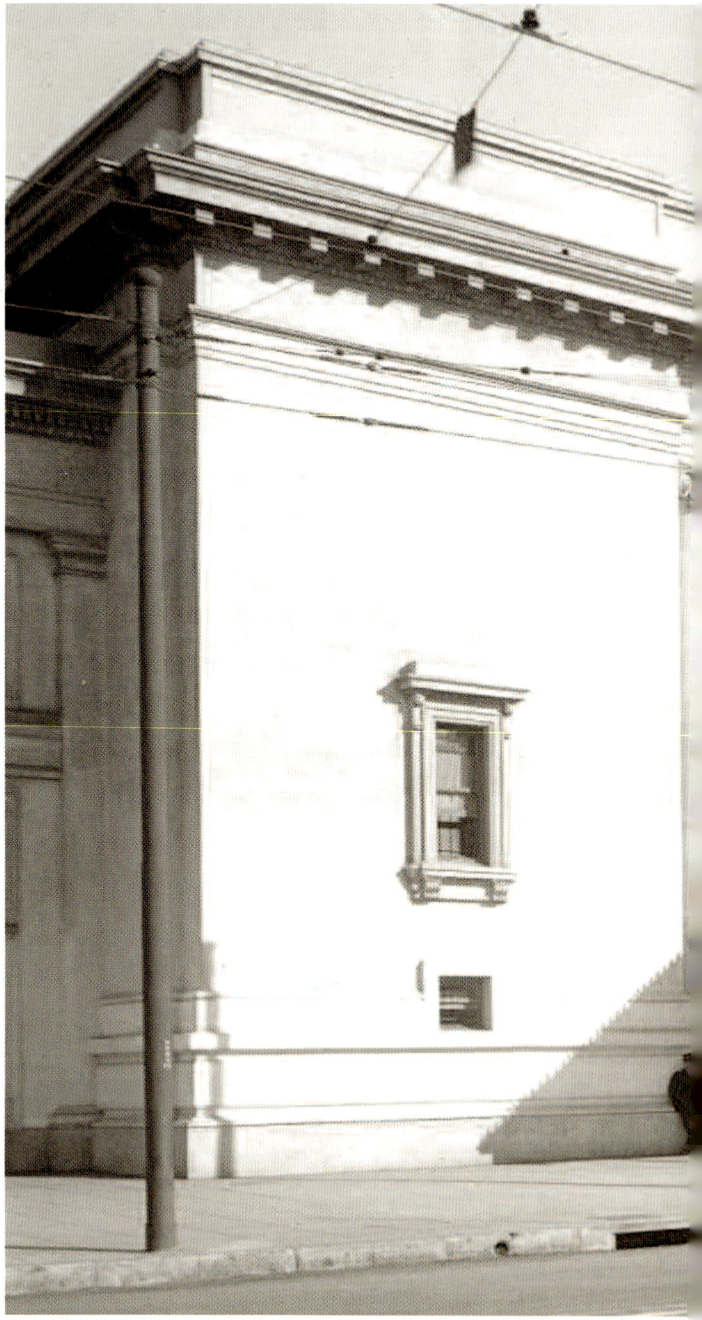

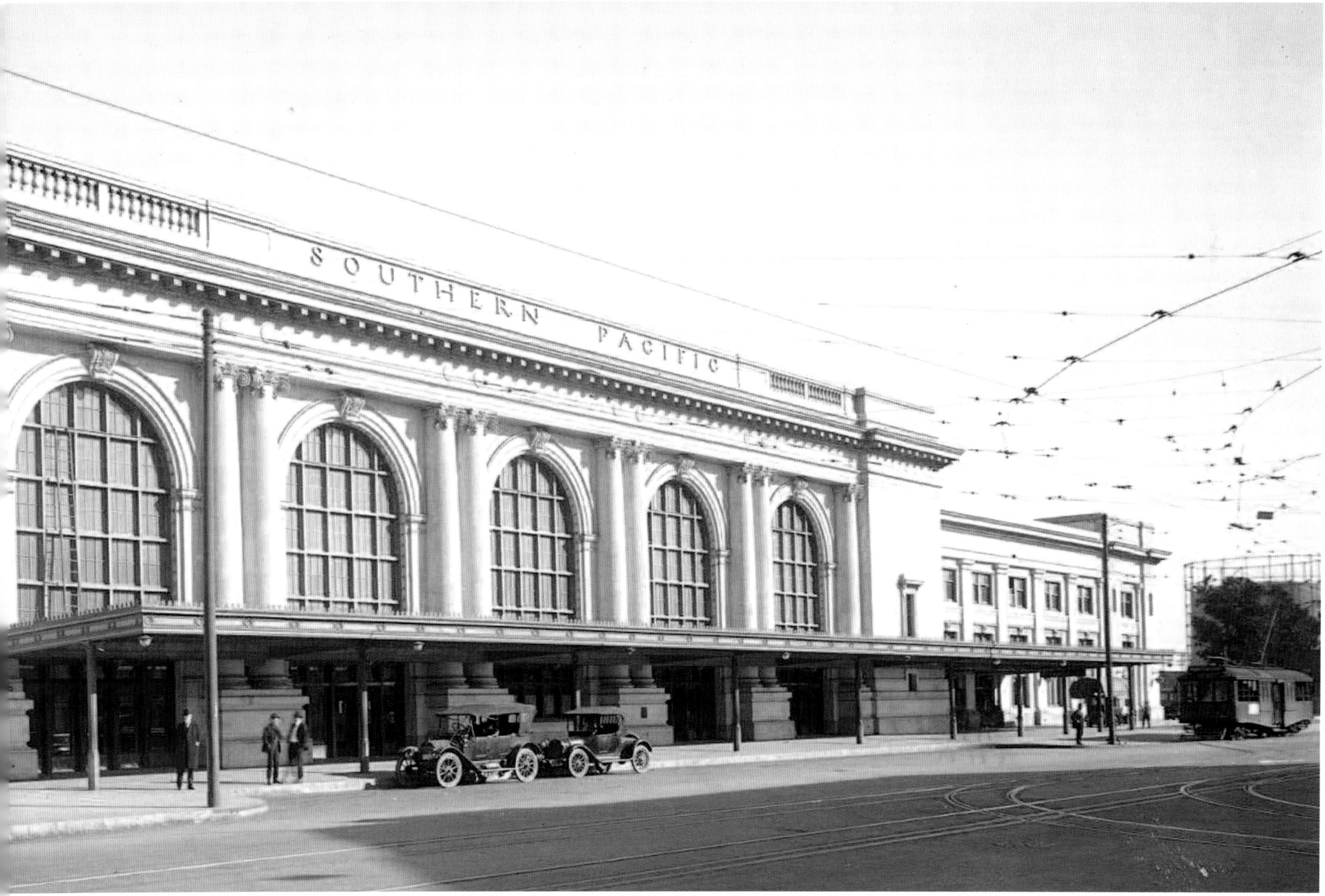
SOUTHERN PACIFIC

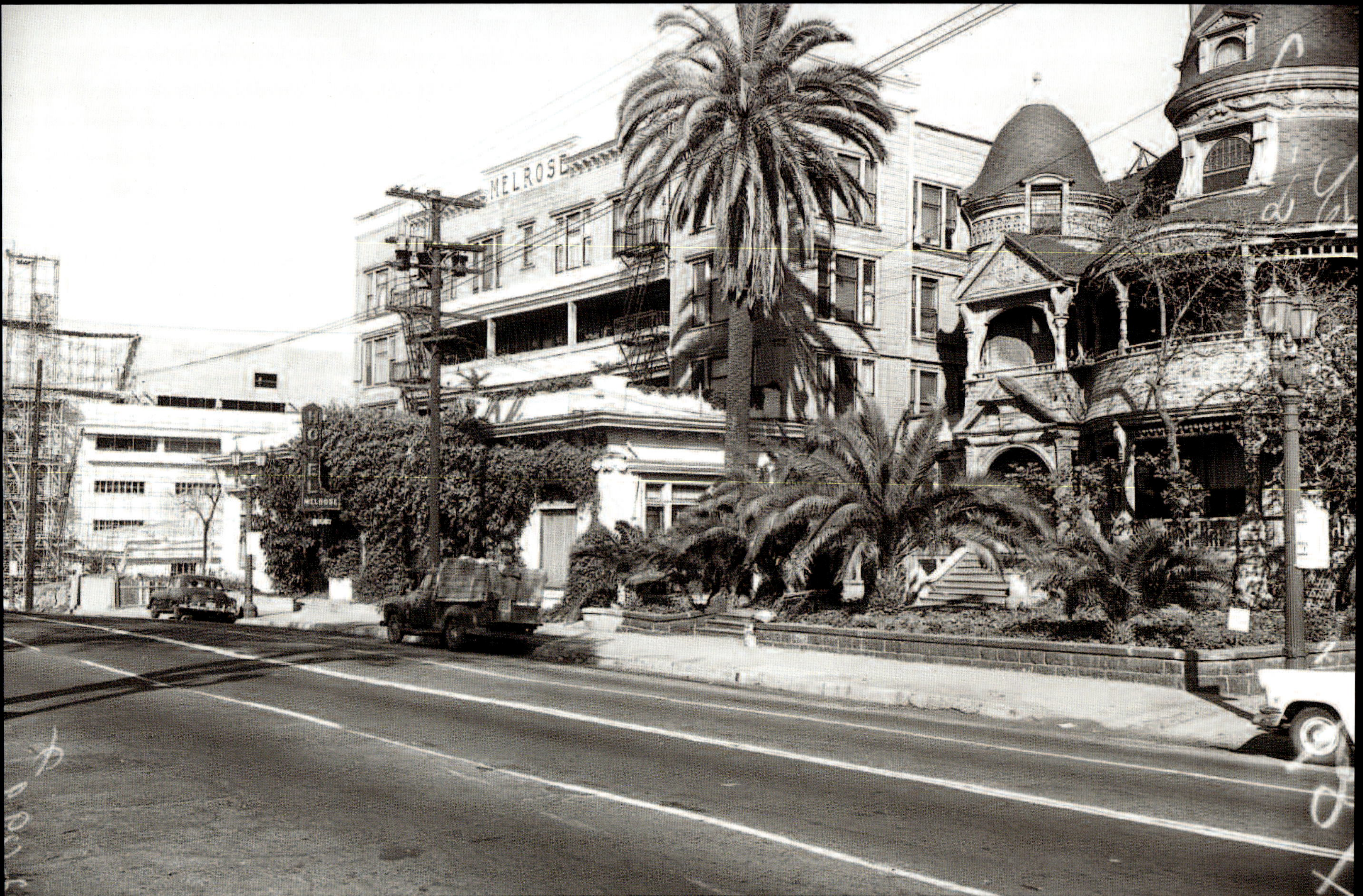
MELROSE
HOTEL
MELROSE

Melrose Hotel, Richelieu Hotel REDEVELOPED 1957

The three "grand dames" of Grand Avenue between First and Second streets weren't Hollywood starlets but historic, Victorian-era hotels. The Melrose Hotel and its annex, along with the Hotel Richelieu, offered tremendous views of the city for around seven decades.

The 30-room Melrose Hotel opened in 1881 on what was then Charity Street. Hotelier Marc W. Connor built the five-story structure at 130 South Grand, the center of high society in Los Angeles at the time.

A local described the hotel as a center of fashionable goings-on and society spectacle, as well as a place of repose for honorable people. A place so popular, in fact, that in 1890 Connor began constructing an annex for the Melrose. The box-like design contrasted sharply with the curves of the Queen Anne-style original. Connor connected the annex to the original via an arcade. In 1901, President McKinley became the first sitting president to visit Los Angeles. Both McKinley and, later, Theodore Roosevelt were said to have stayed at the Melrose.

On February 27, 1911, a suspected arsonist struck the hotel. Smoldering newspapers sent employees—Connor's nephew Mark Bentz who was managing his uncle's hotel, as well as Connor himself—scampering from the basement to the elevator shaft and finally to the back of the hotel. A smoky blaze was doused at each location. No suspects were ever apprehended and no motive was ever discovered.

Lieutenant General Nelson A. Miles called the Melrose Hotel home. This much-decorated soldier was awarded the Medal of Honor for gallantry at the Battle of Chancellorsville during the Civil War. He also served as the military governor in Puerto Rico. He was likely the only Melrose Hotel resident who had a city (Miles City, Montana) and a street (Miles Street in Tucson, Arizona) named for him.

In the 1920s famous Socialist Party mayoral candidate and labor lawyer Job Harriman and his wife moved into the Melrose Hotel. Harriman was a well-known attorney who had run for vice-president on the Socialist ticket in 1900.

The Melrose continued to serve the public through the mid-1950s by which time Bunker Hill had fallen on hard times. The Victorian era long over, the Melrose cupola and original detailing had become woefully out of fashion.

Next door, the Hotel Richelieu had begun its life as a private residence for Richard Larkin and his wife Helen in 1891. By 1893 the couple had sold the home to Chicago businessman Charles Hord who overhauled it and converted it into a first-class hotel, with 39 rooms. The hotel held up well. Like the Melrose it suffered a fire in 1954, but the damage appears to have been minimal.

A planned redevelopment for the entire Bunker Hill neighborhood spelled the end for the Melrose Hotel, its neighbor, the Richelieu Hotel, and many other significant Victorian-era buildings. On July 9, 1957, it took the Community Redevelopment Agency just eight hours to level the Melrose. Many remembered the day President McKinley spoke from the hotel's front porch. Others recalled that Nelson Miles, the commander of the U.S. Army during the Spanish American War had stayed there.

Opera singer Julia de Grazia Doerffel wrote an original poem to express her sadness over the lost hotel titled, *Melrose Hotel. Good Bye!* The poem was discovered in the *Los Angeles Examiner*'s clippings morgue.

The Richelieu had disappeared shortly before the Melrose in 1957, and while the *Los Angeles Times* and local residents paid close attention to the loss of the Melrose, no-one seemed to notice the Richelieu had been torn down. In 1959, two years after the hotels met their demise, the redevelopment plan for the Bunker Hill Project displaced 11,000 residents and demolition of most of the old neighborhood's 396 buildings. Today, the spot where the Melrose and Richelieu hotels once stood serves as a parking garage across the street from the Walt Disney Concert Hall.

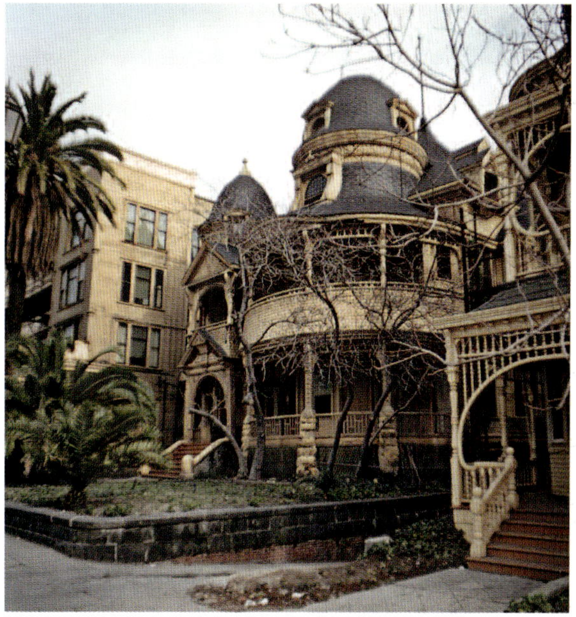

ABOVE *Nearing the end, the two Melrose buildings captured in Kodachrome in the early 1950s.*

OPPOSITE PAGE *The boxy Melrose Hotel annex, which started life as subsidiary to the Queen Anne-style main building, became the entry point in the twentieth century.*

BELOW *The Melrose (left) and the Richelieu (right) some time before 1890, as the Melrose annex is yet to appear to the left of the hotel.*

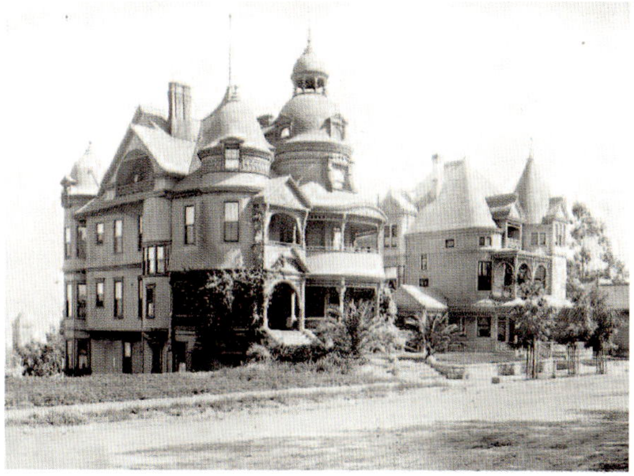

Chavez Ravine EVICTED 1959

In 1844, the Mexican government granted Jose Maria Chavez 83 acres at a spot that became known first as Chavez Canyon, and later as Chavez Ravine. He may have received this real estate in return for his service as a "judge of waters," settling water disputes and later a "judge of the plains," settling cattle disputes.

In 1850, Angelenos used Chavez Canyon as a hospital for members of the Chinese and Latino population who were suffering from smallpox. It was also the site of a Jewish cemetery, established in 1855 by the Hebrew Benevolent Society. Their hilly, three-acre site became surrounded by brick kilns and oil wells over the years and the decision was eventually taken to move the graves out to a cemetery in Boyle Heights. Between 1902 and 1910 all 360 graves were transferred.

The heart of Chavez Canyon took on the name Chavez Ravine and served as home to three Latino communities of La Loma, Palo Verde and Bishop. In 1886, industry poked its head into to the ravine when the City Brick Company started dynamiting some of the hillsides to extract the clay they needed to manufacture their product. At the turn of the century, oil wellheads added to the industrial mix. However families chose to live in the ravine because of housing discrimination in other parts of the city. The ravine served its residents as a self-sufficient and tight-knit community. Its residents ran their own schools and churches and grew their own food.

In 1913, a new wave of Latinos moved into Chavez Ravine when attorney Marshall Stimson paid to relocate 250 families from the Los Angeles River's flood plain.

The oil dried up and residents celebrated in 1926 when they successfully banded together to oust the brick makers who were playing havoc with the environment. On August 20, 1926, the Los Angeles City Council unanimously adopted an ordinance prohibiting the blasting and zoned the area around Chavez Ravine for residential use.

The residents' fight against outsiders determining their future wasn't over, however. In 1937, neighbors learned of plans to stage the Pacific Mercado—an international exposition to celebrate the 400th anniversary of Juan Cabrillo's voyage—and host it in Chavez Ravine. The following year, the idea to host a world's fair in Los Angeles in Chavez Ravine was shot down by the United States Navy who wanted to build an armory in the ravine. The same year, the Los Angeles city engineers had plans on the drawing board to build a highway through the ravine. None of these plans ever came to fruition.

Baseball offered the Latinos their next hurdle, one they would fail to overcome. When the Brooklyn Dodgers announced their desire to come to Los Angeles, the city once again cast its eye on the communities in Chavez Ravine. The city used the concept of eminent domain to force those living in Chavez Ravine to sell their homes so the Dodgers could move in.

In the end, those who refused to sell were physically forced to relocate. On May 9, 1959—a day still remembered in the Latino community as "Black Friday"—armed Los Angeles County Sheriff's deputies arrived with the bulldozers to begin razing the homes and streets to make way for the Dodgers development.

Parts of the ravine survived the destruction and developers sold some of the buildings in Chavez Ravine to Universal Studios at the price of a dollar each. Universal carted these structures to its back lot. Gregory Peck played Atticus Finch in the 1962 movie *To Kill a Mockingbird*. Atticus Finch's "home" in the movie once served as someone's real home in Chavez Ravine.

In October 2008 the city of Los Angeles wiped the name "Chavez Ravine" from the maps when it designated the location as "Dodgertown." The following year the United States Postal Service went along when it assigned "Dodgertown" the Zip Code 90090.

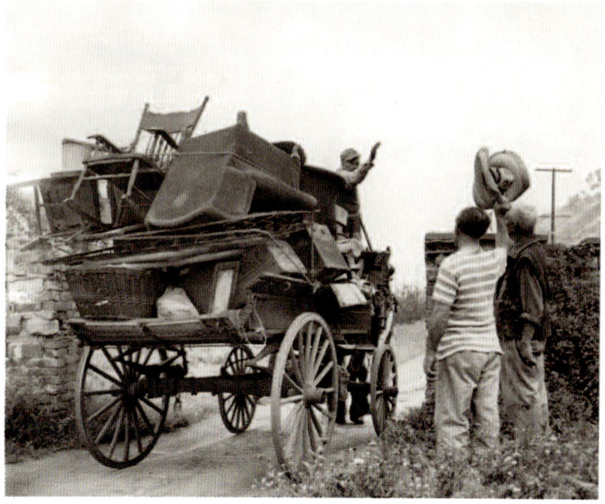

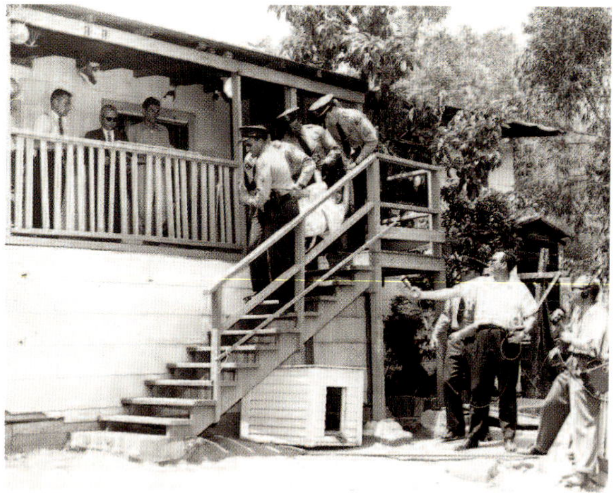

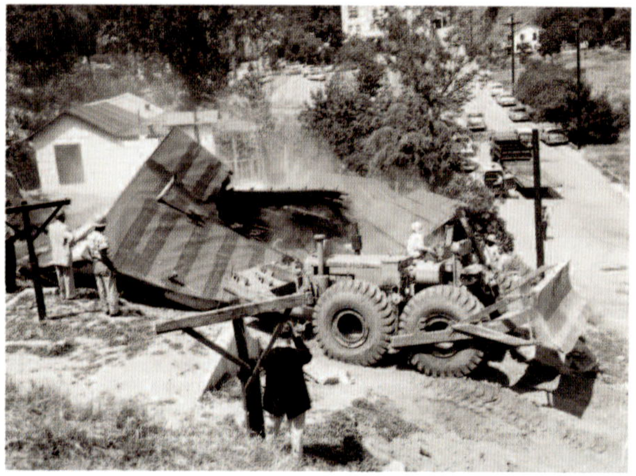

RIGHT *While some families were willing to move, others were forcibly evicted on May 9, 1959. Bulldozers moved in swiftly to make sure there was no re-occupation of the houses.*

OPPOSITE PAGE *With the controversial land purchase swept aside, Los Angeles residents could look forward to hosting a Major League baseball team after groundbreaking began on September 19, 1959.*

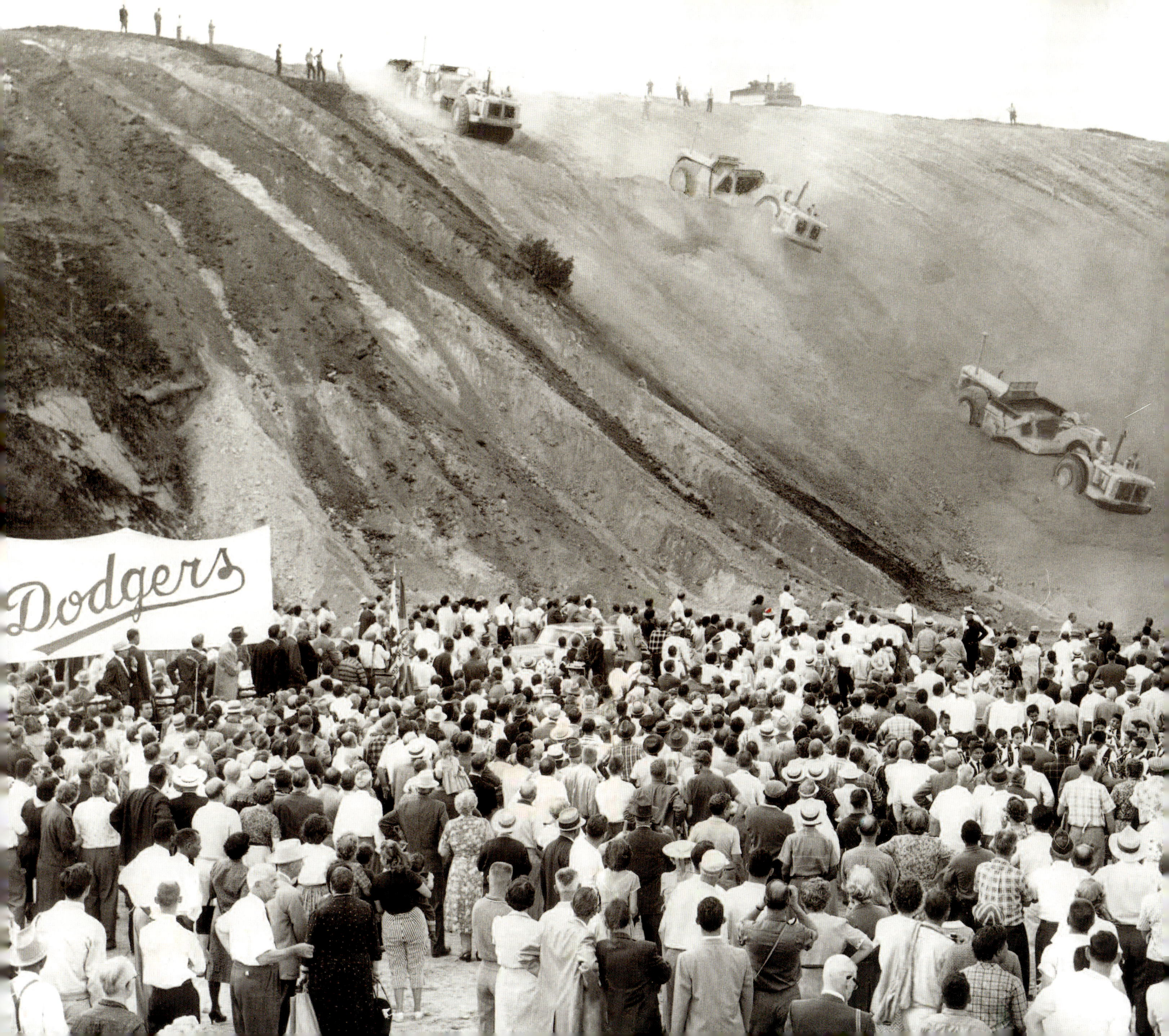
Dodgers

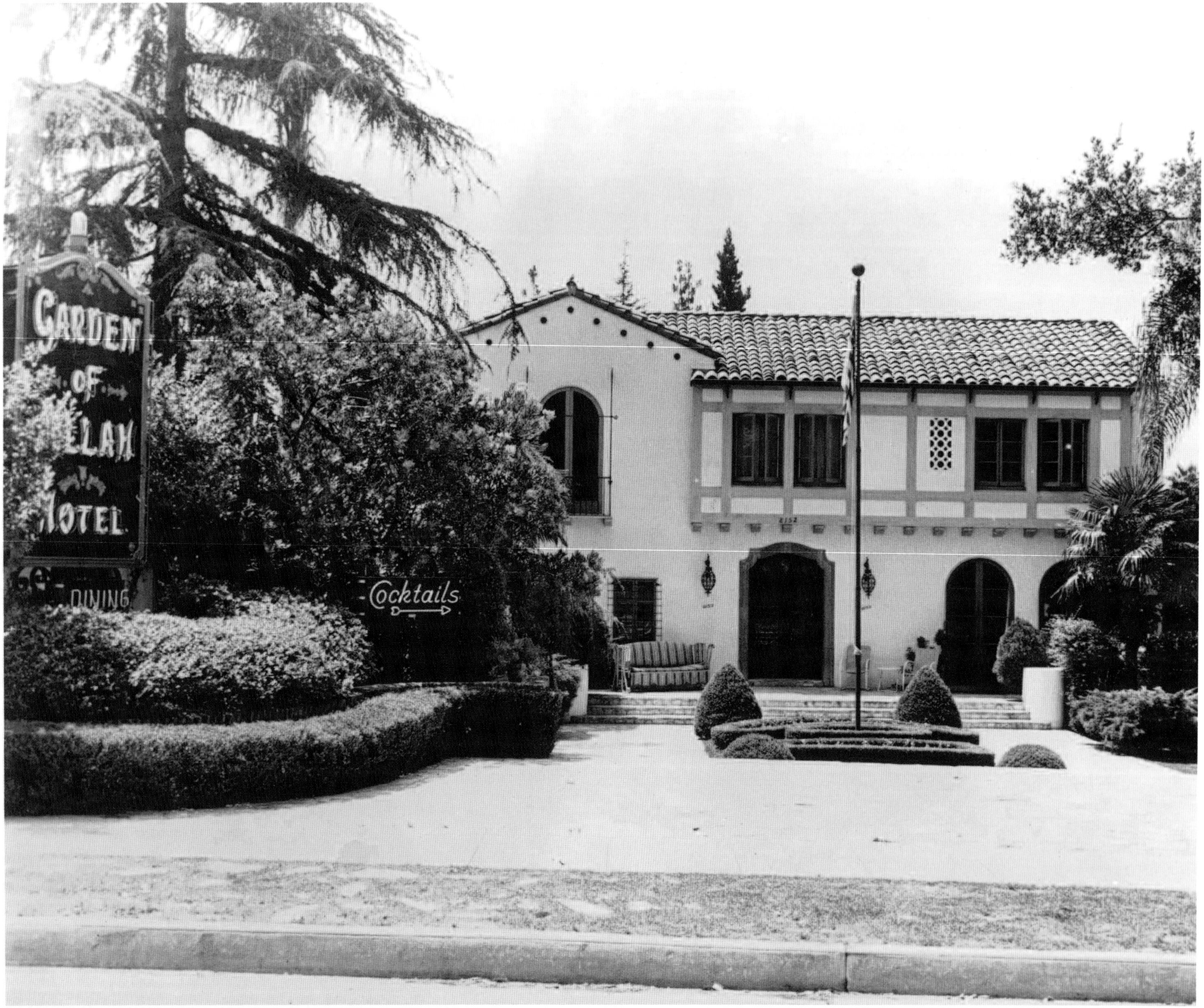
GARDEN
OF
DINING
Cocktails

Garden of Allah TORN DOWN 1959

In the days when Sunset Boulevard was nothing more than a dirt track, real estate developer William H. Hay built his personal residence at number 8152 on two and a half acres. Hay started developing the Crescent Heights area in 1905 and had his 12-room mansion built for him and his wife Katherine there in 1913. Two years later he built another home and put this first residence, "Hayvenhurst" up for sale.

While Hay built homes, Russian-born silent movie actress Alla Nazimova was skyrocketing to stardom. By 1918, Nazimova could command more pay than even Hollywood legend Mary Pickford ($13,000 per week), as well as choose her own scripts, directors and leading men. After the success of her films *Revelation* and *Toys of Fate* showed that the Broadway actress could carry her talent to film, she left for California.

Nazimova acquired Hayvenhurst and its grounds and immediately spent $65,000 remodeling it. Now named "The Garden of Allah" Nazimova discussed literature, art, philosophy and theater with Hollywood's intellectual elite in the equivalent of European salons there.

A decade or so later, Alla's fortunes turned. Her self-produced films had failed to be profitable during the "talkies" era and in an effort to save her financial future, Nazimova took on a couple of investors to convert her Garden of Allah into a residential hotel that would provide some income. She spared no expense on the new effort, constructing 25-guest villas on the grounds and hosting an 18-hour party to celebrate the hotel's opening on January 9, 1927.

Unfortunately, her partners left her high and dry. Within a year she was forced to declare bankruptcy. She sold her property back to Hay in 1928 who ran the hotel through a holding company. The hotel thrived. The Garden of Allah Hotel became synonymous with Hollywood glamour, and home to film stars: Greta Garbo, Errol Flynn and Laurence Olivier, and authors Ernest Hemingway and F. Scott Fitzgerald. Other residents included Ronald Reagan and the Marx Brothers.

Frank Sinatra took up residence here while performing at the Cocoanut Grove in 1941. Humphrey Bogart and Lauren Bacall were rumored to have begun their romance at the Garden of Allah during the filming of *To Have and Have Not* in 1944.

Nazimova returned to the silver screen in 1938. She had supporting roles in *In Our Time*, with stars Ida Lupino and Paul Henreid. She also appeared in the 1944 film *Since You Went Away*, with Claudette Colbert, Shirley Temple and Lionel Barrymore. She moved back to the Garden of Allah and lived in Villa 24 until her death in July 1945.

Some remember her as the "founding mother" of West Hollywood's gay community. She was openly bisexual and had a "lavender marriage" with gay actor Charles Bryant. She had affairs with celebrities that included playwright Mercedes de Acosta, actress Eva Le Gallienne and movie director Dorothy Arzner. She introduced Rudolph Valentino to both his wives. The rumor mill reported that Alla had bedded both these women before they wed Valentino.

By the 1950s the hotel faced stiff competition from larger and more modern hotels. Banker Bart Lytton had purchased the property with the intention of setting up a new branch of the Lytton Savings and Loan.

In August 1959 the hotel held a farewell gala. Guests were asked to dress as celebrities from years past. Among the thousand people who attended were silent-movie star Francis X. Bushman and his wife Iva. Many recalled Bushman for his role as Ben Hur in the 1925 silent version of the film. The Bushmans had also attended the opening party. A screening of Nazimova's 1923 film *Salome* was followed by an all-night party.

The party reflected the Garden of Allah's history as a place of celebrity overindulgence: phony marriages, gallons of Prohibition-era liquor, fist fights, robberies, sex, drugs and feuds. The partygoers recalled how the Garden of Allah helped define bohemian Hollywood.

Like many of the other residents of *Lost Los Angeles*, the Garden of Allah is today a mini mall and parking lot. Plans unveiled in September 2013 for a new mixed-use development on the site expressed an interest in referencing the Hollywood icon that once occupied its location.

If all goes as planned, wreckers will be visiting the site for a second time. This time they'll demolish the strip-mall that stands there today and put up a pair of apartment buildings where Bohemians once partied.

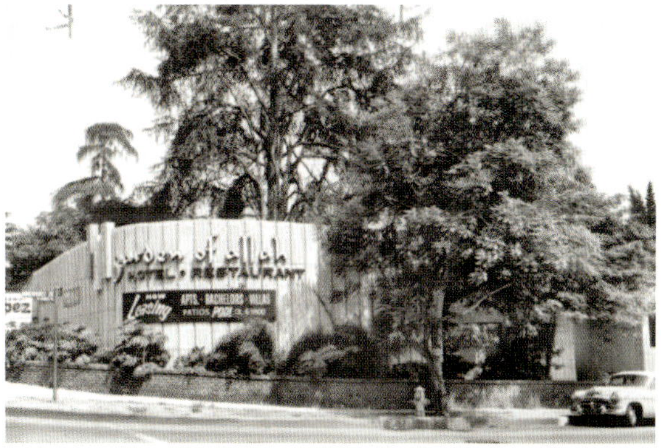

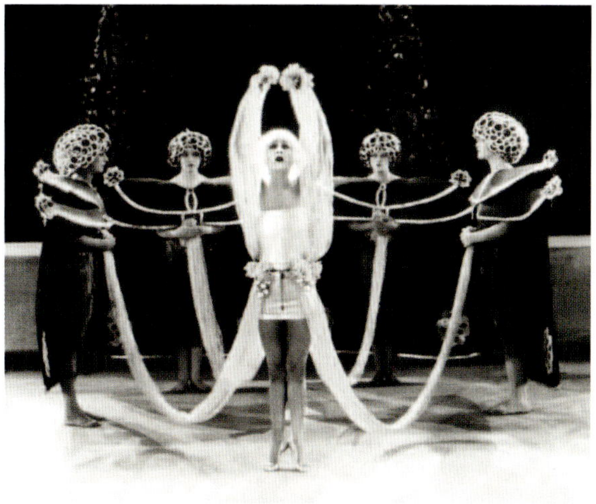

ABOVE RIGHT *In the days just prior to its demolition in 1959, this photo was taken of the entryway to the Garden of Allah Hotel.*

RIGHT *Alla Nazimova appears here in a 1923 promotional photograph for the film* Salome *directed by Charles Bryant.*

OPPOSITE PAGE *The hotel's administration building photographed in the 1930s.*

Grand Central Air Terminal GROUNDED 1959

Nearly every great aviator in the early days of aeronautics knew about Grand Central Air Terminal. Charles Lindbergh began the first west-to-east transcontinental flight here. Amelia Earhart bought her first plane here. Howard Hughes designed and flew his record-setting H-1 racer here.

Begun as a simple grass strip below Leslie Coombs Brand's mansion in Glendale in 1915, Brand's improvements included little more than a hangar built in 1916. By 1923, Brand's strip became a full commercial venture, complete with a suite of investors and the first paved runway west of the Rocky Mountains. A little further down the slope from the original strip, Glendale Municipal Airport soon became a major point of entry for new Los Angeles residents and was reportedly the first airport to offer air service between Los Angeles and New York City. It took the name Grand Central Air Terminal (GCAT) after passing to a new set of venture capitalists.

The popularity of the airline operations in the late 1920s led to the construction of a new terminal in 1929. Designed with the flavor of opulent railroad terminals of the past, the Spanish Colonial Revival building incorporated elements of art deco and functioned as the terminal's flight control tower. It was located at 1310 Air Way between Sonora and Grandview avenues. The following year the terminal was sold again, this time to a commercial group, the Curtiss-Wright Flying Service under the management of Major Corliss C. Moseley.

Many famous films were shot at the airport in the 1930s including Howard Hughes' landmark *Hell's Angels* (1930), *Bright Eyes* (1934) with Shirley Temple, and *Secret Service of the Air* (1939) featuring Ronald Reagan. Another great moment at the GCAT included a pioneering cross-country flight by African American aviators Albert Forsythe and Charles Anderson in 1933.

Moseley continued his operations at the site until the December 7, 1941, attack on Pearl Harbor when airports all over the West Coast were forced to close to private aviation. Heavily camouflaged, the terminal served as a training facility for the U.S. Army Air Force's flying cadets. Hundreds of planes received refurbishment or reconditioning there as part of the war effort.

After World War II and renamed Glendale Central Airport, the facility returned to private ventures. With its newly shortened runway prohibiting larger planes from landing, Glendale lost business. By 1959 the airport closed and Prudential Insurance purchased the property. Soon the area became The Glendale Central Business Park, with its steady tenant The Disney Corporation. Disney eventually purchased the entire former airport site for use as their corporate headquarters.

The original 1929 flight tower building still stands, though it had been deemed unsafe after the 1994 Northridge Earthquake. While Disney has found ways to reuse some of the terminal's original hangars, the architecturally significant terminal hasn't so far been designated a landmark.

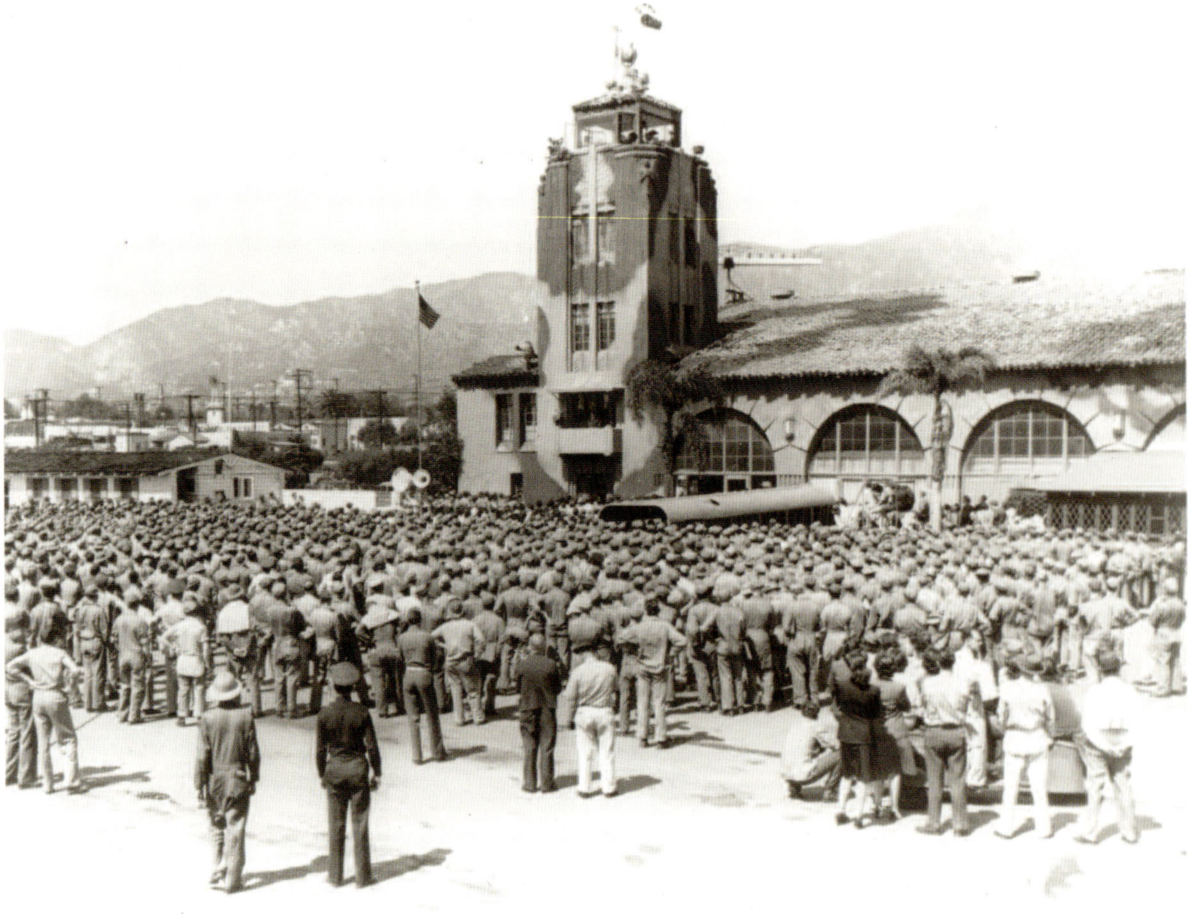

LEFT *Military personnel gather during 1942 in this U.S. War Department photo. The flight tower shows camouflage used to mask the location's true purpose. In this picture, Grand Central Air Terminal staff listen to World War I Canadian flying ace Billy Bishop tell the inspiring story of his 72 victories in the air.*

OPPOSITE PAGE *This photo from 1949 was taken by Hydraulic Specialist Don Ayres who worked at Cal Aero Grand Central from 1949 to 1952.*

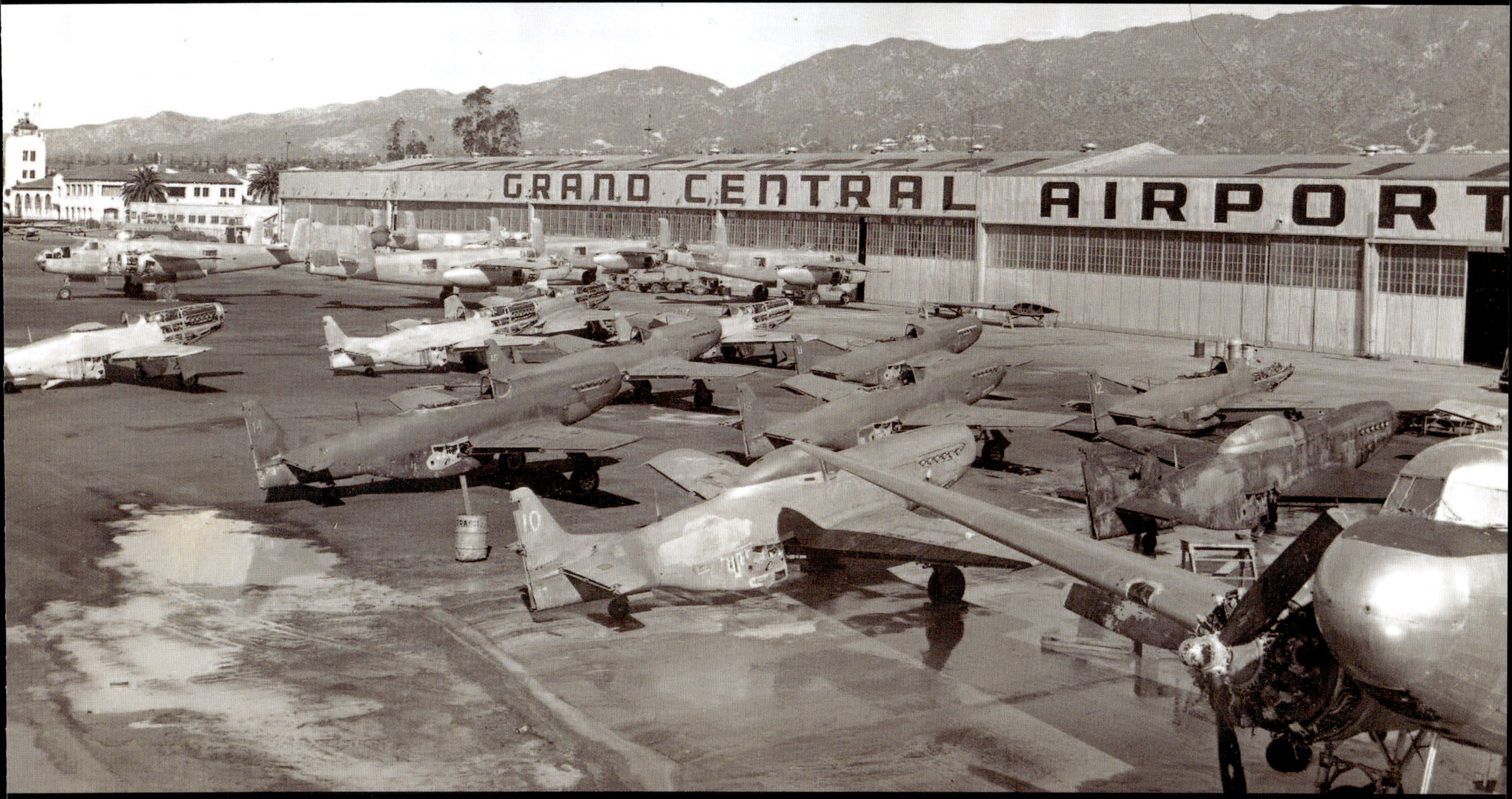
GRAND CENTRAL AIRPORT

Streetcars LAST RUN MARCH 1963

Public transportation arrived in Los Angeles on September 22, 1873, when Charles Dupoy drove his first omnibus into town. The following year a horse-drawn streetcar line, the scheme of attorney Robert M. Widney, began carrying passengers. By the mid-1880s cable cars on the Second Street Cable Railway and The Temple Street Cable Railway had largely replaced the horses.

The city's first electric streetcars began running on the Los Angeles Electric Railway Company line in 1886, and by 1897 electricity was powering all the city's streetcars.

The Los Angeles Railway's "Yellow Cars" and the Pacific Electric Railways' "Red Cars" provided Angelenos a convenient and inexpensive way to get around town in the 20th century. At their peak in 1924 some 1,250 Yellow Cars were running on 20 streetcar lines on 642 miles of track. These cars carried passengers from downtown to neighborhoods in about a six-mile radius of downtown. These included Echo Park, Westlake, Hancock Park, Exposition Park and Lincoln Heights.

The Red Cars of the Pacific Electric Railway began carrying passengers through Los Angeles in 1901. Henry Huntington—the nephew of Central Pacific Railroad mogul Collis Huntington and Isiah Hellman—bankrolled the line.

In 1925, the company opened a mile-long subway that carried passengers on four Pacific Electric Railway lines from downtown Los Angeles to a portal near Beverly and Glendale boulevards. The 250,000-square-foot Subway Terminal Building on Fourth Street, between Olive and Hill streets, served as the hub's focal point with its five wings towering over the site.

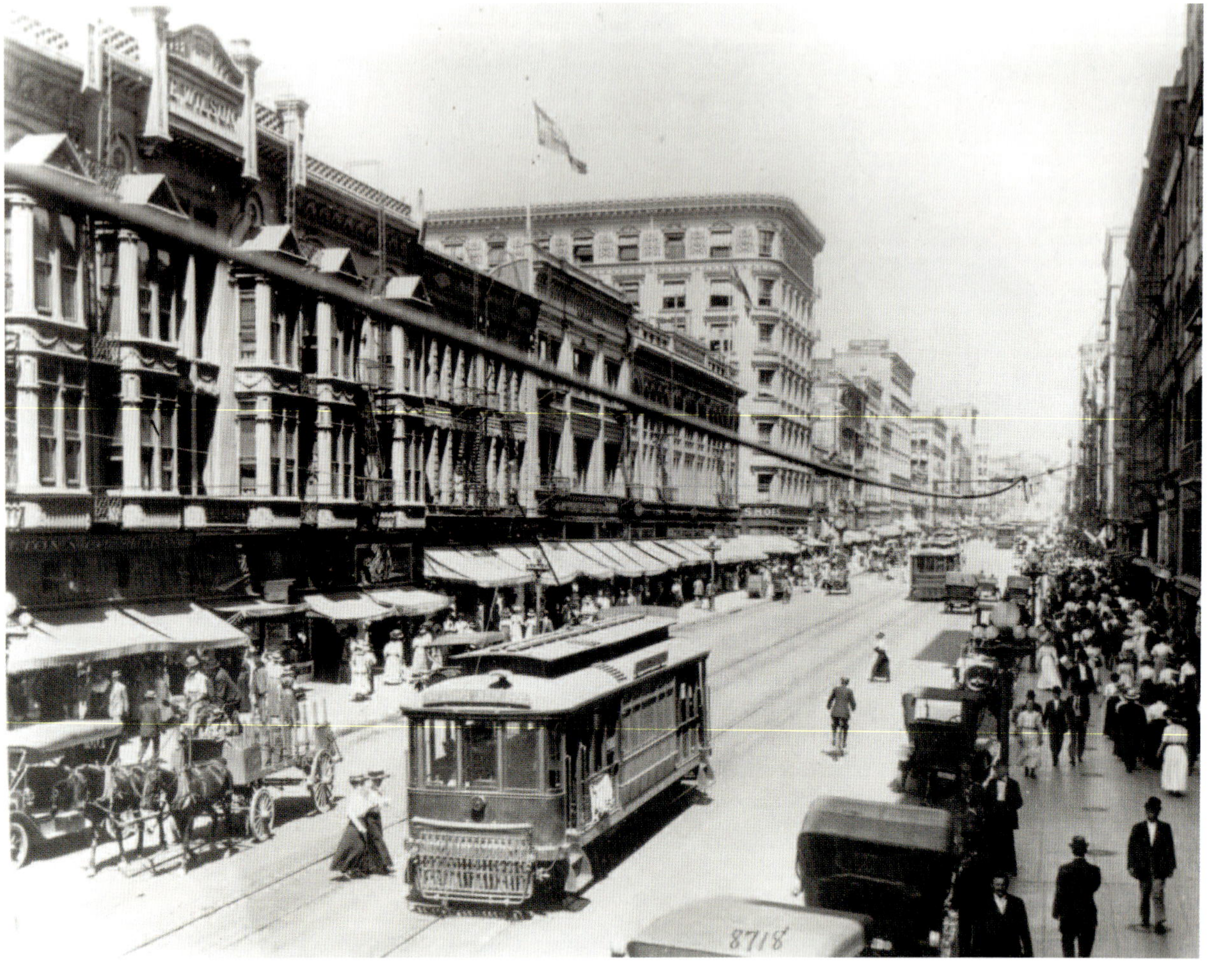

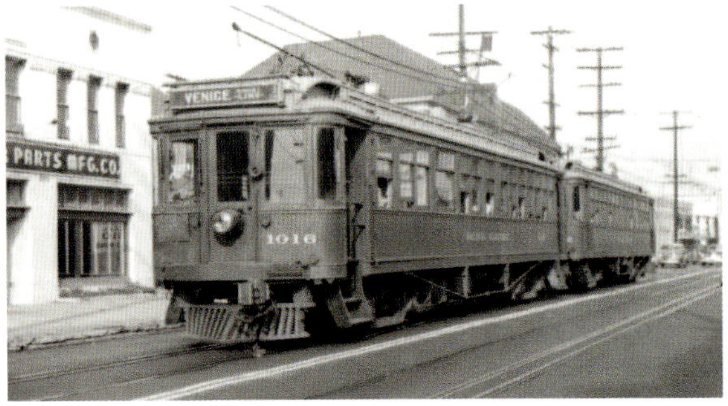

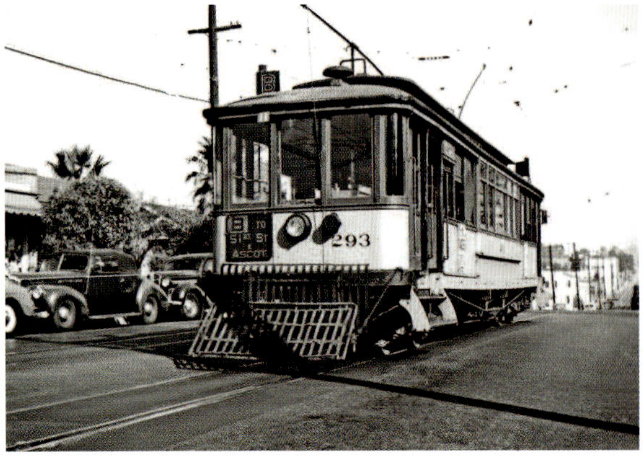

ABOVE *Looking north on Broadway between Fourth and Fifth streets around 1915. The streetcar in the foreground is marked West 11th Street.*

FAR LEFT *A Pacific Electric streetcar on the Venice Short Line photographed by Tom Gray on Venice Boulevard around 1950.*

LEFT *A Los Angeles Transit Lines streetcar photographed by Alan Weeks in 1948 at Evergreen and Brooklyn Avenue.*

OPPOSITE PAGE *A trolley of the Los Angeles Railway Company sometime between 1900 and 1910.*

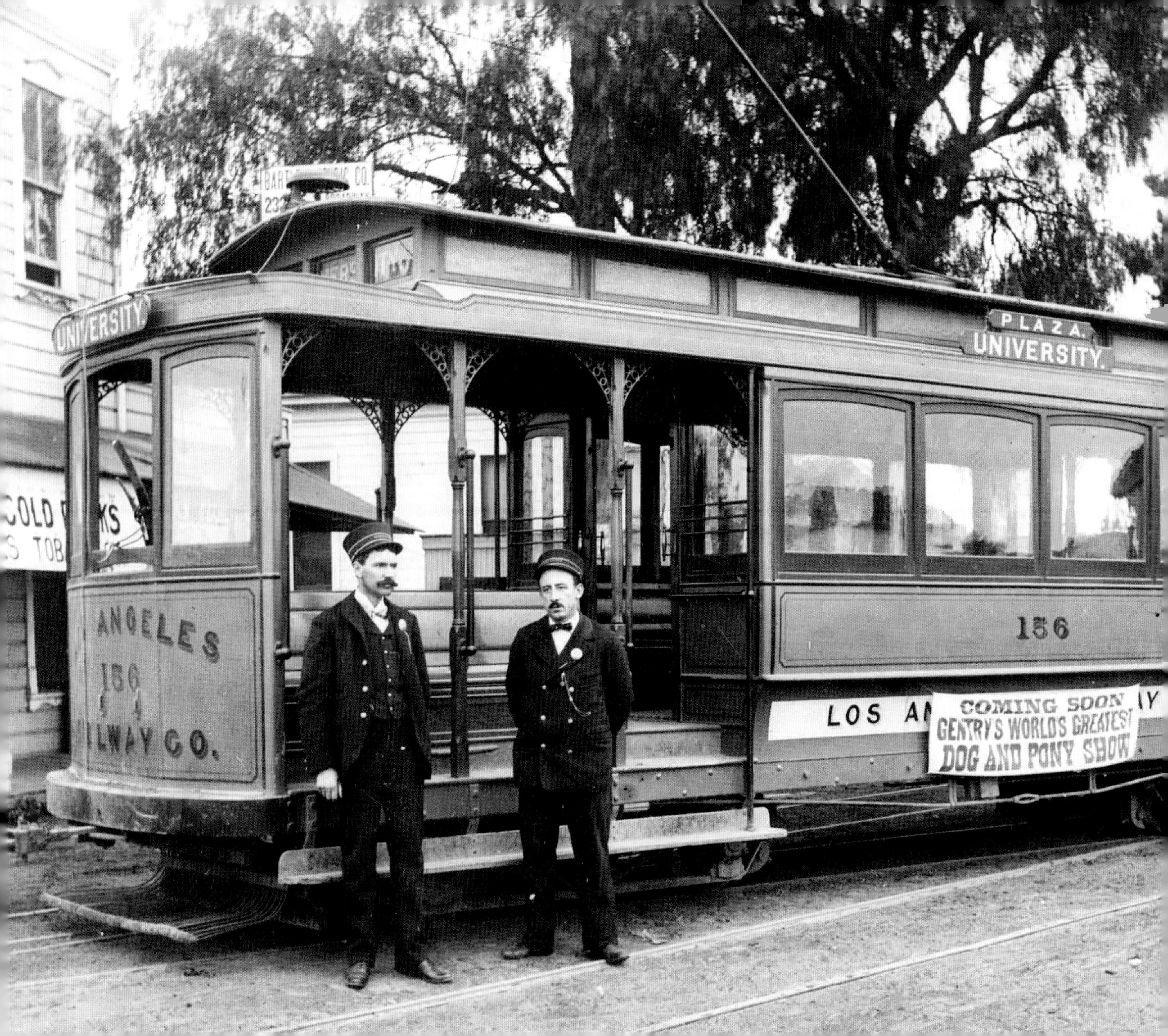
UNIVERSITY.
PLAZA.
UNIVERSITY.
COLD
S TOB
ANGELES
156
LWAY CO.
156
LOS AN
COMING SOON
GENTRY'S WORLDS GREATEST
DOG AND PONY SHOW

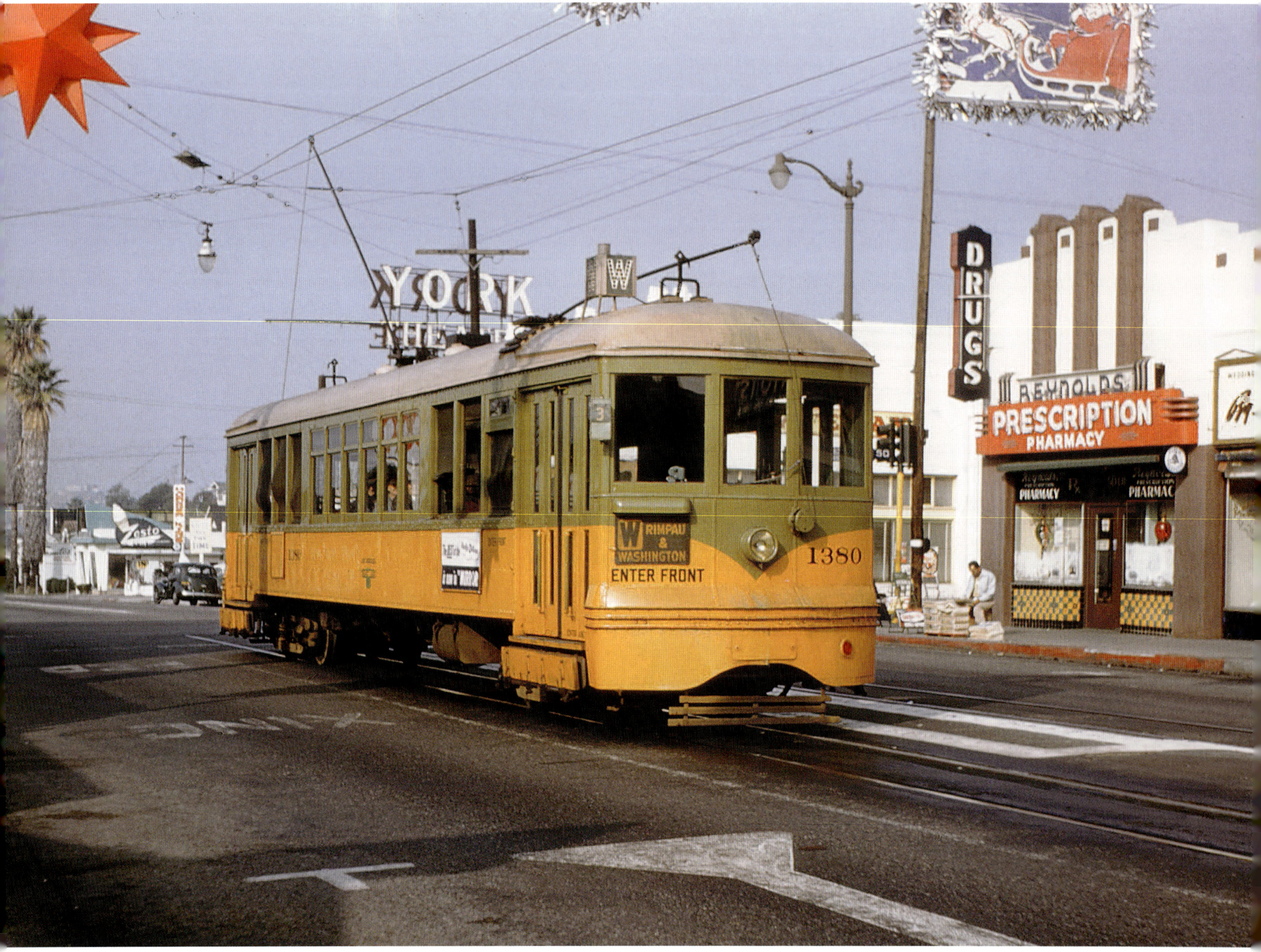
YORK
DRUGS
REYNOLDS
PRESCRIPTION
PHARMACY
W
RIMPAU
&
WASHINGTON
ENTER FRONT
1380
Zesto

By 1933, buses were running in place of some of the Red Cars and Yellow Cars. People driving automobiles instead of riding the streetcars put a dent in business. Decline in ridership worsened in the 1940s and 1950s.

In 1945, E. Roy Fitzgerald's National City Lines purchased the Los Angeles Railway from the Huntington estate. Fitzgerald renamed his acquisition the Los Angeles Transit Lines. He and his brothers played a key role in substituting buses for streetcars not just in Los Angeles, but in countless other cities in the United States. Many accused Fitzgerald of acting as a front man for General Motors in a conspiracy to rid the United States of streetcars and substitute buses in their stead.

The Los Angeles Metropolitan Transit Authority acquired Los Angeles Transit Lines in 1958. Five years later streetcars stopped running in Los Angeles. The last car trundled through the city on March 31, 1963, sporting a weeping face with "Goodbye, forever, old sweethearts and pals!" (lyrics from Buddy Clark's popular song "That Old Gang of Mine") emblazoned on its side.

Today, Los Angeles boasts a modern rail system that includes the Metro Blue Line, Red Line and Green Line. Aficionados have also resurrected the Pacific Electric Red Car Trolley at the Port of Los Angeles.

Streetcar lovers have been laboring to bring that mode of transportation back to downtown Los Angeles. So far the plan remains on the drawing boards with supporters predicting a comeback in 2019.

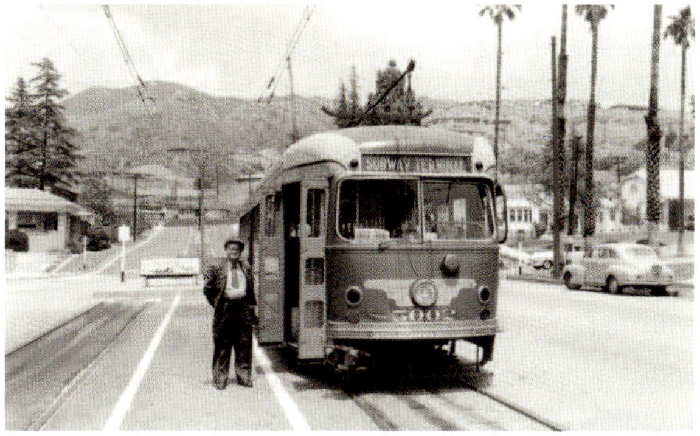

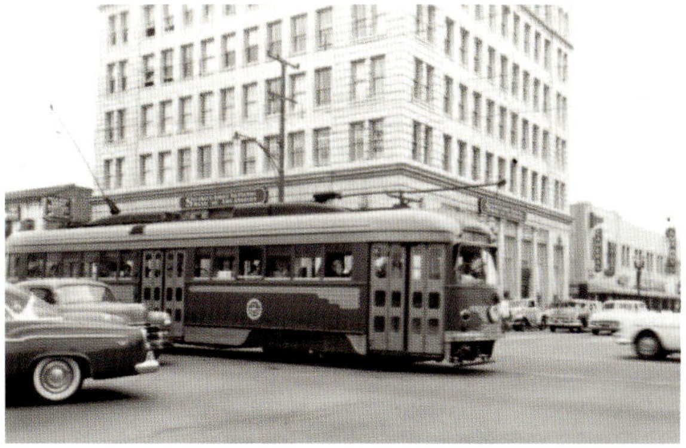

ABOVE RIGHT *A Metropolitan Coach Lines car on the Glendale-Burbank line at Mountain Avenue, 1955.*

RIGHT *Another Metropolitan Coach Lines streetcar, this time at Brand Boulevard and Broadway around 1950.*

BELOW *Los Angeles Transit Lines' LATL 1265 stops for a pedestrian on Market Street in 1954.*

OPPOSITE PAGE *A memory-evoking photo by Alan Weeks of a W Line streetcar on York Boulevard around Christmas 1954. The W was run by Los Angeles Transit Lines.*

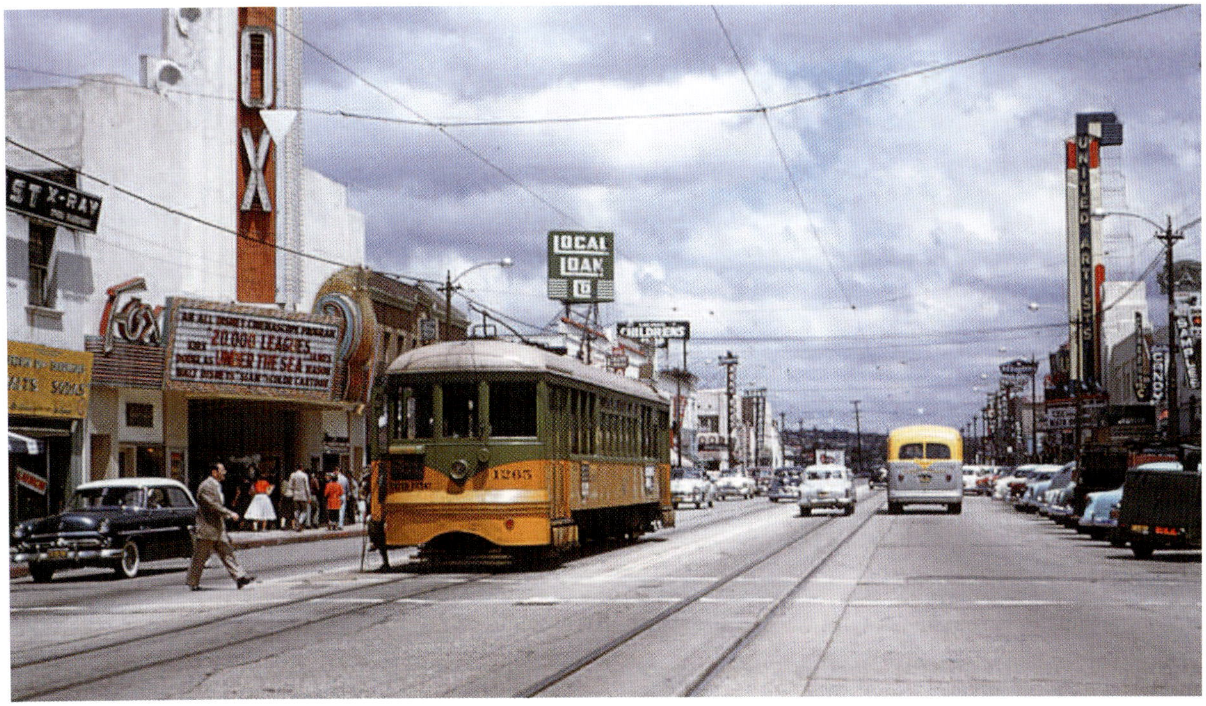

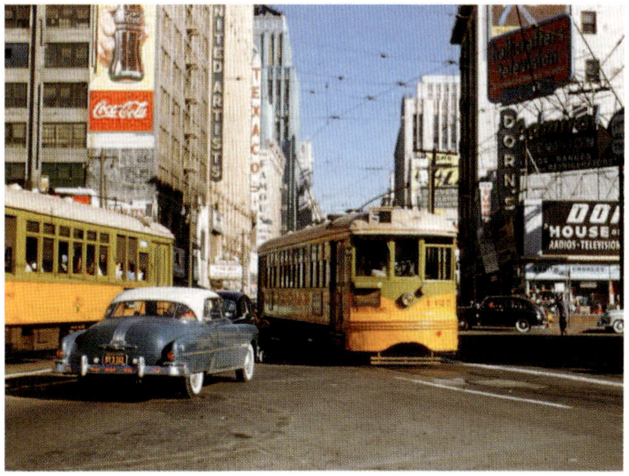

ABOVE *Another LATL streetcar, this time from Line 5 at 10th and Broadway, in the early 1950s. The Metro Transportation Library and Archive contains many more classic streetcar images from around the city.*

Richfield Building DEMOLISHED 1968

In 1928 the Richfield Oil Company turned to architect Stiles O. Clements to build its signature 12-story headquarters on the corner of Sixth and Flower streets. Clements' firm of Morgan, Walls and Clements chose to clad their creation, known as the Richfield Tower, in black and gold terra cotta tile. This symbolized the "black gold" that was Richfield's business. There was nothing phony in the execution of the architects' vision. Artists used pulverized gold dust, which they put into a transparent glazing solution and applied to the tiles that covered the exterior of the structure.

The architects topped the building with a 130-foot-high tower whose lighting simulated an oil-well gusher, a motif that Richfield used at many of its gas stations. The building's total height of 310 feet defied the city's height limitation for buildings, which was only 150 feet at the time. The city did nothing to enforce its building code, and this building opened the door for companies to go high-rise.

Richfield employees could retreat to an "amusement room," which took up the entire top floor of the building. It included a stage, a kitchen, a cafeteria, barber shops, and a ladies' lounge.

Armenian-born sculptor Haig Patigian fashioned the striking exterior sculptures: the building's guardian angels and the golden allegorical figures representing aviation, postal service, industry, and commerce that stood above the entrance.

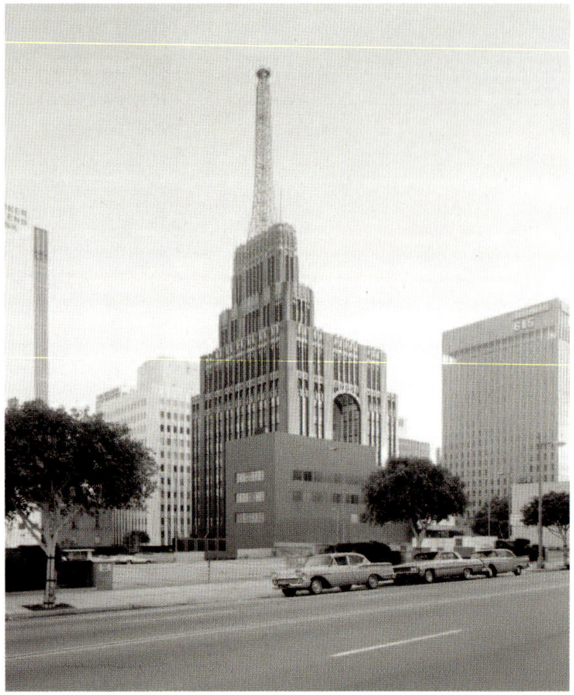

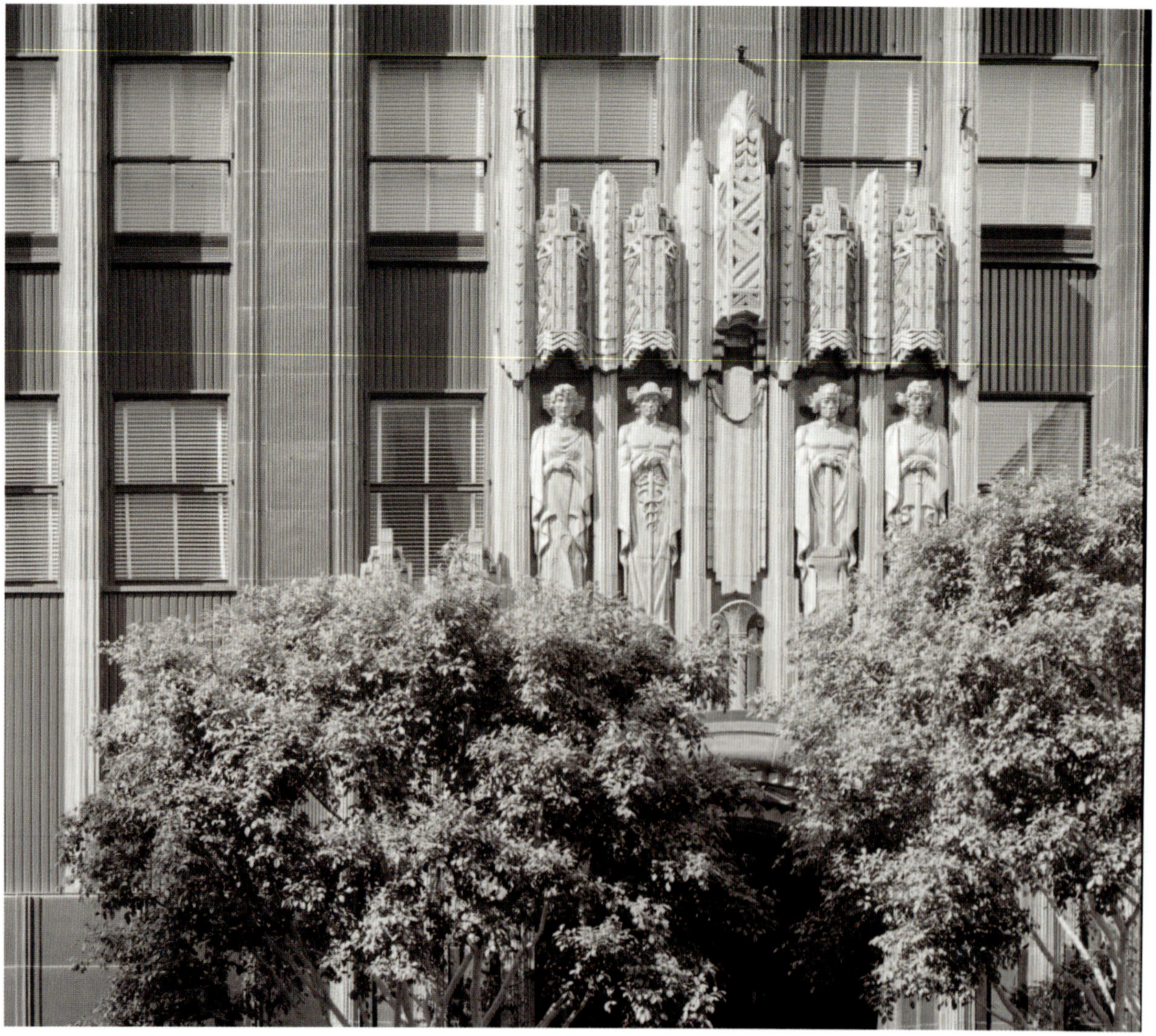

ABOVE *The Richfield Building made a statement both night and day. Each evening the lights on the building's 125-foot-tall tower put on a show that imitated one of the company's oil gushers.*

RIGHT *Golden allegorical figures representing aviation, postal service, industry and commerce stood above the entrance.*

OPPOSITE PAGE *The Richfield Building was best viewed from distance. This photograph was taken looking west near the intersection of West Sixth Street and South Hope Street. The building was shaped like the letter "U." The base of the letter faced Flower Street.*

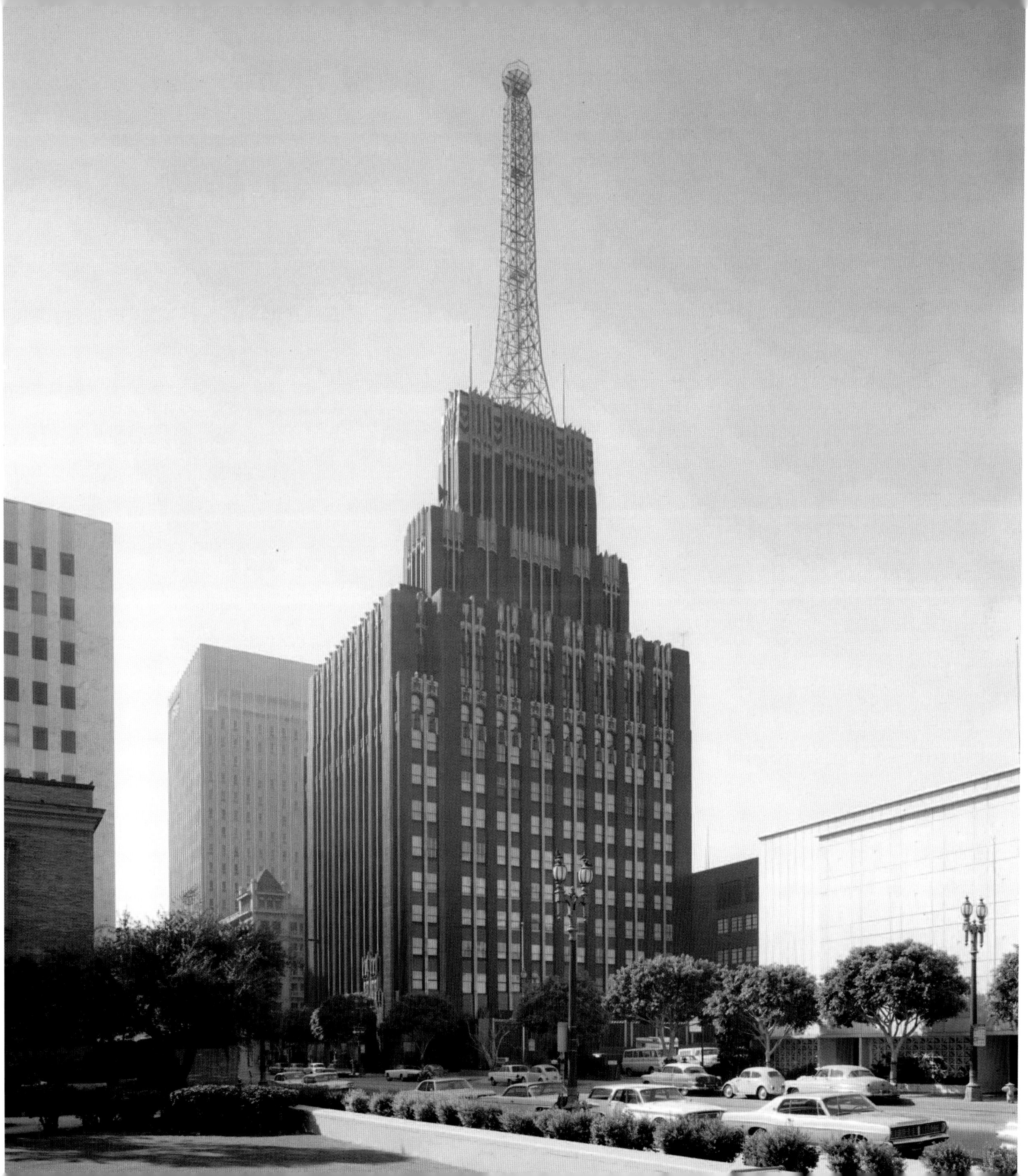

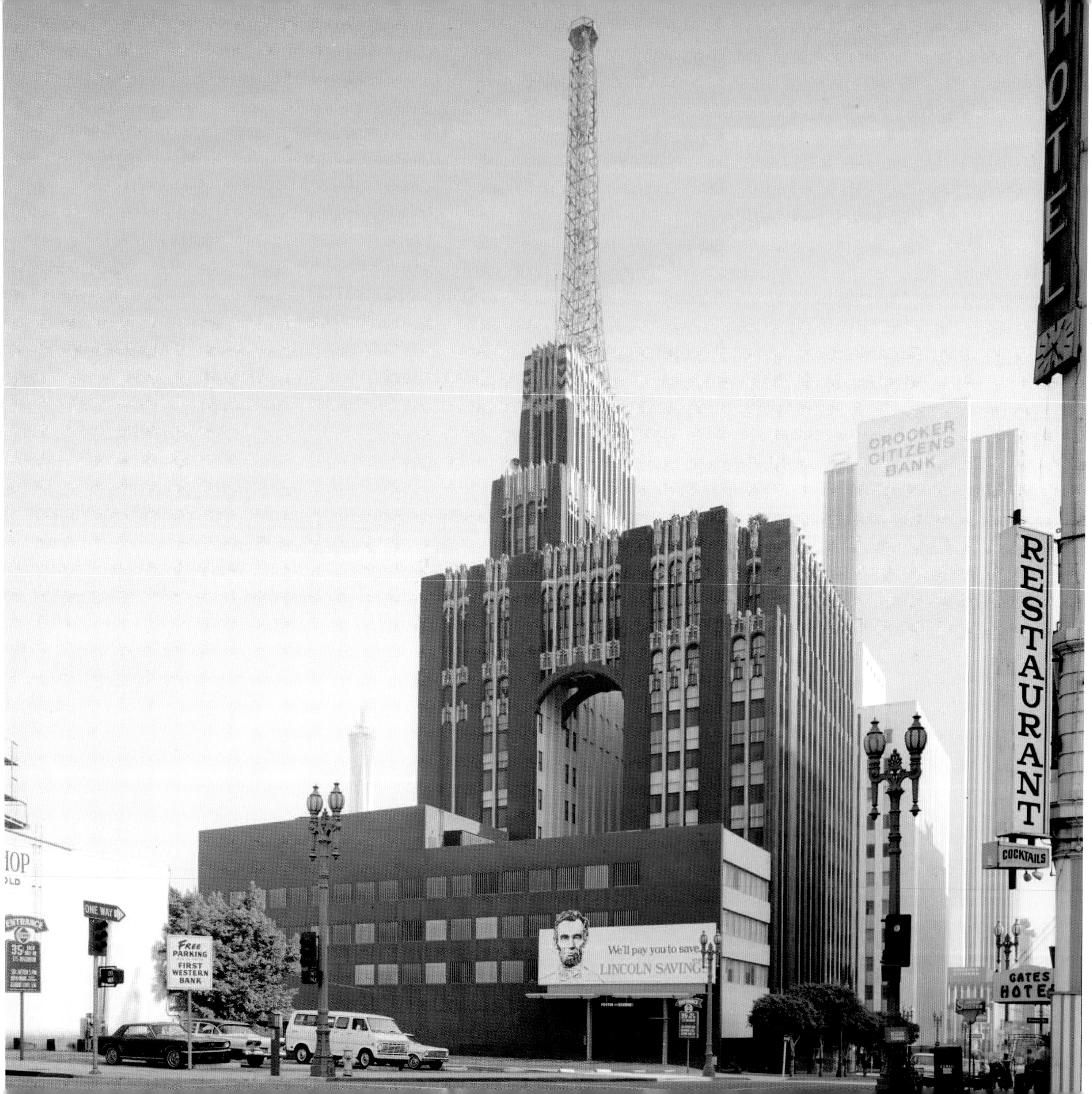
HOTEL
CROCKER CITIZENS BANK
RESTAURANT
COCKTAILS
ONE WAY
ENTRANCE
FREE PARKING
FIRST WESTERN BANK
We'll pay you to save.
LINCOLN SAVING
GATES
HOTE

The Library of Congress called the building "one of the best examples of the 1920s to exuberantly integrate the arts into architecture in a style combining Cubism, applied art and exterior color." Clements later told his friends that the Richfield Building was his favorite project; quite a statement from a man whose firm designed more than sixty buildings including the El Capitan Theatre, Mayan Theatre, KEHE Radio Building and Coulter's Department Store.

Richfield Oil merged with Atlantic Petroleum to form the Atlantic Richfield Company (ARCO) in 1966. The new company viewed the old Richfield headquarters as more of a quaint architectural relic than the HQ for a striving new oil company. Three years after the merger, the new company had the building demolished to make way for the present ARCO Plaza high-rise complex.

Demolition began on November 12, 1968, with wrecking crews stripping out the interior, which continued for several months into 1969. However not all the classic art deco pieces were lost. The 2,500-pound golden angels that adorned the building were sold off at $100 apiece and the company kept hold of the elevator doors.

The Richfield Building was the largest of a number of buildings demolished to make way for the 52-story Atlantic Richfield Plaza, they were all sited on a parcel of land bounded by Fifth Street, Sixth Street, Flower Street and Figueroa Street. A four-story annex to the Richfield building, a small IBM building, an apartment building, Dawson's Bookstore, a car rental agency, and the 11-story Douglas Oil Building all met the wrecking ball so ARCO could build its complex.

ARCO moved out of the buildings in 1999, saying it was too expensive to stay there. City National Bank and Paul Hastings Bank now own the plaza with its twin 669-foot-tall buildings. The complex currently bears the name City National Plaza with one building called City National Tower and the other, Paul Hastings Tower.

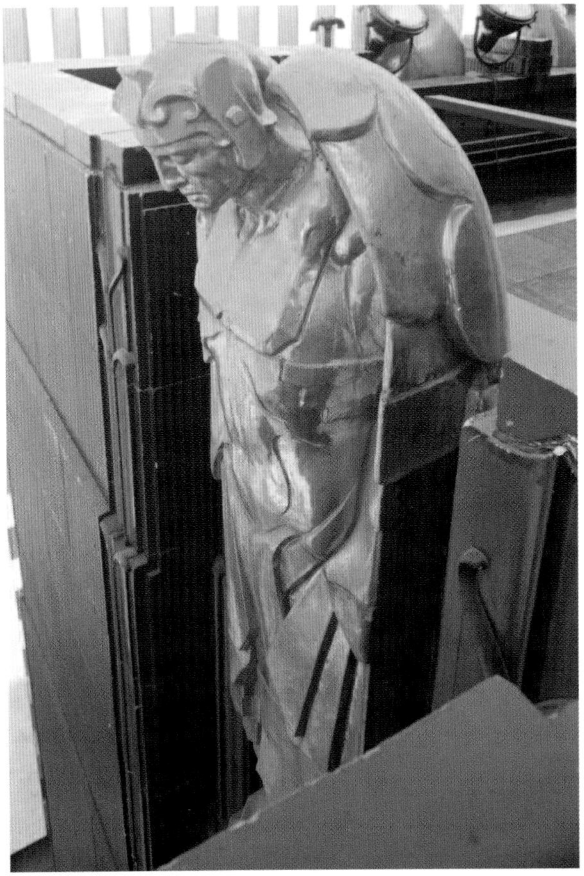

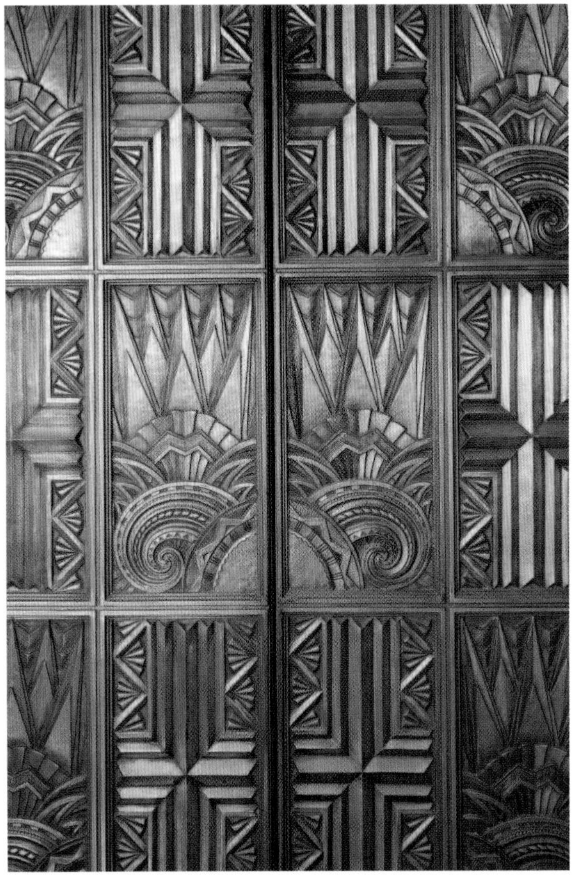

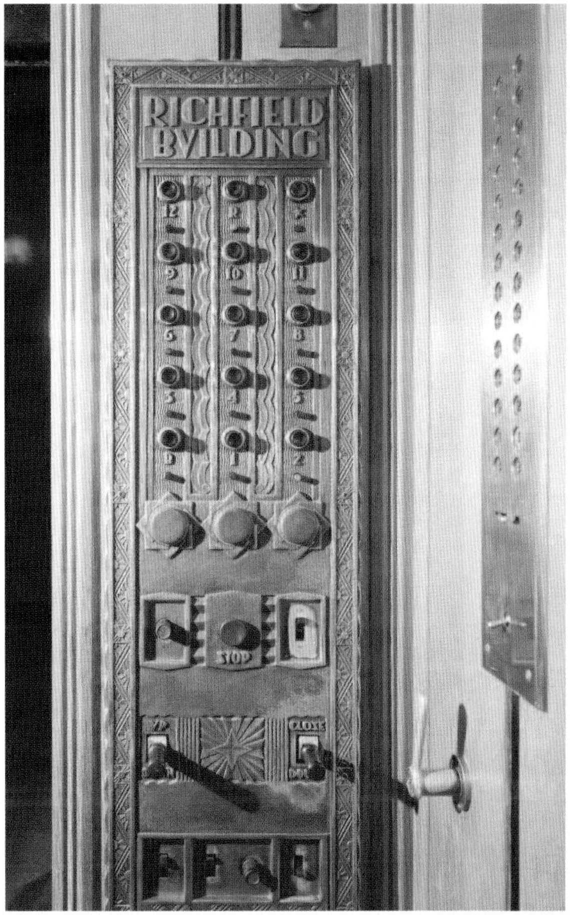

FAR LEFT *One of the 40 golden angels that adorned the Richfield Building looks out onto Los Angeles. When the building was demolished in 1968, the wrecking company offered these monumental works for sale for $100, including two that the wrecker had decapitated. Haig Patigian designed the 2,500-pound angels that were cast and kiln-fired at Gladding, McBean, the same company that produced the tiles that covered the building.*

LEFT *The elevator doors with their art deco design so impressed the new owners of the Atlantic Richfield Company that they salvaged the door panels and used them in the new building.*

ABOVE *This floor selector inside one of the Richfield Building elevators bore the building's name in a classic art deco design.*

OPPOSITE PAGE *The view looking east from West Sixth Street and South Figueroa Street revealed the arch that reached from the third to the eighth floor. The architects added this arch to allow light into the building's central courtyard.*

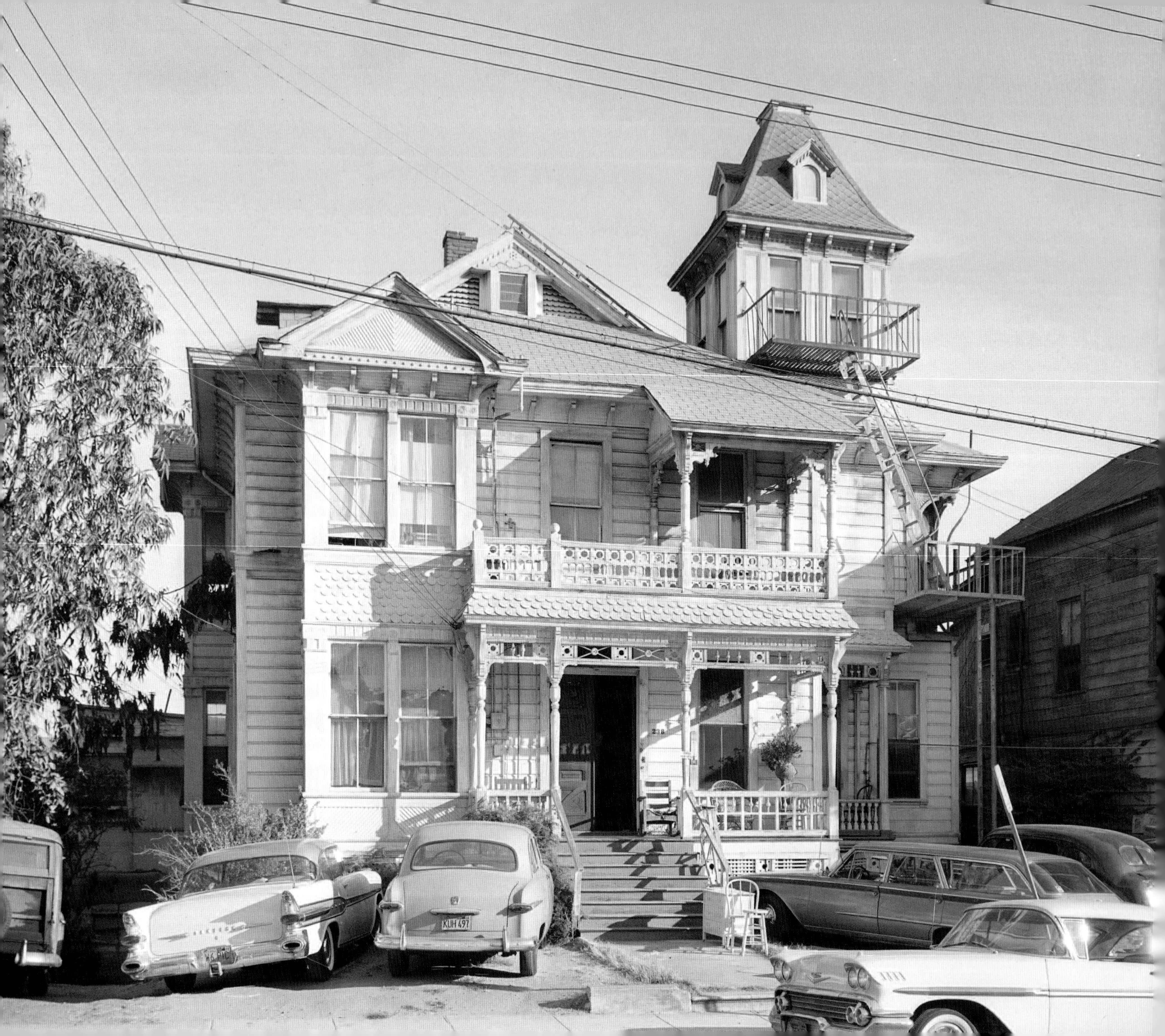
KUH 497

Bunker Hill REDEVELOPED BY 1969

At first Bunker Hill stood above the pueblo as an unnamed, undeveloped promontory. "How Bunker Hill came by its name is somewhat of a mystery," writes Brent C. Dickerson. He thinks that the bunker might relate to nearby Fort Moore. Edward Ord's August 29, 1849, *Plan de la Ciudad de los Angeles* has the name "Bunker Hill" on a spot just west of the intersection of today's First and North Hill streets.

Another tale credits Canadian Prudent Beaudry with naming the hill, but this story can't be reconciled with the fact that Beaudry appeared on the scene in 1867, 18 years after "Bunker Hill" appeared on Ord's map. With an eye on development, Beaudry purchased about 20 acres on and around Bunker Hill at a cost of $517, or $25.85 an acre.

He could do little to develop the property, however, because it had no source or connection to water. He turned to the Los Angeles Water Company for help and was turned down. While undertaking this project Beaudry entered Los Angeles politics. He became the mayor of Los Angeles in 1874.

It took Beaudry until 1875 to build a reservoir that could deliver water to the hill and put a system of roads in place. He was finally able to sell lots and recoup the $95,000 he had invested to improve the barren hill. He promised it would not take long for Bunker Hill to receive the attention it deserved. He was right. By the time he passed away in 1893 the hill had become one of Los Angeles' most fashionable neighborhoods and home to the city's professional elite.

By the time the 20th century had dawned, apartment houses and commercial buildings had begun crowding out the Victorian-era mansions. In 1901, J. W. Eddy opened his Angels Flight funicular that carried riders up Bunker Hill. That same year the Third Street Tunnel began routing streetcars around the hill that some folks downtown now saw as an impediment. In 1928 there was serious talk of removing the hill entirely. The City Council would not go along with the idea and Prudent Beaudry's creation was saved, for now.

The wealthy moved away and Bunker Hill became first a haven for the middle class, then a place for immigrants to find affordable housing. After World War II the neighborhood developed a reputation as a crime-ridden place to avoid. In 1948, the city created the Community Redevelopment Agency, which compiled enough crime data and other information that the city said "proved" that Bunker Hill was a blighted neighborhood. The city adopted the Bunker Hill Urban Renewal Project in 1959, and by 1969 the neighborhood was gone.

OPPOSITE PAGE *In 1878, Judge Julius Brousseau built this home at 238 South Bunker Hill. In 1956, the run-down home was featured in the film* Bus Stop *as the house across the street from Marilyn Monroe's Phoenix apartment. In 1966 it was back on the silver screen when Los Angeles Police Department detectives Glenn Ford and Ricardo Montalban staked it out in* The Money Trap. *As soon the film-makers were gone, the bulldozers moved in.*

FAR LEFT *This small Queen Anne-style cottage represented the second wave of development on Bunker Hill. Wealthy families, like the Crockers, were the first to build here. Like other homes in the neighborhood, this one fell victim to the Bunker Hill Urban Renewal Project in the mid-1960s.*

BELOW LEFT *This home once stood at 245 South Grand Avenue. South Grand Avenue is now just one block from Interstate 101 in an entirely commercial area. Only one home in this neighborhood survived the demolition.*

BELOW *In October 1960 the Historic American Building Survey sent photographer Jack Boucher to photograph "typical houses on Bunker Hill." He photographed homes in an area bounded by Temple, Hill, South Fifth and Figueroa streets. When he photographed these homes, he simply identified them as a row of houses in the Bunker Hill neighborhood.*

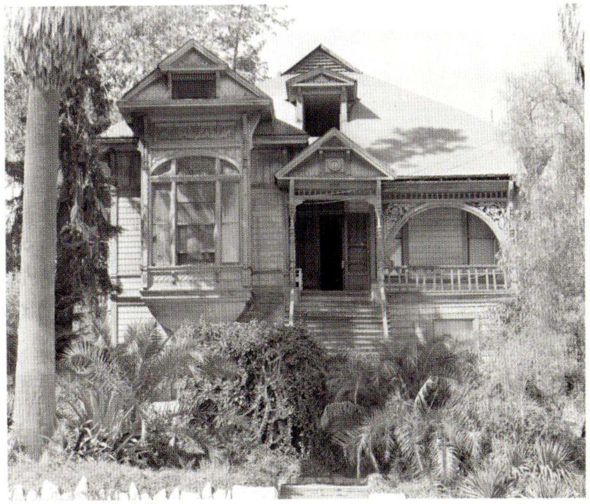

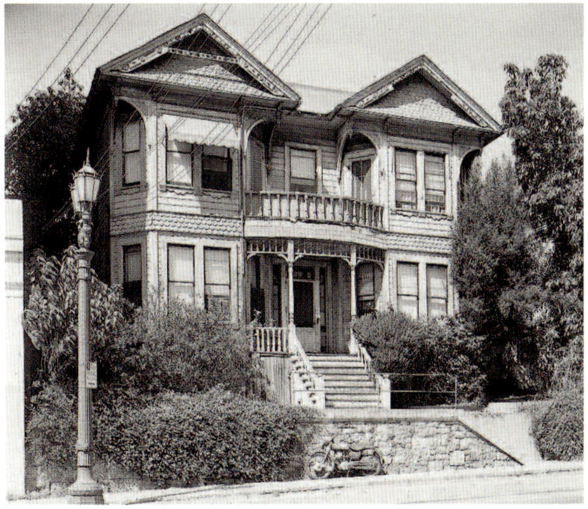

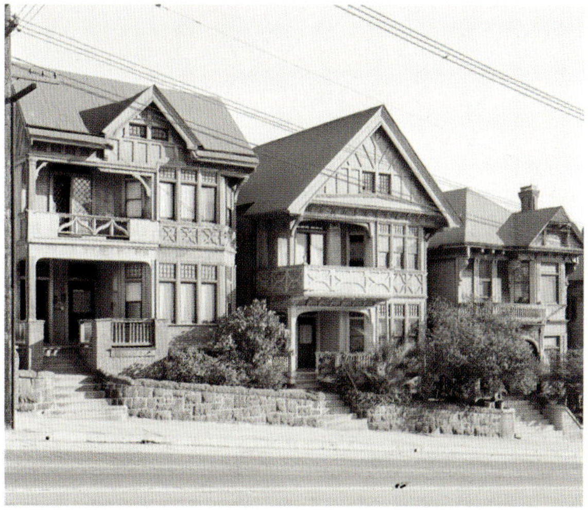

Helms Bakery COMPANY CLOSED 1969

If ever commerce could be charming, it had to be during the days of the milkman, the ice man and the Helms Bakery man. Most suburbanites living in Los Angeles in the 1950s or 1960s would be familiar with the blue-and-yellow bakery trucks that plied city streets delivering fresh bread and pastries until the rise of the supermarkets in the 1960s. Never sold in stores, the Helms brand came to be known for its delivery service and also its service to American athleticism.

Opening in 1931, the bakery was the product of New York expatriate Paul Helms, who began his baking career in 1914 after turning his back on an insurance career. By 1926 his East Coast bakery had expanded to 200 delivery routes, but health troubles forced the 36-year-old to seek out a more suitable climate. Helms and his family moved to Southern California in 1928. His health apparently improved, since three years after moving, he opened his first bakery at Washington and Venice boulevards in Culver City with 32 employees and 11 delivery trucks.

Within a year, Helms landed an incredibly valuable contract for a nascent business: the 1932 Summer Olympics. Taking the slogan "Olympic Games Bakers – Choice of Olympic Champions" the bakery continued supplying the U.S. team as it traveled to London and Helsinki in later years. Soon the Olympic symbol appeared as part of the company logo on bakery vehicles, wrappers and signage on the bakery itself.

In the days before the freeway, Helms trucks ventured out as far as the San Gabriel Valley, an hour or more in each direction. Helms drivers blew a distinctive whistle when they arrived at customers' residences identified with a blue "H" sign in the

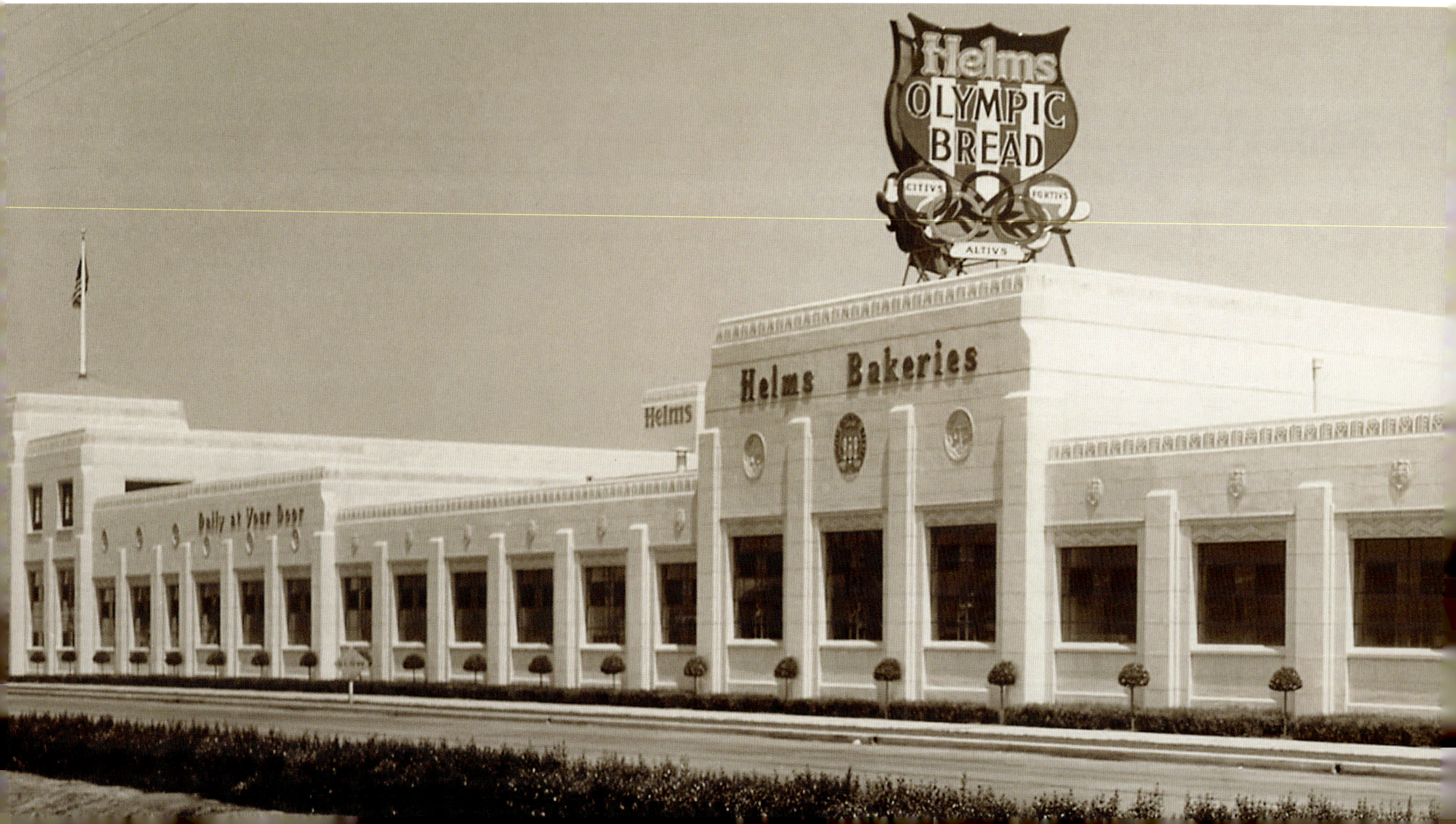

window. This fulfilled the principal slogan of the company: "Daily at your door."

After Paul Helms passed away in 1957, his family continued operating the business, expanding as far as Fresno, San Bernardino and San Diego. Just prior to closing in 1969, the company furnished "the first bread on the moon" for the Apollo 11 landing.

The Helms Bakery delivery model couldn't compete with the more economic model of simply delivering to a grocery store and the company ceased to operate. The grand art deco former bakery in Culver City became a series of commercial operations including restaurants, galleries and even the Helms Bakery Museum, a museum to sports memorabilia originally sponsored by the company back in 1939.

The building still sports the company's original neon sign, and a heroic statue of a seagoing "helmsman" that once graced the front of the bakery now stands in Burton W. Chace Park in Marina Del Rey. In 2003, the Helms Bakery neon sign was restored and rewired to run off solar panels.

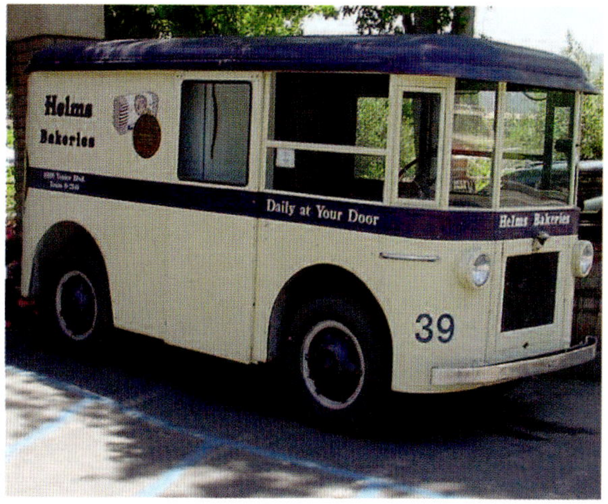

RIGHT *The distinctive blue and yellow design of the Helms delivery van.*

BELOW *Though the bakery is long gone, the elegant art deco building now functions as a museum.*

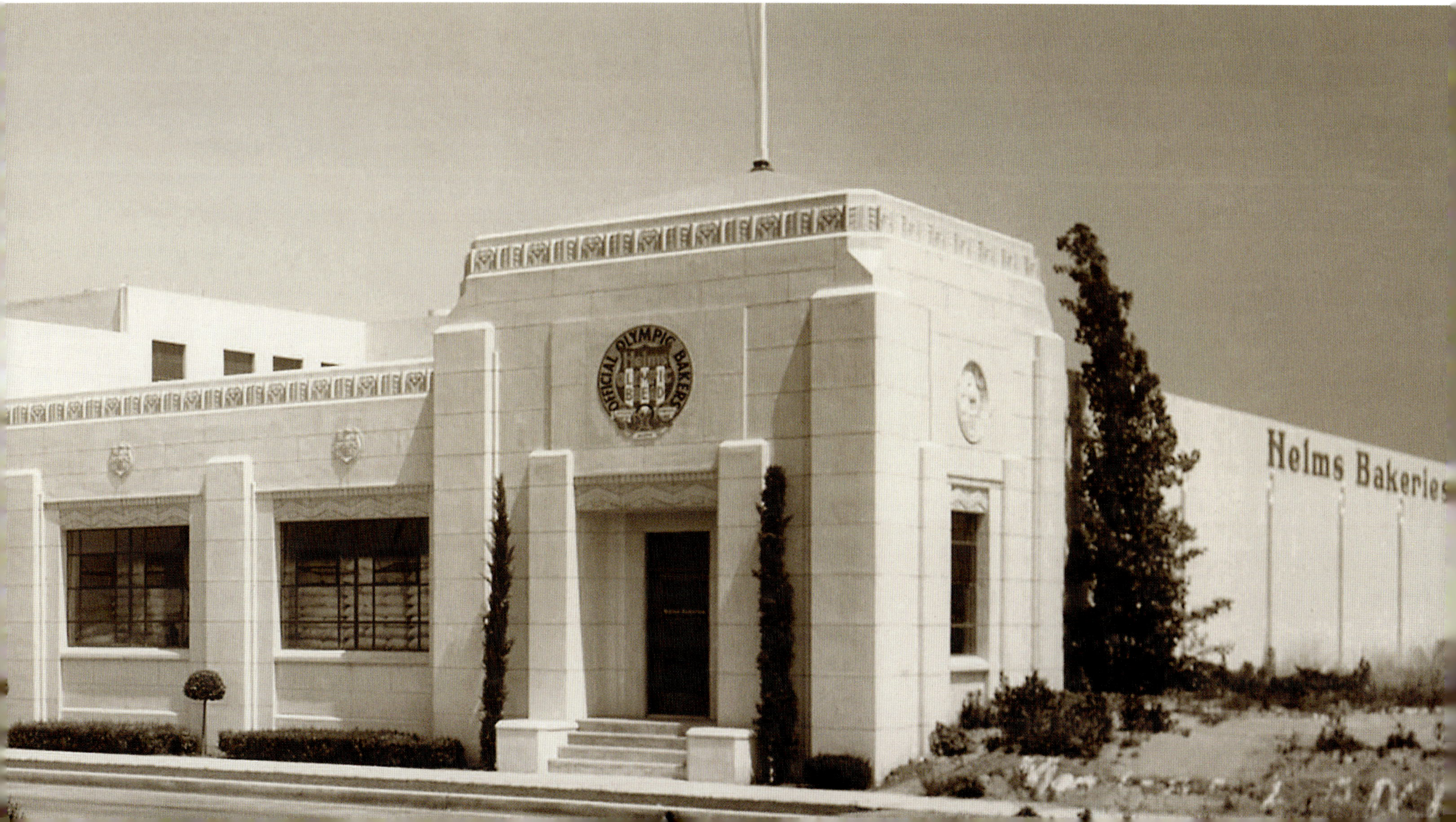

Original Angels Flight MOVED 1969

In 1901, J. W. Eddy built the Los Angeles Incline Railway at Third and Hill Streets to connect downtown with the upper-class residential area of Bunker Hill. Soon renamed Angels Flight and dubbed "the world's shortest railroad," its two counterbalancing white cars, Sinai and Olivet (named after biblical mountains), descended and ascended the hill for one penny each way until 1953, when the price was raised to a nickel for a round-trip. The archway was added in 1908, and in 1930 the cars were painted orange and black. By the 1960s, Bunker Hill had become rundown and was replaced with office buildings and a senior citizens' housing complex. Angels Flight ran for its final time at Third and Hill Street on May 18, 1969 and was dismantled and stored. Thirty years later, in 1996, the new Angels Flight was installed at a new location, half a block south of the original incline. At twenty-five cents a ride, the funicular was highly popular until a fatal accident occurred in February 2001 and it was closed for repair. Angels Flight reopened in 2010 at 50 cents a ride and has been running safely ever since.

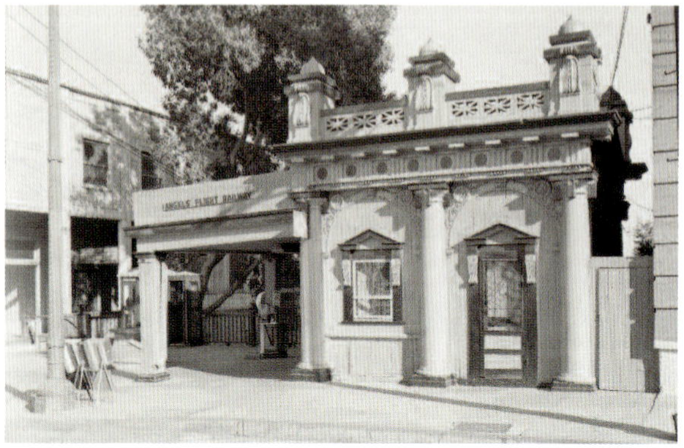

ABOVE *The original upper station photographed in 1960.*

BELOW *Angels Flight as it looked in 1910.*

OPPOSITE PAGE *Angels Flight before the extensive redevelopment of Bunker Hill in the mid-1960s, photographed by Jack Boucher in 1960.*

BELOW RIGHT *A striking contrast is presented in this late 1960s photo of the Flight with all the neighboring Victorian and early 20th-century buildings removed.*

ANGELS FLIGHT CREATOR

Colonel James Ward Eddy lived a full life. He was born on May 30, 1832, in Java, New York. He moved to Illinois in 1853, where he studied law and was admitted to the bar in Chicago in 1855. He knew Abraham Lincoln and worked to help Lincoln win the presidency. He was with Lincoln in Washington when the Civil War broke out in April 1861. He joined Kentucky Senator Cassius M. Clay and Gen. James H. Lane's battalion which was formed to defend the White House during the first month of the war. He returned to Illinois after the war where he served as a as member of the State Legislature. Eddy came west, first to Arizona, where he worked in railroad construction. Eddy, and his wife Isabella, moved to Los Angeles in 1896. Isabella died shortly after they arrived. Eddy married Jane M. Wiswell in 1900. The following year the city granted him a 30-year franchise to operate an inclined railway that he called Angels Flight. The funicular system of two counterbalanced cars traveled up and down parallel tracks and transported passengers up the steep grade on Bunker Hill between Third and Hill streets. The ride lasted one minute and cost one cent. James Ward Eddy died on April 13, 1916, and is buried in the Hollywood Cemetery.

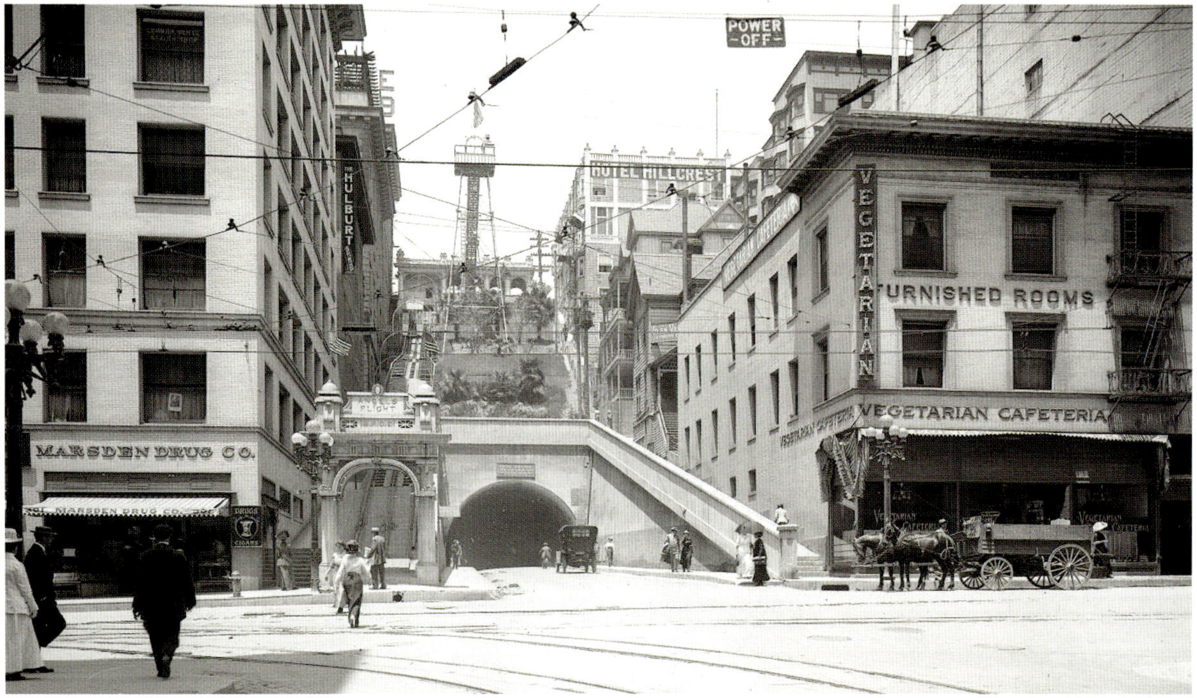

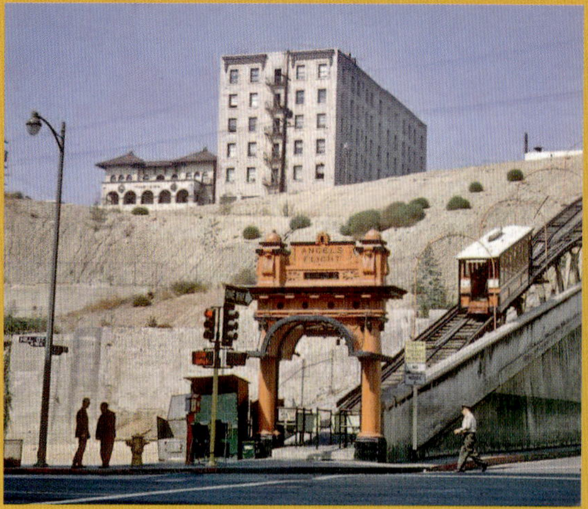

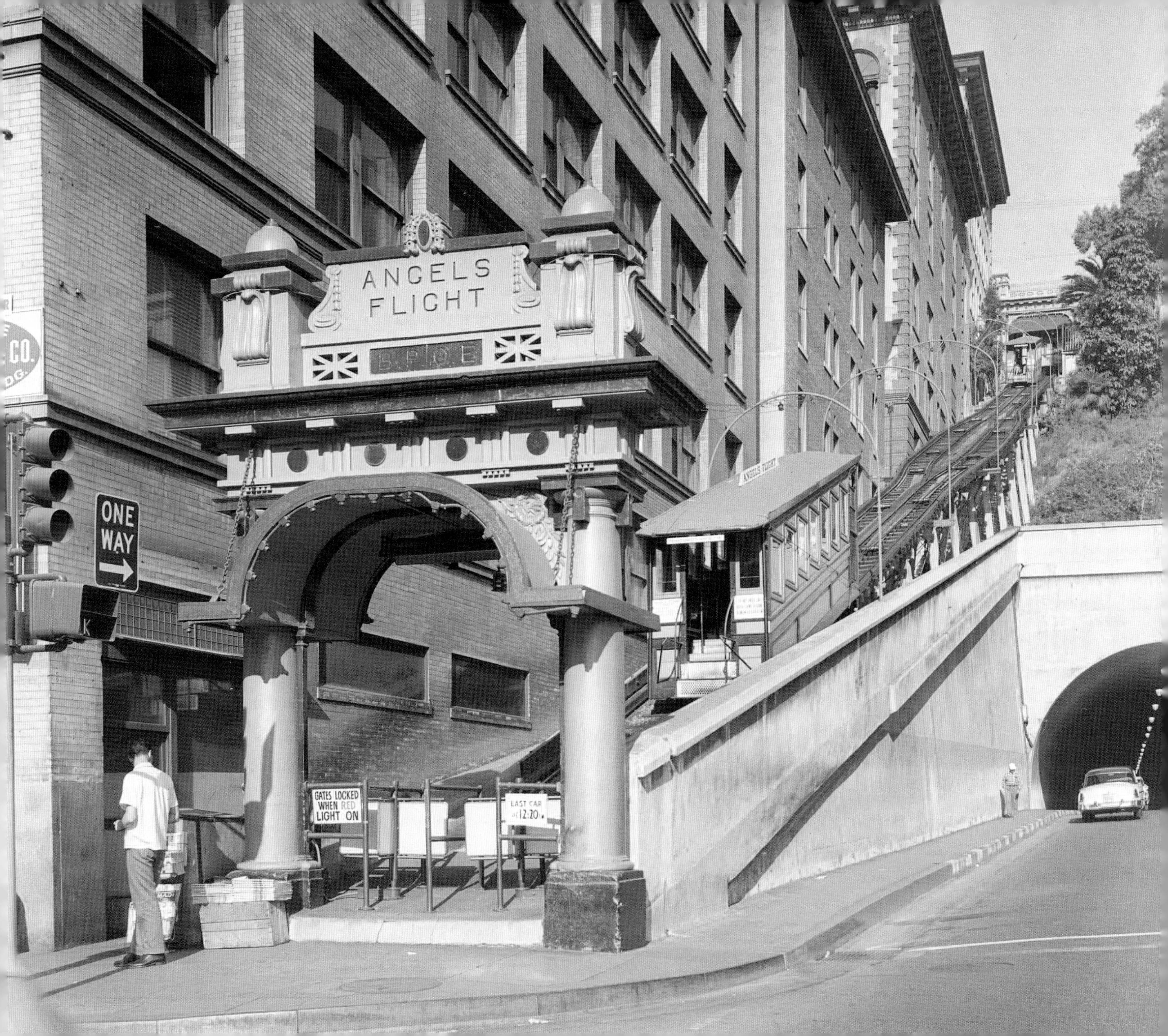
ANGELS
FLIGHT
B.P.O.E
ONE
WAY
ANGELS FLIGHT
GATES LOCKED
WHEN RED
LIGHT ON
LAST CAR
12:20

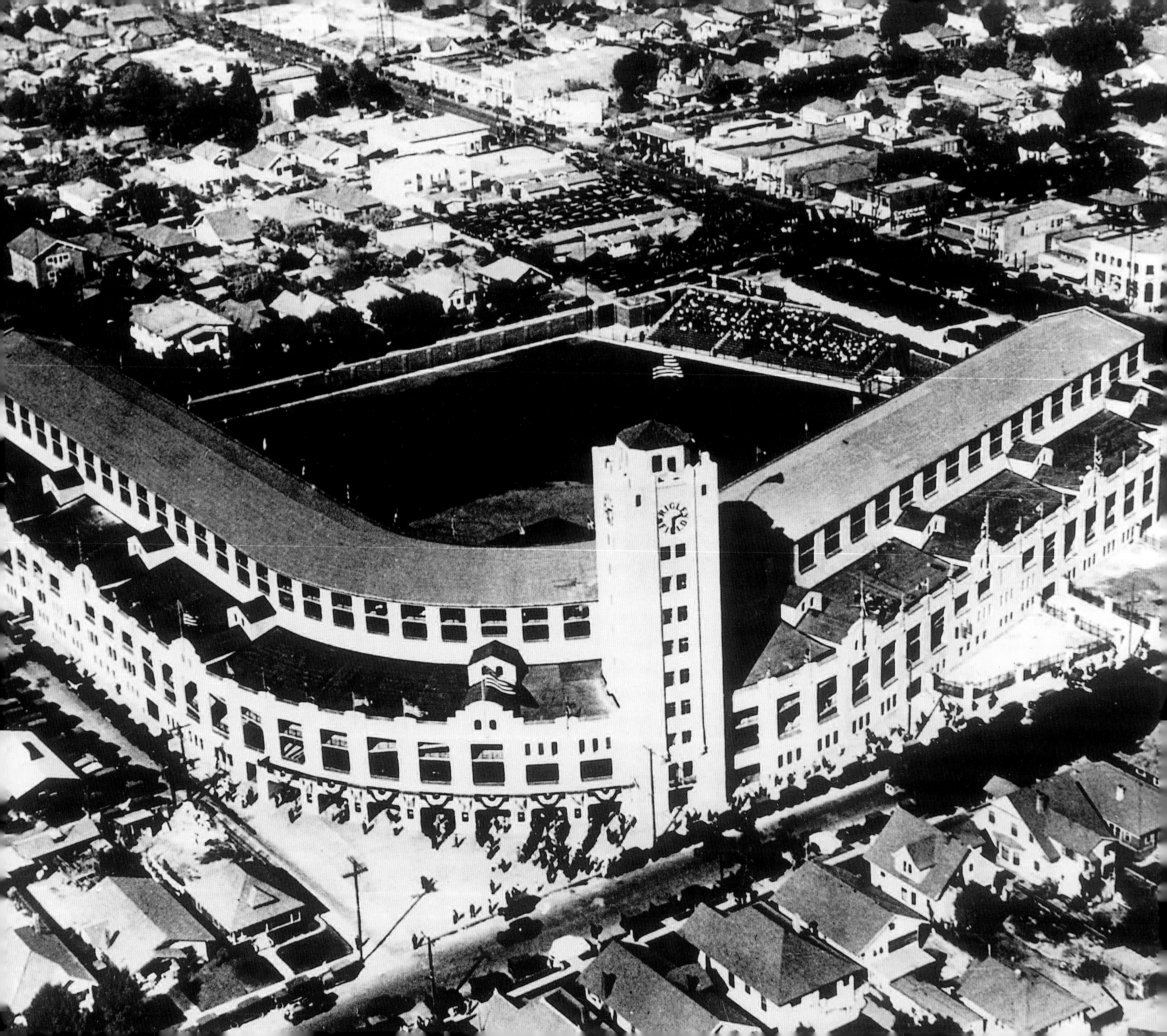

Wrigley Field DEMOLISHED 1969

Few avid Chicago Cubs fans will like to admit their world-renowned Wrigley Field isn't actually the first. Los Angeles can claim the distinction of housing the first Wrigley Field, a minor league park dating to 1925, when the Cubs' Chicago ballpark was still named Cubs Park.

The park's first game on September 29 saw the hometown favorite Los Angeles Angels beat the San Francisco Seals 10-8.

William Wrigley, Jr. the chewing gum magnate owned an incredible portfolio of assets that included both the Angels and the Cubs, most of Santa Catalina Island (a great location for spring training) and commercial ventures from baking powder to clay tiles. Eventually both his baseball teams would play in parks that bore his name.

The Angels moved from their field at Washington Park, which was two blocks west from their original home at Chutes Park. Built in a Spanish style, Los Angeles' Wrigley Field was bounded by Avalon Boulevard, San Pedro, 41st and 42nd streets. The Angels played there for 33 seasons (1925-1957), sharing the park for 11 seasons with the Hollywood Stars, who eventually found their own home at Gilmore Field. The Angels and Stars, while minor league teams, enjoyed quite a bit of success in the Pacific Coast League facing the West Coasts' other up and coming teams.

The field's proximity to Hollywood studios resulted in its appearance in several films. The chosen backdrop for baseball-themed movies, Wrigley Field played a key role in 1927's *Babe Comes Home* featuring Babe Ruth; *The Pride of the Yankees,* written about tragic Yankees' star Lou Gehrig, and classic television shows such as *The Twilight Zone*, *Mannix* and *The Munsters*. Other sporting events held at Wrigley Field over the years included six world-title boxing matches and a U.S. versus England soccer match in 1959.

When the Dodgers moved to Los Angeles from Brooklyn in 1958, the future of Wrigley appeared doubtful. Dodgers owner Walter O'Malley had purchased both the field and the Angels. The park's seating capacity of just 22,000 wouldn't accommodate projected attendance, so instead the Dodgers set up shop at the 93,000-seat Los Angeles Coliseum, bringing their minor league team (the Angels) with them. With the opening of Dodger Stadium in 1961, the Angels began playing there, and Wrigley Field remained without a tenant.

By that time the field belonged to the city of Los Angeles which scheduled various events there, including a civil rights rally featuring Dr. Martin Luther King, Jr. and a few more soccer matches. By 1969 demolition proceeded and Wrigley Field became Gilbert Lindsay Park, a typical city park that features a baseball diamond in the northwest corner of the property. Gilbert Lindsay was a man who began work as a janitor and worked his way up the ranks to become the city's first African-American council member in 1962.

This field, home to Wrigley Little League baseball and softball teams, is still affectionately called Wrigley Field. The site of the original baseball diamond has been converted to the Kedren Community Mental Health Center.

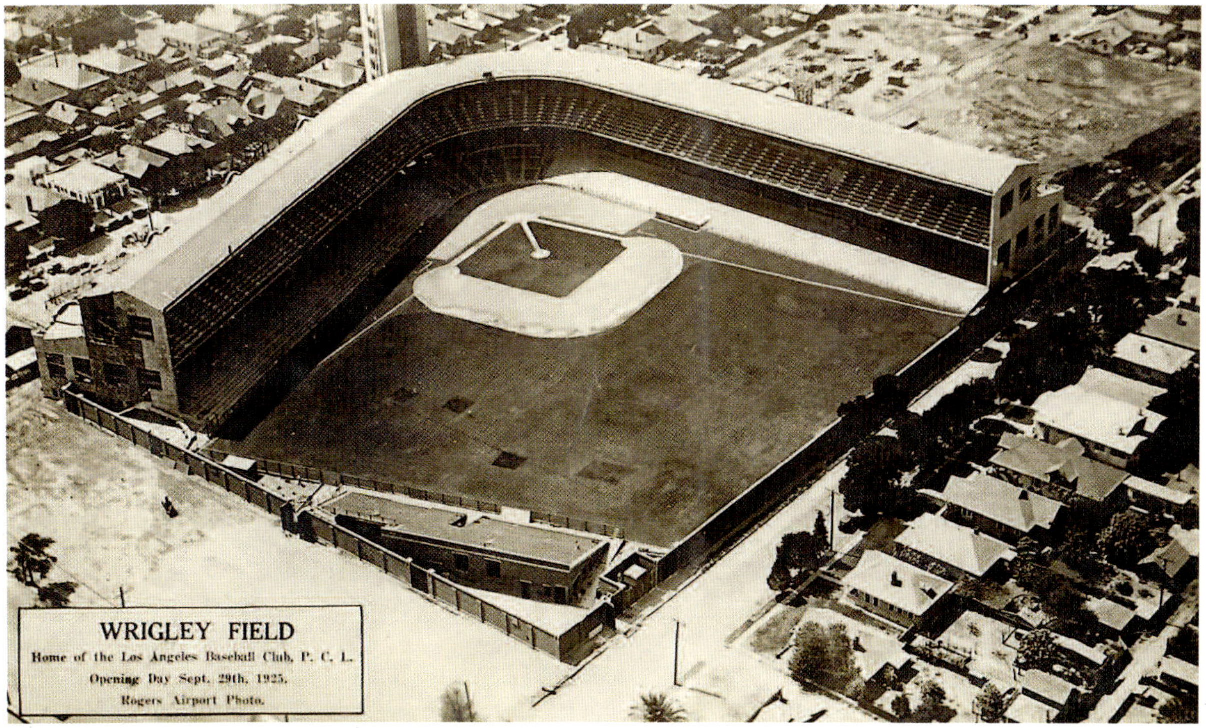

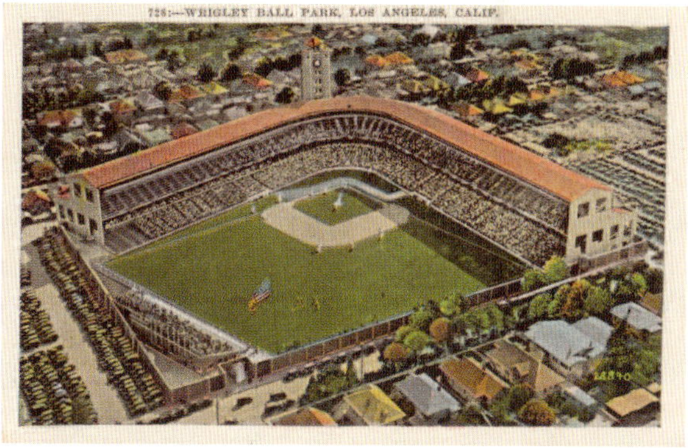

LEFT *This aerial photo of Wrigley Field shows it ready for opening day in 1925.*

ABOVE *A colorized postcard from the 1930s.*

OPPOSITE PAGE *Although the Los Angeles Wrigley Field was the first to take the name, it was designed as a scaled down version of the Chicago stadium, which adopted the name in 1926.*

MGM Back Lots SOLD OFF 1970

Marcus Loewe founded Metro-Goldwyn Pictures in 1924 when he took over and combined Richard Rowland's Metro Picture Corporation and Sam Goldwyn's Goldwyn Pictures Corporation. He brought Louis Mayer in as manager and the following year Loewe added Mayer's name and Metro Goldwyn Mayer was born.

The new company needed a place where they could make their movies and settled on movie producer Thomas Ince's studio in Culver City. Ince built the place in 1915, but soon moved his operations elsewhere. Loewe stepped in and bought up the site in 1924. Under Mayer's management, MGM built six working studios on the 180-acre property.

Shooting began on Lot 2 in 1925 with King Vidor's *The Big Parade*. As more and more films were shot there, the backlots garnered quite a few standing sets. These included "Waterfront Street," where MGM filmed *A Tale of Two Cities* in 1935 and *An American in Paris* in 1951; and "New York City Streets," subsequently immortalized by Gene Kelly in the 1952 film *Singing in the Rain*.

As film production expanded in the 1930s, MGM became a city within a city. Mayer made sure his workers had everything they needed right on site. Makeup could handle 1,200 actors an hour, 12,000 calls per day came into the casting office and the props office handled more than a million items from every country in the world. The MGM music library contained around four million song titles. MGM maintained a 100-man police force among its 4,000 employees.

Mayer could afford to think big. Between 1931 and 1940 MGM banked $93.2 million in profit. During this time, the company accounted for nearly one third of the Academy Award nominations for Best Picture with 27. Five of these films—*The Broadway Melody*, *Grand Hotel*, *Mutiny on the Bounty*, *Gone with the Wind* and *The Great Ziegfeld*—won Academy Awards.

All the glory came crashing down in the 1950s. Despite saving on set-building, the studio hadn't been able to produce many hits. Television had put a dent in movie profits, and by the 1960s the huge lots that had once been the studio's greatest assets presented increased overhead.

The studio's new owner, Kirk Kerkorian, set his sights on other goals (a hotel and casino in Las Vegas) and sold the lots off starting on October 5, 1970.

Hollywood bemoaned the loss of MGM's priceless collection of props sold for pennies in the dollar to save the struggling studio. Actress Debbie Reynolds bought as many of the treasures as she could, hoping to one day open a museum. Many unwanted artifacts were bulldozed into a landfill, including the standing sets. Today, the site of the back lot is tract homes and apartments.

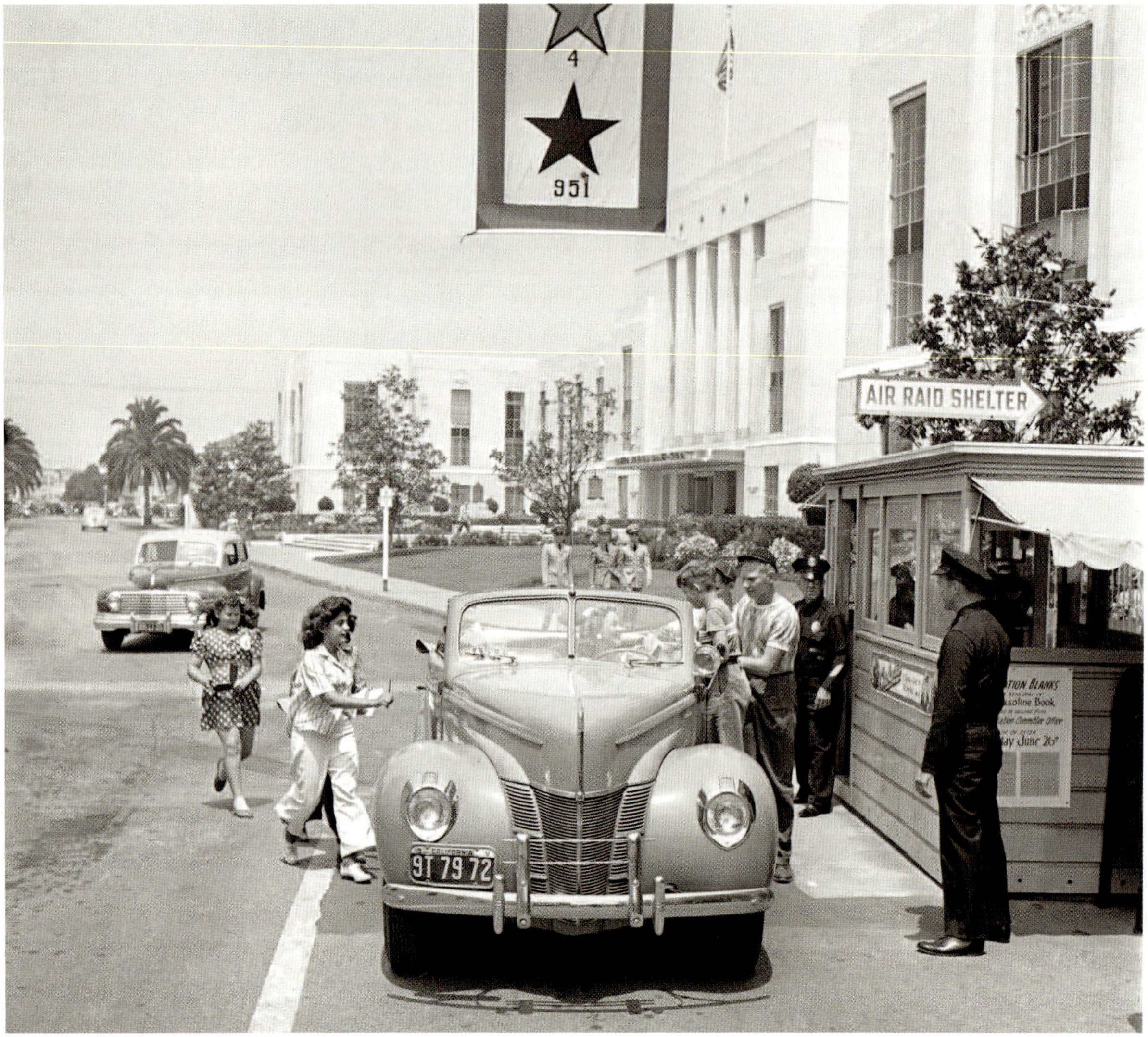

LEFT *This 1943 image shows the MGM entrance gate clogged with fans trying to get an autograph from one of the Wilde Twins (either Lee or Lyn). The air raid shelter sign reflects the nation's wartime readiness, even in Hollywood.*

OPPOSITE PAGE *A circus scene being filmed for the 1925 MGM silent comedy* The Great Love.

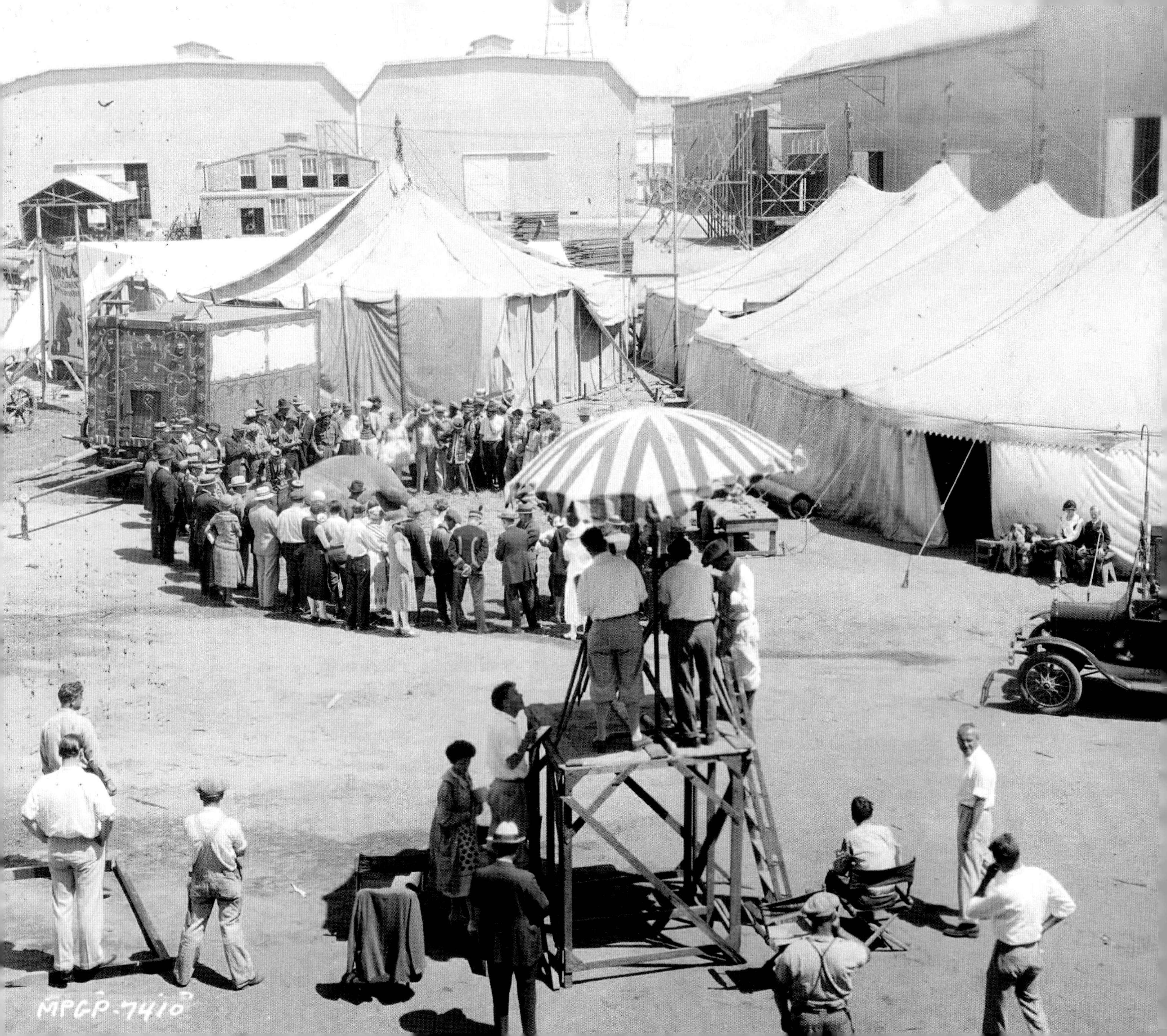
MPGP-7410

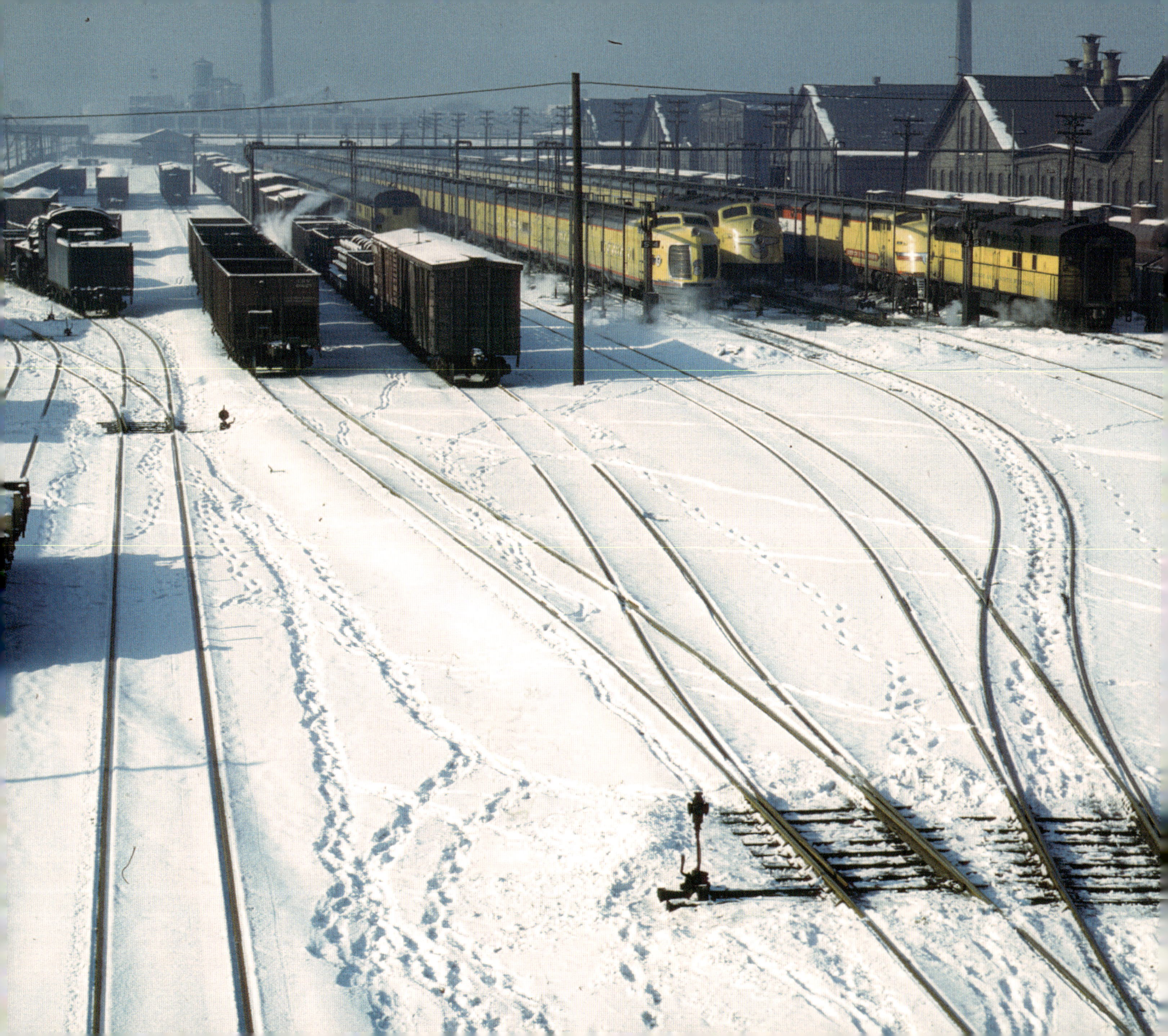

City of Los Angeles Streamliner

SERVICE DISCONTINUED 1971

Union Pacific Railroad's streamlined passenger train, The City of Los Angeles, began service to Chicago on May 15, 1936, just one day after Atchison, Topeka and Santa Fe Railway's new heavyweight Super Chief made its initial run.

Union Pacific's new train also had to compete with The Golden State Limited, a Rock Island Railroad train that had been offering service from Los Angeles to Chicago since 1908.

State-of-the-art diesel locomotives that delivered 5,400 horsepower pulled both the City of Los Angeles and Santa Fe's Super Chief, helping these new streamliners make the trip in just under 40 hours. This shaved a full day off the time the trip took before the advent of the streamliners.

Union Pacific had the locomotives painted "Armor Yellow" with "Leaf Brown" roofs and undersides. They had stainless steel on their "noses," which displayed the Union Pacific herald.

The City of Los Angeles made 23 stops between its hub cities of Los Angeles and Chicago. Passengers enjoyed the scenery as the train carried them through California, Nevada, Utah, Wyoming, Nebraska, Iowa and Illinois. Typically locomotives pulled 17 cars; many were individually named and referenced events in California's history or the names of Southern California towns.

"The Little Nugget" was one of the most famous of these railroad cars. It served as the club lounge for the train's first-class Pullman passengers. In this luxury capacity, she was host to Hollywood's entertainment elite, film stars mingling with movie moguls and agents. The Little Nugget was decked out in Victorian style with red velvet sofas and drapes, bevel-edged mirrors, stars twinkling on the ceiling and caricatures of famous vaudevillians adorning the walls.

The restrooms on the City of Los Angeles had outlets for electric razors and curling irons and diffused lighting fixtures over the mirrors. Accommodations on the train's Pullman sleeping cars varied. Some cars had ten roomettes and six double bedrooms; others offered eleven double bedrooms or five double bedrooms with two compartments and a pair of drawing rooms.

Sleeping-car passengers were welcome to take in the view from the train's dome observation car. "View the historic West and get a front-page lesson in geography on the Domeliner City of Los Angeles," a 1957 brochure invited. Three years later Union Pacific combined the train with the streamliner the City of San Francisco.

On April 30, 1971, the City of Los Angeles left Chicago on the way to its namesake city for the final time. The next day, Amtrak took over long-distance passenger service in the United States. The Union Pacific ended its long-distance rail service when the City of Los Angeles arrived at Los Angeles Union Station for the last time on May 2, 1971.

The Little Nugget lives on and is currently undergoing restoration at the museum in Griffith Park.

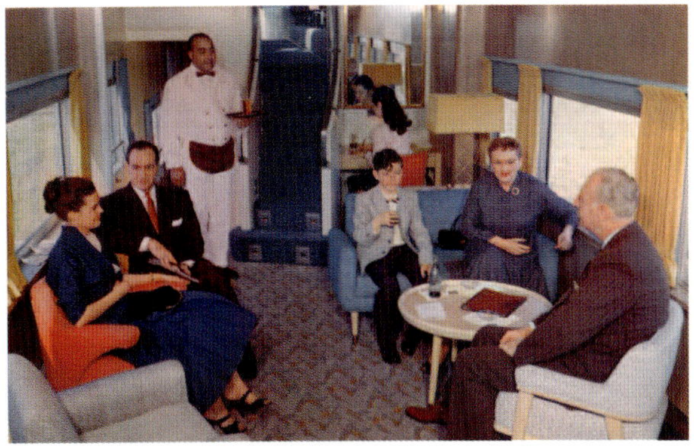

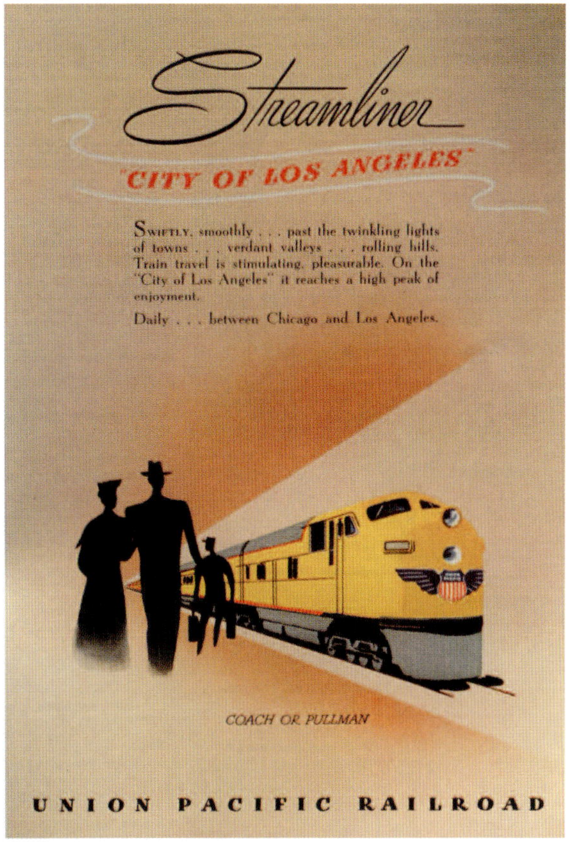

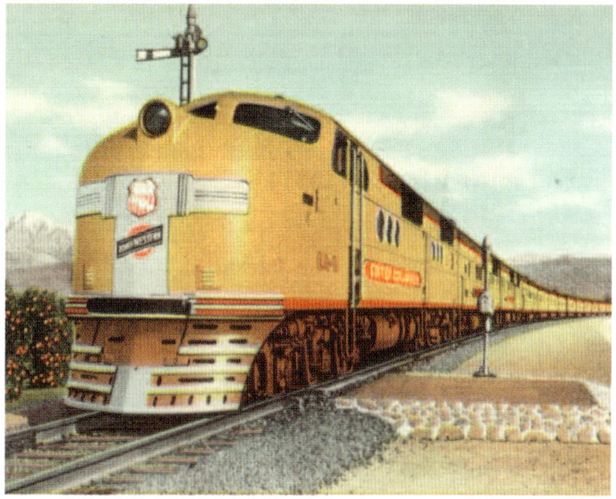

ABOVE *A 1950s postcard view of the train.*

FAR LEFT *A waiter stands by as City of Los Angeles passengers enjoy drinks aboard the train. Union Pacific offered passengers first-class accommodations as it traveled between Los Angeles and Chicago.*

LEFT *A Union Pacific advertising poster promises passengers a smooth ride between Los Angeles and Chicago. Competition for riders was fierce between the Union Pacific's City of Los Angeles and the Atchison, Topeka and Santa Fe's Super Chief. Union Pacific ridership once got a boost when Lucille Ball featured a ride on the City of Los Angeles on the* I Love Lucy *show.*

OPPOSITE PAGE *The City of Denver (left) and the City of Los Angeles (far right) sit waiting in a snowy railyard in Chicago in 1942.*

Pan Pacific Auditorium CLOSED 1972

The Los Angeles architectural firm Wurdeman and Becket designed the Pan-Pacific Auditorium, which opened to great fanfare on May 18, 1935. The Streamline Moderne building with its signature green and white facade stood as a landmark along West Berkeley Boulevard in the city's Fairfax District. The design included four stylized towers and flagpoles that were supposed to remind onlookers of upswept aircraft fins.

The Pan Pacific served the city as the premier location for indoor public events. During the 1940s people flocked here to enjoy national radio broadcasts. In the 1950s they came to watch televised professional wrestling matches. World War II hero Dwight David Eisenhower spoke in front of a capacity crowd of 10,000 people on October 10, 1952, just before he was elected President of the United States. A crowd estimated at 20,000 stood outside and listened to Ike over a public address system.

Elvis Presley sang here to a smaller crowd, just over 9,000, on October 28 and 29, 1957, before he was drafted into the Army. Vice President Richard Nixon addressed a national audience from the Pan-Pacific on November 5, 1960. He didn't fare as well as Eisenhower, three days later he lost the election to John F. Kennedy.

The Ice Capades and the Harlem Globetrotters entertained here. The Los Angeles Monarchs of the Pacific Coast Hockey League played their home games here, as did UCLA and USC's men's basketball teams and UCLA's ice hockey teams.

The building served as the city's primary indoor venue until the larger Los Angeles Convention Center opened in 1972. The Pan Pacific Auditorium closed that same year. Movie producers used the still-attractive exterior as a movie set. The Pan Pacific appeared in the 1975 movie *Funny Lady*, in the 1980 musical *Xanadu* and, finally, in the 1989 movie *Miracle Mile*.

Neighbors worked to have the abandoned building refurbished as an ice-skating rink or a cultural center. Transients began to call the empty building home. They vandalized the interior and started several small fires. Seventeen years of neglect culminated in the building's destruction in a spectacular fire on May 24, 1989.

"The fire began shortly after 7 p.m. At times, flames from the dilapidated, boarded-up auditorium shot 200 feet into the night sky and could be seen from as far away as the Civic Center and the Silver Lake area," the *Los Angeles Times* reported.

Today, a city recreation center occupies Pan Pacific Park. Its new building sports a smaller replica of one of the former auditorium's signature towers. The designers of the entrance to the Disney-MGM studio at Disney World in Orlando, Florida, also drew inspiration from the Pan Pacific Auditorium. That building opened on May 1, 1989, just three weeks before fire destroyed the original. On July 15, 2011, Disney revealed that they had drawn inspiration from the Pan Pacific styling a second time when they unveiled the entrance to the Adventure Park at Disneyland Resort in Anaheim, California.

OPPOSITE PAGE AND BELOW LEFT *The Library of Congress pulled no punches when it described the Pan Pacific in its caption for these circa 1975 photos: "Essentially this building is a shed with an image-imparting entrance facade. The Pan Pacific Auditorium achieves not just the styling of the great streamlined Worlds Fairs of the 1930s, but their festivity and sophistication as well. The four exuberant entrance pylons are carefully scaled to give the building an impressiveness far beyond its actual size."*

BELOW *The derelict Pan Pacific in the mid-1980s, not long before its demise.*

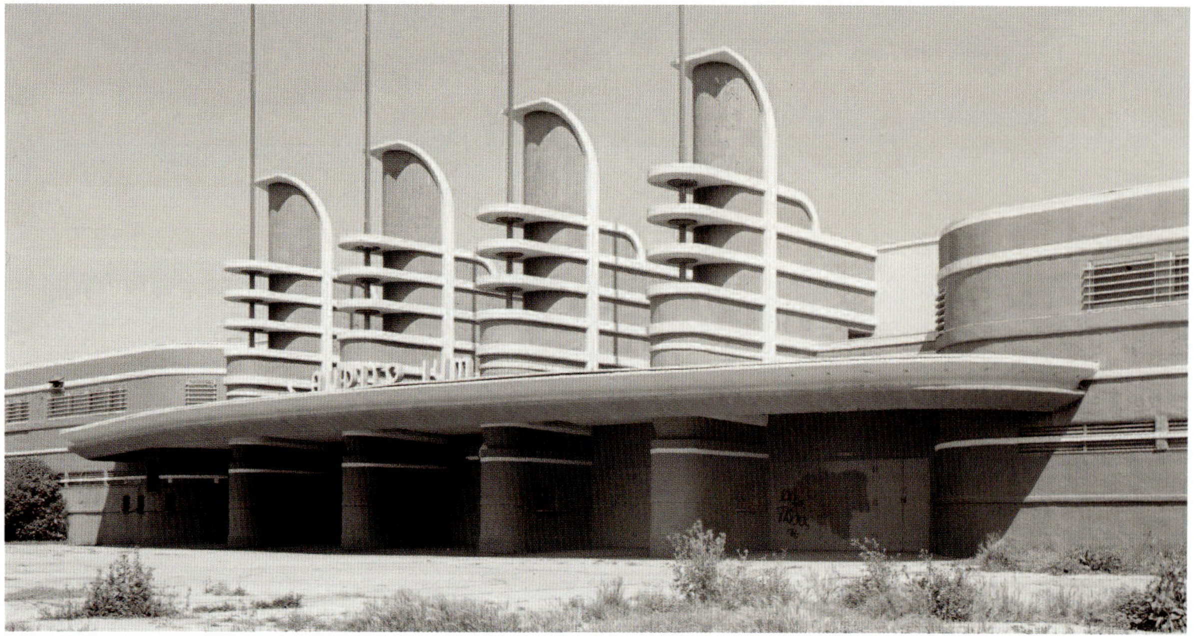

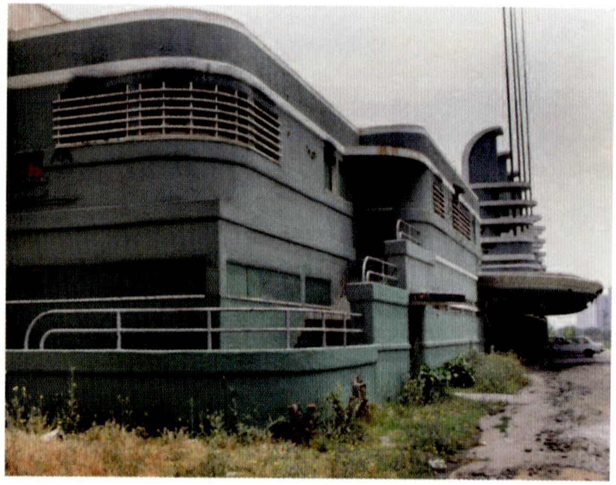

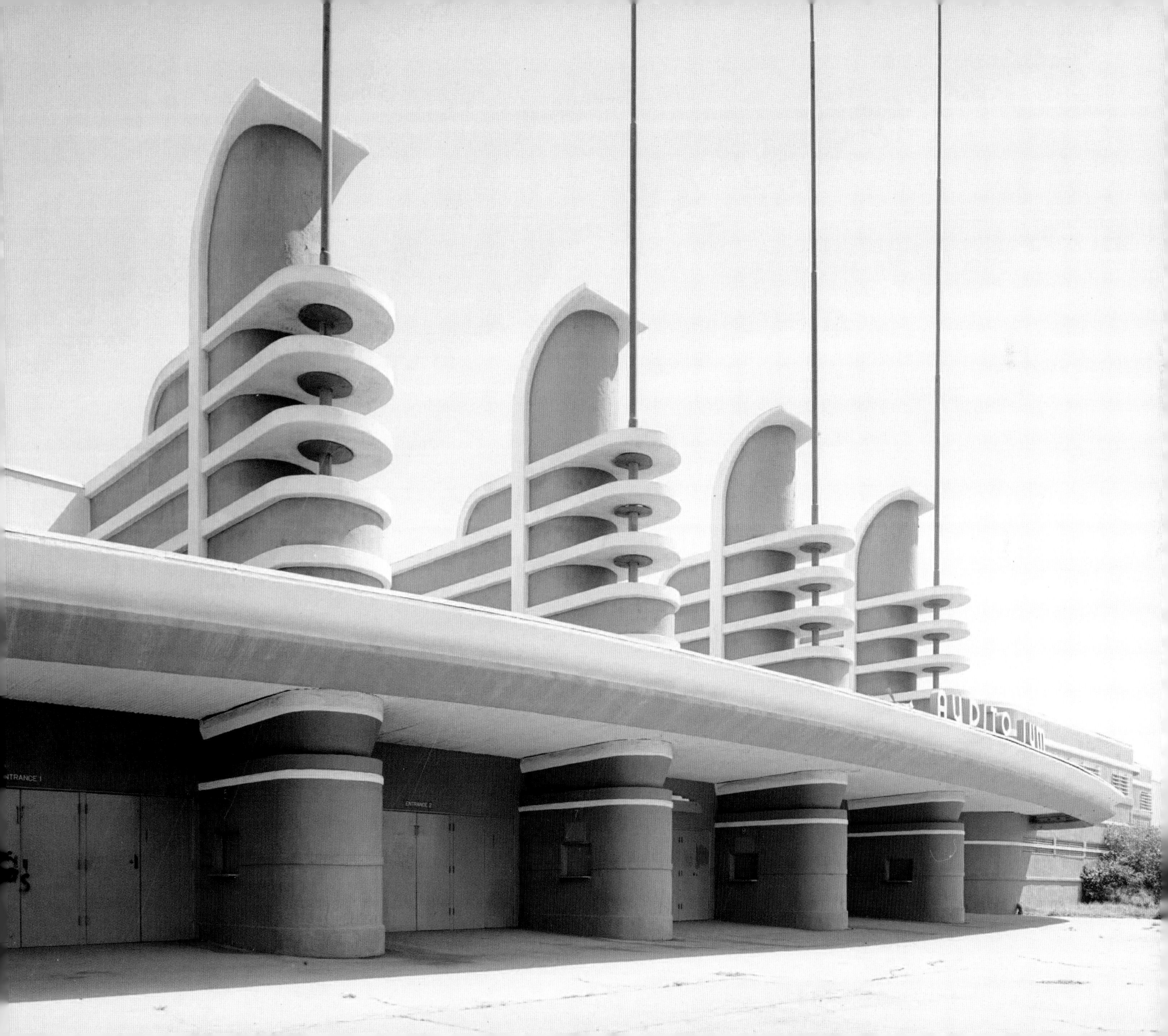
AUDITORIUM
ENTRANCE 1
ENTRANCE 2

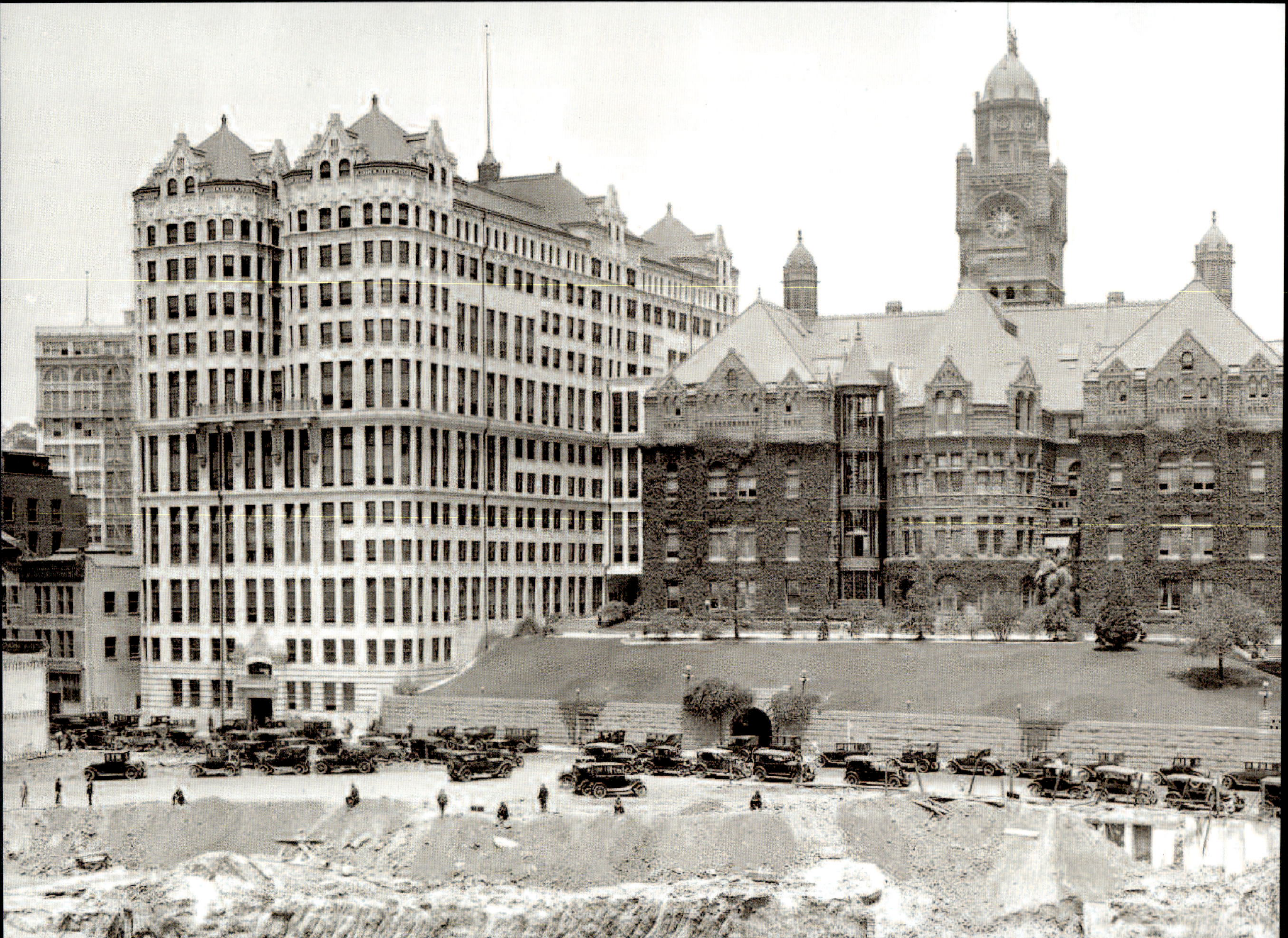

Hall of Records DEMOLISHED IN 1973

Los Angeles County's red-sandstone courthouse was bursting at the seams in 1906, overloaded with documents. The county supervisors decided to do something to relieve the overcrowding. They authorized the expenditure of $1 million to build the county's first Hall of Records. Construction began in 1909 on the 12-story archive right next door to the courthouse. In 1912, county workers moved in. Architects Frank Hudson and William Munsell designed the building to serve not just as the Hall of Records, but to consolidate most county offices under one roof.

They designed a large, light-colored building that divided into two sections halfway up to the top. Large rectangular windows line the perimeter of the building, and molding decorated the top of the structure. Hudson and Munsell crowned the building with some architectural flourishes that included a lavishly ornamented roof.

The design split the building's top six floors into two pairs of wings, which joined at a central elevator shaft. The designers perched the building on a granite base reminiscent of the Romanesque Revival Courthouse next door, but they gave the building a more modern design on its walls, using brick and terra cotta.

While still under construction, the Hall of Records was the target of a dynamite plot that was stopped by an anonymous tip-off. This incident preceded the October 1, 1910, dynamiting of the *Los Angeles Times* building by two weeks. On September 14, two unexploded sticks of dynamite were discovered at the Hall of Records, where non-union iron workers from Llewellyn Iron Works were putting up the building.

When the new Civic Center was becoming a part of the Los Angeles skyline in 1926 the city applied its straight-edge to the jumble of streets in the neighborhood. This included straightening out New High Street, where the Hall of Records stood. This change put the building at an odd angle. It was out of sync with the rest of the new Civic Center, something that tugged at the geometric sensibilities of city planners for many years.

Some suggested rotating the building to fit the new neighborhood that had grown up around it. But that would cost maybe $5 million, five times what it cost to build the Hall of Records in the first place. The county eventually decided it was time for the old building to go.

The Old Hall of Records was demolished in September 1973. At first a parking lot replaced the grand old structure. Today a portion of Grand Park takes up that building's old footprint. The New Hall of Records had already opened in 1962 in a building designed by Richard Neutra.

OPPOSITE PAGE *The Hall of Records and the Los Angeles County Courthouse tower over the building works for the new City Hall.*

BELOW *The photographer stood on what was left of Bunker Hill to capture his panoramic shot of the Los Angeles Civic Center. The State of California Building is tucked behind the Hall of Records.*

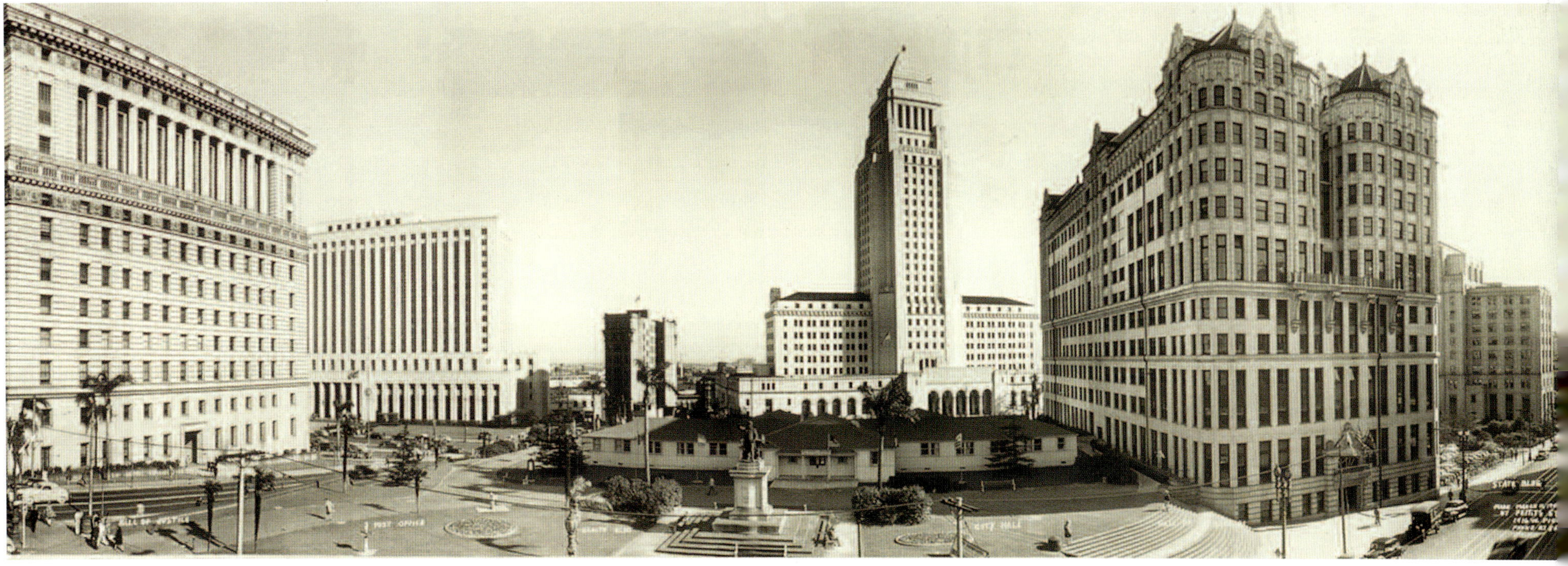

Academy Theater CONVERTED TO A CHURCH 1976

Moviegoers lined up to purchase tickets at the Academy Theater on Manchester Boulevard in Inglewood early Friday, November 17, 1939. The 1,156-seat theater was opening its doors for the first time. The theater had a special treat in store. *Another Thin Man* was premiering that night and Myrna Loy and William Powell who starred in this, and other "Thin Man" films, were going to be in the audience.

Fox West Coast Theaters hired architect Simeon Charles Lee to design the building. Critics called Lee's finished product "the most advanced Streamline Moderne theater in the Los Angeles area." The Chicago native gave the building a special touch: when lit the theater's signature tower—70 feet tall—resembled a spool of film unwinding. Streamline Moderne was essentially the art deco style stripped of its ornamentation and the first to incorporate electric lighting into its design.

Lee began building theaters in 1927—his first creation, the 1927 Tower Theater, still stands on South Broadway as a Los Angeles Historic-Cultural Monument and is listed on the National Register of Historic Places.

Lee had a hand in designing more than 400 theaters in his career. When Lee designed the Academy Theater in 1939 he turned away from styles that looked to the past, like his French Renaissance Tower Theater, to one that looked to the future: Streamline Moderne. "Streamlined styling was evidence of the theater's modernity," writes Maggie Valentine in *The Show Starts on the Sidewalk, An Architectural History of the Movie Theatre*. "Machine-made industrial materials such as glass block, polished aluminum, and chrome tubing—all hard, shiny, and slick—accented the novelty and luxury of the building."

Valentine especially notes the etched-glass figure of a woman holding an Oscar adorning one of the theater's walls.

Critics credit Lee with being the first architect to incorporate the automobile into his designs. He made the parking lot an integral element in the Academy Theater's design.

The 1971 Northridge Earthquake deprived the theater's tower of its signature spool of film. Management replaced the spool with the rings that are still there today. In 1976, five years after the temblor, the theater ended its 37-year run and closed its doors.

Pastor Doyle Hart stepped in and purchased the building. He had moved to California in 1965 and opened the Calvary Temple at Broadway and Manchester Street. Hart's church outgrew the facilities there, and he saw the Academy Theater building as an ideal spot for services: the Academy Theater became the Academy Cathedral. The church is still going strong: the tower lights up each night at sunset and services are held each Sunday morning.

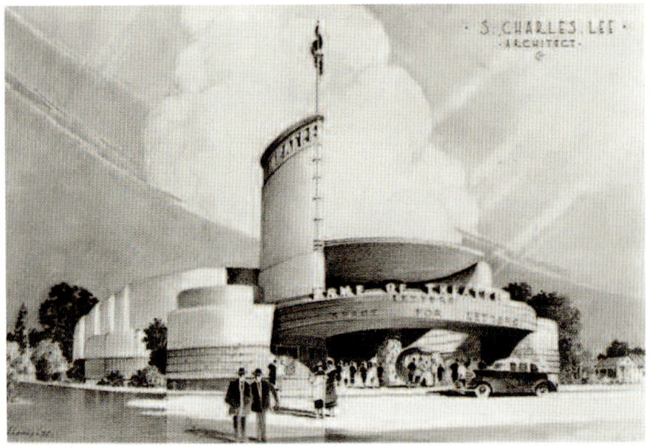

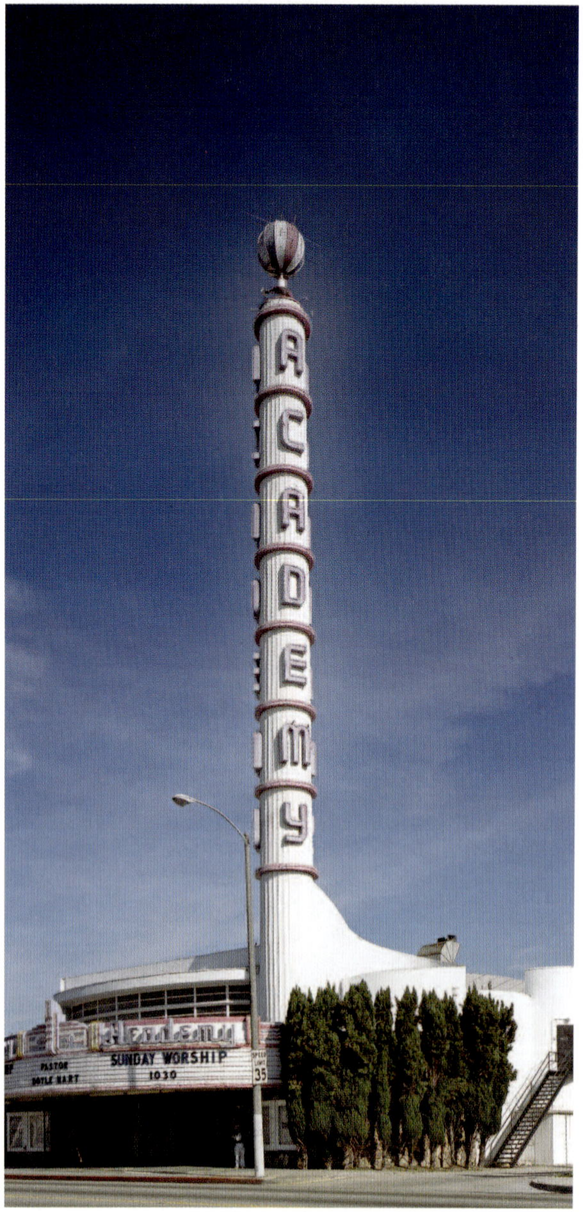

RIGHT *The 1971 Northridge Earthquake damaged the theater's signature marquee. Bands now stand in place of the spools. The new owners still light up the marquee.*

LEFT *Architect S. Charles Lee used this conceptual drawing of the Academy Theater. The final design did not include some of the elements shown here. He simplified the final look of the marquee and the roofline.*

OPPOSITE PAGE *The Academy photographed in its prime in 1939 advertising films starring Humphrey Bogart, Bette Davis and Errol Flynn.*

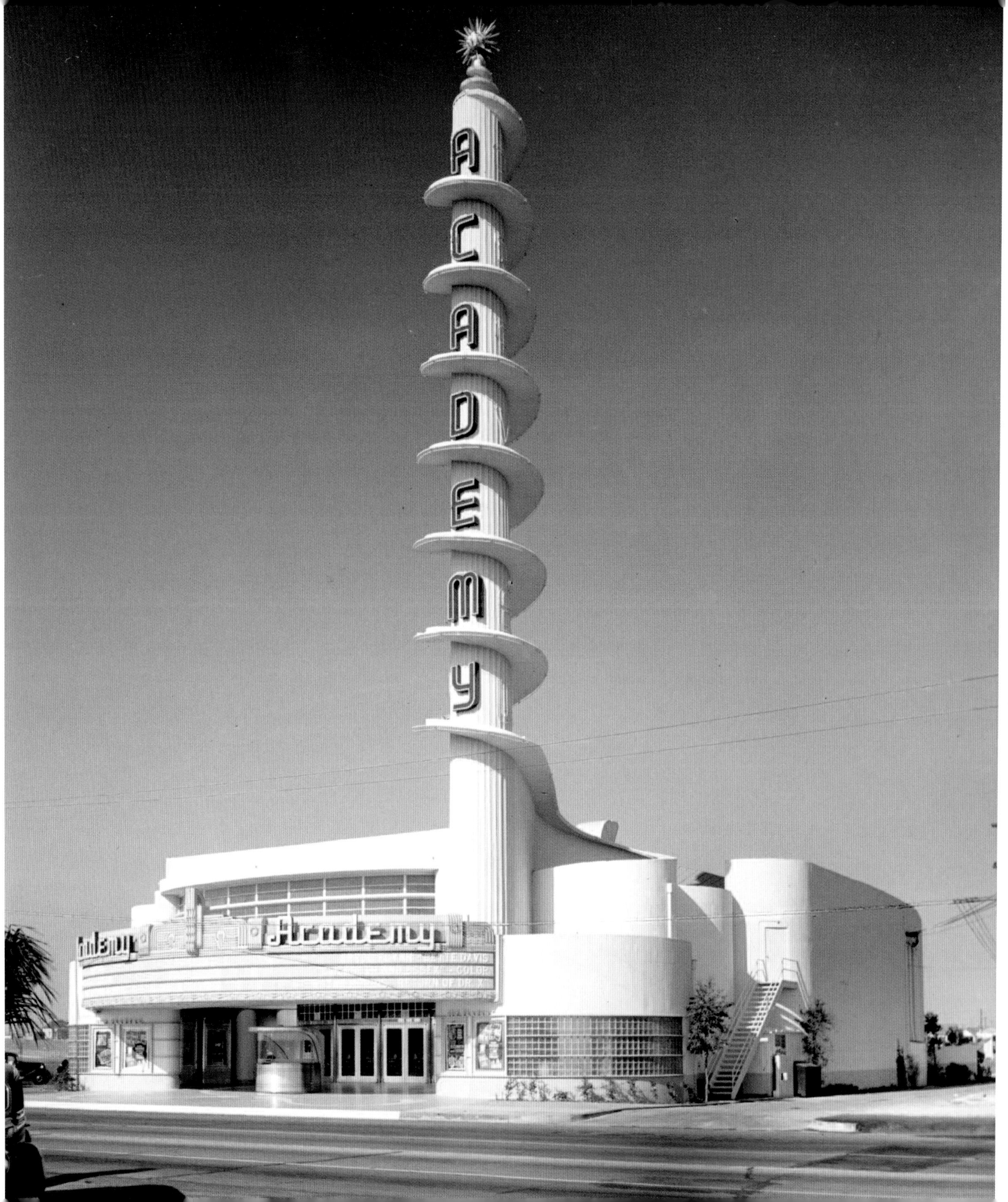
ACADEMY
Academy

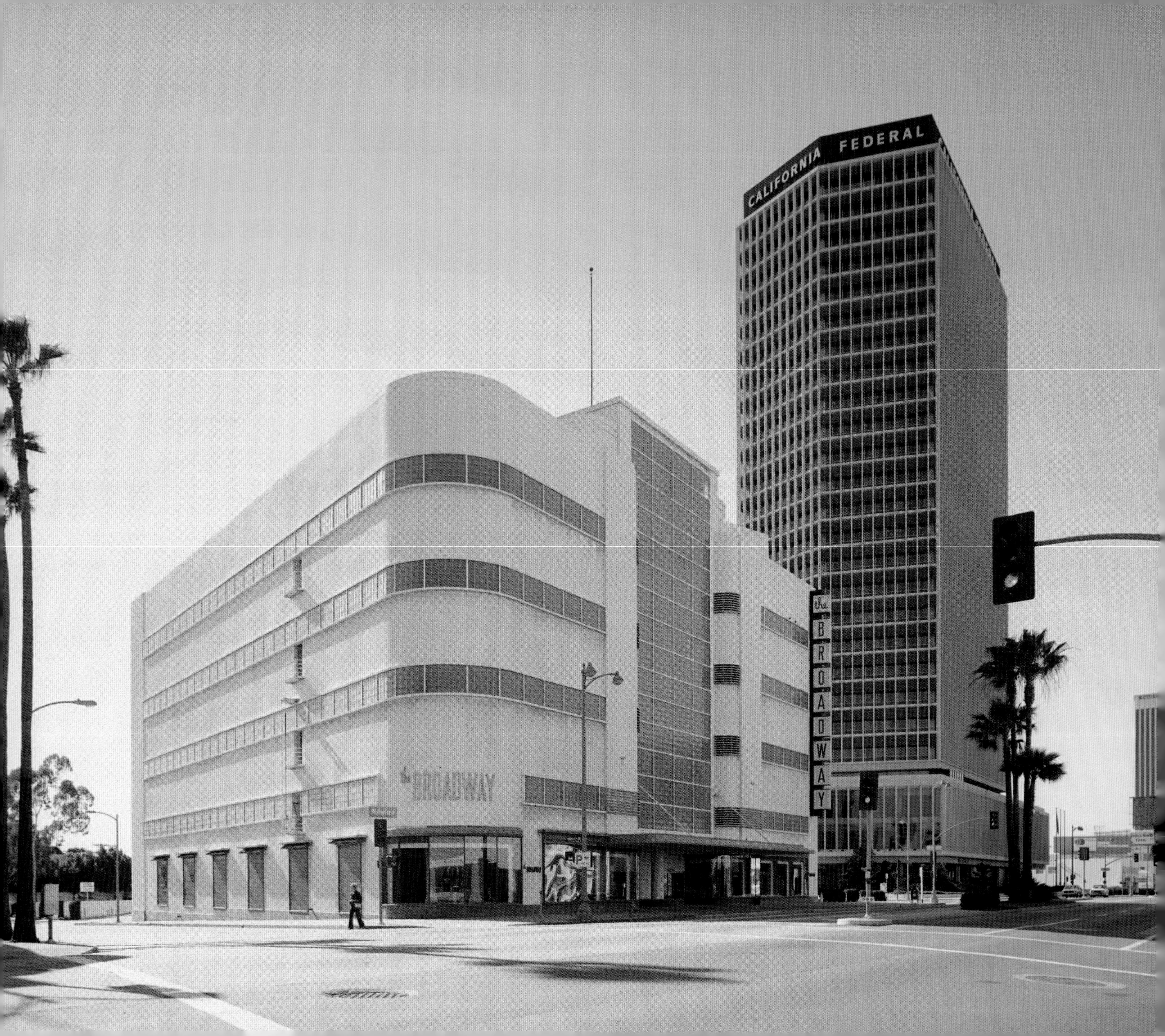

CALIFORNIA FEDERAL
the BROADWAY
the BROADWAY

Coulter's Department Store RAZED 1980

Benjamin F. Coulter founded what is thought to be Los Angeles' oldest dry goods store in 1878, at the corner of Temple and Spring streets. His first store measured just 18 by 20 feet and was stocked with merchandise shipped from New York at the cost of $1,000.

A year after opening, business had grown so substantially that Coulter relocated to the Baker Block where he could stretch out in the luxury of a room that was 115 feet by 20 until 1885. He expanded the operation into a series of department stores located in several spots downtown. He also founded the Coulter Woolen Mills on Figueroa Street to supply his stores with fine blankets and other linens. The Chamber of Commerce reported his stores featured "the latest and most approved forms of counters, show-cases, drawers, shelves and carrier appliances."

Not just a merchant, Coulter was an ordained minister as well, and founded six missions in the city along with the Broadway Church of Christ in 1895. He also helped create a night school for young Japanese men offering lessons in English and the Bible, one of the earliest ministries designed to help Asian immigrants. Coulter proved himself a forward-thinking merchant, sympathetic to demands of organized labor. In 1884, when clerks organized into the Early Closing Association and demanded a closing time of 6:30 p.m. at his and many other merchants' stores, he took a benign view. Just prior to his death in 1911, he presented the city with no less than $150,000 worth of real estate.

By 1906, the company had relocated its headquarters into a building it owned on Broadway between Second and Third streets. This location was known as "the last word in convenience and beauty of appointments" until 1917, when an even larger and more beautiful store opened at the corner of Seventh and Olive streets, historically, the city's main intersection.

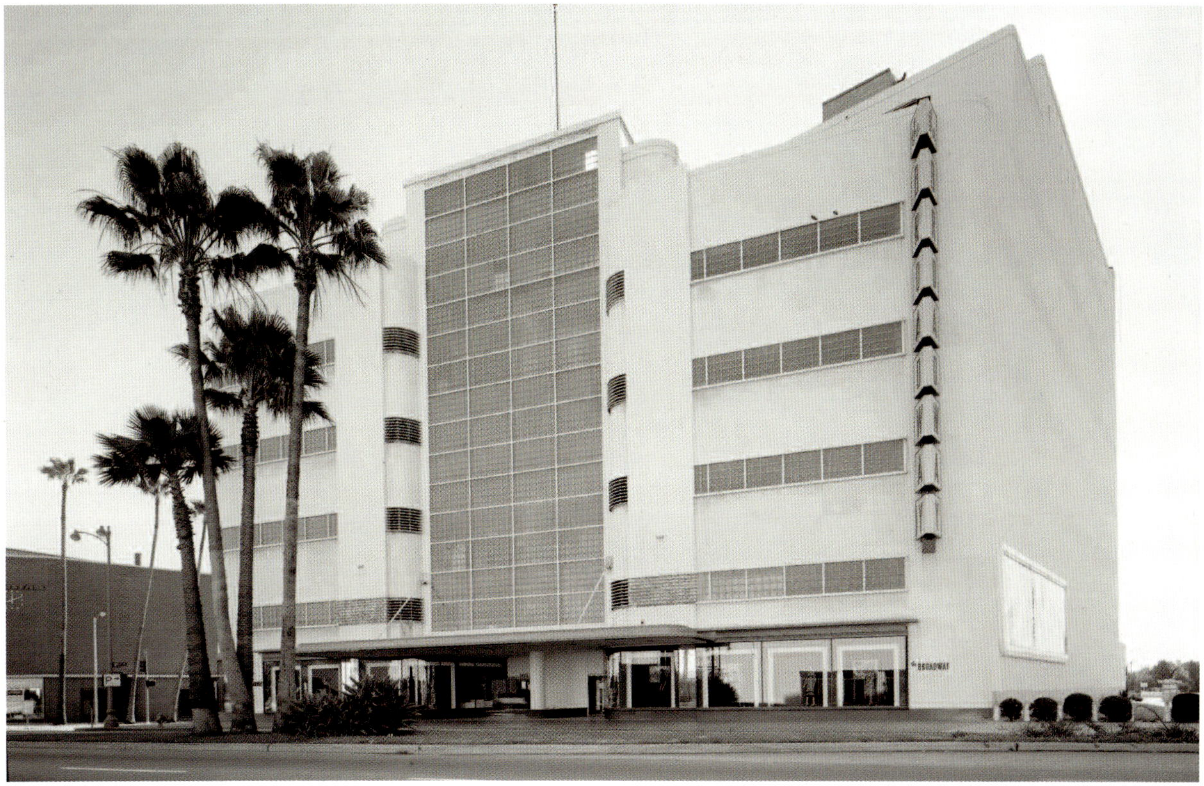

The 1930s demanded that stores address the increasing numbers of people arriving to shop in their automobiles. Architect Stiles O. Clement's name is synonymous with art deco-style architecture in Los Angeles. Most of Stiles' 1930s-era buildings (such as the Richfield Oil Building) have disappeared, but were among the first to accommodate vehicles. As Coulter's planned to move out to the automobile-based Miracle Mile, management called in Stiles to design a new main store. The result was Coulter's Department Store at the corner of Hauser and Wilshire boulevards with its distinctive glass-block layers and main entrance off the parking lot in the rear.

Acquired by The Broadway in 1960, the store stopped selling merchandise in 1979 when the company planned a move to Beverly Center, a mixed-use project that never developed. The plan had called for several blocks along the Miracle Mile to become the Intercontinental Center. The six-story former Coulter's building was razed in 1980 while local residents successfully protested the new development that included a design for a 22-story hotel on the site, putting a stop to the entire project. Until the first decade of the 21st century, the site of Coulter's remained a vacant lot, when a five-story, mixed-use apartment building was constructed there.

LEFT *The Coulter's Department Store Building at 5600 Wilshire Boulevard.*

BELOW *In this postcard view, Coulter's appears part of a bustling scene in the early 1950s.*

OPPOSITE PAGE *Here the Coulter's Building appears in the mid-1970s after it had been acquired by The Broadway.*

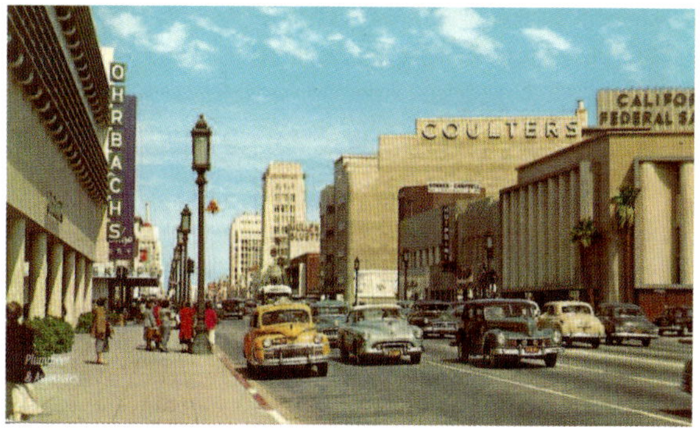

Citrus Groves COMMERCIAL OPERATIONS GONE BY 1980

Beginning with Franciscan Friar Junipero Serra in 1769, active cultivation of citrus fruit in California has continued ever since. Little remains of the verdant citrus groves that once covered downtown Los Angeles on William Wolfskill's land. Living on the very frayed edge of civilization that was Los Angeles in the 1840s, Wolfskill is credited with creating California's first citrus business.

Even as early as 1841, the nutritional value of vitamin C was well known. In the nutrient-deficient gold fields, oranges and their like were essential for fending off scurvy and other ailments brought on by a restricted diet.

Wolfskill owned huge sections of Southern California, including all of what became downtown Los Angeles. He started off with grapes, but after selling citrus fruits at $1 apiece, much of his land—used for everything from wine production to sheep farming—was converted to citrus orchards. Wolfskill seeded his orchards with young trees from the San Gabriel Mission, descendants from the days of Father Serra. Soon he had hundreds of lemon and orange trees.

By 1870, the breeding of the navel orange variety spurred on the industry and supported the state economy as gold veins played out. The sweet, seedless navel had originated as a mutation at a monastery in Brazil and could be harvested while other parts of the country were covered in a blanket of winter. Cuttings from that original plant were brought to Riverside to see if they'd take root. Indeed they did, and without seeds to plant, the fruit became standardized, as the only way to reproduce the tree was by cloning the original plant.

Under the care of spiritualist and suffragist Eliza Tibbets, those original 1873 cuttings gave rise to nearly all the trees in Southern California. By the 1880s, the transcontinental railroad was bringing oranges across the nation, establishing their popularity in eastern markets, and ushering in an economic boom for California. With citrus traveling further than ever, growers found themselves losing out to the railroads. The 1893 Southern California Fruit Exchange cooperative of farmers helped offset the losses.

In 1906, the Citrus Experiment Station was founded to perform experiments in citrus agriculture and it later served as the foundation of the University of California, Riverside. The university today boasts more than 1,000 different citrus types—the most comprehensive collection of its kind. One orange tree in Riverside, still producing fruit at more than 130 years old, has been designated a California Historical Landmark.

Eventually Southern California proved more adept at growing houses than oranges, and much of California's $1 billion annual citrus revenue moved north into the San Joaquin Valley, and today is second only to Florida's mostly juice-oriented crop of oranges. As late as 1970, some 50,000 acres in Los Angeles County still farmed oranges, but the number of acres were dropping in favor of real estate development.

Students and professors at California State University, Northridge moved to have their grove protected as a historic site (and not turned into a parking lot) in 1972. Today this grove of 400 trees is the last in San Fernando Valley.

BELOW *Orange growers in Los Angeles circa 1895.*

BELOW RIGHT *This T. W. Ingersoll stereograph depicts growers picking and packing oranges in the orchards of Los Angeles in 1905.*

OPPOSITE PAGE *The orange harvest in Riverside circa 1898.*

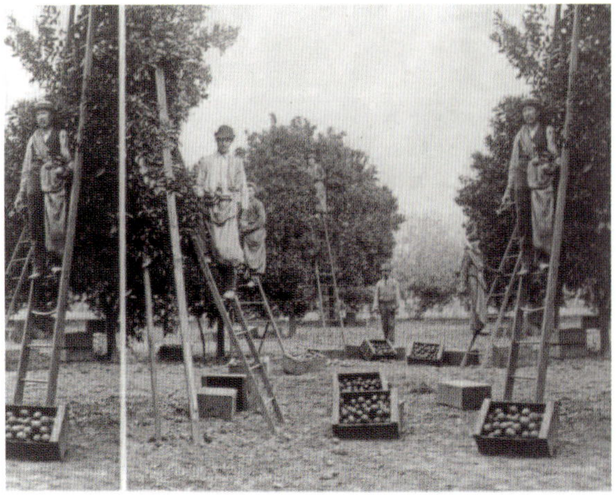

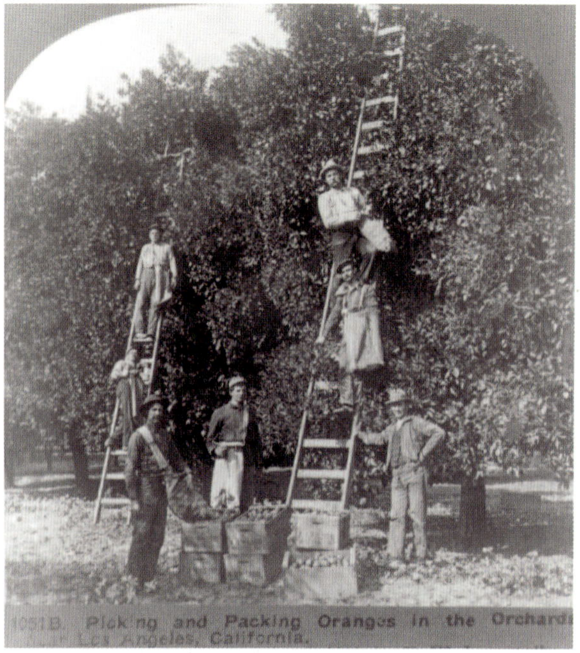

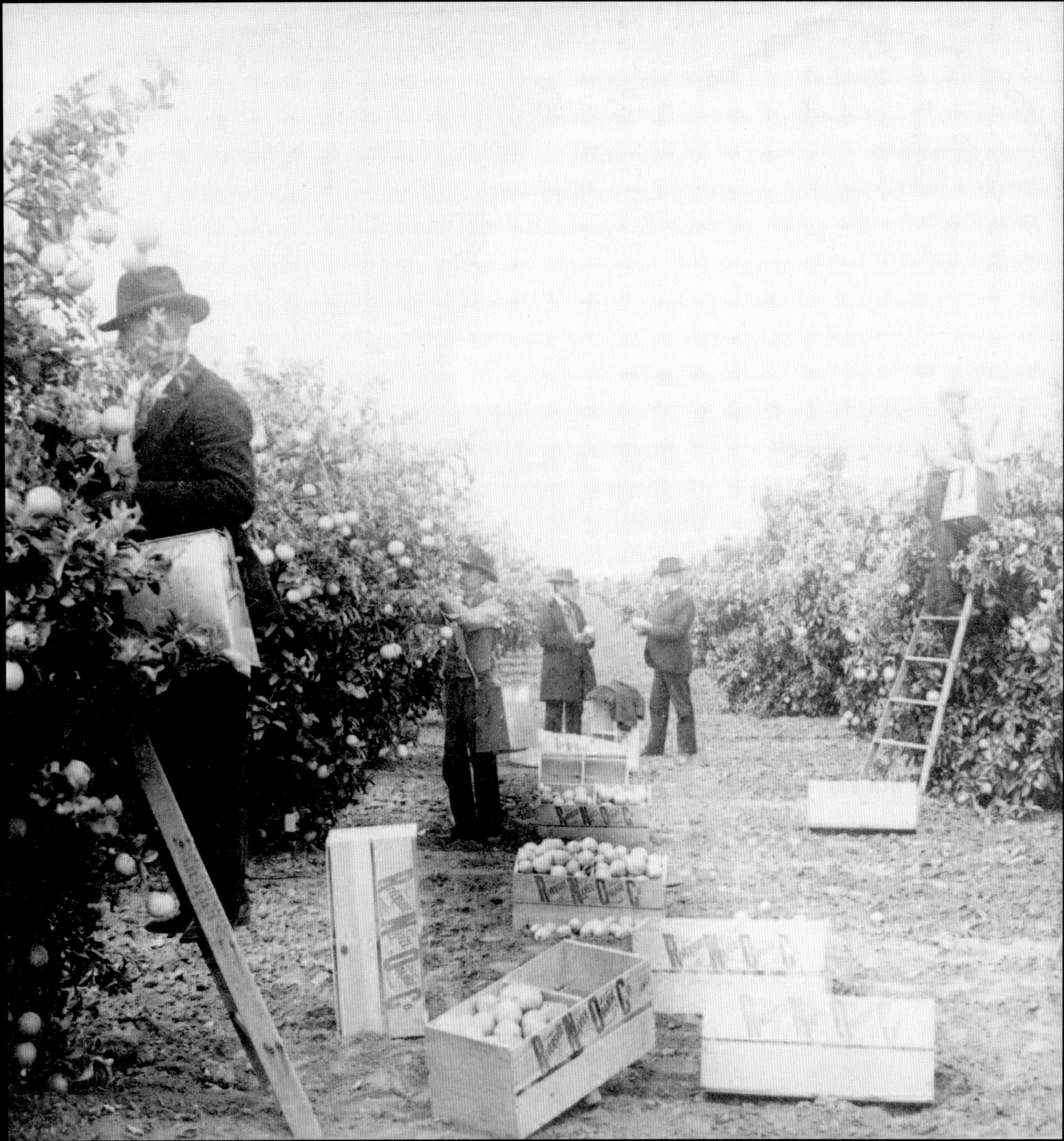

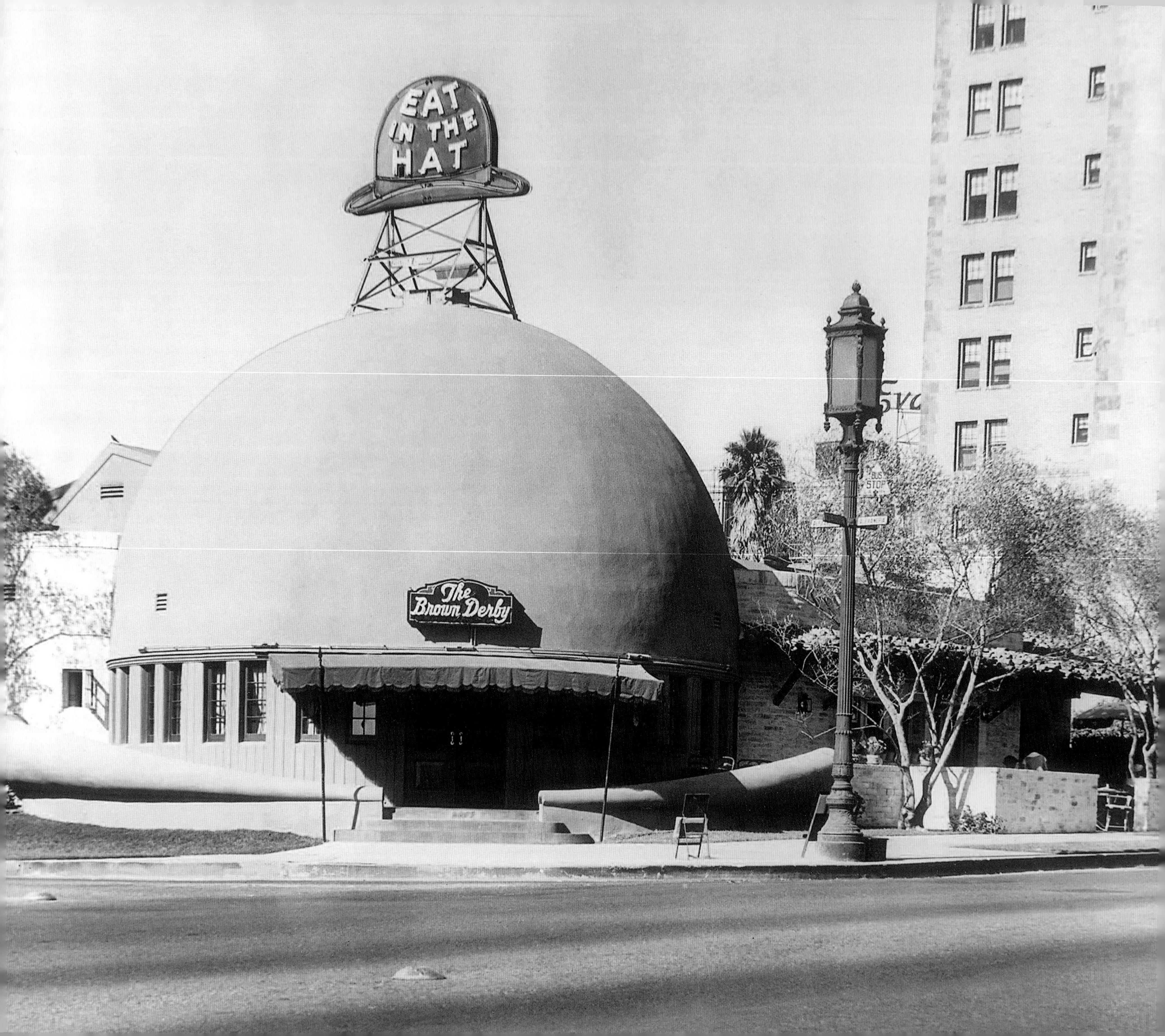
EAT IN THE HAT
The Brown Derby

Brown Derby DOFFED BUT NOT DEMOLISHED 1985

Among the best known works of programmatic architecture, the Brown Derby restaurant opened near Hollywood and Vine on Valentine's Day 1929. The legendary eatery wasn't the first building shaped like a recognizable object, person or creature, nor was it even the first Brown Derby, but it was there that Hollywood legends were made.

Los Angeles car culture encouraged "whimsical" or "novelty" architecture. Shop owners witnessed their customers passing by at ever-increasing speeds, and needed to convey information about their business to them faster than ever. These proprietors turned their entire buildings into signs for their businesses: Randy's Donuts, Tail o' the Pup (hot dogs) or even the tamale-shaped The Tamale, which obviously indicated what was for sale within.

The movement was no joke. Tail o' the Pup was designed by well-known architect Milton J. Black in 1938. Others followed: the 1968 drive-through Donut Hole in La Puente, the Coffee Cup Café at 8901 Pico Boulevard.

In some cases just the presence of a giant character might grab a driver's attention as in the owl overseeing Hoot Hoot I Scream, the pig ready to serve patrons via its mouth at the Pig Café built in 1934 near La Brea and Rosewood avenues, or the toad that presided over the 1931 Toed Inn, originally on Channel Road. The Toed Inn relocated to Wilshire Boulevard in 1938. Some of the sculptures were quite elaborate. The Hoot Hoot I Scream owl's head rotated, and its eyes, made from automobile headlamps, blinked and glowed. Tillie Hattrup ran the owl-themed stand for more than 50 years, first on Valley Boulevard, then moving to 8711 Long Beach Boulevard, before the owl had its wings clipped forever in 1979.

The Brown Derby lives on in other forms. In its heyday, the restaurant boasted four locations: Hollywood, the original on Wilshire Boulevard, the Beverly Hills and one on Los Feliz Boulevard. Hollywood and Beverly Hills folded and were demolished in the 1980s, the Wilshire hat, brimless, was lifted up and deposited behind the Korean shopping center that occupies its former location. The name "Brown Derby" is today a considerable asset, licensed at major tourist locations. Walt Disney Company was the first to snap up the brand and offer Brown-Derby-themed restaurants at its theme parks in 1987.

The Tail o' the Pup at La Cienega and Beverly boulevards and Randy's Donuts in Inglewood both had a difficult time fending off developers in 1985. While both buildings survive, the Tail o' the Pup was moved to a warehouse in 2005 awaiting a new location, as its original site has become a condo and apartment complex. Randy's donut is alive and well, though during the L.A. Kings' 2014 playoff bid it was converted briefly to a hockey puck.

BELOW LEFT *Tamales appeared on the building-sized menu at this eatery. The structure still survives at 6421 Whittier Boulevard in East Los Angeles and is used as a small beauty salon.*

BELOW MIDDLE *The Coffee Cup Café left little doubt as to what was served inside.*

BELOW *The owl whose head rotated and served ice cream to passersby.*

OPPOSITE PAGE *The Wilshire Brown Derby which used to be perched opposite the old Ambassador Hotel.*

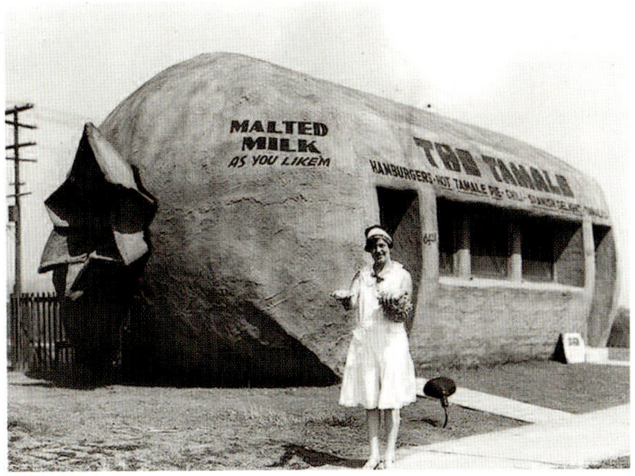

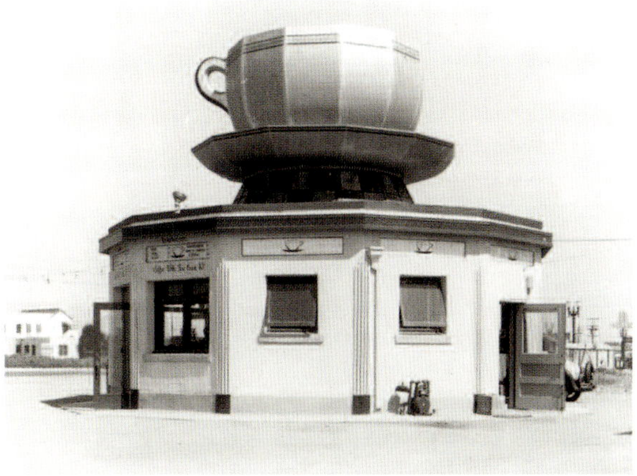

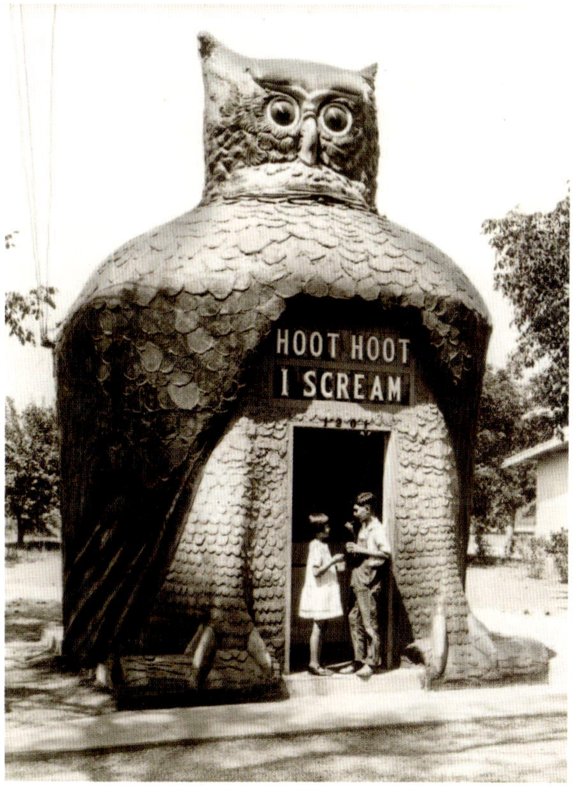

Church of the Open Door

ABANDONED HOPE STREET 1985

Earthquakes always trump historic significance. The 1987 Whittier Temblor knew no difference between a typical Los Angeles residence and the Church of the Open Door, whose holiest of purposes couldn't save it from the quake.

Founder Reuben Archer Torrey served as the church's first pastor. Among the most educated theologians of his day, Torrey came west to establish a new religious university, after having spent two decades traveling the world spreading the word as a missionary and evangelist.

Modeled on the Moody Bible Institute, from 1912 to 1914 Torrey served as the first Dean of the Bible Institute of Los Angeles. In 1913 they moved into the newly built classical structure at the intersection of Hope and Sixth streets. The building contained two auditoriums and two 13-story dormitory towers.

In 1915, Torrey became the first pastor of the Church of the Open Door, which shared the building with the Bible Institute he had founded. Torrey died in 1928 and he was succeeded as pastor by Louis T. Talbot (1932-1948).

The Institute shortened its name to BIOLA University in 1959, the same year the school moved out to La Mirada, leaving the entire building and its two neon-lit "Jesus Saves" signs dating from 1935 and 1937 to the Church. By the 1980s, attendance at the church had dwindled significantly. Church leadership purchased new land in Glendora and looked to sell the deteriorating building to a private developer.

When an initial deal fell through, television preacher Gene Scott attempted to purchase the building. Scott was among the founders at Oral Roberts University of Tulsa, Oklahoma in 1963, and had moved to California during the 1970s. Using fiery sermons and legal manipulations, Scott tried everything to prevent the building and the signs' destruction.

After 72 years, it took the Whittier Narrows earthquake to finally spell doom for the church building. The city building department labelled the property unsafe, the church sold for $20 million to a developer and it came down to be replaced by 555 S. Hope Tower.

As for the Jesus Saves signs, Scott couldn't be deflected from his mission to save them. Despite the church being unwilling to sell them, Scott somehow found them in a scrapyard and had them affixed to the United Artists theater on Broadway, a building that housed Scott's University Cathedral. Though he passed away in 2005, the sign continues to implore the Los Angeles public to embrace a higher power from there.

Gene's wife, Melissa had the other sign moved to Faith Center Church in Glendale in 2011 where she served as a pastor.

Scott's cathedral has been converted to an Ace boutique hotel that has retained the sign. Biola University has sought to get the signs back from the Scott family and the hotel chain, but had to settle for a one-third scale replica incorporated into a mural featuring the lost Church of the Open Door Building in all its former glory. The 38-foot by 59-foot photographic mural appears on the side of a parking structure on the university campus.

The Church of the Open Door itself, after moving to Glendora in 1985, continues to thrive and still meets each Sunday, its congregation numbering about 500 today.

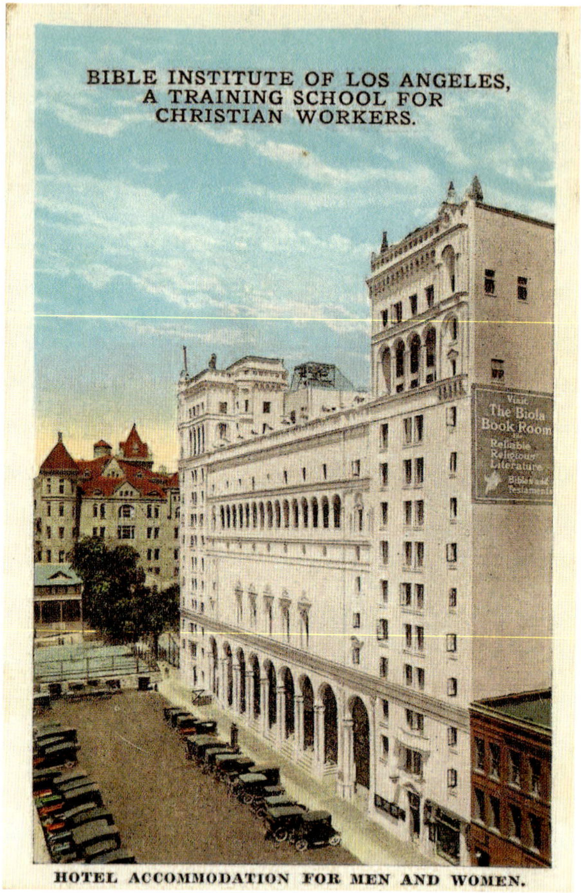

ABOVE *A late 1920s colorized postcard.*

OPPOSITE PAGE *The 13-story Biola University building was a landmark structure in Los Angeles and the "Jesus Saves" signs on top left no doubt as to its mission.*

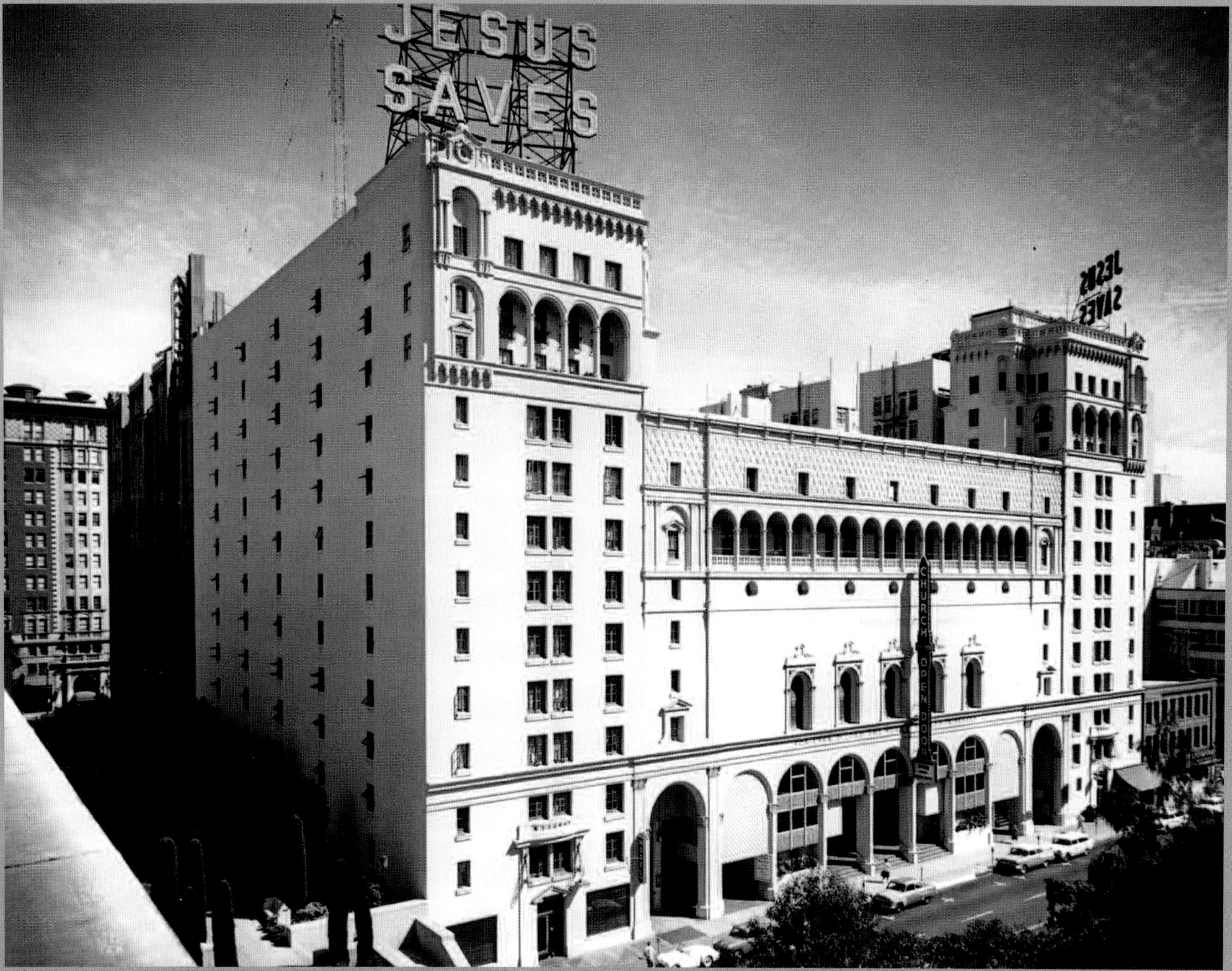
JESUS
SAVES
CHURCH

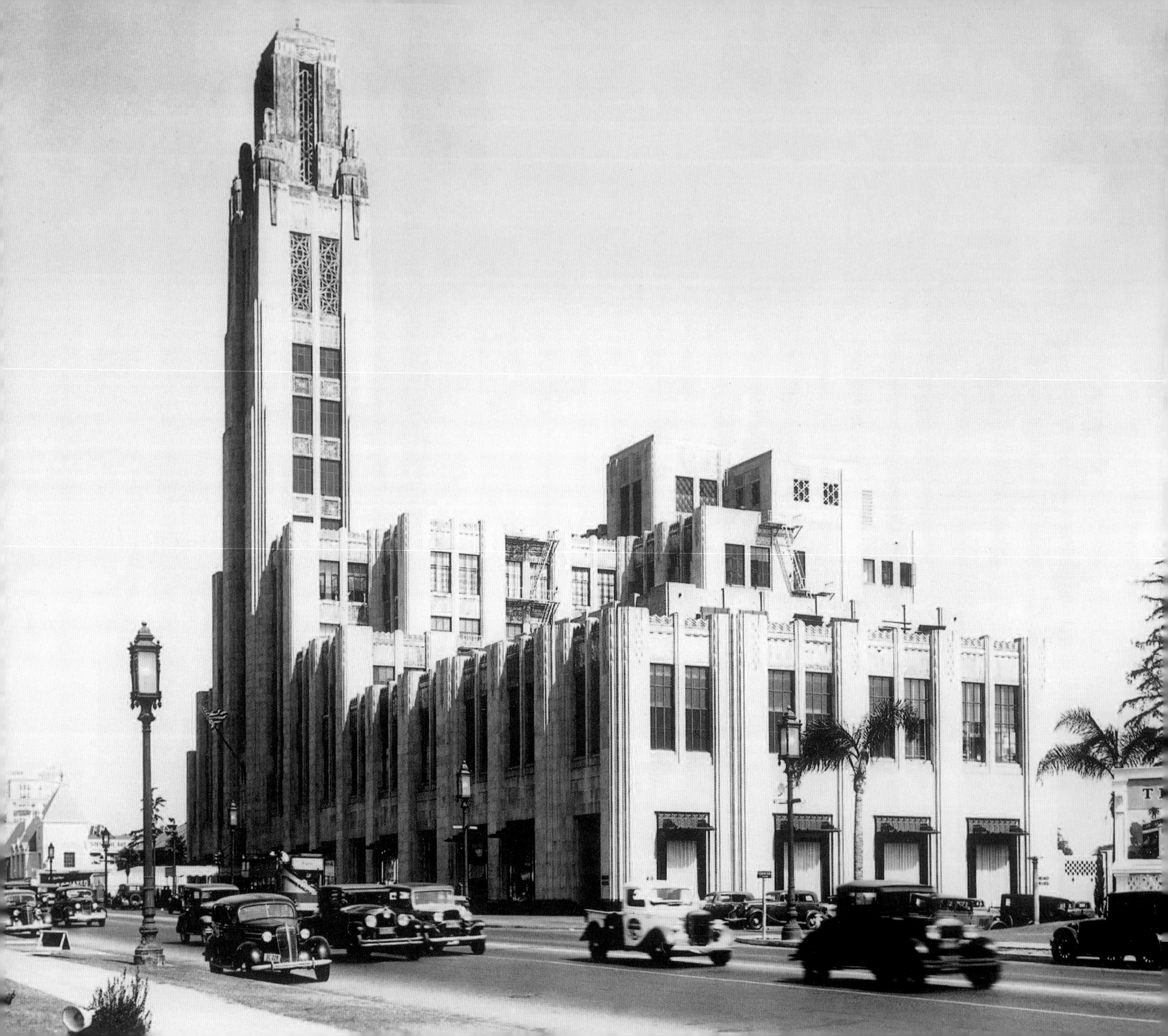

Bullocks Wilshire ABSORBED INTO MACY'S 1988

The unforgettable art deco landmark at 3050 Wilshire Boulevard stands among the many iconic buildings of Los Angeles.

John G. Bullock had already enjoyed success at his luxury department store downtown when he had this satellite location designed by architects John and Donald Parkinson in 1929. Upscale interior design featured a ceiling mural by Herman Sachs. The 241-foot tower's copper sheath has long since been tarnished green but once beamed a light that could be seen for miles. Bullocks Wilshire was among the first stores built to cater to motorists.

Located in a residential district, everything about the building had an eye for the automobile: the landmark tower, the main entrance off the parking lot, sidewalk displays designed to be seen from the street, even valets in fine uniforms. Bullocks helped define design for the automotive age.

Marble halls and floors, elevators lined with brass and nickel, rosewood stands; no expense was spared. The woman's shoe salon was said to have been paneled with wood from a single Central American tree; in the furs *atelier*, the walls were lined with exotic cork in varying shades; other departments featured live mannequins and low-slung racks designed to allow shoppers to take in the magnificence of the building itself.

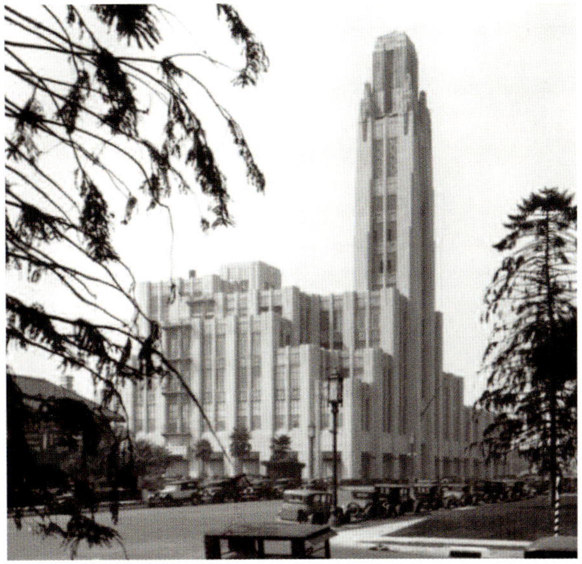

Certain departments functioned as discrete boutiques. The Irene Salon offered the skills of Hollywood costume designer Irene Lentz; The Playdeck offered what's said to be the city's first leisurewear; and the Doggery offered accessories for four-footed residents.

On the top floor, shoppers could enjoy refreshment in the desert-themed tearoom. High society gathered in the women's lounge for fashion shows, or in J. G. Bullocks' elite men's salon: a private suite on the fifth floor where captains of industry enjoyed cocktails and snacks as they watched private modeling sessions.

On any given day, patrons might run into Mae West, John Wayne or Alfred Hitchcock being fitted for a new ensemble, or Marlene Dietrich, Greta Garbo or Walt Disney trying to pick out the perfect gift while at Bullocks. At one point in their teenage years, both First Lady Pat Nixon and future leading actress Angela Lansbury served as sales clerks there.

The building was listed on the National Register of Historic Places in 1978. By 1988, the many branches of Bullocks stores had seen their market change. Department stores increasingly consolidated under fewer and fewer brands and industry leader Macy's purchased the Bullocks chain.

Bullocks Wilshire suffered a break-in, looting and a series of fires during the Los Angeles riots of 1992, but damage was not extensive. Macy's raided the building for its historic artifacts, but under public pressure many of them were returned. In 1994, Federated Department Stores, having acquired Macy's, sold the building to its longtime neighbor, The Southwestern Law School, which proceed to restore it to its original 1929 grandeur.

LEFT *Bullocks Wilshire, shown here in the early 1930s, was designated Los Angeles Historic-Cultural Monument No. 56 in 1968.*

OPPOSITE PAGE *Bullocks was a cathedral of commerce in the 1930s.*

Van de Kamp's BAKERY CLOSED 1990

New York architect J. Edward Hopkins designed Van de Kamp's Bakery headquarters at 2939 Fletcher Drive in Glassell Park. The 1930 building echoed the Dutch Renaissance Revival style intended to resemble a 16th-century Dutch farmhouse. Van de Kamp operated a chain of bakeries and coffee shops in their trademark "windmill" buildings. Neon signs depicting that windmill were seen at grocery stores and atop Van de Kamp's restaurants throughout mid-20th century Los Angeles.

Theodore J. Van de Kamp owned Van de Kamp Bakeries with his brother-in-law Lawrence L. Frank. The pair founded the company in 1915. The company employed more than 500 people at the bakery which also served as headquarters for its chain of 100 bakery outlets.

There were several Van de Kamp restaurants and bakeries around Los Angeles, including one at Wilshire and San Vicente. Unlike Helms, which kept their bakery products limited to their fleet of delivery vans, supermarkets had their own Van de Kamp baked-goods sections.

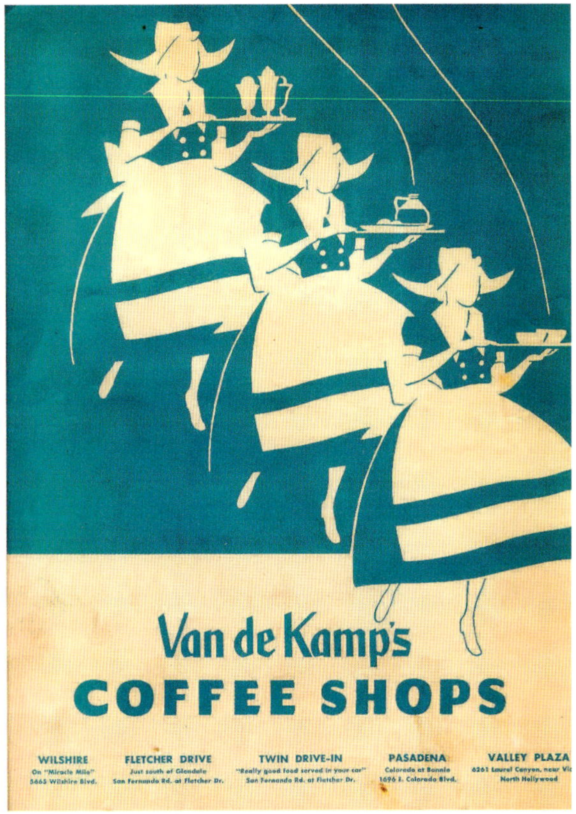

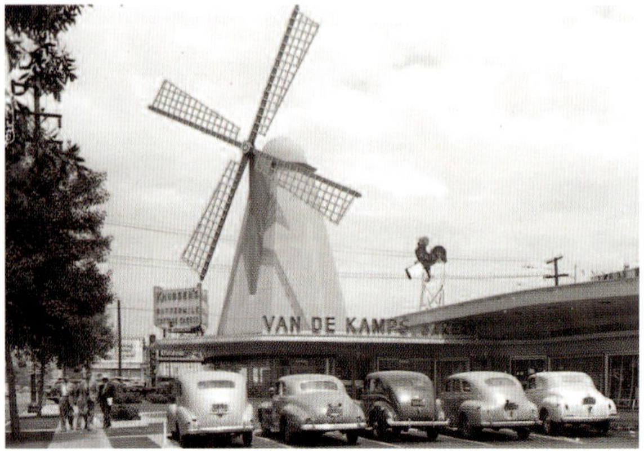

Members of the Van de Kamp family sold their bakery to General Baking Co. in 1956. That company was sold to private investors in 1979, and went bankrupt in October 1990. The Van de Kamp's brand lives on, however. Pinnacle Foods Group now owns the brand, which is also used by Ralph's Supermarkets for their line of baked goods.

In 1997 it appeared that Los Angeles was going to lose the venerable old bakery building itself. "Van de Kamp's Holland Dutch bakery may soon be toast," wrote Larry Gordon in the May 29, 1997, edition of the *Los Angeles Times*. "At least that appears to be the fate of the now-dilapidated hulk that stopped producing meringue pies and macaroons in 1990 and had its Dutch-style facade on Fletcher Drive in northeast Los Angeles declared a city landmark five years ago."

Gordon reported that the city's Cultural Heritage Commission voted unanimously not to block proposed demolition of the building, which at one time was dubbed "the Taj Mahal of bakeries."

This building survived, however, and is still in use. The Los Angeles Community College District spent $72 million to convert the old bakery into a Los Angeles City College satellite campus. However on December 31, 2012, the city prematurely terminated the district's lease after only 19 months of occupancy. The city currently leases the building to a charter school and job training groups. It remains the only example of an industrial plant in the Dutch Renaissance Revival style, while the old windmills can still be spotted on former coffee shops across California.

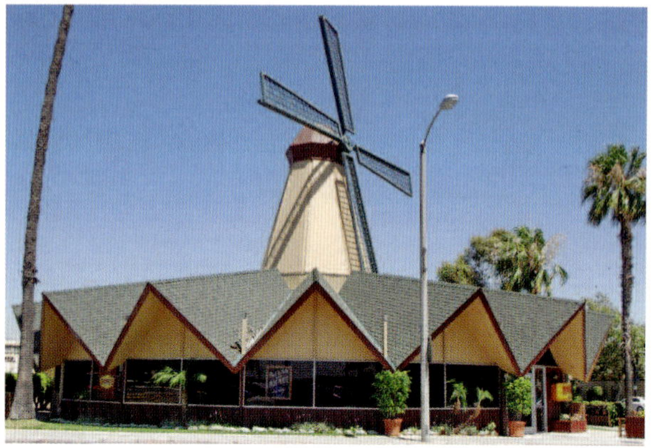

ABOVE *The bakery and the coffee shops are gone, but the Van de Kamp's windmills can still be found.*

LEFT *An advertisement for Van de Kamp's from the 1950s, fittingly done in typical colors of a Delft (Dutch) tile.*

ABOVE LEFT *Van De Kamps Bakery and Coffee Shop with drive-in service, circa 1945. Architect Wayne McAllister designed this Van de Kamp's outlet located at Fletcher Drive and San Fernando Road in Atwater Village.*

OPPOSITE PAGE *Yet another version of the Van de Kamp windmill, this one was at the intersection of West Pico Boulevard and Pelham Avenue.*

BELOW *This photograph snapped on December 17, 1937, shows the Van de Kamp outlet at Beverly Boulevard and Westmoreland Street.*

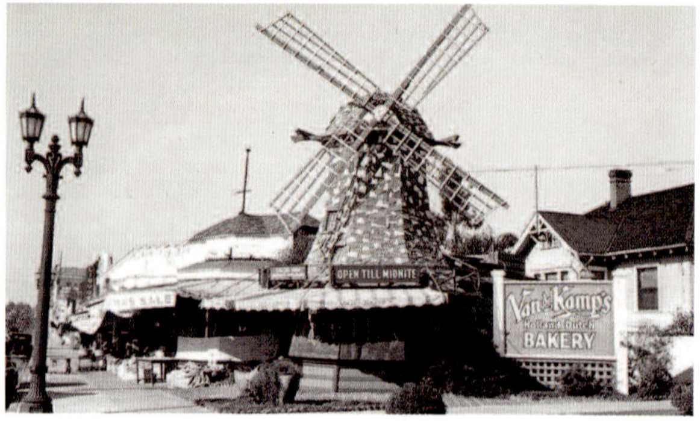

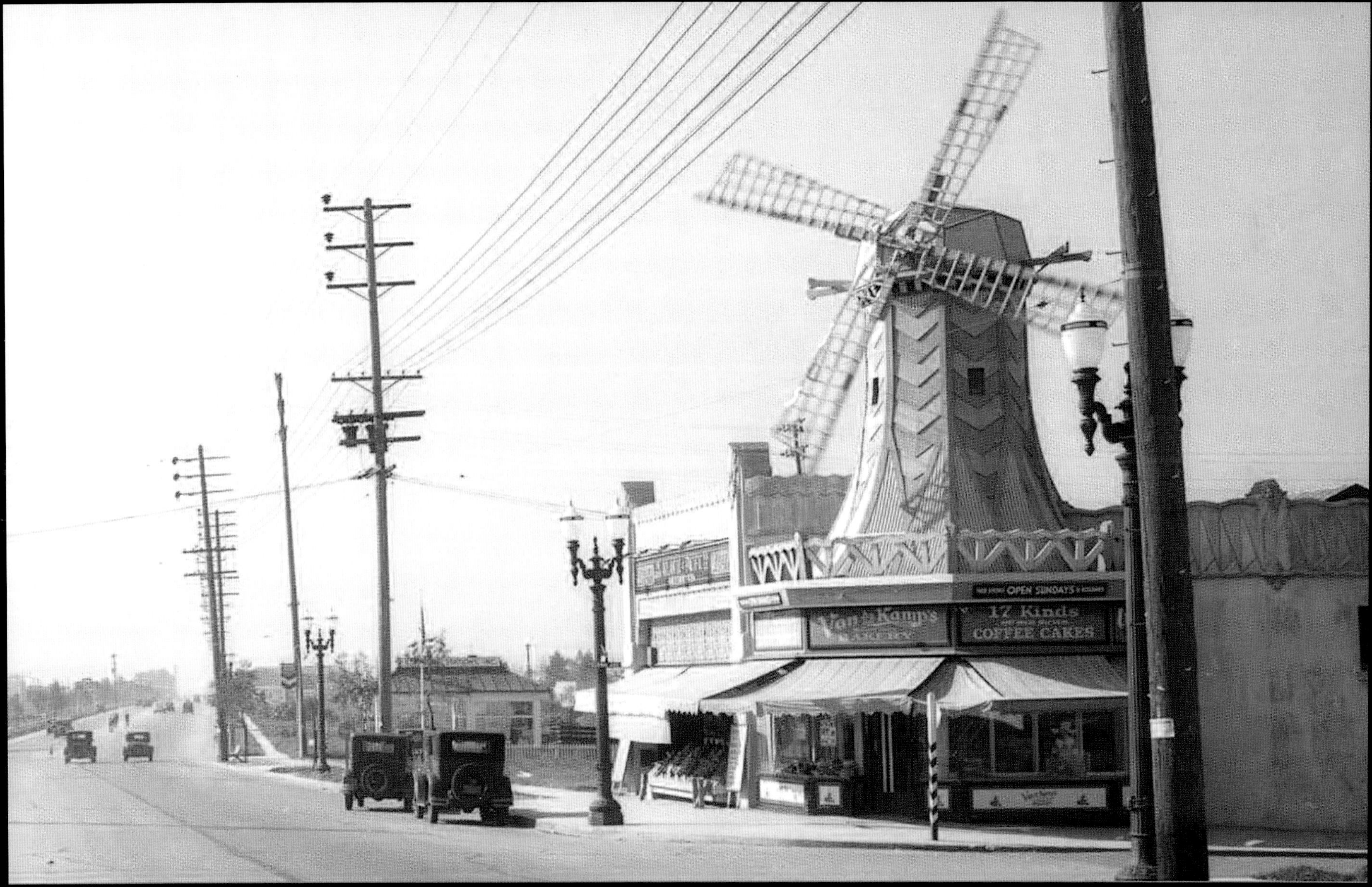
OPEN SUNDAYS
17 Kinds
COFFEE CAKES

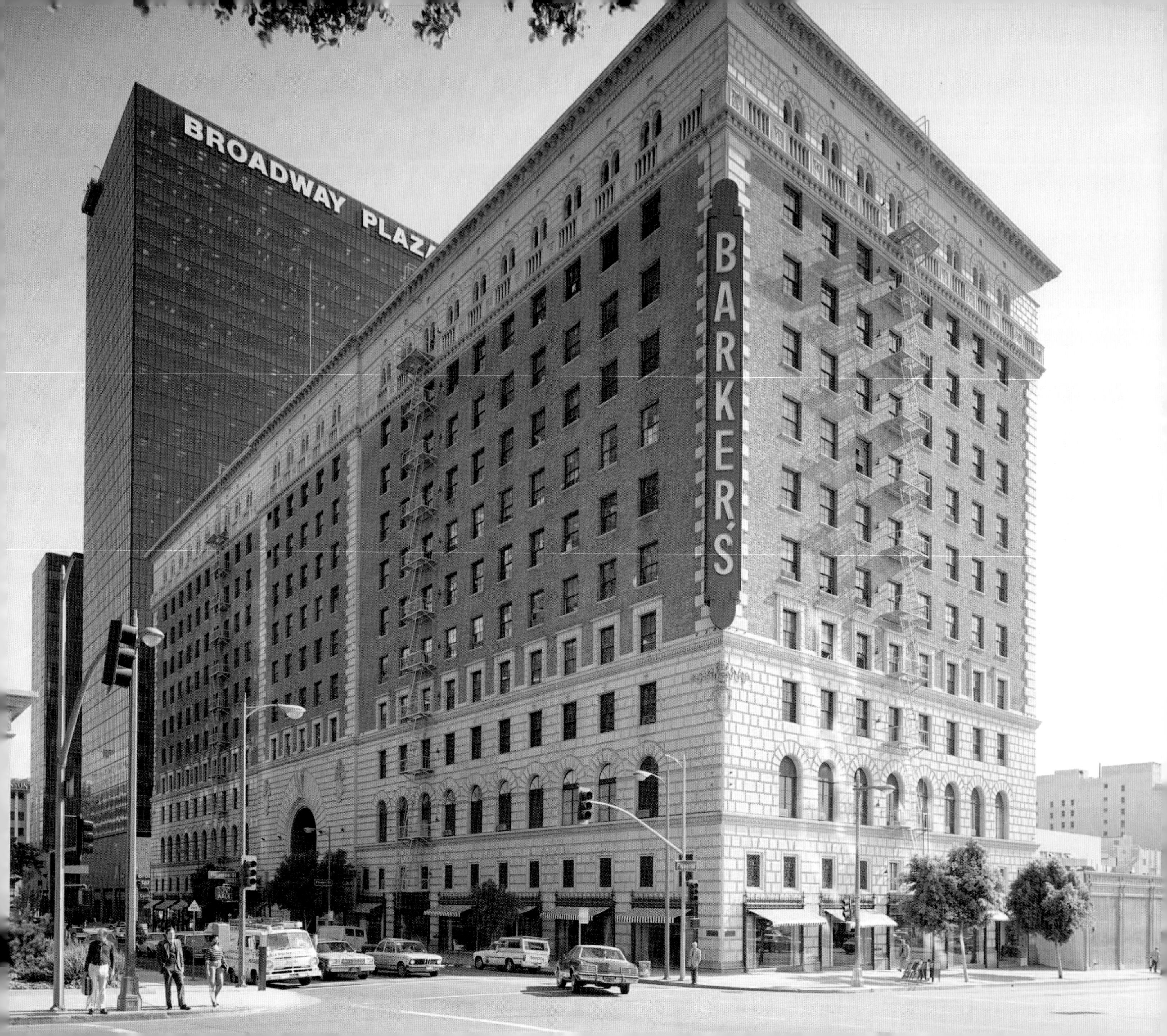
BROADWAY PLAZA
BARKER'S

Barker Bros. Furniture DECLARED BANKRUPT 1992

In a remarkable building in the historic Seventh Street district, the Barker Brothers Furniture Store once sold the finest in home furnishings to the Southern California elite.

Obadiah Truax Barker, a native of Indiana, had fallen in love with Los Angeles in 1880 when the population still hovered around 11,000. Barker could sense the place expanding, he saw the potential for a great city of homes and jumped into the home furnishings business with a partner, Otto Mueller. The story goes that the pair met at a horticulture fair where Barker overheard Mueller complaining that the lone furniture store in town had made it painfully expensive to furnish his home. The partners saw the need for competition and opened a 35-foot-wide store at 113 North Spring Street near Olvera.

Store management passed on to three of Barker's six sons and the company renamed O.T. Barker & Sons after Barker bought out Mueller. By 1887, Barker had all but retired, and his sons renamed his company Barker Brothers in 1898. The store enjoyed immediate success, growing steadily along with the city until moving into its 11-story temple to commercialism at 818 W. Seventh Street, completed in 1926.

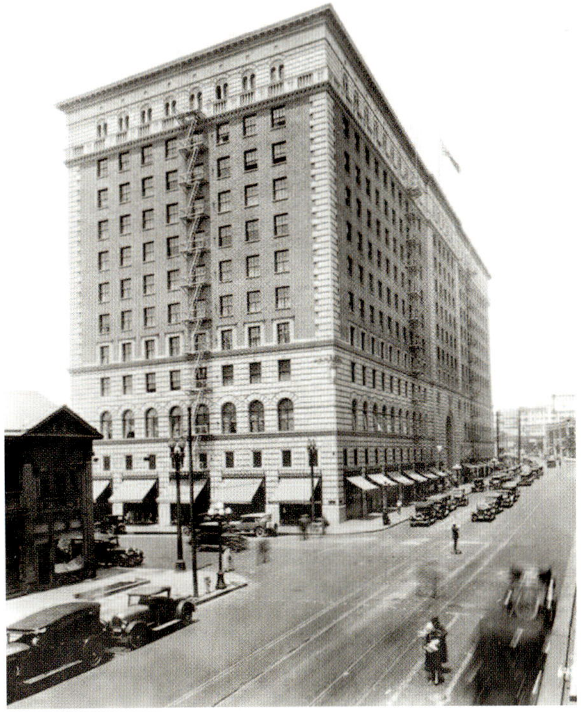

The fine structure, with its walnut paneling and Italian travertine marble, was said to have rivaled any monumental public building of the time. Featuring the fanciest styles of its day, the public regularly plied its halls and 11 elevators in search of the latest trend in furnishing. The building had six additional freight elevators to carry furniture and other merchandise. For nearly a century, Barker Brothers stores served Los Angeles in what seemed an unending era of profit, defining residential style.

Barker Brothers pioneered the concept of selling furniture in staged areas made to look like a room in the prospective buyer's home. The firm also helped architects and designers figure out ways to incorporate Barker Brothers products into their projects. These advisory services included providing floor plans, decorative sketches and color schemes.

At one point, ten stores within Los Angeles formed the Barker Brothers chain. The 1960s and 1970s were a rough time for retailers in city centers around the nation, leaving Barker Brothers with a tough decision over which stores to keep open. In 1984, they sold their last store in Los Angeles, the building at 818 W. Seventh, and fled to the suburbs where they opened 22 new stores.

The plan only sustained the chain another eight years. By 1992, after 111 years of selling furniture, Barker Brothers declared bankruptcy and closed. Since then, the glorious Beaux-Arts Renaissance Revival structure designed by Curlett & Beelman has been converted to a standard corporate office building and just recently underwent a historic restoration of its facade.

BELOW LEFT *A 1926 shot of the Barker Brothers building.*

BELOW *Barker Brothers advertising their "very lovely" silverware in 1929.*

OPPOSITE PAGE *Julius Shulman took this photo of the West Seventh Street store in 1980. Contributing architect Claude W. Beelman was responsible for many classic L.A. buildings including the Eastern Columbia Building on Broadway with its green-tinged terra cotta tiles.*

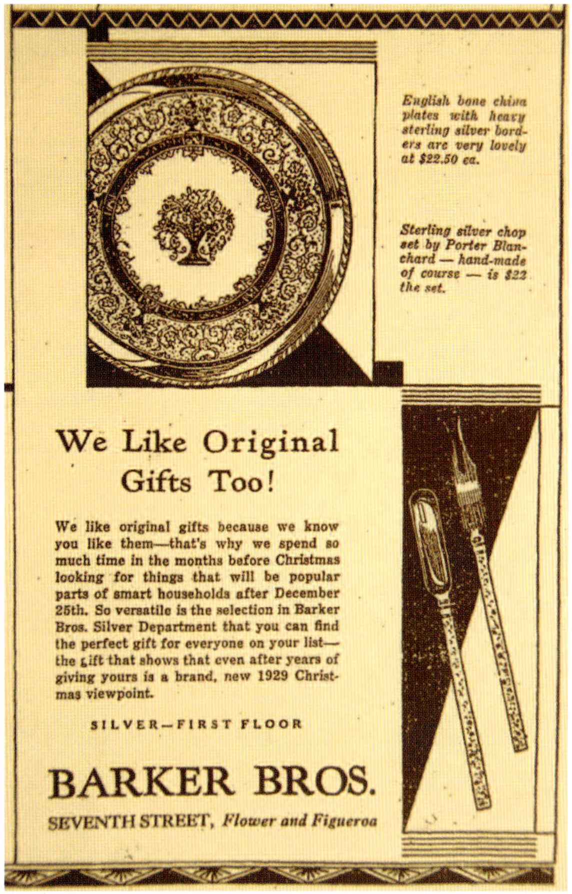

Egyptian Marquee REMOVED 1994

In 1903 Gilbert F. Stevenson and his wife lived at 6712 Hollywood Boulevard, at the corner of McCadden Place. Stevenson, an insurance man, purchased a five-acre lemon ranch as a solid investment. The city was entering a building boom in the teens with Hollywood's population multiplying seven times over in that single decade. Stevenson's lemon trees sat on increasingly valuable real estate.

By 1920, Stevenson had moved to the Santa Monica Hotel, another property he'd invested in. Around the same time, real estate developer Charles E. Toberman was seeking someone to build a high-class theater near his new neighborhoods.

Toberman was a hard man to miss in early Hollywood. According to local legend, he developed 53 subdivisions there, created more than 30 organizations and companies, built 29 commercial buildings and joined 49 clubs, fraternities and civic organizations, including the Masons where he met Gilbert Stevenson.

Soon, with the help of Sid Grauman, whose success with downtown theaters preceded him, Toberman was overseeing the construction of Grauman's Egyptian Theater where Stevenson's lemons once grew. Completed for its premiere showing of *Robin Hood* on October 18, 1922, the theater benefitted from the national craze that followed the discovery of King Tut's tomb that November.

Fronting Hollywood Boulevard with an Egyptian Revival-style building and a vertical sign reading "Grauman's," little else announced the theater from a distance. Grauman had no interest in marquees in the days when movie viewers came every week regardless of what played. By the late 1920s Grauman added promotions to surprise passersby: a pirate ship or steam locomotive, for example, might suddenly appear in the forecourt. Grauman began paying more attention to his Chinese Theater across the street after it opened in 1927. The year following his departure marked a change of approach. A permanent facade reading "Egyptian Theatre" appeared and below, a marquee spelling out movie names and stars—movie audiences were acquiring more discerning tastes.

In 1932, the vertical Grauman's sign was replaced by one reading "Egyptian" on the opposite side of the entrance.

By 1946, movies needed more promotion to compete with television, and elaborate advertisements began occasionally obliterating the marquee. For the premieres of *Duel in the Sun* and *Til Clouds Rolled By* signs featuring the movies' headliners completely covered the marquee and easily tripled its height.

In 1950, the year of Grauman's death, the Egyptian became something new, with a towering concrete facade that would be striped with neon or decorated with movie promotions that distinctly modernized the place.

Fast forward four decades and Hollywood had fallen on hard times. The Egyptian was in decline, a discount movie house offering tickets at less than the 1922 opening's price. In 1992 the theater closed. While workers restored damage sustained in the 1994 Northridge quake, the facade was removed. After a $12.8 million rehabilitation the theater reopened in 1998 with a facade more in keeping with Grauman's original vision of an understated entrance.

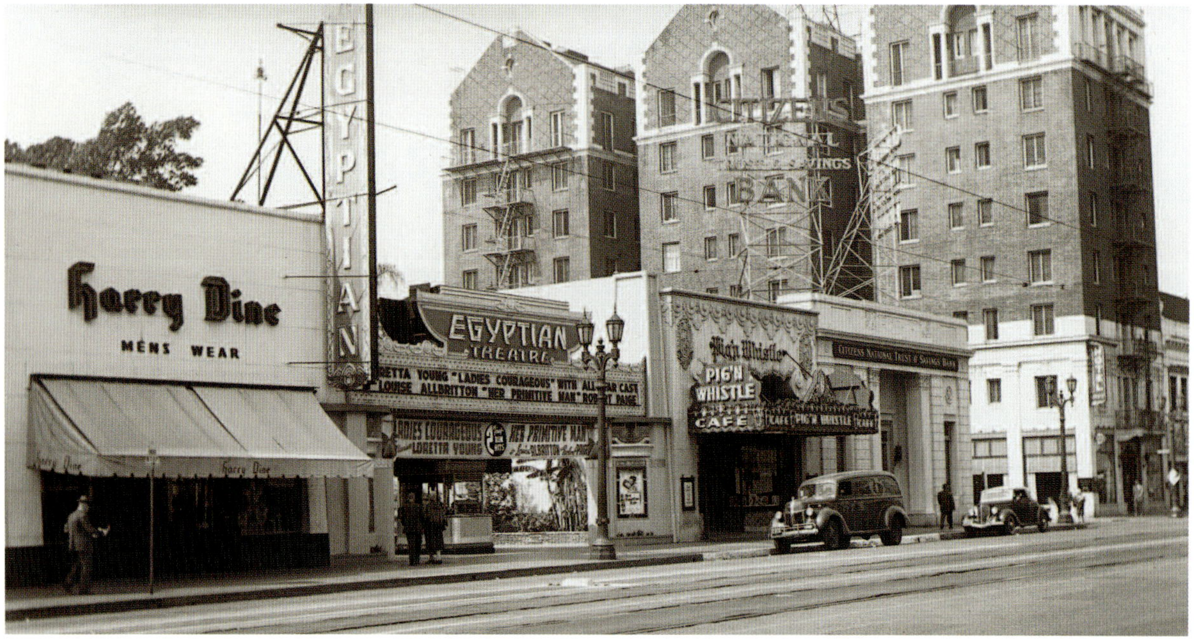

LEFT *The Egyptian photographed in 1944 alongside the Pig'n Whistle cafe, which opened in 1927, closed in 1949, and then reopened in 2001.*

BELOW *The current Egyptian Theatre facade.*

OPPOSITE PAGE *The Egyptian Theatre underwent a major renovation in 1955 that included this huge marquee, a new sign, box office and a redesigned forecourt. The 1955 marquee appears here in 1966 during the movie premiere of* How to Steal a Million.

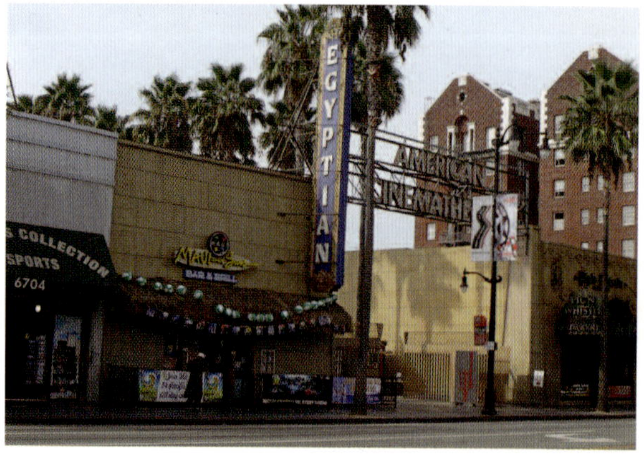

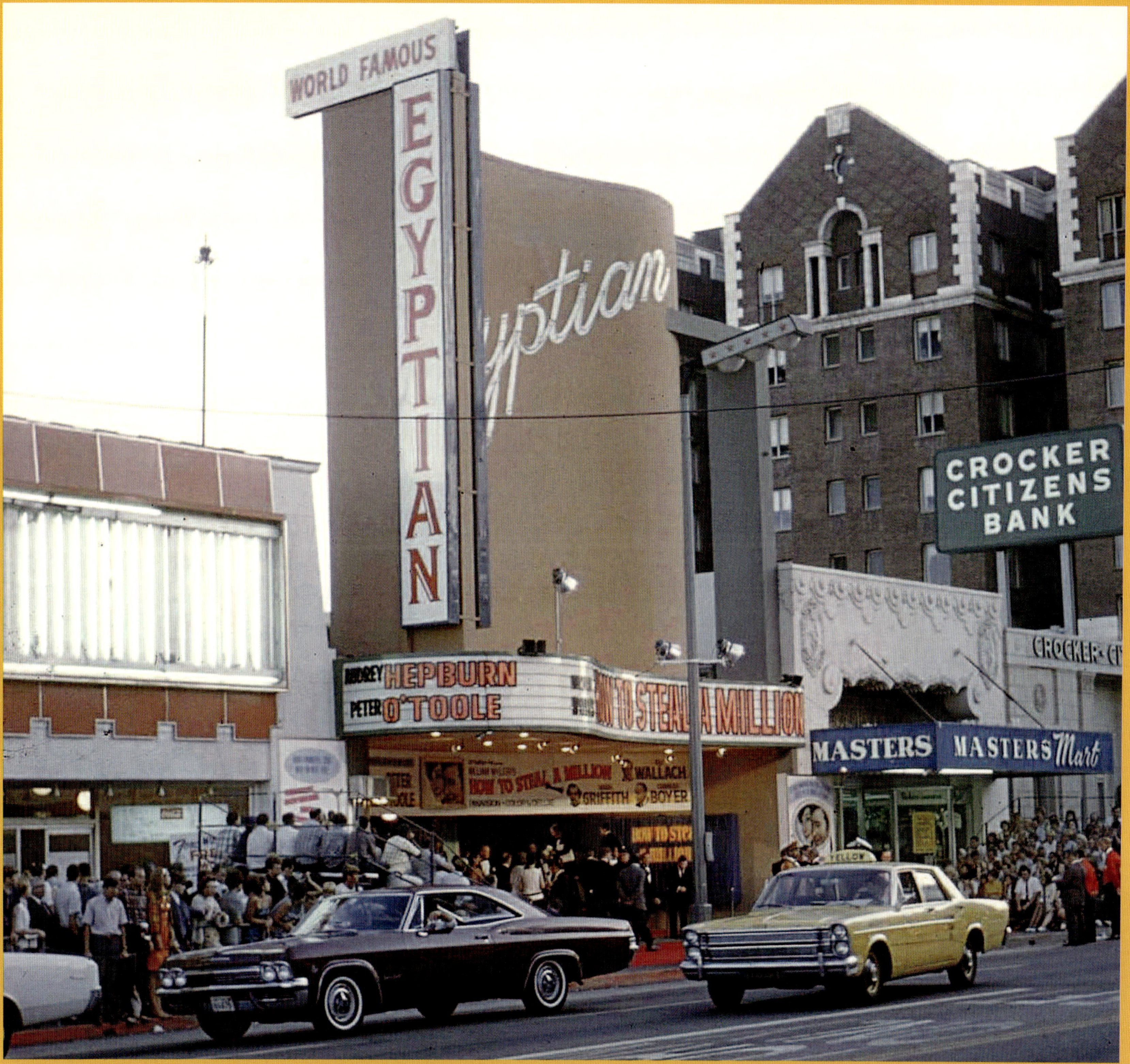
WORLD FAMOUS
EGYPTIAN
CROCKER
CITIZENS
BANK
AUDREY HEPBURN
PETER O'TOOLE
HOW TO STEAL A MILLION
WALLACH
GRIFFITH
BOYER
MASTERS
MASTERS Mart

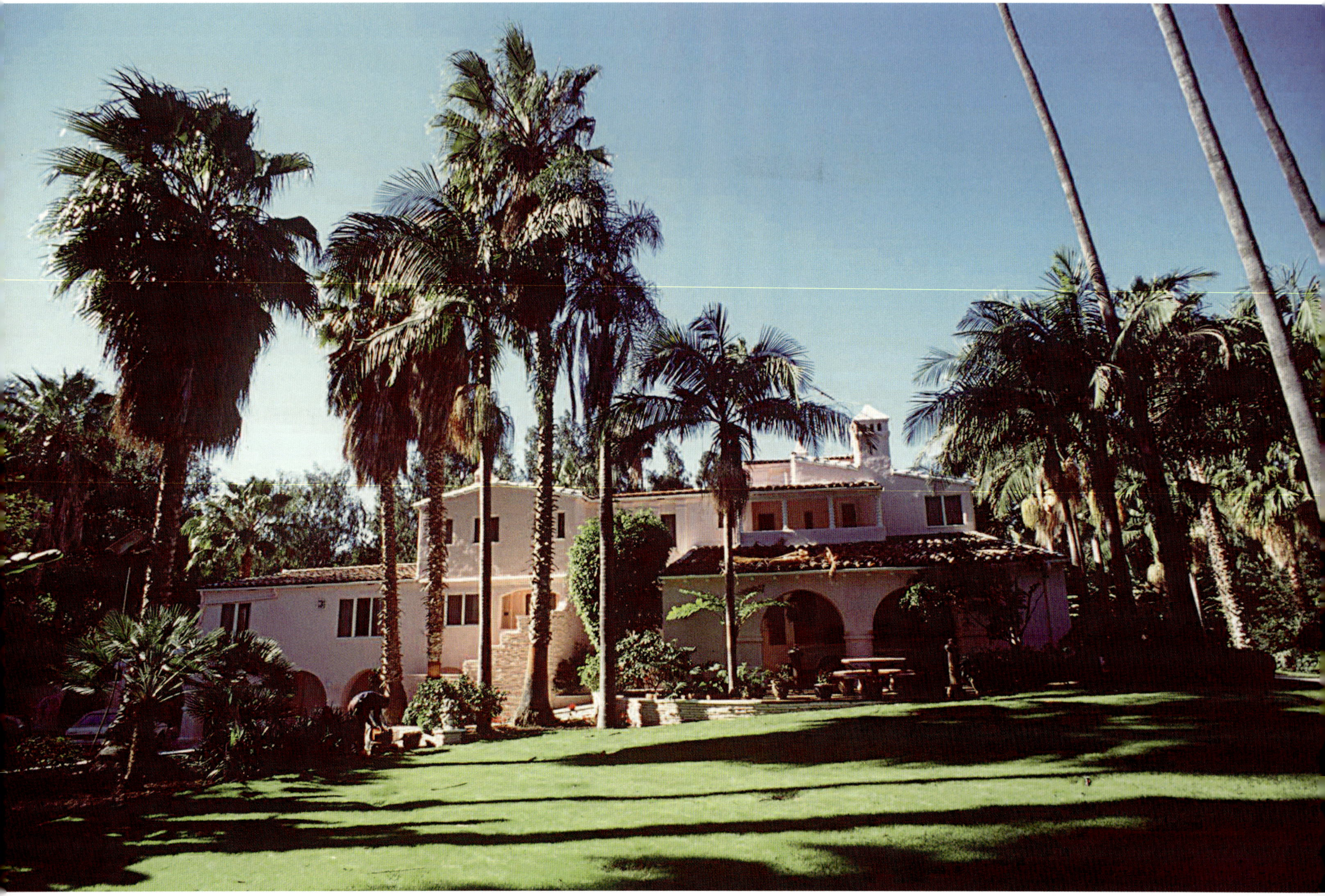

Pink Palace DEMOLISHED 2002

Two of Hollywood's leading starlets in the 1950s and early 1960s, Marilyn Monroe and Jayne Mansfield, lived seemingly parallel lives. Known as the Working Man's Monroe, Mansfield was other studios' answer to 20th Century Fox's exclusive contract with Monroe.

Born Vera Jayne Palmer in Bryn Mawr, Pennsylvania, Mansfield acted on stage and screen, sang and entertained in nightclubs, and was among the early *Playboy* Playmates. As the story goes, Jayne first discovered her penchant for Hollywood glamour during a visit to Los Angeles in 1946 at the age of 13.

Vera Jayne began breaking hearts as a beauty queen, earning titles such as Miss Photoflash, Miss Magnesium Lamp, Miss Fire Prevention Week, Miss Geiger Counter and plenty more, often hiding the fact that she'd married public relations professional Paul Mansfield.

Her constant public attention, wardrobe malfunctions and her oft-repeated 1955 *Playboy* spread helped launch her career. She acted off Broadway, picked up bit parts in films, but her first major screen role came in 1956 playing Jerri Jordan in *The Girl Can't Help It*. She'd moved on to her second husband, body builder Mickey Hargitay by then, and purchased the 40-room mansion built in 1929 and recently vacated by singer and bandleader Rudy Vallee. Built in the Mediterranean style at 10100 Sunset Boulevard in Holmby Hills, Mansfield bought the home not with new Hollywood riches, but with an inheritance from her grandfather.

She promptly remodeled the estate to match her abundant femininity. She had the house painted pink, installed pink furs and a pink, heart-shaped bathtub in the bathroom as well as a fountain "filled with pink champagne" and a bevy of cupid statues bathed in pink fluorescent light on the grounds. Hargitay personally built a pink, heart-shaped swimming pool. Dubbed "the Pink Palace," Mansfield ruled as one of the queens of Hollywood from there.

Much of the decorations and furnishings in the home came free of charge as Mansfield wrote to various companies asking if she could display and represent their products in her new home. She received no less than $150,000 in free samples when the mansion had cost just $76,000.

The very embodiment of the term "sex symbol," Mansfield's major film career was all but finished by the early 1960s when the studios lost interest in busty blonde bombshells, but she still had a devoted fan following and was popular in Europe. Her untimely death at the age of 34 in 1967 (five years after Monroe passed) was decidedly more working class than Hollywood: she was killed in a car crash outside of Biloxi, Mississippi.

After Mansfield's death the home passed to musicians Cass Elliot, who died in 1974, Ringo Starr and then Engelbert Humperdinck. In November 2002 Humperdinck sold the home to the owner of the neighboring property, Owlwood. The new Owlwood comprises a ten-acre estate that includes the site of the former Pink Palace which was torn down.

BELOW *Allan Grant shooting for* Time Life *in 1960 caught the Hollywood sex symbol and her pet dog in one of her opulent Pink Palace bedrooms.*

OPPOSITE PAGE *The image primarily used in real estate advertising to sell Jayne Mansfield's former home.*

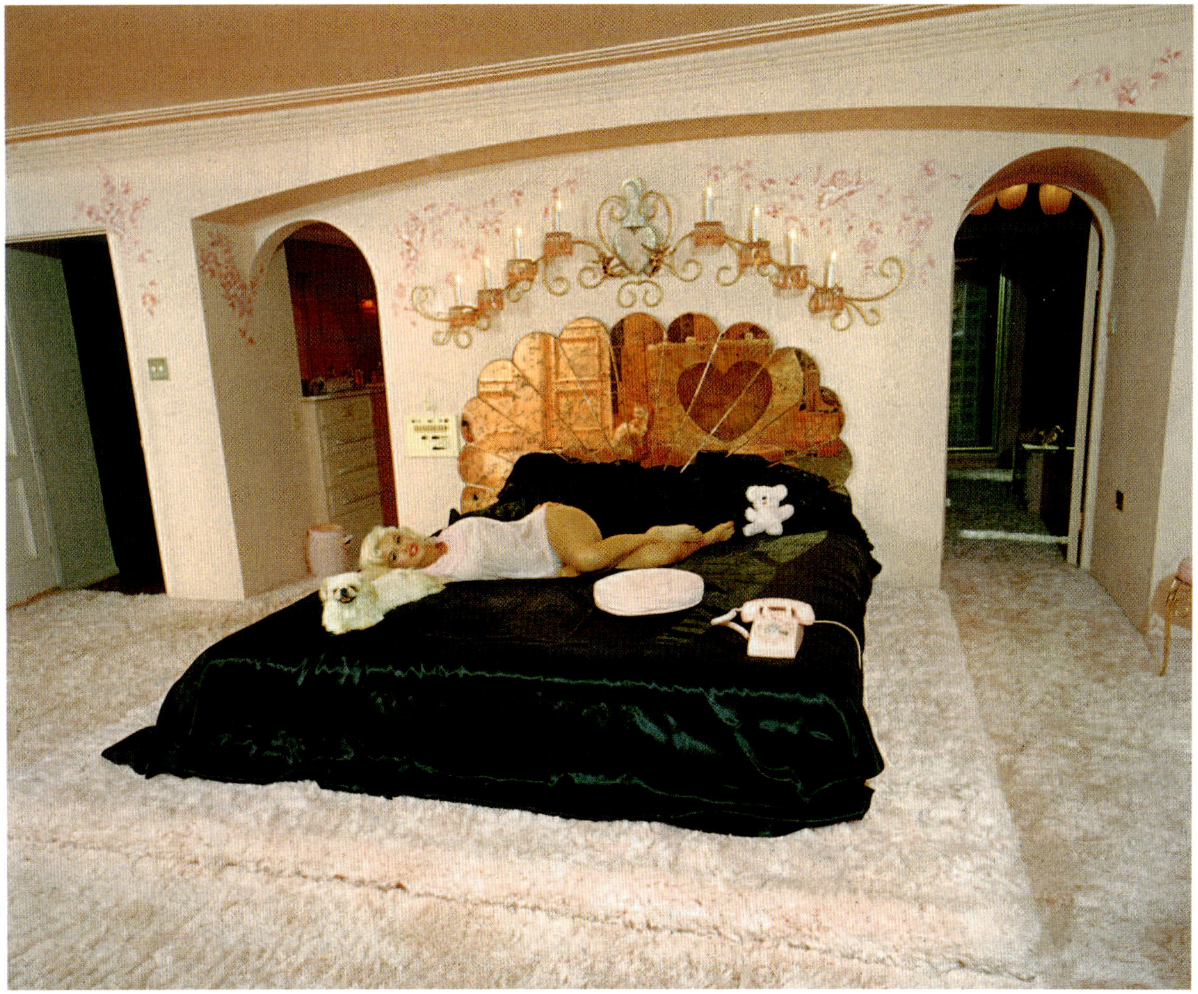

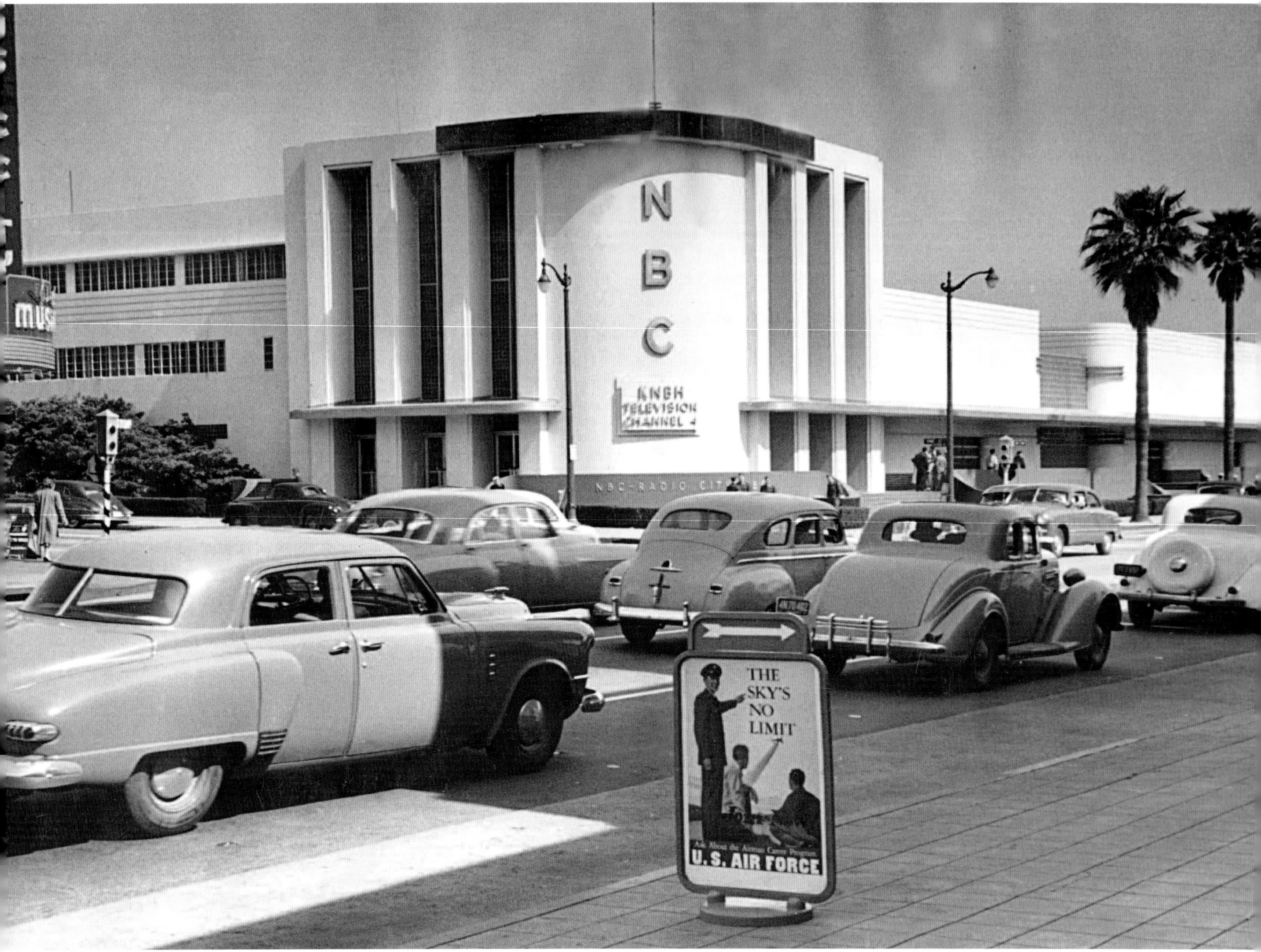
NBC
KNBH
TELEVISION
CHANNEL 4
THE SKY'S NO LIMIT
U.S. AIR FORCE

Radio City LAST BROADCAST 2005

Radio was the first medium to bring the world into people's homes and at one time Hollywood stars looked to radio to build their careers. That perfect synergy led to Hollywood becoming the capital of nationwide broadcasting.

Mention CBS to Americans and few will know the initials come from the company's original name, Columbia Broadcasting System, or that it began as a radio (not television) broadcaster. Ruthless competition between NBC (National Broadcasting Company) and CBS led both companies to establish West Coast headquarters closer to Hollywood's talent in 1938.

CBS Columbia Square was located at 6121 Sunset Boulevard. Constructed at the cost of $2 million, more than any prior broadcasting facility, the new building sat on the site of one of Hollywood's first movie studios belonging to the Nestor Film Company. This example of International Modernist architecture by architect William Lescaze was said to incorporate "many innovations of design, acoustics and control, and will improve the art of broadcasting" according to then-CBS President William Paley. A special day of broadcasts celebrated the facility's opening, ending with "A Salute to Columbia Square" featuring Bob Hope and many other stars. The building also housed the CBS Television Network until 1952 when a separate facility was built.

Between 2004 and 2007 all of these operations moved away to other parts of Los Angeles and its environs. A movement is currently underway to preserve the building, designated a historic site by the city in 2009, while plans circulate to redevelop the site into an office or residential tower.

NBC Radio Network's West Coast headquarters opened at the corner of Sunset and Vine, just a block away from Columbia Square, also in 1938. (The nation's third major network, American Broadcasting Company, or ABC, sat just a few doors down Vine). Nicknamed Radio City, NBC didn't actually produce a Los Angeles radio program from the building when it opened. Instead, content produced in San Francisco was aired in Los Angeles for a time.

With both CBS and ABC in the vicinity, locals began to call the entire neighborhood Radio City. The record shop, Music City, and Capitol Records, both owned by record industry innovator Glenn Wallich, also helped characterize the neighborhood.

Eventually NBC's facility would be too small for television production, and just as CBS created its Television City in 1952, NBC created Color City in 1955, the first facility prepared solely to produce television shows in color. By 1964, NBC's building had been demolished as all production moved to other facilities. Today, on the site of the former Streamline Moderne Building is a branch of the Chase bank.

In 2005 Radio City was truly lost when the last radio broadcast emanated from the neighborhood. Announcers at KNX (1070) signed off for the day at Columbia Square, the last of nearly 70 radio stations based in the area.

OPPOSITE PAGE *NBC originally used the nickname "NBC Radio City" for their headquarters in New York. Their West Coast headquarters made it more formal, emblazoning Radio City on the building. The generation of the 1940s and 1950s, came to know Hollywood as Radio City. The fact that each of the prominent national broadcasters had their headquarters in the neighborhood inspired radio-themed restaurants: Brittingham's Radio Center Restaurant, The Radio Room, The Radio Center Market and even the Radio Motel.*

BELOW FAR LEFT *ABC's Streamline Moderne-style building on Vine Street started life as a bowling lane and recreation center.*

BELOW LEFT *Two different views of the William Lescaze-designed CBS headquarters from the 1930s.*

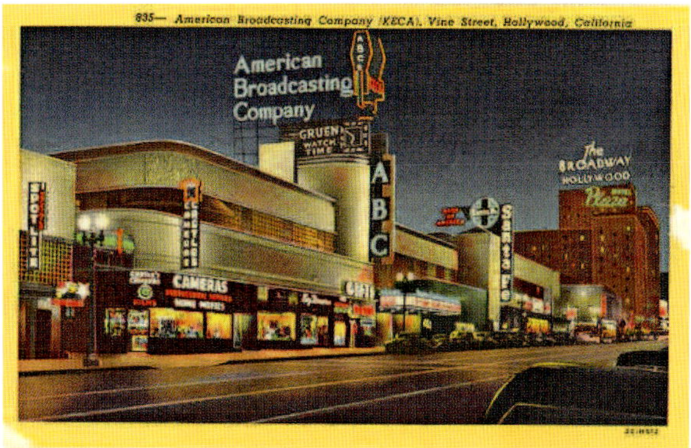

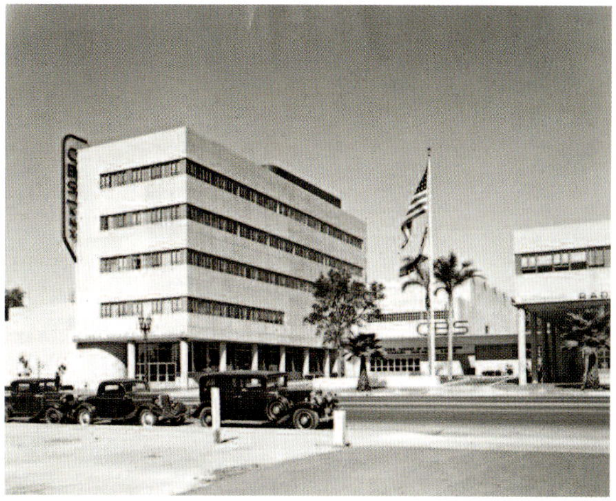

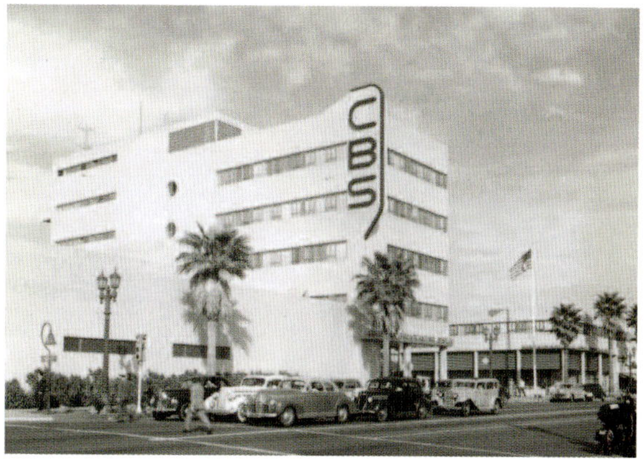

Ambassador Hotel **RAZED 2006**

Steeped in historic significance, the once opulent 400-room Ambassador Hotel provides a stunning example of lost Los Angeles. The imposing building occupied almost 24 acres at 3400 Wilshire Boulevard between Eighth and Catalina streets, nearly to Mariposa Avenue. It hosted the prestigious Cocoanut Grove nightclub and played host to many historic events throughout its 68 years operating as an hotel.

Architect Myron Hunt designed the Ambassador which opened in 1921 on the site of a former dairy farm. Hunt's portfolio of work included the Rose Bowl Stadium, Pasadena Central Library and Huntington Hotel in Pasadena.

At the time of its opening, the hotel joined a chain, the Ambassador Hotels System, which included four other properties: Ambassador New York, Ambassador Atlantic City, Ambassador Santa Barbara and the Alexandria in Los Angeles. The association was short lived. The Santa Barbara property burned a few months after the Ambassador Los Angeles opened. The Alexandria left the chain in 1925, while the Ambassador Palm Beach opened in 1929. During the depression, the chain fell on hard times and dissolved. Ambassador Los Angeles became part of the J. Myer Schine family trust's portfolio.

Several Academy Award ceremonies were held in the hotel, but it wasn't just the entertainment elite who stayed in the hotel's storied hallways. Every sitting president from Herbert Hoover to Richard Nixon is said to have stayed there.

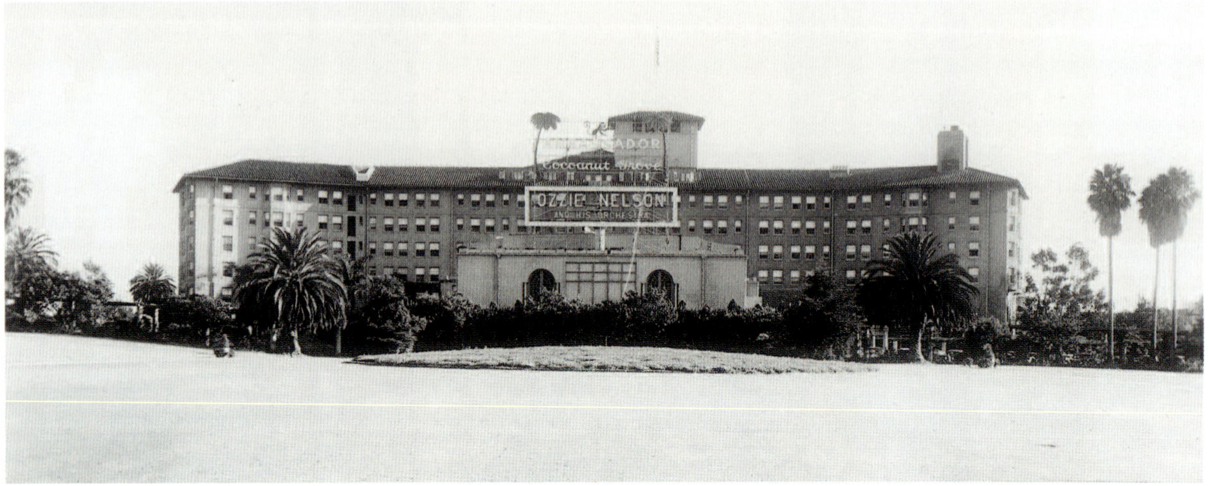

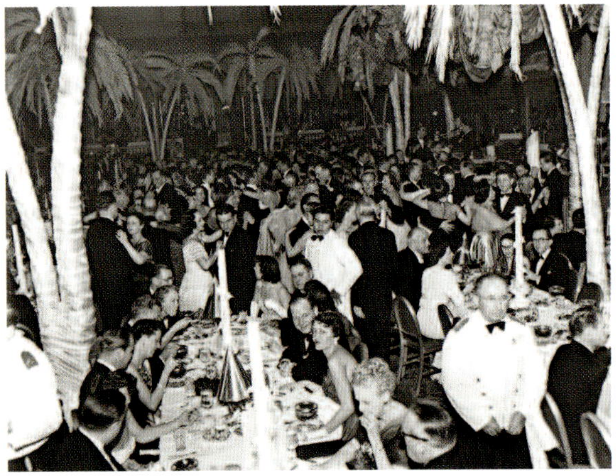

The 1968 assassination of presidential candidate and former U.S. Attorney General, Robert F. Kennedy, along with the wounding of five other people, in a pantry off the Embassy Ballroom created a sense of tragic significance to the place. It marked the start of a downward spiral from which the hotel would never recover.

Managers attempted to revive flagging attendance at the Cocoanut Grove by turning creative control over to the ever-popular Sammy Davis, Jr. in the mid-1970s, but it wasn't enough to turn the venue round.

After selling for $64 million on January 3, 1989, the hotel closed. Though listed on the National Register of Historic Places, and the exclusive category of Historic Hotels of America, a large part of the shuttered hotel fell to the wrecking ball between 2005 and 2006.

The property passed to the Los Angeles Unified School District and has since become the Robert F. Kennedy Community Schools. Elements of the hotel were incorporated in the school's design, including: The Cocoanut Grove, which serves as a 582-seat theater; the 1940s-era, Paul R. Williams-designed coffee shop, which serves as a teachers' lounge; and the intricate vaulted ceiling of the hotel's Embassy Ballroom (the site of Kennedy's final political speech), which was reconstructed as the library for secondary students.

ABOVE *Ozzie Nelson and his band were resident at the Cocoanut Grove through the 1940s. The proximity to Hollywood allowed Nelson to make film appearances and star in Red Skelton's radio show.*

LEFT *A lively crowd gathered at the Cocoanut Grove on December 17, 1949, to enjoy a Candlelight Ball.*

OPPOSITE PAGE *After it closed, the Ambassador was regularly used as a film location and appears in many films including;* Pretty Woman, Forrest Gump, Apollo 13, Beaches, *but particularly noteworthy is* The Thirteenth Floor, *where it was transformed back to its 1937 appearance.*

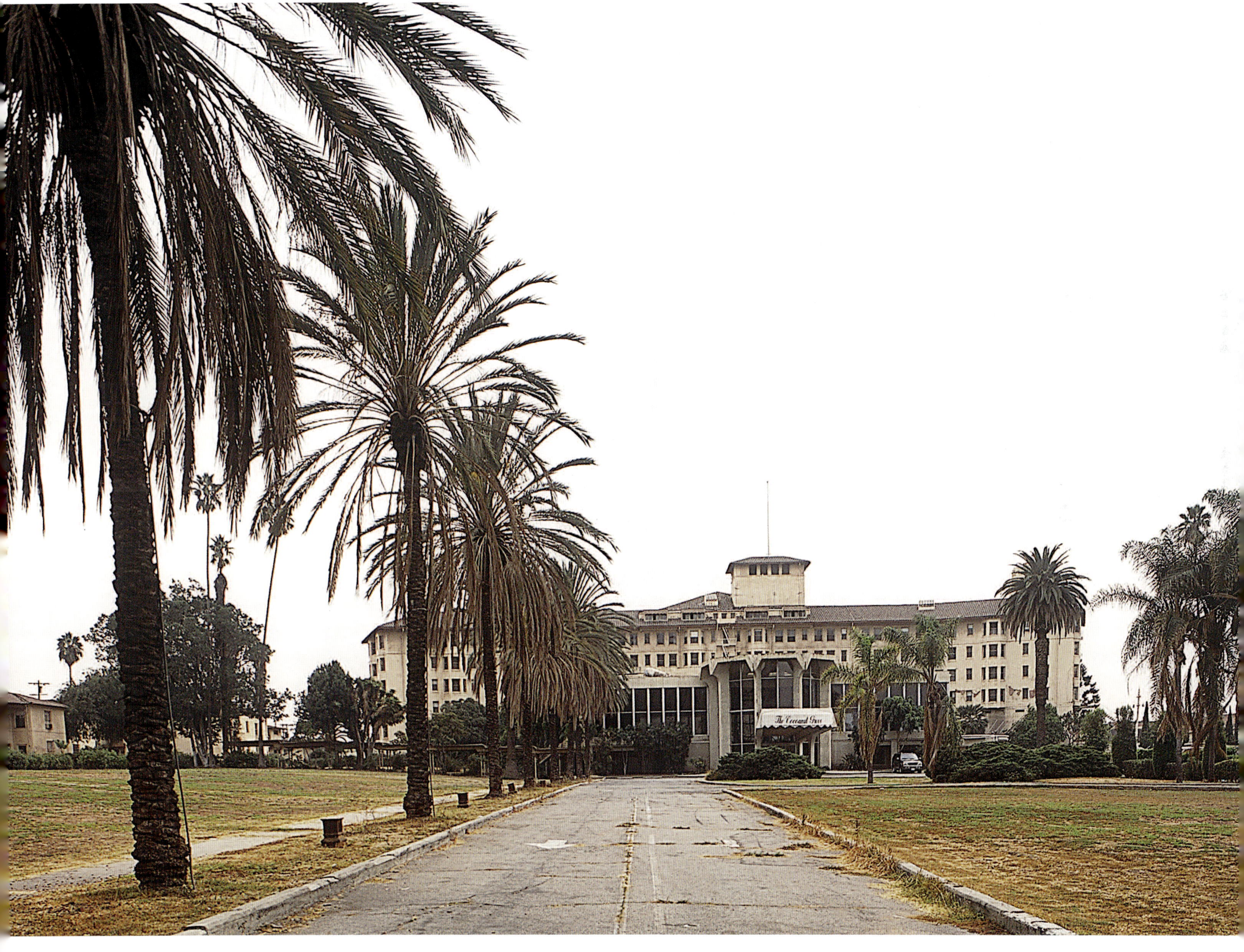

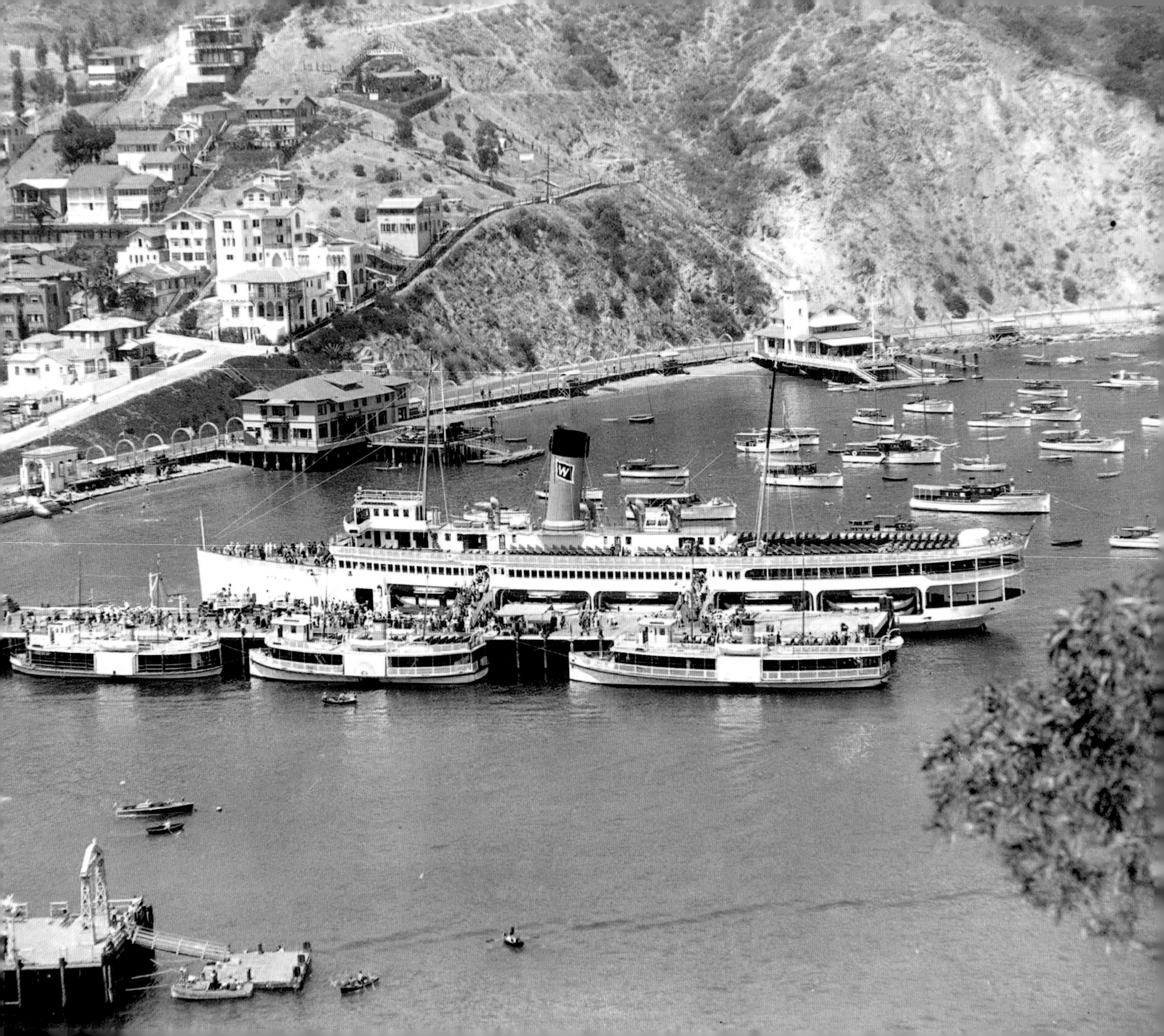

S.S. Catalina CUT UP FOR SCRAP 2009

The S.S. *Catalina*, or "Great White Steamer," as it was affectionately known, first plied the waters between Los Angeles and Santa Catalina island on June 30, 1924. The brainchild of chewing gum millionaire William Wrigley, Jr., this elegant steamship carried passengers from Los Angeles to Wrigley's resort on the Island for the next 51 years. The five-decked craft cost $1,000,000 to build and carried up to 2,000 passengers at a time for the Wilmington Transportation Company, one of Wrigley's holdings.

Wrigley had stumbled upon a fortune while trying to run a soap and baking powder company. The company (which sold for $1.5 billion in 2005) included individually wrapped sticks of chewing gum, as a promotion, with its baking powder and set off a sensation. Before long Wrigley had turned his focus to America's sweet tooth as his gum proved more popular than his baking powder. Wrigley amassed a fortune, and by 1919, he purchased almost the entirety of Santa Catalina.

Wrigley set up public utilities, a hotel and casino, a quarry and tile plant on the island as well as regular steamship service. The regular service, performed by the S.S. *Catalina* and its sister ship, the S.S. *Avalon,* proved very popular. The *Los Angeles Times* described the *Catalina* as "a world of luxurious leather and teak. On the upper deck people danced to swinging big bands. Magicians and clowns entertained passengers. On the lower deck youngsters played hide and seek among the lifeboats, and couples found hidden spots where they could be alone."

Presidents Calvin Coolidge and Herbert Hoover were among the *Catalina's* long list of famous passengers. According to the Steamship Historical Society, the S.S. *Catalina* carried more passengers (25 million) in its five decades of operation than any other vessel of its kind. Some 820,000 of those passengers came during World War II when the *Catalina* moved to San Francisco Bay for active duty as a troop transport.

By the 1970s, a decade after the ship had sold to a group of investors, smaller vessels were proving more efficient at covering the 26-mile trip to Santa Catalina, and the *Catalina* was retired in 1975. The ship sold for $70,000 to real estate developer Hymie Singer as a Valentine's gift for his wife in 1977, and moved from port to port for a time. Proposals for other tours of duty never panned out for the ship and twice it broke free of its moorings. In 1985 Singer moved the ship to Ensenada Harbor where several efforts to revive her as a commercial venture failed. There, the S.S. *Catalina* broke free again and ran up on a sandbar in the harbor in 1997.

For a little over a decade, the ship, listed as a Los Angeles Historic-Cultural Monument and a California Historical Landmark, sank halfway into the mud, decayed, rusted and was looted. The decision to scrap her came in 2009. By 2010, what was left of the S.S. *Catalina* had relocated to Lost Los Angeles.

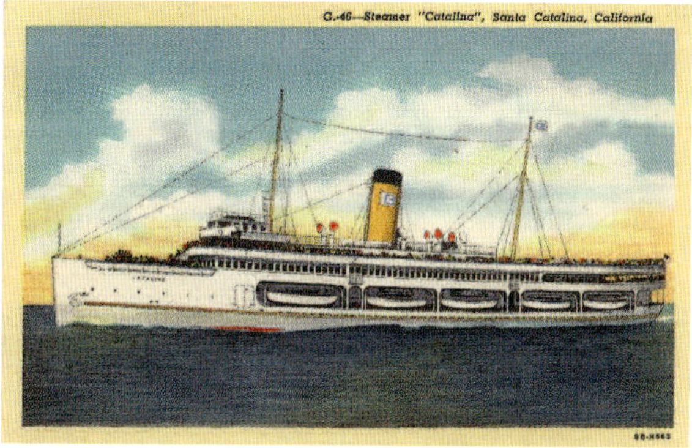

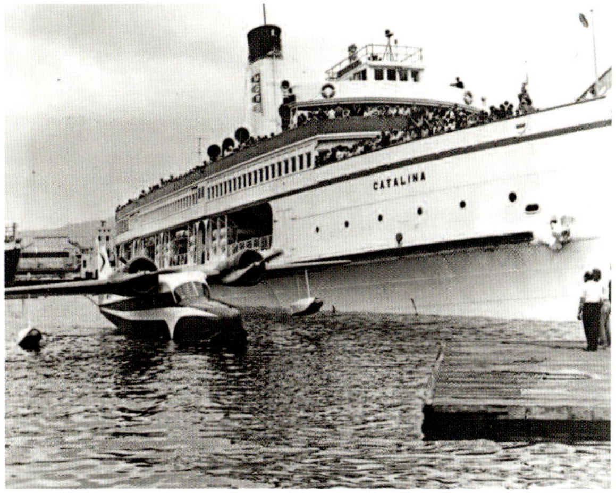

OPPOSITE PAGE *The S.S.* Catalina, *with its smoke stack featuring prominently, waits docked alongside the pier at Avalon on Santa Catalina Island.*

ABOVE RIGHT *A postcard of the* Catalina *in its heyday.*

RIGHT *The historic ship was allowed to sit and rust for twelve years.*

LEFT *There were actually two ways of traveling to Catalina Island, the leisurely way via the SS* Catalina, *or by seaplane using the Grumman Goose seaplane. The seaplanes operated out of Long Beach airport and ran from the 1940s through to the late 1960s.*

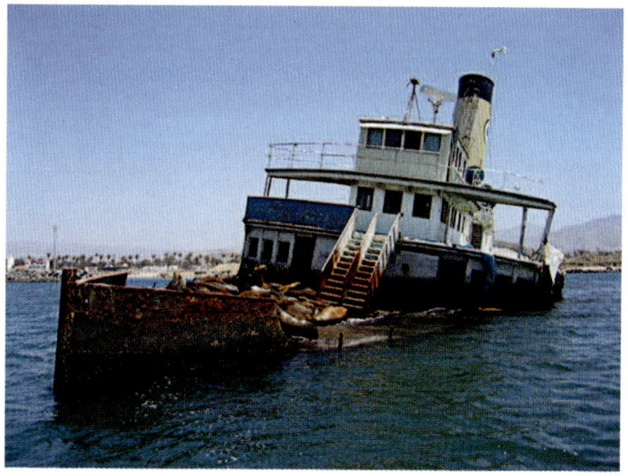

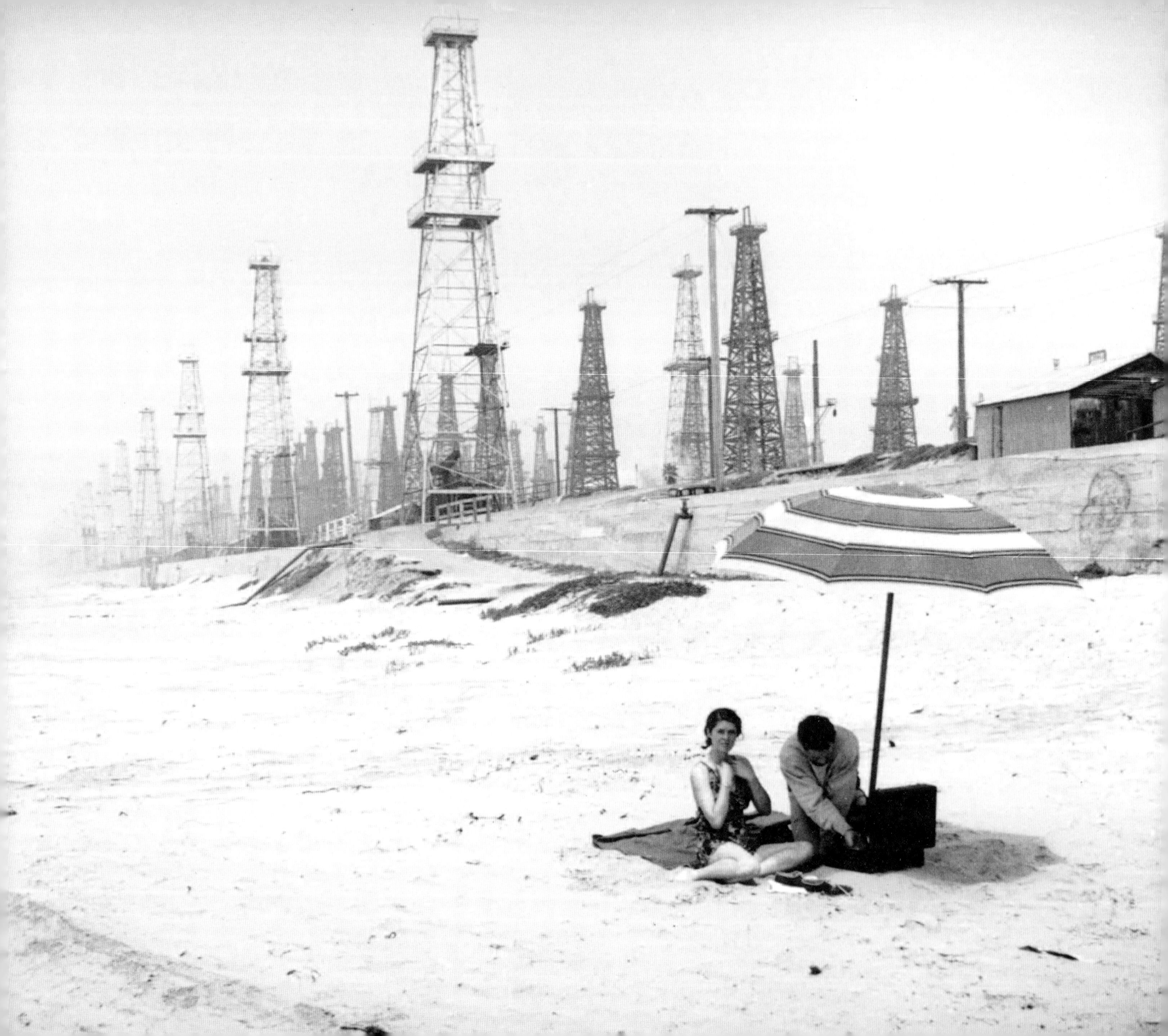

Los Angeles City Oil Field TAPPED OUT 2011

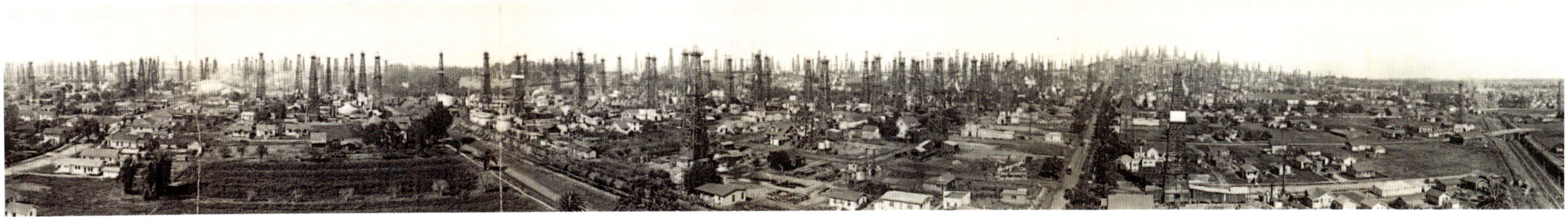

Edwin Doheny was flat broke, but he thought he had a way to strike it rich. He talked his old friend and mining partner Charles A. Canfield into putting up $400 to lease some land near today's Glendale Boulevard and Colton Street, just south of Chavez Ravine.

The pair leased the property and on April 20, 1892, got to work digging a well. John Yewell writes in the *Monterey Herald* that the pair started "with picks and shovels, and at 150 feet resorted to ramming the trunk of a eucalyptus tree into the hole. It was primitive, but it worked. They were soon producing 40 barrels a day."

Doheny had tapped into the Los Angeles City Oil Field. This 780-acre field of dreams was about a quarter mile wide and four miles long. It extended from the area south of today's Dodger Stadium where Doheny and Canfield sunk their well, to Vermont Avenue. By April 20, 1893, wildcatters had sunk 121 wells into this oil field. By 1901, 1,150 active wells had pumped more than 1.8 million barrels of oil.

Doheny and Canfield did not discover this field. California Department of Conservation credits several groups of prospectors and drillers including the Maltman and Ruhland oil companies.

They were also not the first to sink a well here. The 1857 "Dryden Well" was a relatively shallow hand-dug affair near Third and Coronado streets. It produced some heavy oil, tar, and asphaltum during the next 30 years; no-one recorded how much, however. The product was used mostly to oil the streets.

Little remains above ground of the 1,250 wells that were finally drilled into the Los Angeles City Oil Field, and the forest of derricks that once covered hills north of downtown Los Angeles, including Signal Hill.

This was not the only oil field here. At its peak, some 3,700 derricks were busy extracting oil from 55 active oil fields in the Greater Los Angeles Area, including Venice and even Beverly Hills.

Production continues to this day at a reduced level in some of the outer fields. According to the Center for Land Use Interpretation, there are still more urban oil fields in and around the Los Angeles area than anywhere else in the United States. Only now they are heavily disguised in anonymous buildings, the only telltale signs being methane vents on curbs.

Oil still flows from the Sawtelle, Inglewood and Beverly Hills oil fields around Los Angeles. The Beverley Hills Oil Field sports disguised oil towers. These include the fancy Venoco Flower Tower, whose costume could almost fool the passerby and the Plain Exploration and Production Tower on Pico Boulevard.

The vast Los Angeles City Oil Field is all but tapped out; the flow reduced to a dribble. Only one well remains. It still pumps oil at a spot behind a fence on South Mountain View Avenue, one block east of Alvarado Street in the Westlake neighborhood. It produces about three and a half barrels a day.

Urban renewal spelled an end to production in the Los Angeles City Oil Field. Over time, homes, shopping centers and parks had taken over most of the field. Commercial production finally stopped in January 2011, when Allenco Energy capped seven abandoned oil wells in Echo Park to make room for an affordable housing project.

ABOVE *When oil was found at Signal Hill, the wildcatters didn't wait for the population to move out before they started extensive drilling. This panorama is from circa 1923.*

BELOW *This oil well was drilled right in the middle of La Cienega Boulevard. Over the close-to-40 years it was in existence it produced 600,000 barrels of crude oil.*

OPPOSITE PAGE *Oil derricks near Huntington Beach around 1937, one of the many photos from the Herman J. Schultheis Collection at the Los Angeles Public Library. Schultheis was an animator for Walt Disney who was a keen amateur photographer and amassed a huge collection of photos depicting everyday life in Los Angeles.*

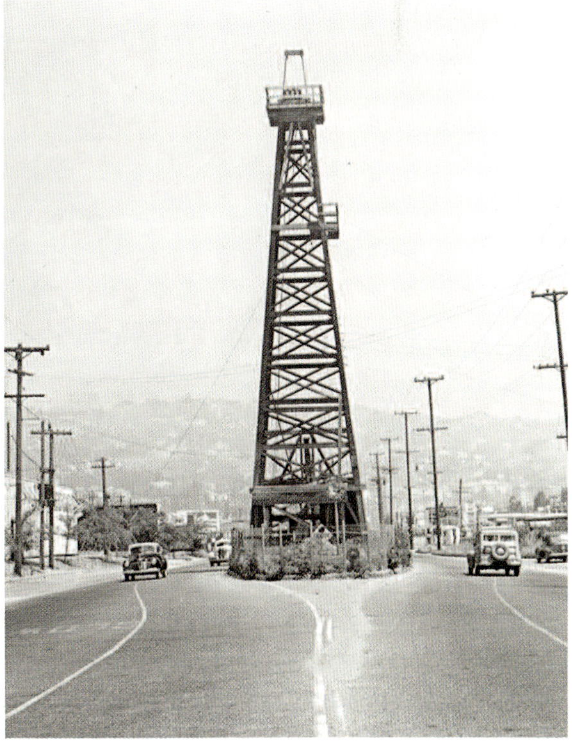

Theme Building Restaurant CLOSED 2013

Once imagined as a giant glass dome containing the airport's central ticketing area, the original plans for the Theme Building at LAX were toned down substantially. They were part of Los Angeles airport's $50 million redevelopment in 1960.

Federal Aviation Administrator Najeed E. Halaby called the Theme Building "the first terminal area designed for the jet age." He even went so far as to say it might rival Disneyland.

Designed by Paul R. Williams, Pereira & Luckman and Robert Herrick Carter it was constructed of 900 tons of steel, with striking 135-foot-tall parabolic arches. In 1961, when the building opened, its space-age Googie style heralded the arrival of the jet age. The future had come. Families ate in the elegant, modern Host International Restaurant, and took in the flavors of international culture while overlooking the planes as they taxied up to the gates.

After being designated a cultural and historic landmark in 1993, and receiving a $4 million renovation, the Disney Corporation established a new restaurant operation called "The Encounter" at the Theme Building in 1997. Disney's careful restoration to the 1960s view of the future as envisioned by the architects had mixed reactions. Ironically, some critics called the redesign, with its giant lava lamps and Tomorrowland futurism, "an overbearing attempt to recreate Disneyland in another venue."

Fans enjoyed what the corporation had done in restoring a piece of 20th-century architecture that would not have withstood the wrecking ball in a city like Las Vegas. However reality intervened. The events of September 11, 2001, forced officials at LAX to close the Theme Building's observation deck to the public. In 2003, a memorial to the victims of the September 11 attacks opened on the grounds. Stucco falling from the arches onto the roof of the restaurant in March 2007 forced the restaurant to close temporarily. After a $12.3 million seismic safety renovation, the observation level reopened in 2010.

But the restaurant closed on December 31, 2013. Today, parents juggle laptops, shoes, belts as well as children, struggling to get through security checkpoints. Few desire risking a trip to the free-standing Encounter followed by the hassle of going back through security again and the restaurant is not seen as a big enough attraction on its own. A January 2014 article in the *Los Angeles Times* reported the restaurant space was seeking a new tenant, with a new vision for the future...

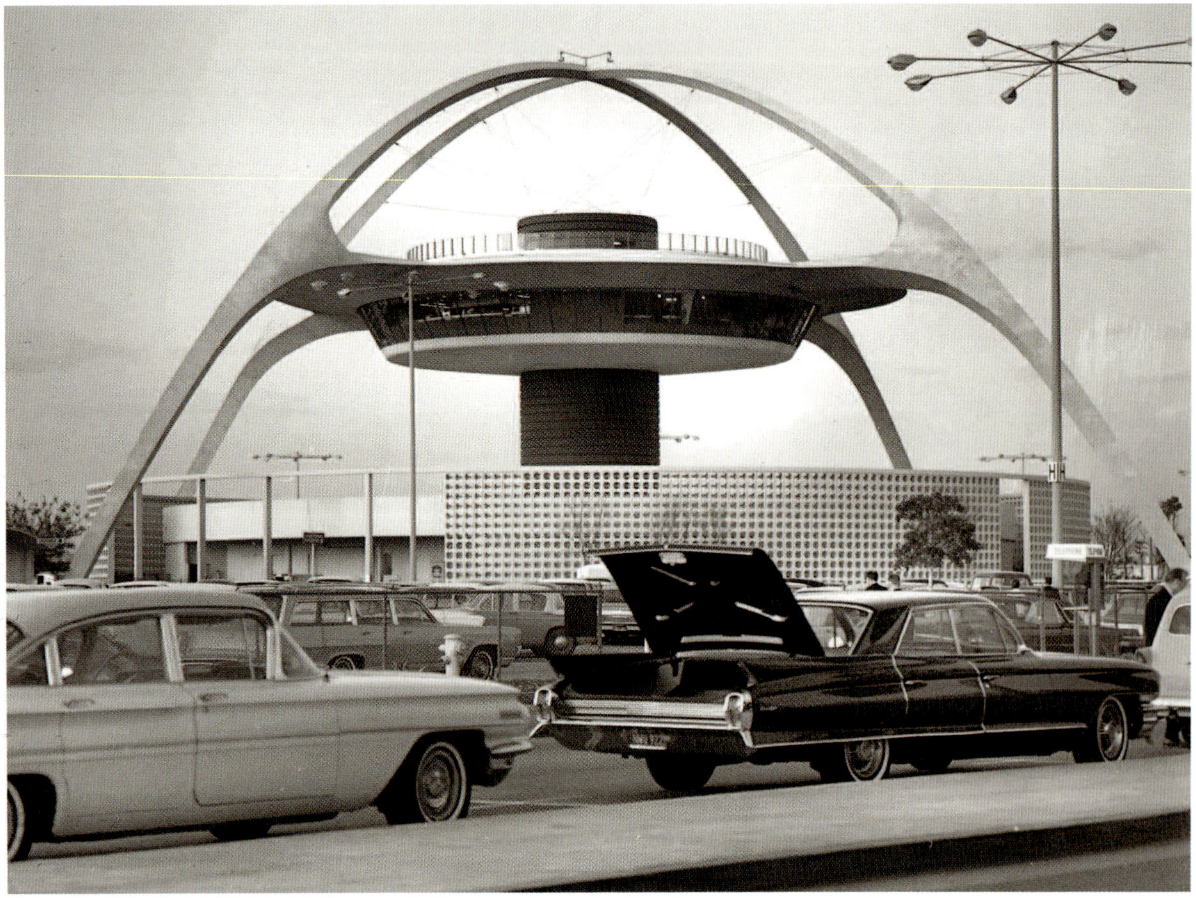

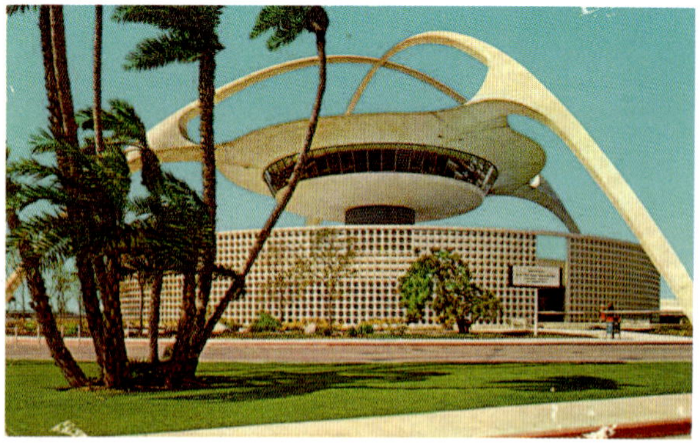

ABOVE *A 1960s color postcard view.*

LEFT *This April 1967 photo shows passengers unloading luggage at the terminal with the Theme Building in the background.*

OPPOSITE PAGE *Waitresses at the Host International Restaurant show off their international garb in this 1962 photograph.*

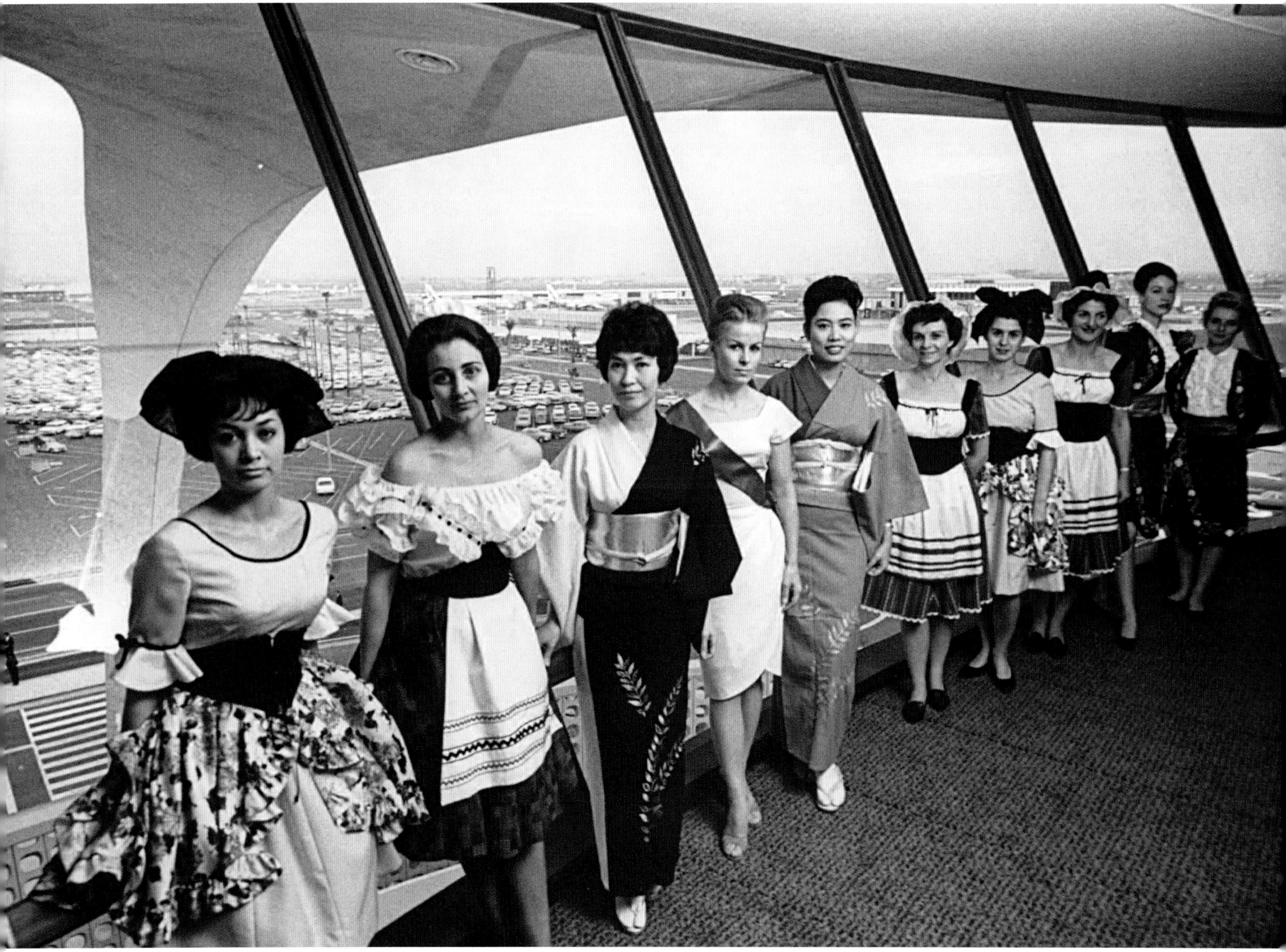

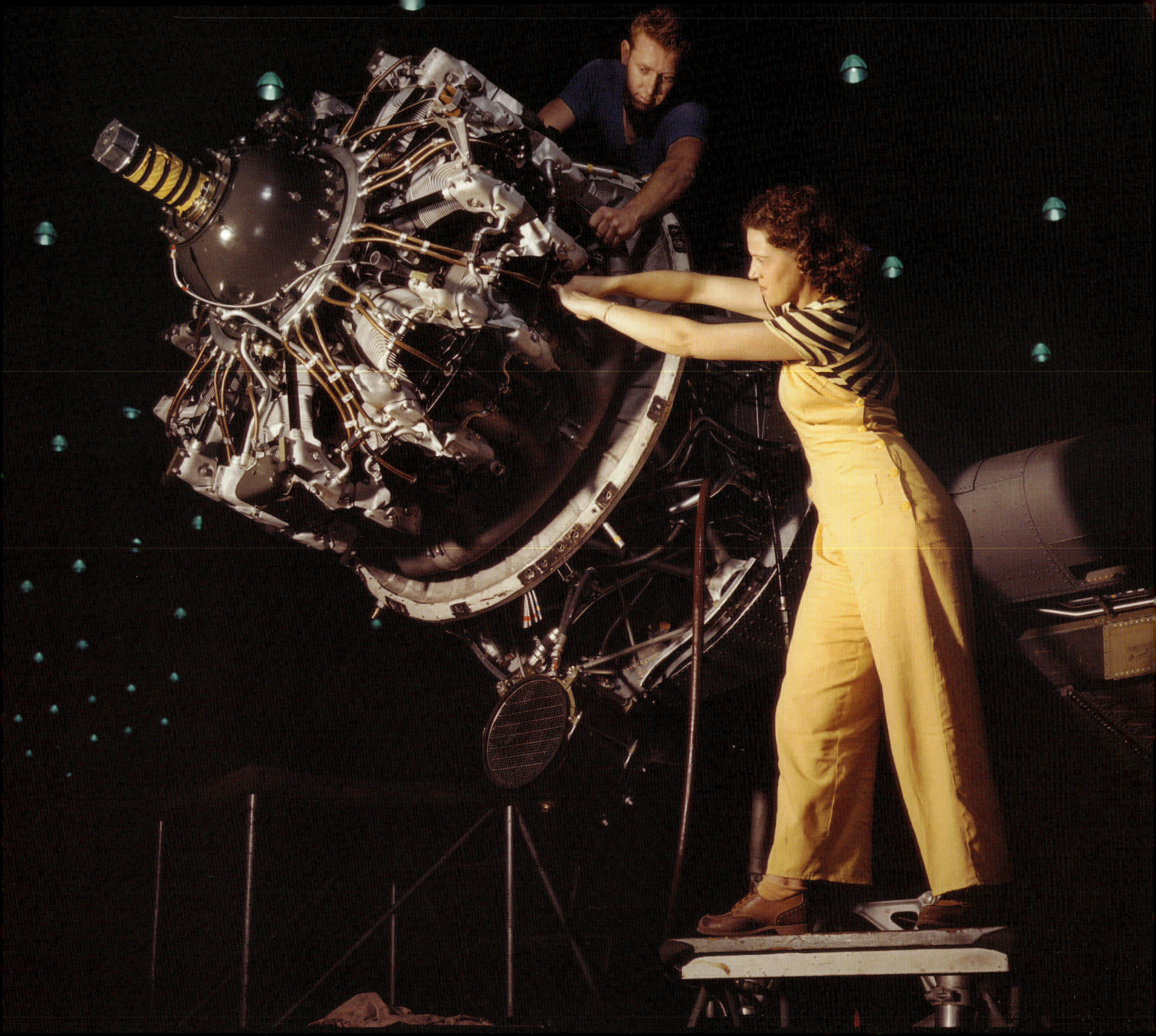

Los Angeles Aero Industry CEASED PRODUCTION 2015

Following the Japanese attack on Pearl Harbor in 1941, industries from Seattle to San Diego burst into life, turning out tanks instead of automobiles, battleships instead of refrigerators, and in the Los Angeles area, bombers instead of movies. Donald Douglas and Alan Lockheed, along with other pioneering aircraft manufacturers, raced to provide President Franklin D. Roosevelt with the weapons he needed. Millionaire playboy Howard Hughes planned to construct the largest troop-transport plane ever flown while his companies based at the Glendale Airfield, and later at the Burbank Airport, secured more mundane war contracts.

Morale was a huge factor following the crushing defeat in Hawaii, and in the spring of 1942, B-25 Mitchell bombers built in Inglewood were winging their way to Tokyo in the Doolittle Raid in the hope of turning the psychological tide.

Meanwhile, photographers did their part promoting the efforts of the factory workers using new color photography that steeped the factories in Hollywood glamour.

The war effort drove decision-making at city hall. When floods threatened the industry, flood control efforts were undertaken. Factories were made to look like non-descript warehouses or subdivisions, while decoys convincing enough to be the set of a film, were constructed in places where minimum damage would be felt.

Communities across the region were involved. Hawthorne's Northrup Aircraft Company built B-17 bombers, Burbank was home to both Lockheed and Vega aircraft companies, Downey was home to the Vultee Aircraft plant, and Santa Monica hosted Douglas Aircraft.

The numbers of planes that were being turned off the production lines by 1945 were staggering. By the end of the war North American Aviation at Inglewood had produced 9,944 P-51 Mustangs and 3,208 B-25 bombers. Vultee had produced 11,687 aircraft, mostly Valiant trainers, while Douglas built 29,385 planes across all their factories with the largest being the 1,422,350 square feet Long Beach facility. In 1945 production came to a crashing halt with a surplus of military aircraft, but the war had created skilled workers and the basis of an industry that was about to move into the jet age and see an unheralded rise in business and leisure travel.

BELOW LEFT *War Department photographer Alfred T. Palmer took this shot of a woman working at North American Aviation of Inglewood in June 1942.*

BELOW *A shot from October 1942 of employees on the "Sunshine" (outdoor) assembly line at North American's plant. The bombers pictured are the B-25 "Billy Mitchell" bombers. This factory also made P-51 "Mustang" fighters.*

OPPOSITE PAGE *During World War II women were able to take a huge step forward in equality, working alongside men in highly technical and detailed capacities. Women helped create everything from airplanes, to battleships, to the atomic bomb. In this 1942 Alfred Palmer photo taken at Douglas Aircraft Company, women were trained to make subtle adjustments and installations to aircraft engines.*

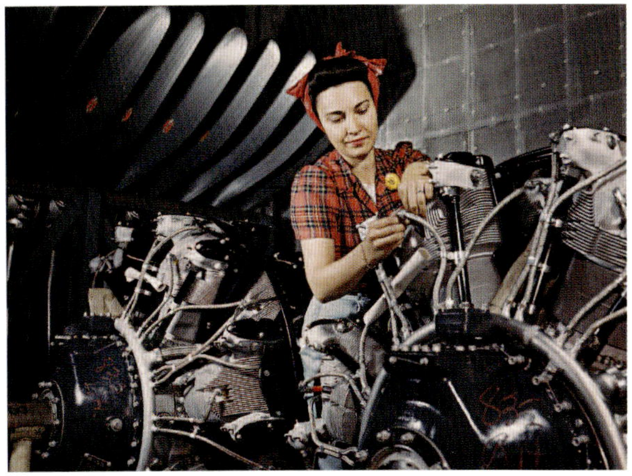

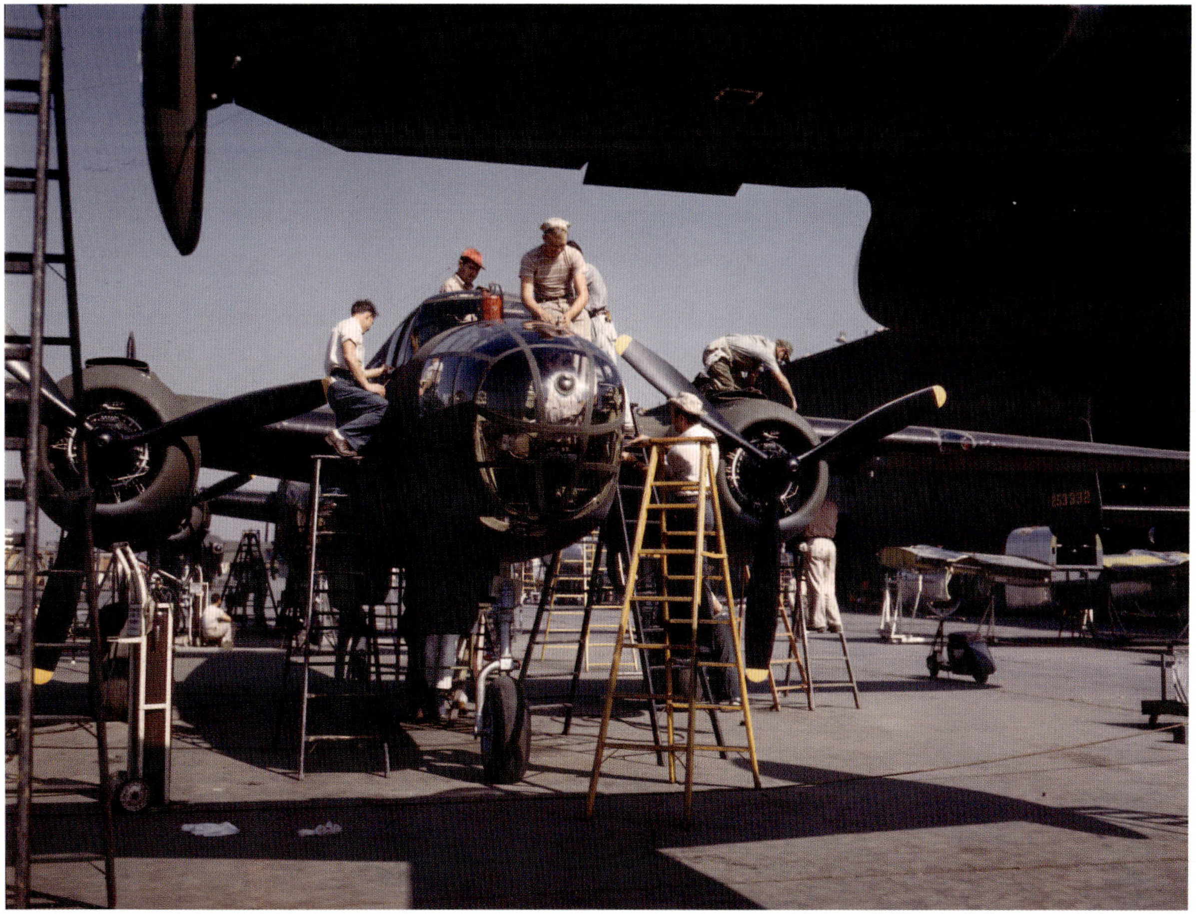

By the time of the Cold War, Los Angeles and the rest of Southern California was home to 15 of the 25 largest aerospace companies in the United States. In 1987 one in ten U.S. jobs in the aerospace industry was held in Los Angeles County.

Today, just a few aerospace companies remain in operation. A wave of consolidations and defense cuts in the 1990s resulted in about half of those jobs (an estimated 142,000) disappearing.

The large cost of developing new planes meant that mergers had started as early as the mid-1960s with Douglas joining forces with McDonnell in 1967 and North American Aviation (owned by General Motors) merging with Rockwell International and then both merged companies eventually being absorbed into Boeing who took control of the huge Long Beach production plant of McDonnell-Douglas.

In September 2013, Boeing announced it would close its Long Beach factory that had been manufacturing the C-17 Globemaster military cargo plane for the U.S. government for the last 20 years and ending the 72-year-run of aircraft production on the site. A lack of new orders, or an interest from Boeing in producing its wide-bodied long-haul Boeing-777X in Long Beach was seen as the root cause. When the production line finally ground to a halt in 2015, it marked the end of nearly a century of aircraft manufacturing in California.

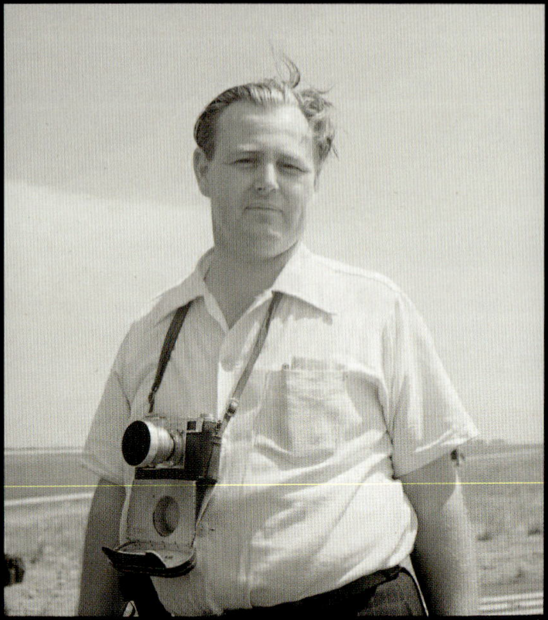

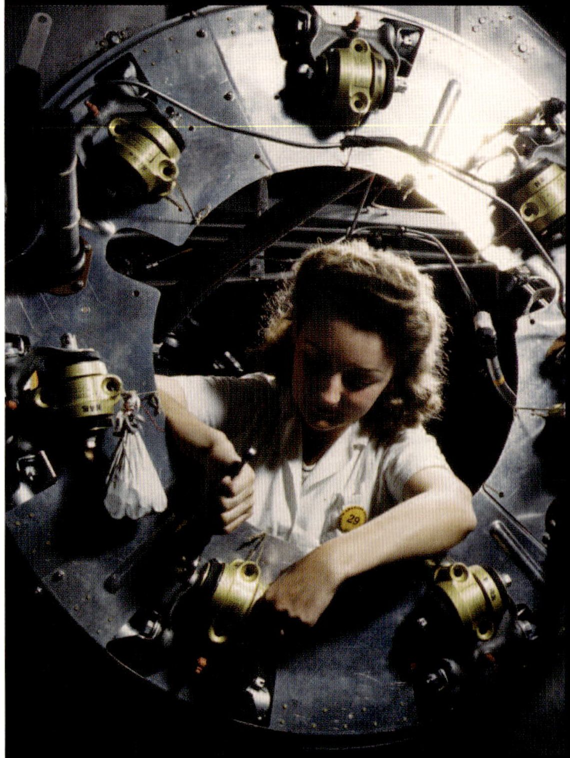

RIGHT *A woman works on part of the cowling for one of the motors for a B-25 bomber, assembled in the engine department of North American Aviation's Inglewood plant.*

OPPOSITE PAGE *Women at the massive Douglas aircraft plant in Long Beach inspect the quality of plane interwings in October 1942 before they are assembled onto a plane fuselage.*

ALFRED T. PALMER

Born in San Jose, California, Alfred T. Palmer moved to Long Beach with his enterprising mother in 1912. When his mother took a job making sandwiches for hikers in Yosemite, Alfred got to meet a young Ansel Adams, who allowed Alfred to carry his tripod. In return, Palmer received a $1 Brownie Box camera. Beginning at age 19, Palmer would travel around the world 23 times aboard the Dollar Steamship Line's *President Monroe* as the company's official staff photographer. By 1938 he had returned to America and was touring the states taking pictures of everything he could, and selling the negatives for $1 apiece for educational books. In June of 1940, while President Roosevelt expanded the U.S. Navy, he also declared the need for the National Defense Advisory Commission of the Office of Emergency Management (OEM). As part of this office, and the new head of the photography department, Palmer was expected to rally and inform citizens about the use of their tax dollars. After Pearl Harbor, Palmer's role stepped up a notch. Now the official photographer for the Office of War Information (OWI), Palmer was given a wider photographic mission to inform. In Palmer's WWII photos, women appeared glamorous, capable and patriotic and helped lead the campaign toward changing public attitudes toward women in the workplace. His work with the New Bureau Negro Press also changed attitudes about African Americans in the labor force. Palmer's photographs were selected to appear at the Museum of Modern Art in 1942 as part of the traveling exhibition *Road to Victory*. Today, the National Archives and the Library of Congress house much of his body of work.

Los Angeles Aero Industry CEASED PRODUCTION 2015

Following the Japanese attack on Pearl Harbor in 1941, industries from Seattle to San Diego burst into life, turning out tanks instead of automobiles, battleships instead of refrigerators, and in the Los Angeles area, bombers instead of movies. Donald Douglas and Alan Lockheed, along with other pioneering aircraft manufacturers, raced to provide President Franklin D. Roosevelt with the weapons he needed. Millionaire playboy Howard Hughes planned to construct the largest troop-transport plane ever flown while his companies based at the Glendale Airfield, and later at the Burbank Airport, secured more mundane war contracts.

Morale was a huge factor following the crushing defeat in Hawaii, and in the spring of 1942, B-25 Mitchell bombers built in Inglewood were winging their way to Tokyo in the Doolittle Raid in the hope of turning the psychological tide.

Meanwhile, photographers did their part promoting the efforts of the factory workers using new color photography that steeped the factories in Hollywood glamour.

The war effort drove decision-making at city hall. When floods threatened the industry, flood control efforts were undertaken. Factories were made to look like non-descript warehouses or subdivisions, while decoys convincing enough to be the set of a film, were constructed in places where minimum damage would be felt.

Communities across the region were involved. Hawthorne's Northrup Aircraft Company built B-17 bombers, Burbank was home to both Lockheed and Vega aircraft companies, Downey was home to the Vultee Aircraft plant, and Santa Monica hosted Douglas Aircraft.

The numbers of planes that were being turned off the production lines by 1945 were staggering. By the end of the war North American Aviation at Inglewood had produced 9,944 P-51 Mustangs and 3,208 B-25 bombers. Vultee had produced 11,687 aircraft, mostly Valiant trainers, while Douglas built 29,385 planes across all their factories with the largest being the 1,422,350 square feet Long Beach facility. In 1945 production came to a crashing halt with a surplus of military aircraft, but the war had created skilled workers and the basis of an industry that was about to move into the jet age and see an unheralded rise in business and leisure travel.

BELOW LEFT *War Department photographer Alfred T. Palmer took this shot of a woman working at North American Aviation of Inglewood in June 1942.*

BELOW *A shot from October 1942 of employees on the "Sunshine" (outdoor) assembly line at North American's plant. The bombers pictured are the B-25 "Billy Mitchell" bombers. This factory also made P-51 "Mustang" fighters.*

OPPOSITE PAGE *During World War II women were able to take a huge step forward in equality, working alongside men in highly technical and detailed capacities. Women helped create everything from airplanes, to battleships, to the atomic bomb. In this 1942 Alfred Palmer photo taken at Douglas Aircraft Company, women were trained to make subtle adjustments and installations to aircraft engines.*

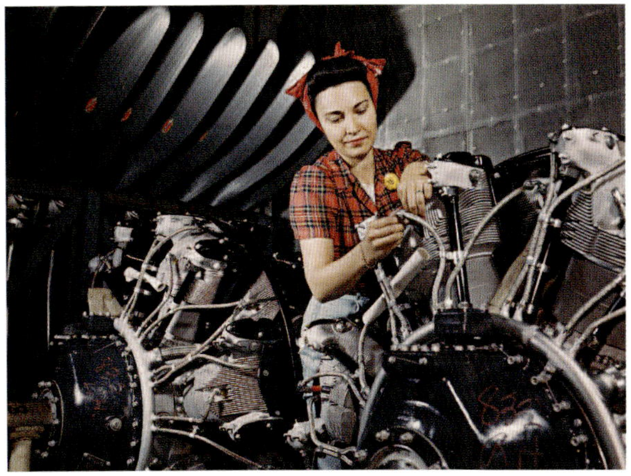

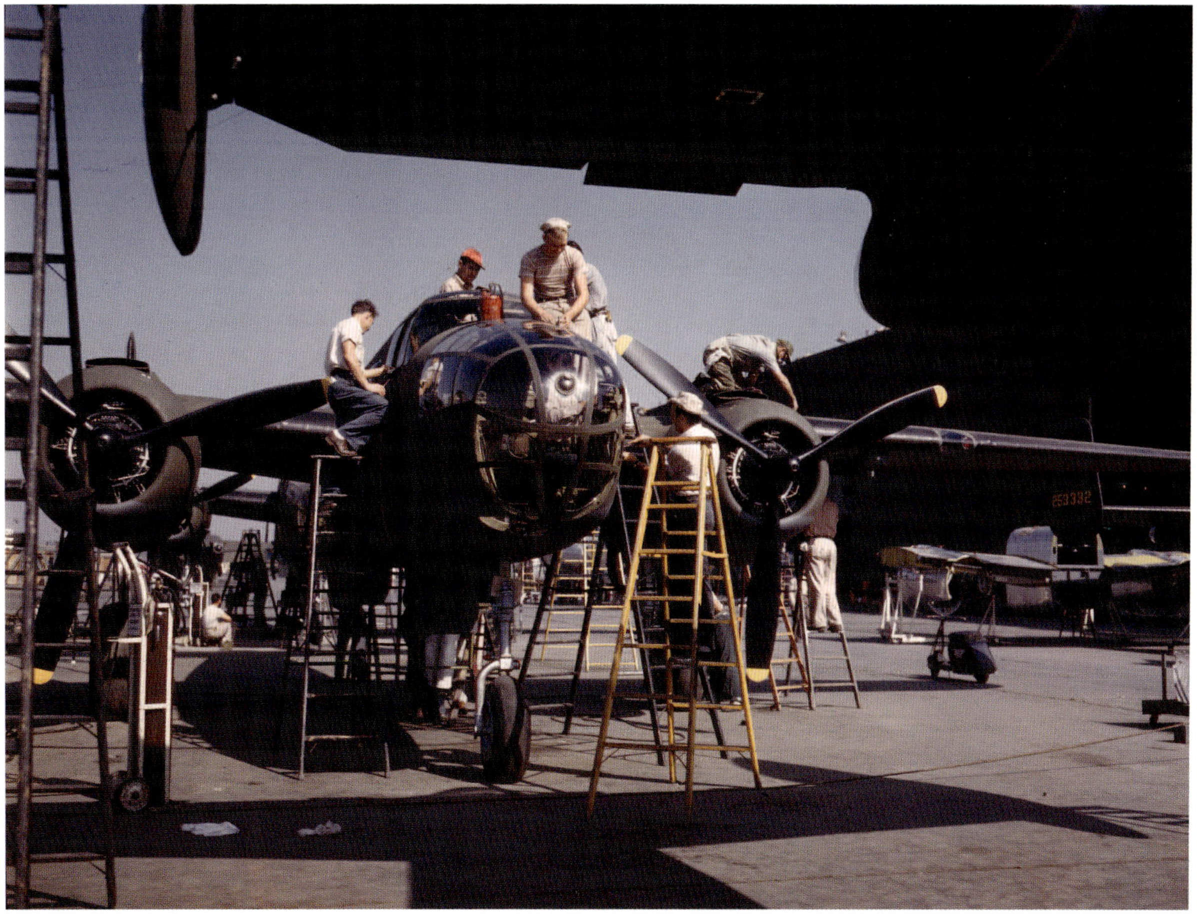

By the time of the Cold War, Los Angeles and the rest of Southern California was home to 15 of the 25 largest aerospace companies in the United States. In 1987 one in ten U.S. jobs in the aerospace industry was held in Los Angeles County.

Today, just a few aerospace companies remain in operation. A wave of consolidations and defense cuts in the 1990s resulted in about half of those jobs (an estimated 142,000) disappearing.

The large cost of developing new planes meant that mergers had started as early as the mid-1960s with Douglas joining forces with McDonnell in 1967 and North American Aviation (owned by General Motors) merging with Rockwell International and then both merged companies eventually being absorbed into Boeing who took control of the huge Long Beach production plant of McDonnell-Douglas.

In September 2013, Boeing announced it would close its Long Beach factory that had been manufacturing the C-17 Globemaster military cargo plane for the U.S. government for the last 20 years and ending the 72-year-run of aircraft production on the site. A lack of new orders, or an interest from Boeing in producing its wide-bodied long-haul Boeing-777X in Long Beach was seen as the root cause. When the production line finally ground to a halt in 2015, it marked the end of nearly a century of aircraft manufacturing in California.

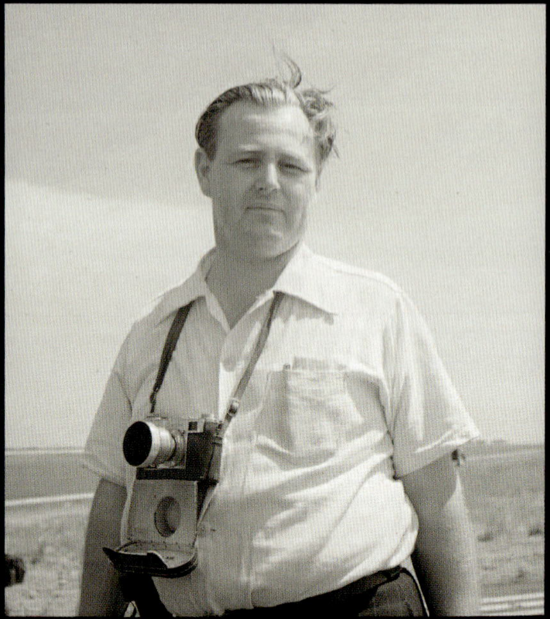

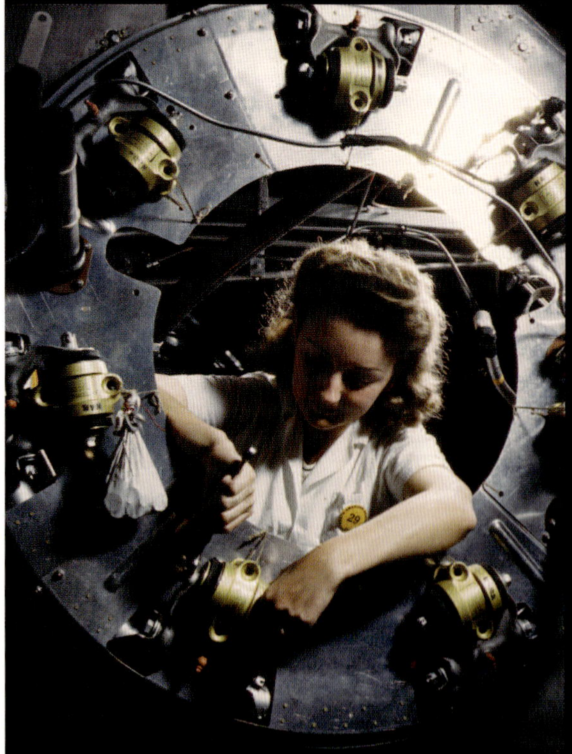

RIGHT *A woman works on part of the cowling for one of the motors for a B-25 bomber, assembled in the engine department of North American Aviation's Inglewood plant.*

OPPOSITE PAGE *Women at the massive Douglas aircraft plant in Long Beach inspect the quality of plane interwings in October 1942 before they are assembled onto a plane fuselage.*

ALFRED T. PALMER

Born in San Jose, California, Alfred T. Palmer moved to Long Beach with his enterprising mother in 1912. When his mother took a job making sandwiches for hikers in Yosemite, Alfred got to meet a young Ansel Adams, who allowed Alfred to carry his tripod. In return, Palmer received a $1 Brownie Box camera. Beginning at age 19, Palmer would travel around the world 23 times aboard the Dollar Steamship Line's *President Monroe* as the company's official staff photographer. By 1938 he had returned to America and was touring the states taking pictures of everything he could, and selling the negatives for $1 apiece for educational books. In June of 1940, while President Roosevelt expanded the U.S. Navy, he also declared the need for the National Defense Advisory Commission of the Office of Emergency Management (OEM). As part of this office, and the new head of the photography department, Palmer was expected to rally and inform citizens about the use of their tax dollars. After Pearl Harbor, Palmer's role stepped up a notch. Now the official photographer for the Office of War Information (OWI), Palmer was given a wider photographic mission to inform. In Palmer's WWII photos, women appeared glamorous, capable and patriotic and helped lead the campaign toward changing public attitudes toward women in the workplace. His work with the New Bureau Negro Press also changed attitudes about African Americans in the labor force. Palmer's photographs were selected to appear at the Museum of Modern Art in 1942 as part of the traveling exhibition *Road to Victory*. Today, the National Archives and the Library of Congress house much of his body of work.

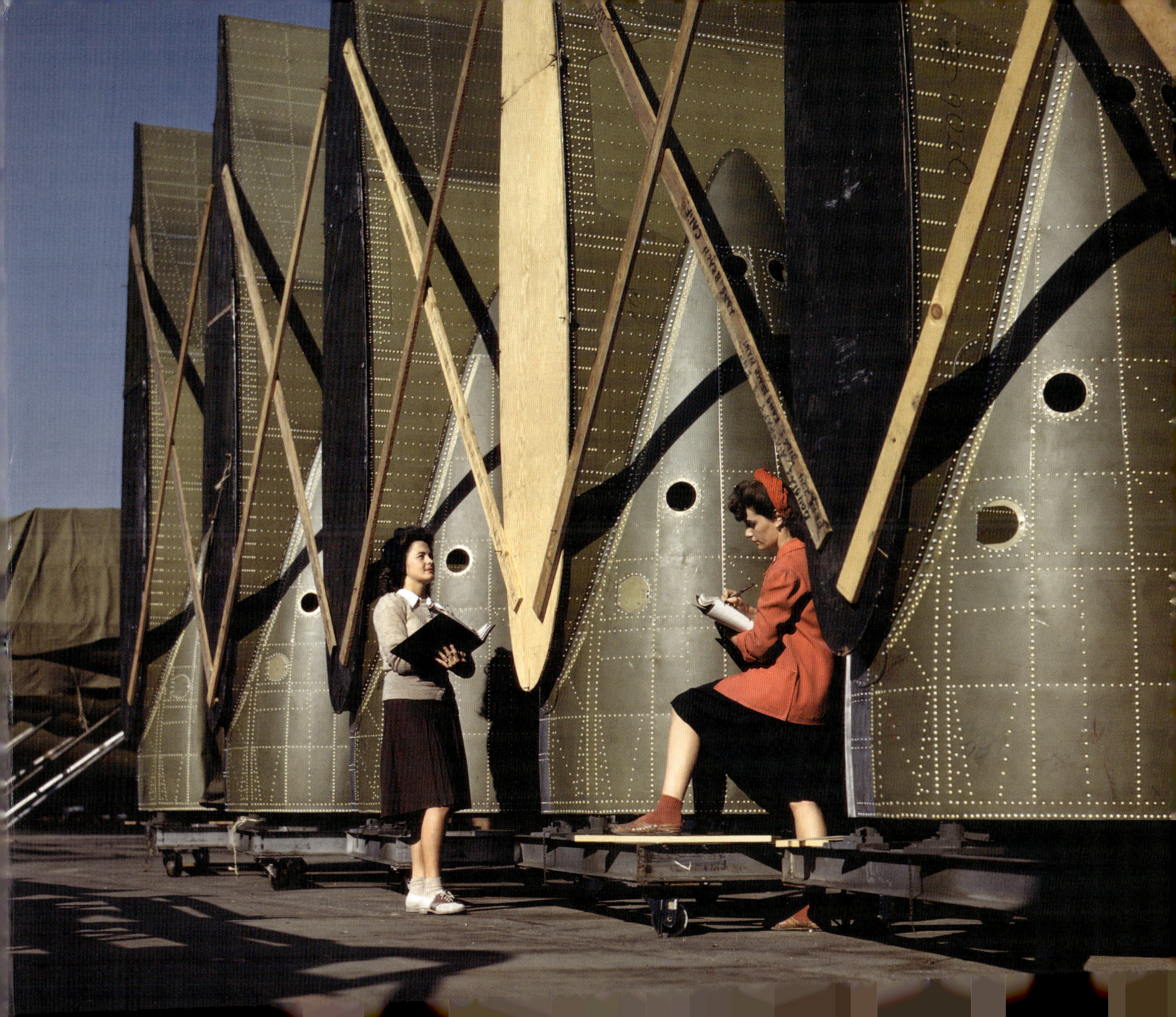

INDEX

OTHER TITLES IN THE SERIES

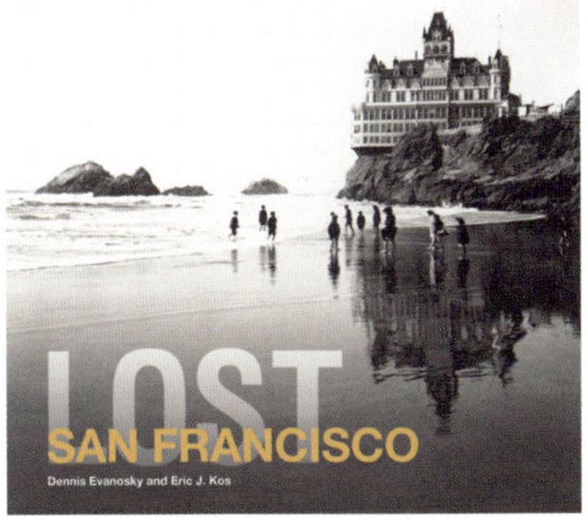

ISBN 9781862059344

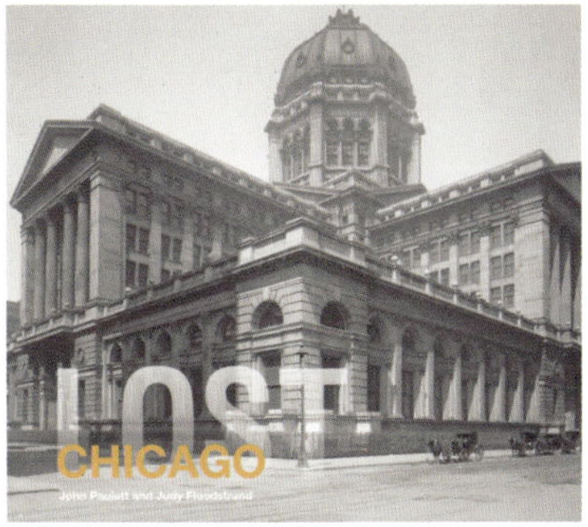

ISBN 9781862059924

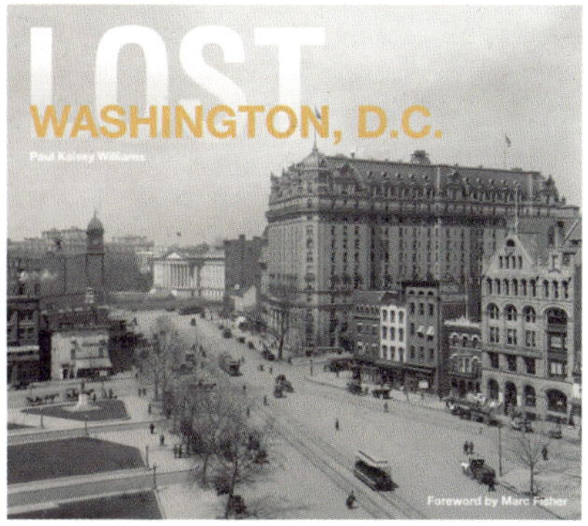

ISBN 9781862059931

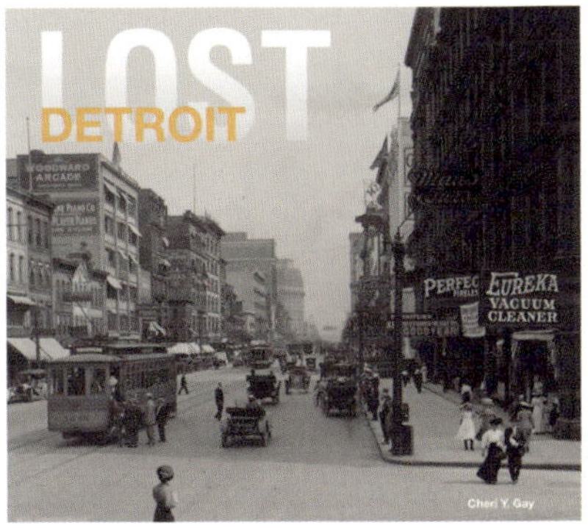

ISBN 9781909108714

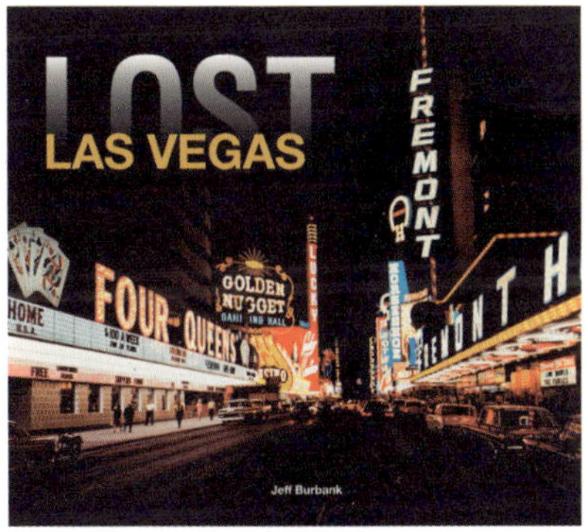

ISBN 9781909815032

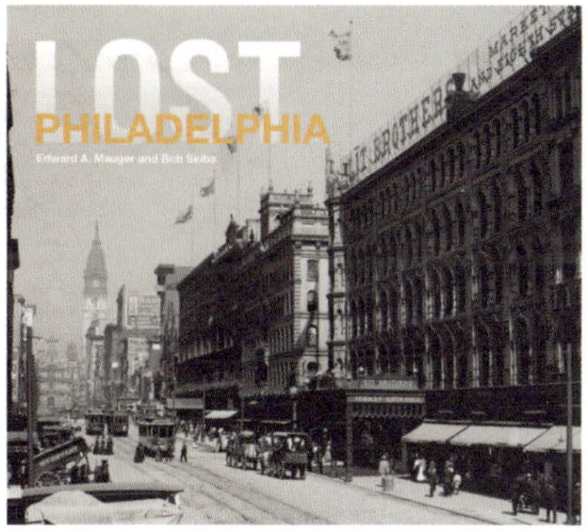

ISBN 9781909108448

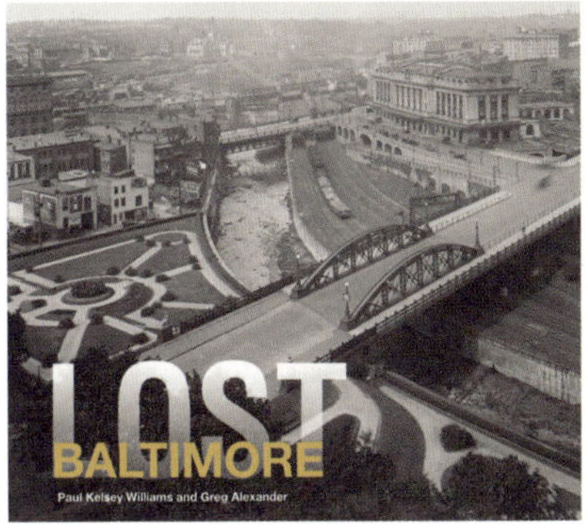

ISBN 9781909108431

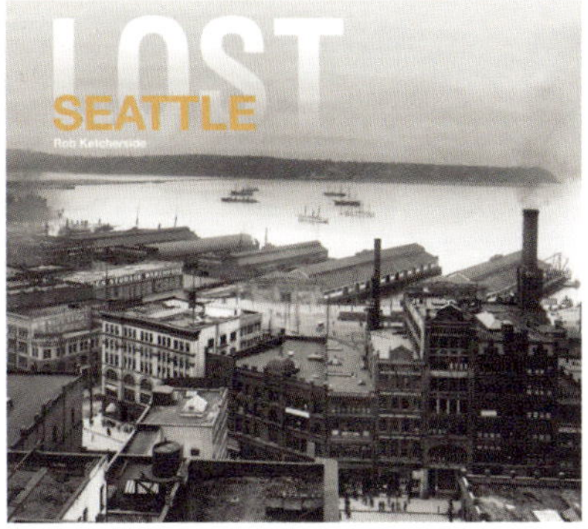

ISBN 9781909108639

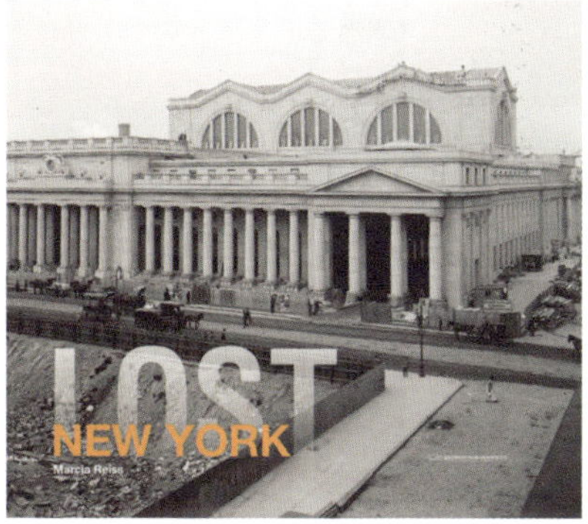

ISBN 9781862059351

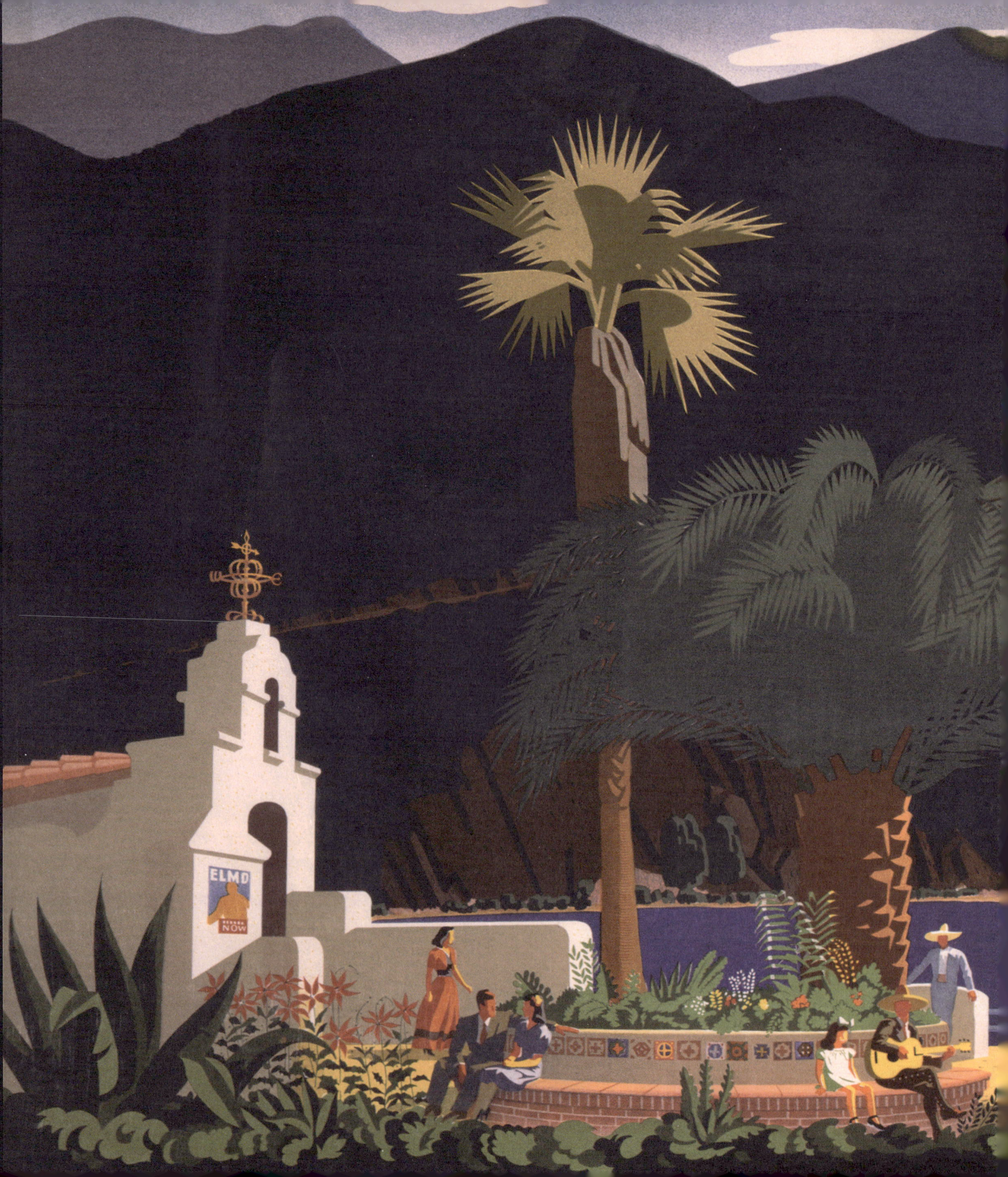
ELMD
NOW